Praise for The Anxious

An outstanding blend of practical information and humor. Dr. DiLeo provides a wealth of useful information in a style that ensures a productive relationship between patient and physician. Dr. DiLeo's insight on pregnancy is so valuable that I plan to recommend this superb contribution to the literature to all of my patients.

> —*Douglas M. Montgomery, M.D., F.A.C.O.G., Chairman of the Department of Obstetrics and Gynecology, Ochsner Clinic Foundation, New Orleans, and specialist in maternal-fetal medicine*

Dr. DiLeo possesses an extremely rare combination of medical expertise, along with the ability to write in an informative and entertaining style, adding strong doses of compassion and wit. I've read just about every pregnancy book available, and many make great bedtime reading (as the medical jargon and dry writing styles often put you right to sleep). This book will not only keep you awake, you will be compelled to read it from cover to cover while you celebrate the miracle of your pregnancy with your favorite book and doctor.

> —*Jeanine Cox, Publisher and Co-founder, BabyZone.com*

As both a surgeon and first time pregnant woman, I had the privilege of reading this book from both perspectives. The unique thing about *The Anxious Parent's Guide to Pregnancy* is that Dr. DiLeo finally provides a guide that interweaves the parent with the obstetrician, the philosophy with the physiology, and the practical with the miraculous. This book is nothing less than a complete celebration of pregnancy and childbirth, but with all the facts. An entertaining read!

True to its title, my anxiety as a prospective mother has been successfully tamed by the perspective Dr. DiLeo instills into even the serious complications that are a part of any thorough discussion of pregnancy. The surgeon in me applauds an important, informative book. The mother in me finds great comfort in the perspective provided, and the woman in me had great fun reading such a charming and funny book about such a serious subject.

> —*Elizabeth Kinsley, M.D., F.A.C.S.*

My professional interests are many, but Dr. DiLeo's take on nutrition in pregnancy is right on. Finally, someone has decided to stop over-complicating the diet for normal pregnancy with ridiculous chapters on calorie counting that no one will follow. And finally, someone has decided to champion the role of nutrition and diet in complications unique to high risk pregnancy. This is the pregnancy book dietitians and nutritionists have been waiting for. And it's fun, too. It's a book that is both delicious and nutritious.

> —*Diana Davis, L.D.N., R.D., licensed nutritionist, holistic Registered Dietitian, certified American Dietetic Association, national lecturer on nutrition and neuro-linguistics.*

the Anxious Parent's Guide to Pregnancy

Pains, Pangs, Thumps, and Twinges— What's Normal, What's Not, When to Worry, and When to Stop and Enjoy Your Pregnancy

GERARD M. DiLEO, M.D.

Contemporary Books

Chicago New York San Francisco Lisbon London Madrid Mexico City
Milan New Delhi San Juan Seoul Singapore Sydney Toronto

Library of Congress Cataloging-in-Publication Data

DiLeo, Gerard M.
    The anxious parent's guide to pregnancy / Gerard M. DiLeo.
       p.   cm.
    Includes index.
    ISBN 0-07-138307-7
    1. Pregnancy.   2. Childbirth.   3. Parenting.   I. Title.

  RG525 .D535   2002
  618.2—dc21   2002022401

To Linda, the mother of our children
To Rosalie, the mother of me

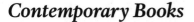

Contemporary Books

A Division of The **McGraw·Hill** Companies

1 2 3 4 5 6 7 8 9 0 AGM/AGM 1 0 9 8 7 6 5 4 3 2

ISBN 0-07-138307-7

This book was set in Janson Text
Printed and bound by Quebecor Martinsburg

Cover and interior design by Jenny Locke

McGraw-Hill books are available at special quantity discounts to use as premiums and sales promotions, or for use in corporate training programs. For more information, please write to the Director of Special Sales, Professional Publishing, McGraw-Hill, Two Penn Plaza, New York, NY 10121-2298. Or contact your local bookstore.

This book is printed on acid-free paper.

R0178862956

Contents

Part Four: The Third Trimester

8: Reaching Critical Mass   137

9: High Risk in the Third Trimester   143

10: Fetal Surveillance in High-Risk Pregnancies   155

Part Eight: Special Conditions in Pregnancy

22: When Life Becomes Complicated   371

Preface

This is more than just a book about pregnancy. It's about life and family too. I've noticed that in most pregnancy books today there's a huge gulf between the actual physiology and the philosophy of reproduction. But both of these things are so beautifully intertwined during pregnancy that I wanted each to help explain the other. In *The Anxious Parent's Guide to Pregnancy*, I feel I've been able to accomplish this. This isn't a book written by a doctor who writes like a doctor; or written by someone who had the quintessential experience and who is trying to write like a doctor. Instead, it is a pregnancy book written by a doctor who writes like a parent. Raising children is a lot more than merely having children, and having them is a lot more fulfilling when you can appreciate the joy in raising them.

As an obstetrician who has taken every single delivery one at a time in a twenty-year career (sometimes two at a time), I have a perspective that goes beyond the sterile collection of lists of other pregnancy books. I do this by using periodic asides, called A-Factors, to allay anxiety. These are bottom-line appraisals of how much concern you should put into a particular subject covered. (Hence the name of this book.) I have also included what I call Fast Forward capsules that summarize explanations, providing quick scans of the most important points of a discussion.

No, I've never had a baby myself. I don't think I could find anything on me that would accommodate ten centimeters dilation. But I have lived with the mother of my children throughout all of our pregnancies, slept in the bed with her, appreciated every symptom and complaint, and shared with her some interesting episodes. My love for her, what she has experienced, and the great things she has done have added considerably to my observations of life in pregnancy beyond mere obstetrics. You can't learn the real meaning of family by reading just a pregnancy book written by a doctor; you can't appreciate what's at stake by reading a birthing enthusiast's manual written in politically correct agenda-ese. It's got to come from the heart of a parent. And this parent just happens to know what's important and what's not; what's likely and what's unlikely; and what's prudent and what's nonsense.

Enjoy this book. It's an easy read, filled with all of the essential information, and tempered by the perspective of someone who has lived childbirth from many angles.

Acknowledgments

This book has been a long time coming. I'd like to thank my patients who have provided me the human perspective of the science of obstetrics that would otherwise be a mere catalog. I'd also like to thank my agent, Peter Miller, who has stood by me longer than he should have. My editor, Matthew Carnicelli, and the production team at Contemporary Books have turned me from a *Saturday Night Live* wannabe into an (almost) serious medical author, and the good people of BabyZone.com have graciously let me contribute to what I think is the best pregnancy and parenting site there is. I'd like to express my gratitude to my office staff, Ann Dalton, Ida Albin, and Marlena Angeletti, who actually bought this pie-in-the-sky story that I was going to be a published author, while helping me keep my office running so well. Thanks to Dr. Nick Landry for taking care of my patients while I was away writing. And one more special thank-you goes to Dr. Elizabeth Kinsley for being a friend, a plastic surgeon, a contributor, and pregnant—all at the same time.

For their support, I'd like to thank my children, Evan, Luke, Blaise, Phoebe, Josh, and Chara, but doubly Luke for showing me the blessings in having a handicapped child. I'm forever indebted to my parents, the late Dr. John DiLeo, for always saying, "Education first," no matter what, and Rosalie DiLeo, for naming me after the patron saint of expectant mothers—who woulda thought?

And most of all, I'd like to thank my wife, Linda, the beautiful woman who gave me such wonderful children and stood behind me throughout the writing of this book, when she had every right to say, "With all of this work, you better frickin' end up on *Oprah*."

First Things First

Planning for Your Pregnancy

Cloned sheep and postmenopausal conceptions may steal all the media attention, but most pregnancies are still the result of good ol' natural sex. IVF, GIFT, ZIFT, AI, and ICSI are all acronyms entering the vocabulary of the mainstream Infertility Nation, the population of which increases as the patience for natural processes wears thin from cycle to unfulfilled cycle. But even though the numbers of children born with the help of technologically begotten conceptions are going up, most children still come from parents who have successfully achieved not IVF (in vitro fertilization), but IBF (in bed fertilization). These Posturepedic parents generally fall into three distinct groups: the Mathematicians, the Merry Wanderers, and the Shocked.

The Mathematicians are the couples who are so serious about planning their life together that they try to plan their pregnancies as well—as if any formula involving children could ever be valid. They call it family planning. I call it chaos theory. Nevertheless, many couples do scheme and plot the perfect time to have the perfect baby for their perfect lives. They consider the optimal financial timing, philosophize about the most successful spacing of siblings, and design the intertwining of family careers. They make coital calendars with X-rated hieroglyphics and coordinate romantic trysts based on urine and little machines. They are devastated when all of the tumblers don't line up the right way in that one month on their calendar circled with the red glitter paint. When their deadlines pass, these couples make it possible for infertility doctors to make a good living.

The Merry Wanderers don't plan to that exact a degree, but instead tread teasingly through an acceptable mind-set in which conception is neither aggressively sought nor avoided—the seductively risky living dangerously approach.

The Shocked are those others who get their snug and warm hedonistically woven rugs pulled out from under them when, in spite of their best efforts, fate steps in with an amazing feat of untimely fertility and ruins their childless carnival and seasonal runs to Club Med.

> **Fast Forward**
>
> Planning the exact timing of a pregnancy is very difficult, even for the most methodical of us. In spite of our best scheming to seek or avoid pregnancy, the timing of pregnancy is often a fatalistic phenomenon.

Except for Immaculate Conceptions, no one can predict exactly when conception will occur, but it probably will occur for most sexually engaged couples. There are infertile couples, but they're the minority that fall through the procreation cracks. When the pregnancy test reads positive (formerly called "The Silence of the Rabbits"), all three groups take out their pencils to calculate their lives around that most profound Holy Day of Obligation, the due date. At this point they are all mathematicians, and it's time to pick out a doctor.

Gender Correctness and Picking the Right Person to Deliver Your Baby

There is no gender-specific advantage in knowledge or skill when it comes to obstetrics. In providing medical care for women, a consensus has been emerging that women do it best. The truth is that it's a great irony that the gender-focused specialty of OB-GYN is gender neutral when it comes to the best doctors. Being of the male persuasion (I was persuaded at my conception), I've had to suffer from the competitive edge female physicians hold over me in the marketplace. It's a great conspiracy against us male doctors in that smart female physicians don't downplay it, and male physicians themselves tap into it when interviewing a prospective associate who has been screened for the "right" marketable gender. The media propagate this thinking: "I went to my gynecologist and *she* told me that. . . ." For all things gynecological, politically correct commercials assume that your gynecologist is a woman. But on the ads for gastritis, diarrhea, and constipation, ". . . my doctor—*he* said to take. . . . "

> ➤ **Fast Forward**
>
> The gender advantage of an obstetrician is mainly a marketing consideration. The best obstetrician for you is the doctor who has proven to be the best gynecologist for you.

I've known women who have actually gone out of town to see a woman doctor who was not as good as the male doctors in her hometown. (Of course, tell a man to see a woman urologist and the bells of chauvinism ring even louder.) Once I had a patient whose husband made her switch to another male doctor because he had five children. Since I had only four, the husband assumed he was more of a family man and therefore less likely to look upon his wife in that way. Men! What can one do?

On the other hand, I've had women come to me, refusing to see a female associate because they felt that women physicians are rougher than men, that the same gender doctor is less understanding. On the doctor end of this are the complaints of superb female gynecologists who have lost patients because they treated them no more special than a male doctor would, but because the expectations were higher, the comparable care was an unforgivable letdown for these disgruntled patients, resulting in anger and flight to—of all things—a male doctor.

This is all asinine, of course. A woman doctor doesn't want to be known as a great gal, but as a great doctor; a male physician doesn't want a patient to go to him just because he's a man any more than he wants a patient to rule him out because of his maleness. No matter what the patients seek in a doctor, no matter what the media assume to be the best gynecologist-patient gender match, no matter how the women's magazines politic in the way of gender correctness, all doctors—male and female—want to be best at being doctors. Male doctors are defensive and huff that you don't have to go to an oncologist who's dying of cancer; female doctors point out that their sex doesn't make them more knowledgeable although less sympathetic. A gynecologist doesn't have to be a man or a woman to do this important work—although a gynecologist is usually a man or a woman because most people, including professionals, are. I'll go out on a limb here and say that men are probably better than women at *taking the credit* for populating the Earth and that women are probably better at doing the actual populating. But the knowledge, skill, dexterity, sensitivity, and reasoning of obstetrics are not better administered by one sex over the other.

Now that I've quashed any assumed gender superiority in OB-GYN, who is the best obstetrician to go to?

You're probably already going to him—or her. (Observing gender neutrality while writing a book about obstetrics is a major distraction, so forgive my using the male and female genders in a polite rotational way. To escape the wrath of the Ellen Jamesians, I will toss his, hers, him, her, he, and she around with responsibly correct reckless abandon.)

Where was I?

You're already going to her—or him. The point is that if you trust your doctor—male or female—as a gynecologist, you should be able to trust your doctor as an obstetrician. They're the same people.

Admittedly, if you're choosing a doctor for the first time, this difficult decision is all the harder when it means selecting an obstetrician because this special kind of doctor must treat two patients simultaneously: you and the child you're carrying. But the sum of the expectant mother and the expected is more than the mere addition of the parts because there is a third entity, the pregnancy itself, which is that symbiotic relationship between mother and child. This third entity has it's own type of respiratory system, circulatory system, and nutritional exchange. For that brief time of gestation there is a different anatomy altogether: the combined mother-child.

To relate properly to an expectant mother (and father), an obstetrician must be able to relate to all kinds of entities—the mother and father individually, the married couple, the developing child, the pregnancy relationship between the mother and child, and the pregnancy relationship among the mother, father, marriage, and child. It can get fairly crowded in this psychodynamic exchange. But the most important relationship is that of the mother and child, because there are diseases of just the mother, diseases of just the fetus, and very strange medical complications that are the result of mother and fetus together.

A lot of this is book knowledge for sure, but there has to be insight as well because as the mother-to-be your thinking is altered as well. Ovarian, pituitary, thyroid, and adrenal hormones jive together with your fervent hopes and dreams to create another thinking and emotional species altogether—the mother-and-child—the pregnancy—a dynamic metabolism honed over the span of evolution to produce a miracle nine months later. Emotional and behavioral aspects of your personality underscore a maternal instinct that comes from deep inside the primitive human brain.

So how does that affect the selection of the doctor who will mastermind your prenatal care? Whether male or female, this doctor better be perfect. At least in your eyes.

Everyone realizes that perfection is an unattainable ideal. But different couples have different priorities as to what constitutes an acceptable level of perfection. You may want the hand-holding type of doctor who will do all the worrying for you, taking both of you through the prenatal course in a mystic cloud of vague pronouncements of well-being. You may want the opposite, a Carl Sagan who will explain the billions and billions of details, pointing out all of the risks and benefits of every option pregnancy has to entertain. You may even want a pal, somewhere in between the first two types, but with enough empathy to struggle with you over a particular decision.

All of these types have successful practices because they attract adequate numbers of patients who seek them out because of their specific approaches. But all obstetricians hope to blend the three types perfectly so that their care is knowledgeable, caring, trustworthy, and endearing.

It is sometimes unfortunate that choosing an obstetrician can be not so much a search for one doctor but an escape from another. Being both an obstetrician and a father, I've had ample opportunity to consider the intricacies of what's important in an obstetrician-patient relationship. A lot of my training in this insight comes from the mistakes of other obstetricians. If you leave one doctor, you no doubt will be switching to another. Your new doctor will be smart to listen to the reasons you switched to her and she will incorporate safeguards into her own practice based on what she can learn from you:

- "I called my doctor for three days and he never returned my call."
- "There are several doctors in the practice, and they all tell me different things."
- "I asked my doctor about this and she just blew me off."

> **Fast Forward**
>
> When choosing an obstetrician, you should be able to take as much time as you need to feel comfortable that your questions have been answered. Ask about the type of practice—solo, group, etc; on call arrangements; and refer to the list of other important questions found in the "Birthing Understanding" in Chapter 12.

Strangely enough, the medical world and patients' reasons for selecting doctors have changed in a very short time. I no longer see people switching doctors because they feel some are knife-happy or too greedy. They seem to switch for failures in the doctor-patient relationship; such a relationship should be professional, but always personable as well. This isn't taught in medical school. A lot of it is innate, but a doctor learns a lot about human nature in the first years of unsupervised private practice too.

As a pregnant woman, you want the best for your unborn child, and you'll usually know after a first visit whether a certain obstetrician's for you. Besides our board exams, we OB doctors must also pass the maternal instinct test.

Two Sides of the Same Coin: Gynecologists and Obstetricians

Your doctor's metamorphosis from gynecologist to obstetrician can be a fuzzy transformation indeed. One positive pregnancy test and he crawls out of his gynecology cocoon as a beautiful obstetrics butterfly. One delivery later and your doctor renews her life cycle by becoming your gynecologist again. The real definition of an OB-GYN doctor, therefore, is based upon what you are—pregnant or not. Your transition from nonpregnant to pregnant walks hand in hand with your doctor's transition from a doctor caring for the nonpregnant woman (gynecologist) to the doctor attending the pregnancy of the child-carrying woman (obstetrician). Because of the fickleness of infertility and the uncertainties of very early pregnancy, an OB-GYN doctor also has to shimmy as both, thinking on two different levels until your particular condition settles toward one of them.

Groups, Solo Doctors, and Midwives

Whether you seek a large group practice or a solo practitioner, there are trade-offs no matter what the flavor. Large groups tend to have a wide variety of personalities to choose from while maintaining a consistent quality of medicine. The many doctors keep each other sharp, and these are the ones most likely to keep up with the medical literature in a timely manner. A large group is also more likely to have subspecialists easily available because the volume of patients can justify the expense of a consultant on the payroll. But this volume also tends to depersonalize your experience. You may not see the same doctor twice in a row, which can be disturbing when you are being followed for a problem that may span several visits. Also, this is exactly the type of situation that might result in two doctors advising two different things. On the other hand, coverage for emergencies is usually better in a large group, the shared on-call schedule so infrequent for a particular doctor that she is well rested, fresh, cheerful, and keen. The flip side of this is that you probably won't be delivered by your chosen doctor. Perhaps not even by a doctor at all.

Midwives have been successfully attending deliveries for thousands of years. Today's certified nurse midwives work in hospitals and are backed up by obstetricians in case of complications. I myself like midwives. A midwife walked me through my very first delivery, and demonstrated a technique I have maintained all of these years. (She later went on to become an obstetrician, mainly out of political frustration.) Midwifery is not to be confused with home delivery, which I address with no small amount of commotion in "Controversies in Obstetrics" in Chapter 22. In my opinion, a normal vaginal delivery in a hospital or birthing center, attended by a certified nurse midwife, backed up by an obstetrician, is as good as a delivery by an obstetrician. It may even be better since midwifery entails more of a total psychodynamic approach. Large groups are usually the ones that routinely employ midwives.

The small group or solo practitioner won't be as swank as the large group, but you're likely to spend much more one-on-one quality time with the same doctor throughout your pregnancy. Also, since there's usually a financial penalty to her when another doctor covers for her and delivers your baby, you're more likely to have her at your delivery. But she'll be running late for many of your appointments, at the mercy of her other patients who may be laboring or delivering during the office hours you were scheduled for.

> **Fast Forward**
>
> Group practices are swankier than solo practices and the individual doctors are exposed to influences that keep them sharp, but they're more impersonal and you won't see the same doctor for each visit throughout the pregnancy.
>
> A solo doctor will be dedicated to you and can better assure you of being there for your delivery, but he must be there for all of his other deliveries, meaning that you should bring a lot of reading material to each appointment.
>
> Nurse midwives offer all of the advantages of an obstetrician when backed up by an obstetrician, and promise their patients more of a total experience.
>
> Doctors who are employees of a hospital or HMO will be forced to practice along fiscally sound guidelines. Although this may be medically sound, you may notice a difference.

Employee doctors are a strange breed. On one level they don't care how much time they spend on each patient because they're on a salary; but on another level they may get fired for not being productive enough. This is particularly true if they're employees of an HMO. When the turnover is high for employee doctors, there can be many reasons, but the fact that the turnover is high says it all.

If You Choose to Forgo an Obstetrician

The safety of your pregnancy depends on the quality of person to whom you're entrusting your baby, his eighty years or so of life, your own life, and . . . you get the point. I deal with home deliveries in detail in "Controversies in Obstetrics" (Chapter 22), but here are the questions you need answers to:

Is there some sort of certification your midwife has passed, or is she some sort of grandfathered (grandmothered?) provider? What amount of continuing medical education has she taken in the last two years? Does she have the official backup of an obstetrician ready to take you on as a surprise obstetrical complication? And if so, does that doctor have an arrangement with other doctors to deal with this sort of thing should he be off? Or are you on your own if you need transport to a hospital nearby, taking potluck with whatever doctor is on the indigent "life-and-limb" unassigned patient list for that day?

How heroic is she when it comes to pulling off that difficult vaginal delivery she sees as a victory, and does this victory conflict with what's best for your baby? What is her protocol with fetal assessment during labor and how well does she respect signs of fetal distress, like meconium?

> **Fast Forward**
>
> Since your baby is so important, investigate a home delivery advocate before allowing this type of delivery. Don't assume expertise without checking her out. Many are self-appointed experts. Be assured of proper backup.

If you're not comfortable with any of her answers, that's your maternal instinct flaring its nostrils. If her answers are well-thought-out and give reasonable explanations, then the only peril left to deal with is the controversy over home delivery.

Choosing the Right Hospital

The greatest doctor or midwife in the world will be inadequate if the facilities are. The ideal hospital for pregnancy, labor, and delivery is one that has in-house anesthesia; a Level III neonatal nursery (that designation means they can handle anything); neonatologists to run the Level III nursery; nursing personnel whose numbers aren't continually adjusted based on the hospital census; private rooms that transform themselves for labor, delivery, and recovery (LDR rooms); pediatric cardiovascular and neurosurgeons; and protocols intuitively sensitive to your needs. There are only a couple of hospitals that meet all of these criteria. One is in Shangri-la, the other is in Oz.

All of this stuff costs money. With the diminishing reimbursements to hospitals by third-party providers, cost containment has made this type of hospital very unlikely. Some endowed large city centers come close, but gilded edges tarnish very easily.

We're talking trade-offs here, aren't we? Not when your baby is concerned, we're not! Well . . . maybe.

So what are the deal breakers? If you can't have it all, what should you have? Twenty-four-hour in-house anesthesia is an assurance for safety that can't be replaced. If you have anesthesia available to you anytime, even at three in the morning, that means that there's C-section readiness should your baby take a bad turn during your labor. It also means that you can have your epidural immediately if you decide that Lamaze is for the birds, that you hate your husband (the callous brute), and that jumping out of the window might seem reasonable.

Fast Forward

Twenty-four-hour in-house anesthesia and a decent nursery should be the deal breakers when it comes to choosing a hospital.

There should be at least a Level II nursery, which has a neonatologist who can take action when surprises happen. A good Level II nursery can handle a lot of difficult situations or at least stabilize a baby for transport to a Level III nursery should the need arise.

Even if you're planning natural childbirth, anesthesia capability is crucial to assure you adequate care in an unforeseen emergency. A Level II nursery is a close second. The candlelight dinner—that marketing perk that whispers, "We care"—should be a distant consideration. If they care, they'll pay for in-house anesthesia and a good neonatologist.

The Best Prenatal Care Begins Before Conception

Maybe you're too late for this section, but if you're not yet pregnant, then heed this call: obstetrically speaking, the best prenatal care begins before you conceive. And if you can't exactly determine when that will happen, the safest way is to stay prepared, to modify your lifestyle as if pregnancy could happen at any time.

Fast Forward

Your baby is what you were! Conditions during conception may reflect what was happening three months earlier, when your egg began its journey to the surface of the ovary for ovulation.

Recent studies have shown that the extra ingredients in prenatal vitamins, started a few cycles before conception, can lower your risk of genetic problems and miscarriage. Many researchers feel that when a woman ovulates, the egg's journey to the ovary's surface actually began three cycles earlier. Knowing this, beginning the specially formulated prenatal vitamins three months before your conception makes a lot of sense. And this certainly makes one stop and think about what may have been eaten, consumed, or inhaled over the previous quarter year. Men too have to understand that prior exposure to dangerous substances can affect the ultimate sperm produced. Party on, Garth? Having a baby is an adult decision, and nothing underscores this more than realizing that adult decisions require thinking about the future, even if it's only three months at a time.

The Ten Commandments of Pregnancy

The number ten has always meant something special to human beings. For example, our entire counting system is set on base ten. There were Ten Commandments for goodness' sake. Now scientists feel, as difficult as this is to imagine, that there are actually ten dimensions. So when I cite the important considerations in pregnancy, I don't have to wonder how many to list. I choose ten of course, and I do this for an extremely relevant and scientifically significant reason: That's the number of fingers and toes parents count at their very first perusal of their newborn child.

There are, however, countless considerations, not just ten, when it comes to pregnancy. No matter how many books you read, documentaries you watch, or support groups you attend, there's nothing like actually having a baby to demonstrate how little we all know about this baby business. There could just as easily be a hundred or a thousand points to make about pregnancy. Since space is limited, I'll present ten really good pointers:

1. Get pregnant for the right reasons. There are a lot of wrong reasons to get pregnant. A child is too important to create for frivolous, careless, or selfish reasons. Your decision to have a baby should be based on wanting a child, wanting to raise a child, wanting to make the world better because of how you raise your child.
2. Be a good mother and father before conception. This means being a good husband and wife before exposing children to the complex psychodynamics that constitute a marriage. It's best for all future children if both of you are secure in your relationship before making the next leap toward a family.

3. Be good parents during the conception process. This involves being sensitive to what you expose yourself to during this time. Smoking, alcohol, and drugs are implicated in abnormal pregnancies and pregnancy complications, as well as in miscarriage. Even the guy's exposure to such substances can have an impact so it's best if a safe lifestyle is equally espoused by both of you. Since the very egg you conceive with begins its maturation a few months before actually being released, waiting three months will allow conception with an unpolluted egg, so to speak.

4. Be a good mother in early pregnancy. Ditto on the smoking, alcohol, and drugs. Your obstetrician can give you a list of medications acceptable in pregnancy. Weeks six through nine (four through seven after conception) are crucial to your infant's organ development, so this is the time of highest risk. It is therefore prudent for you and your unborn baby to be evaluated as soon as pregnancy is suspected.

5. Know the warning signals that should prompt a call to your doctor during your pregnancy. Bleeding, leakage of fluid, and decreased fetal movement are the big three, but ask your doctor. (All of the red flags will be discussed in chapters that follow.)

6. Stay active and fit. Your exercise regimen before conception need only be modified slightly to avoid undue stress on your ligaments and joints, which will tend to loosen somewhat during pregnancy. You must take care not to get overheated, however, because an increase in your core body temperature may affect your baby's development or heart rate (hot tubs included), although this has never been proven. But don't be sedentary. Cardiovascular fitness helps labor and delivery substantially. Statistics for healthy labor and delivery outcomes weigh heavily on the side of physical fitness. And speaking of weighing heavily . . .

7. Concentrate on good nutrition. High-protein, low-fat, low-sugar diets are the best way to go, but fanaticism is to be avoided. After all, you should enjoy life too. Potato chips in your fourteenth week aren't the best choice, but they won't give your child Attention Deficit Disorder.

8. Attend childbirth preparation classes. At least for your first baby. Really. In spite of what I'm about to say. True, your first impression of the instructors may be that these are geeky people who for some strange reason chose this to be their holy mission; but these classes fill in a lot of the blanks that regular OB visits may leave. Although it is best if the Ob-Gyn

you choose helps clarify and explain the varied aspects of your pregnancy, there's nothing like the detailed education of childbirth classes—for husband and wife. You should be aware that many of these instructors sometimes have a political agenda, downplaying epidurals and other pain management as unsatisfactory alternatives to more natural approaches. This sort of thinking won't bother you if you're planning on a natural childbirth, but if you're an admitted coward, the denunciations of modern pain relief will give you anxiety. If you ignore the tirades, you can otherwise rely on the medical information as accurate. You'll know when self-appointed birthing guru hooey interweaves with legitimate medical information when you look over at your spouse and see that one raised eyebrow. If you can't swing the time to do the classes, I suppose you had better read the rest of this book.

9. Trust your doctor. Many pregnancy books encourage you to challenge any aspect of your prenatal care. Unfortunately, some of these authors unilaterally decree what issues are apparently unethical, be it indications for C-section, usage of labor inducers, or other judgment considerations. But when it comes right down to it, you either trust your doctor or you don't. If you do, you'll feel comfortable with the rationale for any decisions that need to be made. If you don't, you're going to the wrong doctor.

10. Appreciate the important things in your life. Realize that you're going to have to put yourself second for a while. Realize that although children are hard work, they give back more than they take. Know that if you're anguishing over birth contracts and fashionable delivery methods, it's not how you have the baby but how you raise the baby. Let me repeat that because it's a theme that is the basis of all that's important in life:
It's not how you have the baby, it's how you raise the baby.

Besides reading a book on pregnancy, you might also pick up a book on parenting because after you have your baby, your obstetrician's job is over. Yours is just beginning.

Q & A

The "Q & A" section is a great way to shed light on finer points that tend to get lost in categorizations in the text. At the end of each part, I include actual questions that have been sent to me, along with the answers I have given. They're typical of the actual conversational tone in the doctor-patient relationship. This gives more of a "press the flesh" treatment on described problems, individualizing issues that come up but are generally ignored in the clear but otherwise incomplete chapter explanations.

Relationship with Your Obstetrician

Question: I chose my obstetrician carefully, but I find that she uses a nurse for the routine visits so I have yet to even meet her. How should I approach this uncomfortable situation?

Answer: Welcome to managed care. Enter the physician extender. With reimbursements going down and overhead going up, the only way doctors can maintain their income is to deal with more volume. But a doctor can only see so many people. If a doctor properly supervises her practice, the use of a physician extender like a nurse practitioner is safe, ethical, and financially necessary in these troubled times of managed care. If the doctor is responsible, so will be her supervision.

Prenatal Vitamins

Question: I can't swallow those big vitamin pills—they make me gag. What if I don't take them at all?

Answer: Some women cannot swallow the big horse pills that most prenatal vitamins are without gagging. If there is any degree of morning sickness, prenatal vitamins can make this worse. The iron in them generates burps and aggravates the esophageal reflux that pregnancy is famous for, seriously challenging the self-esteem of any lady who fancies herself demure. If it's the sheer size of the pill, and you can't break them into halves or thirds (which is OK) your doctor may have to prescribe chewable or liquid vitamins to overcome these difficulties. Sometimes it's wise to just wait a few weeks, then restart a vitamin because vitamins are more than just a good idea. They are an important component of modern prenatal care. But they have to be tolerated to do any good.

Previous Surgery on the Cervix

Question: I've had my cervix frozen twice for dysplasia (precancerous cells). Will this affect my fertility or pregnancies?

Answer: The cervix is that structurally strong opening that holds a pregnancy in until labor causes enough force to push a baby against it, allowing dilation. One would think that any destructive procedure, like freezing the cervix to cause a "freezer burn" of precancerous tissue (called cryosurgery), could weaken the strength of the cervix and make premature delivery more likely. In my experience I haven't found that to be so, even with multiple episodes of cyrosurgery (and laser too). Of course, some women have a congenital weakness of the cervix already, so it's hard to say whether preterm delivery is really a complication of cryosurgery or laser treatment, instead of just a bad cervix to begin with. Theoretically, cryo might cause scarring, interfering with the passage of sperm or with dilation during labor. A gentle probing can solve the first problem, and if necessary, a C-section will tackle the latter.

► Fast Forward

Conservative treatment for cervical dysplasia usually doesn't interfere with pregnancy or delivery.

In spite of theoretical dangers, freezing and other techniques to destroy precancerous cells (dysplasia) are for all practical purposes fairly harmless out in the real world. This is because the real functioning portion is the internal cervix, which lies well up the cervical canal, well out of the way of the more superficial zone of destruction. Seldom do destructive procedures go that deeply. Except for cone biopsies.

A cone biopsy is the most aggressive way to remove abnormal uterine tissue. This technique is usually reserved for particularly severe cases (borderline cancer) or when it's not known how far up the cervix the abnormal tissue extends. A scalpel is used to remove a cone-shaped chunk of the cervix, and this excision, along with the added tissue damage caused by suturing and by cauterizing to control bleeding, might get close to the internal opening of the cervix (the "internal os").

But cryo and laser are not even in the same ballpark. The only problem that could remain is that the sampling area for Pap smears could get scarred up the canal, making it more difficult to get an adequate Pap, which of course is very important when a woman has had dysplasia already.

Keeping a Previous Abortion a Secret from Your Doctor

Question: I've had an abortion, and now that I'm pregnant again I'm wondering if keeping this information from my doctor will affect the care. Does he really have to know?

Answer: Not really. If you didn't have any serious complications related to the abortion, like a postoperative infection that might have scarred the inside of your uterus or another medical condition that became evident only after the challenge of an operative procedure (the actual termination), then I can't see how this information would be crucial.

However, do you really want this type of relationship with your doctor? You certainly depend on honesty from him; shouldn't he expect the same from you? Yours is a lie of exclusion. A doctor-patient relationship goes both ways. If he's professional, regardless of his views on abortion (and I'm sure this is why you ask), he should treat you no differently because of that information. If you can't fess up, then there's a serious problem with the doctor-patient relationship.

The Big Question

And I'd like to end this with a ringer question:

Question: Is it how you have the baby?

Answer: No, it's how you raise the baby.

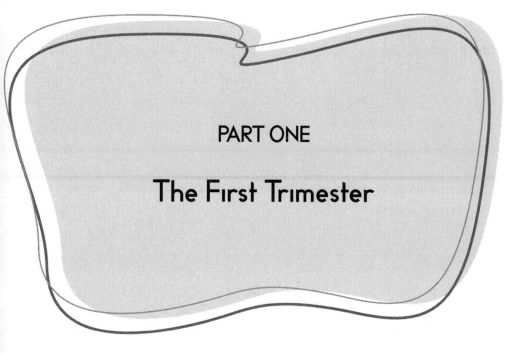

PART ONE

The First Trimester

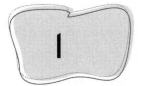

So You Went and Got Pregnant

The Womb of the Unknown Pregnancy: The Art of Classical Obstetrics

With the advent of ultrasound and near-perfect urine and blood tests, the diagnosis of pregnancy is pretty much a no-brainer for today's lab-connected physician. But there is a certain romance of sorts in the history of pregnancy diagnosis before these modern aids were in common use. Doctors used to be trained differently—to use judgment and diagnostic skills that today seem obsolete.

Yesteryear's medical books, incorporating the intrigue and romance of physiologic processes, were so beautifully written that it's hard for me to ever throw any of them away. Looking through them is a journey back into the wonders of the art of diagnosis. Today you're handed ultrasound pictures of your baby on a silver platter and your doctor is spoon-fed rising values of hCG, the pregnancy hormone, almost before your period is late. In earlier nonsophisticated times, many women couldn't get the diagnosis of their "delicate condition" until midpregnancy. We should never pine for a return to those days, but it is fun to see the diagnosis through the eyes of old-time medicine, like watching a child's wonder at the simplest of things we take for granted every day. Pregnancy is and has always been a beautiful experience; and although the science of obstetrics has made for a better pregnancy, the beauty of the art of medicine has been somewhat lost. But as a Rembrandt in an attic remains beautiful even if there's no one there to appreciate it, so it goes with the signs and symptoms that were noted in years past.

Back in the "olden times," circa 1960 (last century, remember?), the "old time" diagnostics were grouped into three classifications:

Presumptive Evidence of Pregnancy: This category includes mainly things you yourself notice, like no period, breast tenderness, nausea, frequency of urination, and fatigue.

Probable Evidence of Pregnancy: These are changes that your doctor will notice, like increased size of your uterus, softening of your uterus, and ballottement (the fetal bounce).

Positive Signs of Pregnancy: These are the "f'sure" things, like fetal heart tones, fetal movement, and ultrasound pictures.

Of course, modern diagnostic techniques make a lot of the presumptive and probable signs and symptoms of pregnancy obsolete and quaint diagnostic tools, placing them nostalgically into the Dark Ages.

Your Due Date: Fun with Arithmetic

The due date is referred to as the estimated date of confinement (EDC). This is a throwback to the days when a woman was confined to bed and home for a period of time after birth until convalescence was complete. It was a term contemporary with the "lying-in" which meant the same thing.

By the time your period is late, that period that doesn't come, you are already two weeks past the time of conception. According to the usual way pregnancy is calculated, you are considered four weeks pregnant. At least we obstetricians call it four weeks because we count from the last regular men-

Fast Forward

The Gregorian calendar and the OB calendar don't jive. The OB calendar uses perfect four-week months—lunar months—while the Gregorian calendar uses months of thirty, thirty-one, and even twenty-eight and twenty-nine days. The forty weeks of pregnancy take up nine months according to that calendar.

strual period. But since no one is pregnant before conception, this is a source of confusion on every pregnancy until the way we count is explained.

The normal human gestation (the period of time it takes for a baby to be grown in the womb) is about 280 days. Divided into perfect four-week months, this comes out to ten perfect months. But Julius Caesar and Pope Gregory XIII, the architects of the modern calendar, were thinking of anything but gestation when, as the sing-song goes, "Thirty days hath September, April, June, and November." (It goes without saying that all the rest but one have thirty-one.) If an obstetrician had designed the calendar, every month would have twenty-eight days ("and no more"), comprising thirteen perfect four-week months per year. Actually, this "OB year" would be just a little short, the real solar year being thirteen perfect months and about one and a quarter days. (I know I could figure out something to do with that extra one day, five hours, and forty-nine minutes.)

It is no coincidence that the average menstrual cycle lasts twenty-eight days. These intervals have been called lunar months in the past, coinciding with the repetitive phases of the moon. The word *menses*, from which menstrual cycle is derived, is a Latin connection with the word for moon. Periods historically coming every lunar month only serve to teach us how very implanted we are into this world, its spin, and its satellite. Over the long spans of evolution the exact relationships have been lost, but it makes sense that the pineal gland in your head, a vestige of a third eye that in lower animals responds to light and helps with circadian rhythm and that is involved with pigmentary changes affected by estrogen and progesterone, is linked to the periodic light phases of the moon and the mysteriously related menses.

Each time the modern calendar month goes beyond twenty-eight days, the perfect gestation of ten perfect months gets out of synch with it. The two days here and three days there eat into that tenth perfect month, so that by the printed calendar of today a pregnancy lasts nine months. So when exactly is your due date? As I said before, the due date is called the estimated day of confinement (EDC) because traditionally women were confined to bed, "lying in," from the day of delivery until convalescence was complete. LMP (last menstrual period) is the only observable event from which to calculate a pregnancy without the aid of ultrasound. EDC and LMP combine in the following formula for calculating your due date:

$$EDC = (LMP - 3 \text{ months}) + 7 \text{ days}$$

While the due date is usually designated as the day forty weeks after the first day of the last regular menstrual period, it's not a true due "date" because there is too much variation in the general population. Since term is anywhere from thirty-eight to forty-two weeks, it's really a "due month."

Pregnancy Rules for Husbands

Rule #1: You should never use the *Sports Illustrated Swimsuit Calendar* to track your wife's pregnancy.

The Maternal-Fetal Person

Your pregnancy, along with the resultant delivery of a life as complex as another human being, requires extraordinary changes in your body to create the shared physiology between you and your developing child. We tend to think of the expectant mother and the developing child as two different beings, but the combination is actually a different creature altogether—the mother-child entity. Who is this person?

This is someone very different from either you or your baby taken alone. Since a mother doesn't "fade out" as the baby "fades in" (although you may want to argue this later on), the third trimester sports quite an extra amount of metabolism. Naturally, the brunt of these changes has to be borne by you, while all the baby has to do by the end is be born.

Having a baby grow inside of you is like having a tumor in many ways. (Having twins grow inside of you is like having a Buick.) For the most part the changes you will notice are due to the hormonal new world order. The major pregnancy hormones are estrogen, progesterone, human chronic gonadotropin (hCG), human placental lactogen (hPL), and prolactin (the milk letdown hormone). Each of these has a role in manipulating the maternal-fetal physiology in preparation for the birth of your offspring. Estrogen and progesterone also figure prominently in preparing your body for actual conception, the preparation known as the menstrual cycle. In short, estrogen helps build up the lining of your uterus (womb), and then after ovulation progesterone helps mature this tissue so that a conception will have a suitable bed of tissue in which to implant.

Your hormone shifts and cycles, strangely enough, all start off with a hormonal blueprint called cholesterol. Much maligned for its heart disease implications, it's actually a necessary substance. That's because if you remove a certain carbon group—voilà!—it becomes a precursor hormone called pregnenolone. Then from pregnenolone are derived estrogen, progesterone, and testosterone, among other things. If you were to watch the molecules vacillate back and forth on some type of biochemistry instant replay VCR, you would see a time lapse of fluttering side molecules around an unchanging core chemical structure that is the skeleton of cholesterol.

Just like a period is the end of a sentence, so too the menstrual period is the end of your preparation for pregnancy when the receptive lining of your uterus goes unfulfilled. But this is a period at the end of a run-on sentence because as one cycle's tissue bed collapses, the hormone sequences are restarting to try again for your next cycle.

At the point when a fertilized egg does bury itself into the cozy lining of your uterus, local reactions at the implantation site begin a chemical chain reaction that signals your body to maintain hormonal levels so that the status quo is preserved. A longer cycle is now begun—one that will last forty weeks, until your uterus is emptied not of unused uterine lining, but of a baby. As the new maternal-fetal person, you walk into your doctor's office.

Prenatal Care

Unless you're under the care of a midwife who visits you at home, getting pregnant begins a series of visits to the obstetrician's office. The types and frequency of visits are as varied as the doctors who attend the deliveries. In this respect the entire prenatal course is punctuated by a doctor's care plan that he has developed over the years and then fine-tunes to the unique presentation of your pregnancy.

There are two types of prenatal populations:

- Those pregnancies where everything is perfect.
- The rest of us!

The perfect pregnancy won't exist until we use our knowledge of the human genome to get Barbie and Ken into the process and then follow up with cloning and mail order (without the shipping and handling). Of course, first we'll have to work out the problem of Barbie and Ken having no genitalia.

Fast Forward

Either you're normal or you're not. Not so fast on the self-appointed "normal" tag—even the smallest concerns will warrant the melodramatic "high-risk" label so as to watch suspect conditions more closely.

While we wait for that controversial merger of Mattel, Dow, and UpJohn that will give us the perfect pregnancy, we have to focus our attention according to relative scales, and to this end obstetricians think in terms of normal and high-risk pregnancies. These two groups are the most generalized divisions of surveillance for an obstetrician watching a pregnancy. "Normal" and "high-risk"—these are humorous designations in that if there's any problem at all, a doctor will consider the patient and pregnancy high risk.

Melodramatic? Perhaps, but there's just too much at stake otherwise. Every pregnancy is of ultimate importance. In your pregnancy anything that goes "Boo!" should be taken seriously.

Normal Pregnancy in the First Trimester

In a so-called normal pregnancy you can expect your obstetrician to see you every three to four weeks in the beginning, then tighten up the frequency of visits as your pregnancy advances, until the time of those weekly visits during "countdown time" in the last month. As I mentioned in Chapter 1, during your pregnancy you can expect there to be a hair-trigger to reclassifying you as high risk should anything stray from normal parameters. High blood pressure, spilling of protein in the urine, fetal growth abnormalities, abnormal ultrasound—any number of things will justify moving you from the normal to the high-risk category. Of course, that's what obstetrics is all about—knowing which patients need extra care.

Until the completion of the first twelve weeks of pregnancy (ten weeks after conception), known collectively as the first trimester, your prenatal care will consist primarily of documentation of a healthy pregnancy, the general medical considerations as they pertain to your pregnancy, and addressing any questions you may have. Since pregnancy is a natural process, there usually aren't any extraordinary measures taken to watch you, beyond having you check in for your weight and blood pressure as well as "dipstick" tests to look for illnesses that give themselves away by spilling warnings into your urine. In fact it's hard to hear the fetal heartbeat with a Doppler before ten weeks, so a lot of this documentation of a healthy pregnancy consists of nothing more than a documentation of exclusions: no vaginal bleeding, no unusual vaginal discharges, no fevers, no unusual pain, and no troubling medical peculiarities. A lot of this is recording an interval history since your last visit and marking down mere measurements of the weight, blood pressure, and urinalysis, so this is a time when a doctor who has physician extenders (nurse practitioners, etc.) uses them.

Of course ultrasound gives your doctor the opportunity to peek in at a very early time, but because it is early in gestation, even those measurements are limited. With many managed care insurance companies authorizing only one measly (editorial rhetoric) ultrasound per pregnancy, your doctor may want to wait a bit so as to get the most information from the one ultrasound.

The first trimester is also a clearinghouse time of sorts to separate the normal from the high-risk patient. For this reason everyone initially undergoes an evaluation that consists of a physical exam and laboratory investigations (cultures and blood work). The first trimester will usually label you with something early if you're going to end up in the high-risk category later on.

A-FACTOR
Remember, the high-risk club has very lax membership criteria, so don't flip out if you find yourself in it.

The real hubbub of the first trimester is vigilance against miscarriage. (Part Two of this book will deal with all aspects of abnormal pregnancies in the first trimester.) The first twelve weeks of pregnancy is the time when miscarriage is most likely and up to 20 percent of diagnosed pregnancies end up miscarrying due to genetic mishaps at conception. But assuming all is well and normal and in every way unsuspicious, you can expect your normal pregnancy to involve monthly visits usually until the end of your second trimester (twenty-four weeks).

Prenatal Care in the First Trimester

Medical History
On your initial visit you will be asked a number of questions, either with a question sheet or by interview (or both), so as to record or update a careful

history, depending on whether you are a new patient or not. Prior records from your last doctor or from consultants (like infertility specialists) who have been caring for you will be sent for. If there's a history of preexisting conditions—hypertension, irritable bowel disease, diabetes, thyroid, etc.—that will mean you're out of the normal pregnancy group. If your history isn't obtained by the doctor herself, you will probably be questioned by her regarding any unusual things that came out of the inquiries so far.

Fast Forward

The initial work-up in normal pregnancy is a careful history and a thorough exam that includes vaginal cultures for STDs, a Pap smear, and a determination to see if the uterine size is appropriate for the gestational age (the result of which may prompt an ultrasound).

Blood work will check for anemia, syphilis, hepatitis (disease or carrier), HIV (AIDS virus), blood type, immunity to rubella, and perhaps immunity to toxoplasmosis or chicken pox. Racial genetic concerns are addressed, like sickle cell and Tay-Sachs.

Sensitivity to the risk of miscarriage is heightened during the first trimester.

You will be appraised of the protocols unique to your doctor and given instructions, precautions, and prenatal vitamins, among other things.

The Initial Physical Exam

In addition to routine blood work and vaginal cultures, the initial physical exam will be used to assess both your general maternal health and the size of your uterus. If it's too early to hear your baby's heartbeat, then your doctor will compare the size of your uterus to the size expected for the supposed gestational age. For instance, if you're six weeks pregnant, but your uterus is twelve weeks by size on the exam, either the estimate of gestational age is wrong, or you've got twins (or fibroids). On the other hand, if you're twelve weeks along, but the size of your uterus by exam is less than six weeks, either you had a delay of your ovulation, making dating of your pregnancy from your last menstrual period inaccurate; there's a problem with your baby's growth, which would constitute a miscarriage concern; or you're not pregnant at all.

Fast Forward

The size of your uterus must be reconciled with the gestational age of your baby, or there's something wrong. Twins, misjudgment of dates, and even nonpregnancy should be suspected if dates don't equal size.

Measuring Your Pelvis

There are manual measurements of your pelvis at the initial exam. By manual, I really do mean by hand. In the course of your vaginal examination your doctor will size up your pelvic measurements by comparing them with her own hand measurements. Over the years your doctor has come to know a personal yardstick—her own hand—and by seeing how her examining fingers lay down against the length and width of your pelvis she can determine the likelihood of a successful passage of your baby through your pelvis. When it's done with X rays (rare in today's modern obstetrics), this is called *pelvimetry*. When it's done with your doctor's hand, it's called skill.

Fast Forward

Chances of a successful vaginal delivery first and foremost depend on an adequately sized pelvis to accommodate your baby. Your doctor can get a pretty good idea by simply measuring your pelvis with her hands and fingers during the vaginal exam. You won't even know she did it, as it's part of the vaginal exam.

Blood Work and Other Lab Tests

Routine blood work will check for anemia, immunity to rubella (German measles), blood type, diseases such as syphilis and hepatitis, thyroid function, and exposure to HIV, the virus that causes AIDS. Routine cultures will be done for chlamydia, gonorrhea, and perhaps Group B strep, although the strep culture is usually done later, around thirty-six weeks (see Chapters 8 and 9). And you should have a Pap smear because no prenatal care is adequate without a recent one (less than one year old by your due date). Life with cats, normal or otherwise, should prompt a test for immunity to toxoplasmosis. (This may be your husband's grand opportunity—the callous brute—to lobby for getting rid of the cat, which isn't necessary if you wash your hands after any feline handling.) If you can't remember having had chicken pox, there's a test for that too.

Abnormal functioning of the thyroid gland can cause problems with the development of your baby, so testing for that is thrown in as a good idea, although most people with thyroid problems already know it. A screen for cystic fibrosis can be offered as well.

The test for gestational diabetes, typically done at twenty-four to twenty-six weeks, should also be done early in pregnancy if there are some warning signals for diabetes, like yeast infections, history of previous gestational diabetes, large babies, or sugar in the urine.

HIV, the virus responsible for AIDS, has been an official part of prenatal screening since 1985. Although still considered a fatal disease, on the obstetrical side of things we've made great progress in preventing its transmission to the fetus, so it's a must-have on any initial prenatal screening.

Unless you were born under a red sun or you and your husband were both virgins when you met each other, either of you may have a little souvenir from love lives past. Absolute fidelity and undisputed monogamy are not protection from the past. Don't be insulted when your doctor checks you for gonorrhea, chlamydia, syphilis, and other things. Even a condition without symptoms can be "anything but" in your newborn. Likewise, screens for drug abuse may be routine in your doctor's protocol. Your doctor may do it on everyone, not just the patients with the Marilyn Manson tattoos.

If there is a discrepancy between how far along you are supposed to be and the size of your uterus on pelvic exam, this would be an excellent indication for an early ultrasound to see what the story is. If this pans out to a miscarriage scare, there are extra blood tests that can be done to check appropriate progress of your pregnancy. If everything between the date and size jibes and all else seems well, depending on your obstetrician, an initial early ultrasound might be done anyway to demonstrate to you a normal-appearing fetus, confirm the agreement with your date based on your last menstrual period, and to begin the actual bonding process. (Seeing your child for the first time is a moving experience—worth the price, even if your cold-blooded insurance company doesn't agree.) Except for a change in the due date, which may just be arithmetic, any other ultrasound surprises (like twins, for instance) will be your ticket out of the normal pregnancy group.

Many obstetricians prefer getting two ultrasounds before twenty weeks because while the accuracy of the dating of the pregnancy falls off dramatically in later pregnancy, most babies grow at about the same rate before twenty weeks, making that a good time in which to compare your baby with what's considered normal growth. The first ultrasound is often obtained at or before twelve weeks. The second one, if that is the usual practice of your doctor, will be obtained at least a month later so that an expected and appropriate interval of growth can be documented.

The use of ultrasound is a financially controversial matter. Insurance companies will point to studies that indicate that routine use of ultrasound will not change the pregnancy outcomes of the general population. But of course we're not talking about the general population—we're talking about you. Enjoy a doctor who likes ultrasound.

During the first trimester, the staple of each visit is blood pressure, weight, and the urine values for sugar (glucose) and protein. The weight becomes important when following a patient with morning sickness. Actual weight loss, which will prompt weekly or even daily visits instead of monthly, can result when morning sickness worsens into what's called *hyperemesis gravidarum*, a nausea bad enough to seriously jeopardize your nutrition. Unless you have chronic hypertension or kidney disease, you shouldn't have blood pressure problems or protein spilling into the urine, which are more likely to be problems later in the third trimester.

Since the first trimester is the time zone of highest risk of miscarriage, any bleeding will prompt ultrasounds more often, sometimes even weekly. You'll be out of the normal group for this as well, and a series of blood levels of the pregnancy hormone, hCG, will be drawn to watch for ensuing miscarriage, ectopic pregnancy, or resolution toward a normal pregnancy.

Fetal heart tones are difficult to hear during the first trimester, so hearing the heartbeat will have to wait until the second trimester.

The perfect pregnancy patient gets booted out of the Perfect Pregnancy Club for even the slightest physiologic indiscretion. Back at Louisiana State University we used to have a moderate-risk pregnancy clinic as a joke, to take time off, because there is the normal pregnancy for some and the high-risk for everyone else. There was no such thing as a moderate-risk pregnancy—that clinic was empty. But most patients start out in the Perfect Pregnancy Club until they are ousted for this problem or that. Depending on what your problem is, you may have close to a normal sequence of visits or at the other extreme may be seen every day in the hospital for a serious problem that requires complete bed rest and jeopardizes your baby and/or you.

In the first trimester, problems that can make you high risk include:

- Bleeding (threatened miscarriage)
- Unusual pelvic pain (prompting worries of possible ectopic pregnancy)
- Chronic hypertension
- Preexisting medical conditions, such as hypertension, heart disease, diabetes, asthma, thyroid disease, etc.
- Medication exposure (either necessary medication for a preexisting medical condition or exposure to medicines before you knew you were pregnant)
- History of previous miscarriage, preterm labor, premature delivery, congenital abnormalities, stillbirth, or neonatal death
- Family history of congenital abnormality or stillbirth
- Multiple gestation (twins, triplets, and so on)
- Smoking
- Alcohol or drug abuse
- Abnormal Pap smear

Preexisting medical conditions can make for tricky pregnancy management because some treatments may be safe for you, but they may not be safe for your developing baby. Sometimes the risks have to be weighed against the benefits, with trade-offs involved for the fetal as well as for your maternal side.

Regarding what separates normal pregnancies from high-risk ones, every doctor has his list—a routine for keeping an eye out for warning signals in each of those perfect pregnancies. Those patients who are or become "high risk" have a series of appointments tailored just for them. In your visits to your obstetrician, you should have all of the screenings that this year has to offer—not last year's obstetrics. You should expect your doctor to follow your pregnancy appropriately, whether you're high risk or normal. And you should presume that he knows the difference.

A Typical Time Line During Prenatal Care in Private Practice

First trimester—up to twelve weeks

Initial prenatal visit:

- History or history update
- Thorough physical exam—documentation of pregnancy and estimation of due date (gestational age)
- Arrangement for initial blood work—standard cultures for gonorrhea, chlamydia
- Pap smear, unless you've had one recently. Listen for fetal heart tones if initial visit occurs at twelve to thirteen weeks gestation. Possibly arrange an ultrasound. Arrange for perinatal consultation for risk factors, including age above thirty-five.
- Request for old records if pertinent

Subsequent visits every three to four weeks:

- Documentation of blood pressure, weight, urine tests for protein and glucose
- Questions and answers to specific concerns
- Reconciliation of ultrasound to gestation age

Battle of the Bulge: Changes in Your Body

Now that you've gone and gotten yourself pregnant, there is a knocking at the door. At first it's a polite, little tapping. Then there's a more urgent rapping. By the third trimester pregnancy is pounding on the door, rattling the metal cup against the prison bars. Since human gestation is long, you have some time to get used to it (as if that's possible). The first trimester is that polite first knocking.

Estrogen

Estrogen and progesterone cycle up and down each menstrual cycle much like a thermostat. When there's a lot, less is made, and when there's too little, more is made. It's a merry-go-round every month, a dance of hormones at a party that awaits your guest of honor. When implantation occurs, a maternal-fetal communication begins within you, an informational exchange between you and your developing child made up of biochemical and hormonal signals. During the first trimester estrogen is mostly produced by the placenta; until near the end of the pregnancy the amount circulating in your body is a thousand times the amount you have when not pregnant. Estrogen makes everything grow by improving the blood supply. This will have impact on your breasts, moles, and spider veins.

Progesterone

Unlike estrogen, which is manufactured by the placenta, progesterone comes from the cholesterol connection in your blood. Progesterone is a potent anti-inflammatory, possibly contributing to your blunted immune system so you won't reject your baby. It is also a smooth muscle relaxant, slowing down gastric emptying to give you heartburn and acid reflux, and decreasing the tone of your bowels, leading to constipation. It also increases the oiliness of your skin, so if you're the fairest in all the land, you'll be shocked to see that first zit in five years rear its ugly little head. Its relaxant properties may play a role in keeping your uterus from contracting until term.

Estrogen and progesterone together help control the onset of breast milk, keeping the floodgates closed by inhibiting the breasts' response to prolactin, the milk letdown hormone. Their levels plunge at delivery, allowing prolactin to stimulate the flow.

Human Placental Lactogen (hPL)

Human placental lactogen is made by the placenta and is a growth hormone. It affects your metabolism by breaking down fat to provide nutrition for your baby.

> **Fast Forward**
> Estrogen, progesterone, hCG, hPL, and prolactin are the major pregnancy hormones. Thyroid and adrenal hormones from both you and your baby play roles as well.

Human Gonadotropic Hormone (hCG)

Except for some very weird and rare ovarian tumors, hCG is a pregnancy exclusive. We use this fact to our advantage by using it as a pregnancy test. We can even tell how well the pregnancy is going by measuring the increases in the amounts of hCG, which should double every two days or so in the early part of the first trimester.

The level of hCG plateaus near the end of the first trimester, leading us to believe it may have something to do with morning sickness. Not only does morning sickness usually fade away coincidental with the plateau of the hCG levels, but half of the hCG molecule is identical to half of the thyroid-stimulating hormone, itself a cause of nausea. The most apparent biological effect of hCG is to regulate progesterone production from the site on your ovary where you ovulated, that part of the ovary remaining as something called the *corpus luteum*. This progesterone regulation plays a role in sexual differentiation of your baby.

Prolactin

Prolactin, the milk letdown hormone, acts when the estrogen and progesterone decrease at the end of pregnancy. Thyroid hormones, insulin, and other things work together to pull this off, but prolactin is the main regulator for the onset and regulation of lactation.

Nutrition: Eating Right for the Mother-Child

Pregnancy books are famous for flipping out over the subject of nutrition. You can't blame these authors. Nutrition is certainly crucial in pregnancy, and it would seem that any author would be remiss in leaving out detailed instructions on how to pursue the perfect pregnancy nutritional state. It would seem. Along comes *The Anxious Parent's Guide to Pregnancy*, and I've decided to be flip about it rather than flip out about it.

Don't get me wrong—this is an important subject. It's just that you've had a lot of practice seeking good nutrition before becoming pregnant. The other pregnancy books spend a lot of time breaking down each kumquat into calories, ergs, joules, and whatever else would make a biochemist wax nostalgic. There are recipes, food groupings, and complex caloric formulas. All of this content certainly makes for a thorough-looking treatment on the subject.

The truth is that you are not going to alter your life around the arithmetic of nutrition. You're not going to concoct meals based on the recipes suggested or keep a food diary to tabulate your intake. I know. I've seen a generation of pregnant women, visit by visit, pound for pound. In the real world pregnant women keep eating like they've always eaten and alter their diets only slightly so as to pursue the few extra requirements of pregnancy (while obeying any nausea and acquiescing to any cravings).

Those extra requirements are all you really have to know. Face it, you already know whether you eat well or not. Donuts are poison if that's all you eat. But if you eat meals that encompass a high-protein, somewhat low-fat, somewhat low-sugar breakdown, you won't have to alter your diet much at all.

What Are the Extra Nutritional Requirements of Pregnancy?

Here's the lowdown:

You need about three hundred extra calories a day for the extra metabolism that pregnancy creates, spread evenly over all of the food groups. For the most part, this is almost a negligible amount, squandered in a single craving. If you're exercising, you need to taper this requirement up accordingly. Your own body will give you the telltale urge of hunger.

Since pregnancy is a natural process, a good, healthy diet will supply you with most of what you need before and during pregnancy. Boosting intake of some items, however, will benefit you. Extra folate (folic acid) taken at least one month before conception and during the first trimester will decrease your chances of neural tube defects—i.e., spina bifida and devastating abnormalities of the baby's central nervous system. The FDA, recognizing the importance of folate, orders folate supplementation of grains in this country. Folate is also found in leafy vegetables like lettuce, beans, and peas, and in citrus juices. The amount of folate seems to vary with whatever study is most recent, but the minimum should be at least 0.4 mg (400 micrograms), which is the amount contained in most nonprescription vitamins. In my practice I use a full 1 mg (1,000 micrograms), which is easy to arrange since that's the amount in most prescription prenatal vitamins.

Fast Forward

Folate (folic acid), iron, zinc, and calcium are owed special attention since they are needed in greater quantity during pregnancy. Prescription prenatal vitamins usually do a good job, but sometimes more iron is needed than those vitamins include.

A good, healthy diet means no alcohol, tobacco, substance abuse, fad diets, or psychiatric eating disorders. In the absence of these dietary abnormalities, it's easy to keep up with most of the usual vitamins except for B6 (which seems to protect against morning sickness), D, E, and the folate mentioned above. More minerals are needed during pregnancy, so iron is given to prevent anemia, extra zinc to make up for iron's interference with zinc absorption, and calcium. The biochemical importance of these substances is very complex, and since I don't want to induce an irretrievable coma, suffice it to say that most prescription prenatal vitamins take care of the extra vitamin and mineral demands of pregnancy. Except for anemia. An extra iron supplement is sometimes necessary, assuming your doctor has ruled out nonpregnancy causes like sickle-cell anemia, thalassemia, or other inherited anemias.

It's good to spread your food intake over several small meals instead of the usual three square meals a day. I hate to make eating in pregnancy sound like you're strapping on a feedbag, but it's less of a social gathering around the table and more of a matter of keeping you and your baby properly fueled. By equilibrating a stable blood sugar level all day, meals spread out throughout the day will prevent dizziness and fatigue. Merely skipping one meal is enough to have you swagger to a chair with dizziness. Also, this way of eating is more likely to keep some food in the stomach all of the time, buffering acid and decreasing heartburn. Six small feedings (sorry) are better than three larger meals.

Fast Forward

Eat right to begin with, and then . . .

- You need three hundred extra calories a day (more if you exercise) and extra folate, iron, zinc, and calcium.
- Eat many small meals instead of three large ones.
- Don't skip any meals.
- Take your prenatal vitamins.
- Don't lose weight—especially on purpose.
- If you begin a pregnancy with special considerations (being a vegetarian, allergies to certain foods, diabetes, etc.), you'll need a dietitian/ nutritionist.

All of the food groups are a tidy way of thinking about types of food, but don't eat just one group for a single meal. The way to go is to have an even mix, every meal.

Of all of the vitamins championed in pregnancy, folic acid (also called folate, a B vitamin) seems to have particular importance in your baby's neurological development. Your prenatal vitamin gives you what you need for that, but leafy green vegetables, asparagus, whole grains, liver, beans, and peas are a good source.

There are changes in your blood during pregnancy, and iron is essential to the goings-on. All in all, you make more blood in pregnancy so that in that bloodletting experience known as delivery, you'll break even on the deal. But you'll definitely get a little anemic because the amount of plasma increase is more than the amount of red blood cell increase. Since the blood count is a comparison of red blood cells to plasma, this anemia is a little bogus, but the bottom line is that iron is necessary for red blood cell production. Therefore, extra iron is needed in your diet. Again, your prenatal vitamins will satisfy this extra need, but things like liver, spinach, and green leafy vegetables are good sources of iron. Oh, yes, and sardines, as my nutritionist sources tell me.

There's a lot of bone-making going on in your baby. If you don't take enough calcium in, your baby will sift what he needs first, leaving the rest for you. If your diet includes dairy products, you're fine. Zinc and other minerals are important, but these and the protein, fat, and sugars you need should come naturally from a healthy diet.

Take your prenatal vitamins. Take one made by a big company because the big companies are the ones who spent the money making sure their vita-

▶ Fast Forward

Don't go overboard about diet and nutrition. If you eat well already, take your vitamins and let your body urge you toward the extra calories needed. If you don't eat well, if your doctor thinks you don't eat well, if you're gaining too much or losing, or if you just don't know, forget your doctor or any book. See a dietitian/nutritionist and do it right. I love them and no doctor will ever do nutrition better than they will.

Dietitians/nutritionists rule!

mins are adequate. Stay away from fitness gurus who construct a combination of ingredients under the guise of holistic holiness—they're not dietitians and you're just another sale to them. Diets that have a particular hole here or there will be nicely supplemented by a prescription prenatal vitamin.

And there you are.

Normally, I'd say, "End of subject," and move on. Except that I want to make a very important point: nutritionists and registered dietitians spend years studying what they do. Your doctor merely takes a few nutrition courses in med school. Whole books have been written on nutrition, and any pregnancy book that claims to be a nutrition model for you, with just a section or a chapter, insults the whole science of dietetics. If you know you don't eat healthily, or if your doctor feels your weight gain (or loss) is suspect, don't fool around with books. Sit down with a dietitian/nutritionist and develop a problem list and solution protocol specifically tailored for you and your pregnancy. You shouldn't get it from your doctor, either—it must be a properly credentialed dietitian/nutritionist because they're the ones who do this. If you were to have any other problem in pregnancy, you would go to the expert, so your nutrition should be no different. If you have no medical dietary concerns and eat a healthy diet, my general guidelines are plenty enough. If there's doubt, let the pros deal with it.

Unfortunately, the insurance companies (who *pledge* to care about you until they *have* to care about you) won't pay for a dietitian, so you'll have to spring for it. But it's only going to be about a hundred dollars, tops, and it'll be the best bargain of your pregnancy. While I can't say enough about my respect for the important work that these professionals do, I also can't say enough about my disdain for the attitude of insurers who won't authorize a dietitian if you were to have hypertension, diabetes, milk intolerance, or any condition that would make one mandatory. They just don't care. (Stronger piece to follow in "Controversies in Obstetrics" in Chapter 22.)

If you really must know, the four major food groups are:

1. Meats, fish, and poultry (including eggs)
2. Dairy group (be careful, ice cream can be a Svengali)
3. Fruits and vegetables—for vitamins C and A.
4. Bread, cereals, legumes, and peas

Vegetarians can get their iron from beans and their protein from beans and nuts. But beware and remember the famous children's rhyme:

Beans, beans, they're good for your heart.
Beans, beans, they make you fart.
The more you fart, the better you feel,
So eat your beans at every meal.

Now on that note I can truly say, "End of subject."

3

The Initial Trials of Pregnancy

It's hard enough trying not to sweat the normal things in your life—exercise, diet, and generally the stuff that you can mind your own business about. In pregnancy, however, there are things that come after you, whether you like it or not. The hormones of pregnancy—the mother-child—are what bring on those little surprises that make you wonder what you've gotten yourself into. "The Initial Trials of Pregnancy," alternately, could be called "The Initial Mis-

Fast Forward

The initial trials of pregnancy:

- Breast tenderness
- Stretch marks (mainly on breasts in first trimester)
- Pigmentation changes and spider veins
- Headaches
- Decreased tolerance for exercise
- Heartburn
- Constipation
- Shift in figure
- Cravings
- Weight gain
- Morning sickness, evening sickness, anytime sickness
- Hyperemesis—exaggerated morning sickness

eries of Pregnancy," depending on whether you see your uterus as half empty or half full.

Breast Tenderness

The sex connection aside, the breasts are two glands, and being glands, they do what glands do best—they secrete. Of course they secrete sustenance during the bonding of newborn to mother. Glands are not inert globs of tissue, but dynamic clusters of cells that are provoked by a stimulus to function. In the case of the breasts, this function is the production and release of mother's milk. Estrogen, being the great stimulator of growth that it is, in increased amounts enhances the size of your milk ducts. The result is enlargement of your breasts. The nerves around the ducts are also made more responsive owing to the extra blood flow, which you will perceive as tenderness in early pregnancy. This tenderness is also related to your breasts' response to the increased estrogen and the amount of that increase. Every woman is different in early pregnancy, some experiencing exquisite tenderness in the breasts, others worrying that the breasts are not sensitive enough. (By now it has become a famous cliché that painful breasts imply a healthy pregnancy because this is direct evidence of a hearty amount of estrogen to support the pregnancy. But since tenderness is a result of the breasts' sensitivity to amounts of increased estrogen, and not necessarily a specific amount of estrogen, this isn't a guaranteed truism. Similar "truisms" are propagated in early pregnancy, e.g., concerning nausea—see page 52.)

Because of changes that ready the breasts for delivering the goods, the nipples widen and there is a deeper pigmentation. Also, if your breasts enlarge at a rate such that the elasticity of your skin is challenged, damage to the skin will be seen as stretch marks (striae).

Stretch Marks (Striae)

Stretch marks on the abdomen can be seen in the second trimester. Striae on the breasts, however, can appear in the first trimester. Sometimes they're not noticed at all until after delivery (which will be a shock if you think you had escaped them) because increased pigmentation and seasonal sun exposure can camouflage even a significant array of them.

Fast Forward
Tanning beds are poison and cause terminal cosmetic prunosis.

Tanning beds aren't a good idea. Besides making you prone to skin cancer and providing you a chance to become Miss Prune in 2020, they can deepen the damage at the tearing level of the stretch marks. Additionally, they can cause dehydration, which isn't a danger to your metabolism since you'll gulp down a health drink right after, but which will thin out the stretched, damaged tissue being irradiated, worsening any vulnerability. I suggest you get your Vitamin D with your prenatal vitamins.

Spider Veins (Telangiectasias)

These are the spider veins that swell from the extra estrogen. They'll probably shrink or disappear after your baby's born. More white women get them than black women, but this may only be that they're more noticeable on light skin.

Pigmentation

Estrogen and progesterone affect hormones (such as MSH—melanocyte-stimulating hormone) that stimulate the deposit of pigment in the skin. I mentioned darkened nipples above, but sometimes there can be an exaggerated pigmentation in other areas. *Linea nigra* is a pigmentation of the midline from your navel to your pubic area; most women develop this discoloration to some extent. There is also something called *chloasma*, the mask of pregnancy, which can be seen in varying degrees in half of pregnancies. This darkening of the face may continue after delivery if birth control pills (which, like pregnancy, are also an estrogen and progesterone source) are taken. Brunettes are the most vulnerable. The admonishments against sun exposure and tanning beds go for hyperpigmentation too.

Everyone wants to be normal, and you are your own best expert. Unfortunately, you're also your own worst critic, so it's unsettling if you notice any of these changes. Reassurance lies in the fact that all of these changes are reversible after delivery. Even your stretch marks can fade over time and with increased tone.

Headaches

Headaches are common in early pregnancy, especially in the first trimester when the hormones are racing to unprecedented levels. The problem is that there are a lot of hormonal surges happening at once. Headaches tend to fizzle after the first trimester, either because the surges stabilize or because you're dealing better with the headaches or with the stress that causes them. If you smoke (not that you would do such a stupid thing during pregnancy, right?), you can add another powerful headache ingredient to the mix.

The most common cause of headaches in pregnancy, though, is stress. Fear of the unknown while physically trying to carry on life as usual with all of your body changes will produce an occasional four-hour throbbing for sure. Migraines, on the other hand, are not the body's adaptation to stress, but truly abnormal processes and therefore harder to manage. Thankfully, migraines usually improve in pregnancy; stress headaches usually get worse and more frequent.

Your doctor is somewhat limited as to what to offer you during your pregnancy when you have a headache. The famous recommendation is to lie quietly in a dark room with a cool rag on your forehead. Yeah, right. That'll happen.

Fast Forward

Headaches are common in the first trimester until a lot of the hormones level out. Acetaminophen is safe by private practice standards. NSAIDs are potentially hazardous. A migraine sufferer used to Imitrex shouldn't use it without the permission of her doctor. Narcotics, under your doctor's direction, should be safe, but can perhaps worsen a stress headache.

You'll get little sympathy for that headache that just won't go away if you're a smoker.

But assuming you can stop the entire world and everyone you need to interact with, this is a good technique. Even though there are some liver toxicity concerns, doctors use extra-strength acetaminophen anyway because no one sees liver toxicity from an occasional dose. "NSAIDs" (such as Advil,

Nuprin, Motrin, etc.) are out because they can cause complications with the pregnancy and have definite effects on your blood-clotting system, which is already a little weird from the pregnancy itself. If you've taken an Advil instead of a Tylenol, don't panic. The studies don't label a pregnancy exposed to an occasional NSAID as doomed; they just indicate that it's an unwise choice compared to acetaminophen.

For headaches resistant to acetaminophen, narcotics have a time-honored safety. But beware—I've found narcotics (Tylenol #2 and #3, Vicodin, Loricet, etc.) to sometimes make stress headaches worse. Imitrex is the darling drug for migraine sufferers. So far, it hasn't been shown to do any harm to babies, but there hasn't been enough volume of data yet to recommend Imitrex with a completely clear conscience. Surely Imitrex exposure before you found out you were pregnant should not cause you worry.

Fast Forward

If you're used to a certain exercise regimen before you were pregnant, you should be able to continue it, modified only by changes in stamina and changes in the space you occupy. You should shy away from high-impact or joint-challenging maneuvers or routines that prolong a persistent rise in your body temperature.

Change in Response to Exercise

Because of the tremendous changes in your blood volume and your physiology's response to this change by your cardiovascular system, you would think that being pregnant would bring about big changes in your ability to adjust to even a moderate aerobic program. Actually, the maximum amount of exercise that you can tolerate goes down only a little. If you were used to a certain program of exercise before becoming pregnant, you should be able to continue it into your pregnancy at only a slightly reduced rate. As pregnancy continues, the larger uterus and pendulous weight of your breasts may interfere by throwing off your center of gravity and making you feel like you're 99 percent belly, but for the most part exercise should be continued because it's good for you and your pregnancy.

Temperature increase is somewhat focused toward the fetus in early pregnancy, and raising your body temperature may have some theoretical effect, but there really hasn't been any such effect noted in humans, all of the data being in animal studies only. In fact, even rigorous routines in the first trimester haven't shown any deleterious effects. The fetus is usually a degree warmer than you are, so piling a sauna or a soak in the hot tub on top of that will tend to make your obstetrician nervous. She'll tell you not to, and even though she won't be able to back it up, anything that would make your doctor nervous should make you nervous too. And just because she can't back up her warnings now doesn't mean that her next journal won't have a smoking gun alarm about such things. A good, yet unscientific, rule of thumb is that you shouldn't do anything in your pregnancy that would make your own doctor nervous about her own or his loved one's pregnancy.

Athletes of maximum effort—triathletes, marathoners, and the like—sometimes suffer exercise-related amenorrhea (their periods stop). These individuals have a deficiency of progesterone, necessary in the second half of the cycle to provide for implantation or subsequent periods. Indirectly there is probably a problem with ovulation, which is why the second half of the cycle (and with it progesterone) is faulty. This type of extreme exercise would really frighten an obstetrician, but such scares are rare since a woman with an exertion-related amenorrhea rarely conceives. And even if she were to conceive, this would make more of an impact in the first few weeks, if at all. Exercise-related disruption of such an early pregnancy would probably result in a "silent" miscarriage, lost in a shuffle of irregular bleeding misinterpreted as the usual sporadic cycle.

I once had a patient who ran five miles a day throughout her pregnancy. For twins! She did great. She didn't listen to my advice; of course, neither did her husband when the infertility specialist had told him to give up—that he would never father a child with such a lousy sperm count. Doctors—what the hell do they know?

Heartburn

Pyrosis is the medical term for heartburn. It's common in pregnancy for several reasons:

1. Progesterone, abundant in pregnancy, slows down the movement of the gastrointestinal tract, causing decreased stomach emptying—that feeling that the food is just sitting there . . . because it is. The additional decreased motility and tone of the esophagus also lessens its pressure, which then is less of a barrier to stomach acid refluxing upward. That stuff burns!

> **Fast Forward**
>
> Heartburn is caused by both mechanical changes (cramming two people into the space of one) and chemical changes (effects from progesterone and abuse from normal acids).

2. The distortion of the anatomy due to pregnancy results from many different organs fighting it out for space, and the stomach is no exception in this turf battle. The stomach is displaced, altering the emptying of its contents and acid.

3. The opening in the diaphragm through which the esophagus passes (from the chest into the abdomen) widens in pregnancy. It becomes a physiologic hiatal hernia, and if a stomach portion slides up through it, this can also cause interference with stomach acid going back down. Once again, esophageal reflux. This particular aspect of heartburn is worse when lying flat instead of in a slightly elevated head-up angle: in a flat position the top of the stomach can slide up through this hernia (also called a "sliding" hernia). Propping yourself up will allow gravity to do its thing and the stomach can fall back down into place. Sorry, but you wouldn't be a good candidate for the International Space Station.

   We doctors dread trying to advise a patient on what to do for her hiatal hernia and her feet swelling because elevating your head while elevating your legs above the level of your heart will possibly make necessary an orthopedic consultation.

4. Due to the increased amount of iron, prenatal vitamins can be irritating to the stomach. Sometimes it's necessary to put the vitamins on hold for a couple of weeks. (Prenatal vitamins are a great idea—especially to get your folic acid—but they're not a deal breaker. We got by for millions of years before prenatal vitamins.)

The most conservative treatment for stomach upset is an antacid other than sodium bicarbonate (the sodium in sodium bicarbonate can cause considerable swelling). Milk of Magnesia, Maalox, and so forth are all good choices. The trick you have to remember is to use these about twenty minutes before you eat, otherwise you're just pouring it over the food and it won't act as well as an antacid at the site of acid production, the stomach lining.

More aggressive approaches use agents that decrease the secretion of acid, like cimetidine (Tagamet). These agents are for the most part safe (except for Cytotec, which can induce abortion or preterm labor).

Constipation

Progesterone again plays mischief—this time with your bowels by relaxing them, thereby slowing them down. Your large intestines play a major role in your state of hydration. The longer feces sit in your bowels, the longer the intestines can reabsorb water and dry this material out. The result is a harder stool, namely, constipation. (Of course you're a lady, so such things really aren't a part of your world.) A further side effect of this may be the development of hemorrhoids, varicose veins around the anus that fill with the straining associated with trying to eliminate a particularly disobedient stool. But you should get used to disobedience—you're going to be a mom.

Shift of Your Figure

You're going to panic a little bit in very early pregnancy when those Calvin Kleins don't zip up the way they did just weeks ago. After all, just how much weight can you gain in that short a period of time? The actual problem isn't weight gain, but a shift in the figure. In fact if you were to weigh yourself right at the time you had your corporal argument with Calvin, you would be surprised that you probably hadn't gained any weight at all. So what's happening?

Hormones again, I'm afraid. Just as the lack of hormones will tend to shift the figure of a menopausal woman, a surge of them will likewise have an effect. Calvin Kleins are rather unforgiving to childbearing hips, which in your case are already in progress. Added to this is an evenly distributed swelling of tissue known as fluid retention, thanks to sodium retention, further thanks to estrogen. (This same problem is seen before a period.) Hand in hand with figure shifts is the subject of weight gain.

Cravings: "I Can't Believe I Ate the Whole Thing"

By the seventh month of pregnancy, your unborn baby is responsive to the tastes of different substances. Unfortunately, there isn't much of a menu, but we won't go into that. On the other hand, you can hop into a car and ride out to obtain whatever taste your heart desires. Or send your husband, who will gain weight along with you during the pregnancy, but probably won't lose it afterward like you will.

Your husband will enjoy your cravings too, because suddenly there is gustatory anarchy at the hands of runaway hormones. Men don't balk when they see the double-stuffed Oreos arrive with the rest of the groceries.

Taste is very closely related to smell, using many of the same nerves and areas of the brain. The taste buds on your tongue are more richly vascular in pregnancy, changing the taste of many things for you. Suddenly even Dr Pepper tastes pretty good. This vascular effect is evident in everything in your pregnancy, from your gums that bleed so easily with teeth brushing to the growth spurt of skin tags (molluscum gravidarum) and moles that have better blood supplies around which to flourish. The pregnancy's estrogen increase is a great stimulant for blood vessel development and thus nutrition for all of your tissues, be it nasal mucosa, taste buds, or even cancer.

Cravings are a natural part of pregnancy, with a complex set of factors contributing to a need to wolf down the hankering du jour. Sugar metabolism is altered, causing the insulin the pancreas manufactures to be less effective. Fat is stored at a different rate; protein is metabolized differently. The need for vitamins is increased, influencing your desire to consume a particular food choice. A natural nurturing instinct causes you to choose greater portions of some items than you used to. Salt metabolism changes, affecting thirst. There are, I'm sure, a host of yet-to-be discovered influences on why a woman craves certain things while pregnant. And of course there are the more richly supplied taste buds.

In my practice I tend to be fairly forgiving of mild diet fluctuations. The overall nutritional picture must be balanced, of course, and the requirements of necessary items be satisfied, but for the most part weight gain is over maligned. In fact recent reports have indicated that the traditional recommendation of gaining twenty-two to twenty-seven pounds may be unfairly limiting to the woman who may gain five or so more pounds than this. When it comes right down to it, each maternal-fetal unit is unique, and there is no formula that will fit everyone. We know that there needs to be a diet adequate in calories, protein, essential fatty acids, minerals, and vitamins, but we also have to tolerate the occasional cravings that cumulatively may add only a few more pounds. Perhaps some humoral, endocrine, metabolic need is driving you to get some nutrient, even if it's coming in the form of french fries. (I once read a recommendation to avoid Mexican food, which made me wonder, what are pregnant Mexicans supposed to eat?)

But anything that's not done in moderation can have bad effects. If crave-binging becomes a substantial part of your diet, modern prenatal care will have to step in.

And now, the list everyone's been waiting for:

The Ten Most Popular Cravings During Pregnancy in My Obstetrical Practice

1. Pickles at the deli counter
2. City Park hot dogs (chili mandatory)
3. Anything from Baskin-Robbins (except the nonfat stuff)
4. Shoney's breakfast bar
5. Hot tamales
6. Meatballs and spaghetti
7. Popcorn
8. Anything left on any family member's plate (more likely than not you will choose to overserve each member at mealtime)
9. Mylanta
10. More popcorn

And now it's time to turn to the unfunny side of cravings.

Weight Gain

Because hunger in pregnancy isn't like normal hunger (it's more like alien-space-monster hunger), weight gain is always a concern. Luckily, in today's modern obstetrics it's more of a cosmetic concern. Weight gain is more an issue in the later trimesters, but weight is not the harbinger of doom it once was, promising one complication after another. In the past one out of every two hundred C-section patients died, so it was in the patient's and the doctor's best interests to be militant about weight gain, a cofactor of risk for this mode of delivery. Now with later-generation antibiotics and improved surgical techniques, women seldom experience even moderate complications with C-sections. With this drop in fretting have come less rigorous attitudes about weight gain when not associated with diabetes. Some people are lucky and get everything for free, but for you it might be pay now or pay later because less rigorous attitudes about weight gain may also be an important factor in the rise in the C-section rate. No matter how safe it's become, it's still an operation. If that's important to you, you'll have to deal responsibly, against great odds, with your weight gain.

Fast Forward

With some slight variations, weight gain due to your pregnancy will be twenty-five to thirty pounds. Anything else is you—either abnormal fluid retention due to pregnancy complications, or—dare I say it?—caloric indiscretions. But this is somewhat unfair because there really should be an expected increase in your own fat due to pregnancy, which is all part of extra energy pathways used in the altered physiology of pregnancy.

Like I said, it's an alien hunger. An alien has taken over your body and plugged an input-output signal jack right into that part of your brain that begs, "Feed me! I want it, I need it, I've got to have it now!" This hunger is like the Terminator: You can't reason with it, you can't argue with it, you can't beg for mercy. All you can do is hop in your car and run for your life . . . to the deli. True, there is a breaking point after which weight gain does become a grave medical concern, but it's at a much heftier pound mark than it used to be.

Pregnancy Rules for Husbands

Rule #2: No garment—no shorts, no skirt, no slacks—ever, ever, in any way makes a woman's behind look big. Ever.

There are pounds that are solely the result of the pregnancy. The rest is you. A general breakdown at term goes thus:

> Fetus: 7.5 lb
> Placenta: 1.5
> Amniotic fluid: 2.0
> Uterus: 2.0
> Extra blood: 3.0
> Fluid retention: 4.0
> Maternal variation: 5–10
> TOTAL: 25–30 lb

Sudden weight gain can be a sign of sudden fluid retention—a warning signal for pregnancy-induced hypertension (preeclampsia), a toxic condition we'll talk about in Chapter 7.

Pregnancy Rules for Husbands

Rule #3: Don't ever show the slightest hesitation in affirming Rule #2 when asked. Hesitation is tantamount to a *Yes.*

Morning Sickness: The Nausea and Vomiting

Of all the things that may make you suspect you're pregnant—breast tenderness due to stimulation of breast tissue by estrogen; loss of usual figure even before any weight is gained, which is also a hormonal effect; constipation due to progesterone slowing down the intestinal tract; mood swings, also hormonal—there's nothing as miserable for you in early pregnancy as the severe nausea that can happen. This so-called morning sickness actually can be anytime and can even last all day long (and all night too). Many theorize that the rise in the pregnancy hormone hCG, one part of which at a microscopic level resembles thyroid hormone, causes nausea in a way similar to the way hyperthyroidism can cause it. Others think it's the estrogen, known to increase blood flow to the taste buds and affect taste and cravings negatively as well as positively. Since taste is almost identical to smell, this would explain the reason some smells set off a wave of nausea.

> **Fast Forward**
>
> Nausea happens. On the other hand, if you're nausea free, don't assume it's a troubled pregnancy or you might make yourself throw up from worry.

Cranial Nerve One, the olfactory nerve, the first major nerve to come out of our brains, goes to the front of our heads as the first point of contact to the world, bypassing the pecking order of even our eyes, which use Cranial Nerve Two. It's a definite "dis" to sense organs we deem more important, but perhaps such sensitivity to smells had some survival value for a pregnant cavewoman, allowing her to avoid bad things by their bad smells long before they could be seen. In modern times about the worst thing you can smell before it's dangerous is bad food in the refrigerator.

True, many are blessed with having no nausea whatsoever, but many suffer greatly, even to a point wherein they need to be hospitalized overnight to be rehydrated with IV solutions. When nausea is this bad, we refer to it as hyperemesis gravidarum, which is a vicious cycle: nausea causes dehydration, dehydration worsens the nausea, and further nausea causes further dehydration. This sequence can be broken by rehydrating with a simple overnight IV, which is often enough to get a woman stable enough to begin eating again.

Usually when the amount of rising hCG plateaus (at about ten weeks), the nausea subsides. There are exceptions, with lingerings into the second trimester, but by this time the nausea is much more tolerable.

> **Fast Forward**
>
> Assuming a pregnancy is going great by the amount of nausea is no compensation for the misery that nausea is, and it's no acceptable trade-off for the nutritional deficiency and dehydration it can cause.

There are few feelings as bad as the helplessness of nausea, and on one level we obstetricians find reassurance in this misery because it means the hormones are raging and the pregnancy is probably strong. But the nutritional shutdown is never normal. The dehydration is never normal. A mixed blessing, for sure, but I'd just as soon skip this type of reassurance because it's a bad type of suffering. And it happens that a lot of the suffering goes unimproved in spite of our best efforts.

The word *teleological* refers to something that has a purpose or specific design, as in nature. It is a romantic notion to suppose that the nausea and vomiting of pregnancy is a teleological condition, along with cravings. That is, there's something unique to a particular pregnancy that would make certain foods harmful to that specific fetus and other foods particularly beneficial. Unfortunately, teleological theories will always be cloaked heavily in ignorance and even superstition because you cannot study them scientifically. It's enough to make you throw up!

Hyperemesis gravidarum is an excessive amount of nausea and vomiting, interfering with nutrition and hydration. Any nausea and accompanying vomiting that causes weight loss or in which a woman cannot hold down any of her meals without vomiting—that is, any nausea severe enough to compromise nutrition—is what we call excessive.

Bendectin was an effective treatment for nausea. A combination of vitamin B_6 (pyridoxine) and an antihistamine, doxylamine, it is still marketed in Canada as the drug Diclectin. In 1983 it was voluntarily removed from the U.S. market by its manufacturer, weary of defending it. Its bad rep was much more of a populist uprising fueled by tabloid accusations of babies being deformed because of its use; scientifically it could never be proved that it caused any more developmental defects than were present in the general population (defects were no greater in Bendectin users than in non-Bendectin users). But the witch hunt and mob frenzy prevailed, and Bendectin is no longer available in the United States except by a little creative alchemy (see page 58). Personally, I miss the stuff. I used it before 1983, and it really helped a lot of my patients. Other antihistamines have been used for nausea as well, by calming the labyrinthine inner ear.

So what are we left with? One nonprescription remedy and a handful of prescription drugs.

Emetrol, an over-the-counter mixture of sugar syrups and phosphoric acid (phosphorylated carbohydrate solution), acts by soothing the actual wall of the gastrointestinal tract. But since hyperemesis more than likely originates in the head, not the stomach, it might help—but it might not.

Prescription Medicines for Treating Nausea

Compazine (prochlorperazine) and Phenergan (promethazine) are considered phenothiazine-like drugs, meaning that they act centrally in the brain to relieve nausea.

An allergic reaction to phenothiazines is not like a reaction to other drugs. With other drugs one may develop hives. But phenothiazine reactions can include abnormal eye movements, protruding tongue, and a feeling of tongue thickness along with difficulty speaking. You'll wonder if you're having a stroke. Called *oculogyric* symptoms, these will worry a patient greatly (understandably so!) until a trip to the ER for a Benadryl shot—the same thing as for hives—which will usually cure the problem.

Tigan (trimethobenzamide) is an actual antiemetic (antinausea medication), probably related to anesthetics.

I've saved the best for last. Zofran (ondansetron) is a newer very powerful antiemetic that seems safe. In fact, in spite of its recent introduction, it's a Category B drug. It has no real toxic levels and doesn't seem to interact badly with other drugs. It's used to great effect for nausea after surgery, but it is extremely expensive. (You get what you pay for!) Home health agencies have even used it in a pump delivery system to great effect, saving a lot of hospital time. It's also available in pill form. HMOs, forever worried about the current fiscal quarter instead of the long term, generally decline to pay for a Zofran pump at home. Capitalism—actually, fiscal quarter capitalism—prevails. (Think of the HMO CEO on his yacht every time you throw up as one of life's accurate, intuitive metaphors.) Zofran represents a major leap in controlling nausea, and I say that based on my own clinical experience with it—it's awesome.

Reglan (FDA Category B) helps with nausea by helping to empty the stomach the right way—down instead of up.

Wait a minute! I'm pregnant! These are drugs!

FDA Drug Risk Categorization

The FDA has a classification of drug risk to the fetus that runs from "Category A" (safest) to "X" (known danger—don't use!):

Category A: Controlled studies in women fail to demonstrate a risk to the fetus in the first trimester (and there is no evidence of a risk in later trimesters), and the possibility of fetal harm appears remote.

Category B: Either animal-reproduction studies have not demonstrated a fetal risk but there are no controlled studies in pregnant women, or animal-reproduction studies have shown an adverse effect (other than a decrease in fertility) that was not confirmed in controlled

studies in women in the first trimester (and there is no evidence of a
risk in later trimesters).

Category C: Either studies in animals have revealed adverse effects on
the fetus (teratogenic or embryocidal or other) and there are no
controlled studies in women, or studies in women and animals are not
available. Drugs should be given only if the potential benefit justifies the
potential risk to the fetus.

Category D: There is positive evidence of human fetal risk, but the
benefits from use in pregnant women may be acceptable despite the risk
(e.g., if the drug is needed in a life-threatening situation or for a serious
disease for which safer drugs cannot be used or are ineffective).

Category X: Studies in animals or human beings have demonstrated
fetal abnormalities, or there is evidence of fetal risk based on human
experience or both, and the risk of the use of the drug in pregnant
women clearly outweighs any possible benefit. The drug is
contraindicated in women who are or may become pregnant.

Drug Risks in the Real World

Reading these designations without a doctor's experience of having been out
in the real world of private practice, you probably think that avoiding any category greater than "B" would be a fundamental principle upon which to base
all pharmaceutical decisions. But I *have* been out in the real world of private
practice, and so has your doctor. Typically, we both will use Categories A and
B without hesitation. Category C, in the real world, isn't the quantum leap in
risk it seems to be. Your doctor will use Category C with little worry, even
for illnesses that aren't life-threatening.

When the FDA cites these definitions, it is telling the absolute truth. It's
what you can count on as the most cautious position. But your doctor will use
these categories as guidelines, and then mix them with logic, medicinal track
records, and anecdotal stories from his experience and that of his peers to
make a conclusion about the drug as it applies to you.

Asthmatics must breathe, so a Category C drug that works better than a
Category B is a better choice. Otherwise, such a patient may end up in the
hospital needing Category D rescue. My point is that your doctor will weigh
the risk versus benefit of any drug and individualize his choices specifically for
you. Your doctor doesn't want trouble. He doesn't want to cause an unhealthy

baby. He surely doesn't want a lawsuit. He practices obstetrics for the love of what obstetrics is all about and would never knowingly do anything that would hurt your baby. If he makes a choice for a Category C drug, in spite of how ominous the designation is defined, he has chosen this path as the best thing for you and your pregnancy. Bottom line: your doctor uses Category C all of the time and without worry. Bad news travels fast. If there's a drug that doesn't treat a baby well, your doctor will know about it and act responsibly in avoiding it. I can't tell you how many times I've used Categories A through C in my twenty years of private practice with no problems at all.

Category D can get pretty creepy, and these are used for life-threatening illness—epilepsy for example. Even so, babies are tough. Depending on when in your pregnancy you take the medicine or how much and for how long, the majority will do fine even if a minority does terribly. The mother must live or everything is lost. I submit that it's more dangerous for your baby if you don't use a seat belt than if you use a properly supervised Category D drug. And if you smoke, well, don't get me started.

Other Causes of Nausea

Before slapping down that drug card, though, you need to know that hyperemesis, although common, is abnormal. Your doctor needs to rule out other causes of extreme nausea and vomiting in pregnancy. Other causes are:

- Hyperthyroidism
- Gallbladder disease
- Appendicitis
- Other gastrointestinal problems, such as irritable bowel disease (Crohn's disease or ulcerative colitis), ulcers, hepatitis, pancreatitis, obstruction of the intestinal tract from adhesions, etc.

Your doctor may want to try other ways to address hyperemesis before jumping to prescriptions:

- Change your diet to be low in fat and sugar with a lot of vegetables and fruits. Many homeopathic clinicians feel the liver is bearing the brunt of the pregnancy, causing the nausea, so a diet that doesn't stress the liver is seen as an answer to decreasing the nausea.

- Eliminate caffeine and of course nicotine.
- Raise Bendectin from the dead! Even though Bendectin is no longer commercially available, many obstetricians and gastroenterologists consulted by them are making their own. It is simply a combination of pyridoxine (Vitamin B_6) + one half of a Unisom tablet. Or you can jump the border and get some Diclectin from our friends to the north.
- Acupressure—pressure on the NeiGuan Pressure Point (P6). This spot is about two inches below the wrist crease that divides the underside of your wrist from your hand, between the two tendons. Since organized medicine usually doesn't study holistic approaches until it's realized that someone, somewhere, is making billions from it, you won't yet find a lot of legitimate material on this and other similar methods. But so far the studies disagree as to whether acupressure helps with hyperemesis or not. It probably works for some women. Patients who try it and don't improve will probably suspect it's voodoo, and they'll be pretty upset when their insurance doesn't cover it under the voodoo rider of their policy. The truth is that it isn't voodoo. There really is something to pressure points. Unfortunately, many who champion a particular procedure promote it as an end-all; heightened expectations, when unfulfilled, lead to scorn by organized medicine and patients alike.
- Hypnotherapy—the problem with this is that it's a long therapy during which time the nausea of pregnancy may abate on its own.
- Herbal remedies—ginger has been used for centuries for nausea. Avoid high doses. One cup of ginger tea is not a high dose.
- Tincture of time—since morning sickness and its wicked stepmother, hyperemesis, are usually self-resolving, time-related conditions, the passage of time may prove the most beneficial treatment when all else fails.

Management of Nausea (in Chronological Order)

1. Thyroid function tests to rule out hyperthyroidism; hCG determination to rule out hydatidiform mole-like conditions; gallbladder ultrasound to rule out gallbladder disease or gallstones; other studies to rule out liver disease and pancreatitis.
2. Avoid foods known to worsen the situation, like dairy products or fatty foods.
3. Emetrol, homemade Bendectin (pyridoxine + Unisom), herbal ginger tea.

4. Prescribe Compazine, Phenergan, Tigan, or Reglan.

5. Prescribe Zofran.

6. Parenteral hydration. *Parenteral* is a word used to mean administering by intravenous route—by an IV infusion. The dehydration from nausea and vomiting can make the nausea worse—a vicious cycle that spirals down—and fluids via an IV can break this chain. Usually one overnight stay in the hospital with a liter or two of merely physiologic solution through an IV can cure a severe hyperemesis episode.

7. Use of a Zofran pump to continuously deliver a dose of Zofran, managed by a home health company, like Matria. This is expensive, and some managed care companies won't pay for it.

8. Order a psychiatric evaluation. Yes, some patients just may have a psychosis or neurosis, but it's interesting to note that this cause is considered very unlikely as compared to a generation ago when this would have topped the list of causes.

Nausea's not cute, even though it's the running joke of identification with the otherwise joyous condition of pregnancy. Throwing up is a massive physical upheaval that you're powerless to help. I know. I've been to college fraternity parties—I've called Ralph on the big porcelain phone myself. But whether it's teleological or merely the unfortunate chemical struggle between two persons occupying the same body, it can have serious consequences if unremitting for any period of time. All of our treatments are Band-Aids at best. But what I've presented here is what we have. So far.

Fetal Development in the First Trimester

By the end of the first trimester, your baby is about twenty-two inches long with the beginnings of hair, nails, and bones. Genitalia are beginning to show a particular gender. Weeks six through nine are particularly sensitive times for avoiding exposure to substances that are known to cause abnormalities because this is a time called organogenesis when all of the organs are laid down and their architecture completed. Your baby is termed a fetus after about eight weeks, which is important for medical books and arguments on both sides of the abortion issue, but to you and your husband this is your baby, your child. The embryo's development into the fetus is the anatomy, but your child is the person you carry. We can talk about symptoms and signs and miseries and effects, but the whole thing is about you and your husband having a child. Hopefully this book will help address the need for clinical information, but on each page—sometimes between the lines, sometimes overtly—there's a message in the bottle, just as sure as there's a child in your pregnancy.

And it gets better. With the second trimester, teleological gives way to existential.

Q & A—The First Trimester

Timing of First OB Appointment

Question: I'm newly pregnant and the first appointment opening my doctor had for me was in a month. How long can I wait without any evaluation whatsoever?

Answer: Assuming you're already an established patient and you've kept up with your regular appointments up to now, your doctor seems to be comfortable with the appointment schedule for your first pregnancy office visit. After all, she's your doctor, so she should know.

Fast Forward

There is some leeway in timing the first appointment during the first trimester because usually first trimester–related problems like miscarriage are unalterable. Preexisting conditions like heart disease or diabetes or pregnancy-related conditions like severe morning sickness should put you on the fast track to see your doctor.

If you're going to her for the first time and you have some special consideration that might jeopardize your pregnancy (like heart disease or diabetes), a good receptionist will be able to glean details that might warrant the bureaucratic card-shuffling needed to get you in sooner. If you have such a condition, report it; otherwise it will be assumed that you have no special need to be seen any sooner than the normal schedule allows.

Except for nutrition and vitamin supplementation needs, if you're up to date on your visits anyway, there isn't much in the first trimester a doctor's visit can do to alter what happens before the transition into the second trimester.

Running, Exercise, and Low Progesterone

Question: I'm seven weeks along and I'm an avid runner. My doctor advised me not to run because of low progesterone. She has me on Prometrium. Why can't I run?

Answer: Your doctor is a believer in exercise-related amenorrhea, or in your case exercise-related hypoprogesteronemia (a fancy term for low progesterone). Ovarian progesterone is made in the second half of the menstrual cycle, and it prepares the lining of your uterus for implantation. When pregnancy occurs, this second half of the cycle continues until term, when progesterone finally falls off. But there's a transition near the end of the first trimester; at that point the placenta takes over your ovary's job of making the progesterone. If there's a lag between your ovary making it and the time the placenta takes over, the lining of the uterus may not be at its best. The faulty lining poses a risk for the implantation, and miscarriage is a risk . . . theoretically. This is why doctors use progesterone to supplement those with inadequate progesterone levels. She also wants you to cool it on the running. Will your disregard of her recommendations cause a miscarriage? Probably not if you're on Prometrium anyway. But I could be wrong. What if you have a miscarriage just because your pregnancy fell into that 20 percent of diagnosed pregnancies that miscarry anyway? Wouldn't you like to know you did everything you could to prevent it?

This is all very controversial because many people think that even with low progesterone a good pregnancy can carry and that even with adequate progesterone a faulty pregnancy can miscarry. The good thing is that progesterone is harmless to the baby, even if it tends to make you sleepy and constipated.

> **Fast Forward**
> Strenuous exercise may not be harmful, but in high-risk pregnancy, cooling it won't hurt. Progesterone pills also won't hurt since low progesterone has been associated with strenuous exercise and miscarriage.

Safety of Ultrasound

Question: My doctor is worried about a threatened miscarriage. Besides all of the blood work, she has ordered many ultrasounds. I'm worried about the radiation. Can a baby get too much ultrasound?

Answer: Ultrasound has been used in obstetrics for more than thirty years now. We live in a brave, new world in which we should wonder what anything can do to us. But the fast pace of technology means that there are just too many things to investigate to come up with a solid conclusion about one thing in particular. Alarmists have tried to blame everything on ultrasound, from childhood leukemias to Sudden Infant Death Syndrome (SIDS), without any meaningful conclusions.

> **Fast Forward**
>
> Ultrasound is safe in pregnancy, and its value is priceless (information for your doctor and reassurance for you) when used to follow a particular concern. You should like a doctor who likes ultrasound.

If you're worried about radiation, then you need to look around. The telephone company has been bouncing microwaves off of us ever since the first satellites. Cell phones, microwave ovens, VCRs, and even your own body give off radiation. Radio, television, and even light are radiation. And the most exposure comes from places you take for granted: the ground, as radon, which is a breakdown of natural uranium; outer space, in the form of cosmic rays that are passing through your body all of the time at great speeds; and that nuclear bomb 93 million miles away we call our sun. Let's face it, we're an irradiated species. And we're all lucky that there hasn't been a supernova within our light-year neighborhood, or we'd all die from the radiation burst. So we walk, talk, conceive, and deliver with radiation. Godzilla would argue, but radiation per se isn't the worry. It's the type of radiation, how long, how much, and at what gestational age. For the record, ultrasound doesn't worry me. It's as inconsequential as the sun, unless you use a tanning bed, and you know how I feel about that during pregnancy. Besides tissue-toxic radiation used in cancer therapy, X rays are the only medical radiation source of concern, and even they aren't bad during a pregnancy if the right precautions are taken.

If your doctor wants to follow an important concern with ultrasound, let her. It's an added benefit that you get to see your baby too, so enjoy the visit and the reassurance.

Horror Stories Relatives Tell You

Question: Now that I'm finally pregnant, all of my relatives and friends are giving me all kinds of advice and describing the horrible details of all of their compli-

cations. Are these things I should ask my doctor about? What should I tell these people?

Answer: Tell them, politely of course, to mind their own business.

Since you say you're "finally" pregnant, that tells me that you had some trouble already. The last thing you need is to worry about things like Aunt Zelda's uterus falling out of her at the mall the day after Thanksgiving or how your friend's epidural never worked, so she had to go through four days of The Labor from Hell.

Those were those people—this is you. Don't listen to any of it. They're all stories that are anecdotal, don't apply across blood or friendship lines, and are usually melodramaticized for notoriety's sake.

A little trick I pioneered at Charity Hospital was to double the amount of drinking and smoking a patient said they did and to halve the amount of bleeding they claimed to bleed. You can treat these melodramas like bleeding—cut them in half and you're likely to get a more accurate rendition. Nevertheless, it's all of the good outcomes that you never hear people rambling on about, just the complications. No wonder they'll stand more prominently in your fears. Just remember that for every disaster you hear about, cut it in half so it's demoted to a mere complication, and then assume there are a hundred uneventful outcomes for every one of those. That's the perspective on Aunt Zelda's uterus twitching to everyone's horror in front of the Gap.

True Story of a History I Took at Charity Hospital

Me:	Do you drink any?
Patient:	Yeah, I suppose I do.
Me:	How much?
Patient:	Oh, I guess I drink quite a bit.
Me:	How much is "quite a bit"?
Patient:	I do go on, now, y'know.
Me:	Yes, but how much? Like a pint a day?
Patient:	A pint! Shit, I spill that much, boy!

Look for other current questions and updates regarding the first trimester at BabyZone.com, by going to babyzone.com/features/expertsqa.

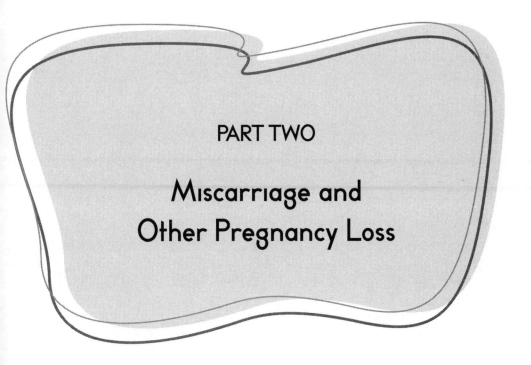

PART TWO

Miscarriage and
Other Pregnancy Loss

4

The Reality of Miscarriage

If you bought this book after your first trimester, you can skip this part because miscarriage usually occurs in the first ten weeks of pregnancy. Or you could read it anyway so that you can appreciate the turning point you've reached—the second trimester. You've made it out of miscarriage territory. Sure, there are the unusual incidents of fetal demise in midpregnancy and even at term, but these are the exception and nowhere near the proportion that miscarriage reaches in the first trimester. But your first trimester is a dramatic example of how, in these shells—our bodies—we live our mortal lives at the mercy of the biological rules that govern survival: sometimes bad things happen. One such very bad thing is miscarriage.

There are those who say miscarriage is a very good thing that assures the health of our species. But couples aren't thinking about the species when they choose to have a child. No one thanks Darwin for miscarriages. Sometimes God gets the brunt of misdirected anger, but it is in fact misdirected for building such a complex creature as a human being who is exceedingly special.

Each person is a unique individual who is the result of infinitesimal odds. We take this for granted because we look around at everyone and see, well, everyone. But each and every person we encounter—all those people in the elevator with us, in those partially obstructed seats at the rock concert, in line at the DMV, in the stadium doing the wave—they've all made it through a process much more challenging than winning all the Grand Slams in a year.

Every person is in the winner's circle, which is why everyone is a winner deserving great respect.

But sometimes there's an elimination in the finals. In spite of victorious conception against all odds, the nine-month plan to become a human being can go awry anyway, and a pregnancy can still fail.

Nature's Way

Miscarriage is nature's way of discarding a pregnancy that didn't proceed in a way compatible with life. Even though it may be a mere disposal from an evolutionary standpoint, to prospective parents it is a real tragedy—hopes and dreams and a certain romantic vision of their child-to-be dashed before their broken hearts. But the fact remains that it happens for a reason.

As physicians, we obstetricians have two obligations. We must treat the discarding aspect of miscarriage scientifically but treat the human tragedy aspect with compassion and understanding. There's even the possibility that we're out of the loop because miscarriage often happens very early. Even before implantation. A woman may not even miss a period. When one realizes how many things must go perfectly to make a baby, it's a wonder that it happens at all.

Miracle is never a worn out word for a baby. Usually after about the twelfth week of pregnancy the chances of miscarriage plunge. In fact, pregnancy loss after twelve weeks is almost always due to a rare catastrophic event or an even rarer genetic mishap that took a little longer to make trouble.

Progesterone, a major female hormone necessary in pregnancy, can be a factor in preventable miscarriage. A normal pregnancy may be in trouble because the mother's progesterone level is low. Oral progesterone can correct this, and the medicine can be withdrawn near the end of the first trimester when the baby's own placenta manufactures enough for the pregnancy. This is not to be confused with the opposite—a low progesterone level because the pregnancy is doomed to miscarriage. In this case, administering the hormone only delays the inevitable, a miscarriage occurring after withdrawing the progesterone when ultrasound or hCG hormonal levels bear out the truth. It's often impossible to tell the difference between the two instances, but many doctors feel they would rather delay an inevitable miscarriage than write off a normal baby. In the literature the success of progesterone therapy is controversial, but infertility specialists use it frequently to protect their hard-earned pregnancies. It's safe, which is reassuring after the DES debacle of the last generation. (DES, an estrogen, was given to prevent miscarriage in the 1950s. It didn't work and caused abnormalities in the babies exposed.)

Miscarriage occurs in about a fifth of all clinically diagnosed pregnancies. This is a staggering amount of anguish since most couples never consider this possibility when they choose to have a child. Almost always it is because of some random genetic mismatch unsuited to progressing all the way. Once again, we're at the mercy of the biological rules. It is nature's way of assuring a continuing healthy species. Miscarriage can also happen because of infection; maternal diseases like lupus, diabetes, and thyroid problems; and abnormalities with the anatomy of a woman's reproductive tract. The sad fact is that it does happen, and people are blindsided by this loss. Sometimes it happens to the same couple more than once, prompting evaluation for known causes. But it's frustrating that most of the time there is no known cause, and the couple feels they are being sent away with only an invitation to return to the obstetrician for the next try—as if finally pulling it off tomorrow would undo today's tragedy.

This is the illusion, especially in a couple's eyes who feel that the loss is their own private catastrophe they can't seem to share enough with others no matter how hard they try. And they are somewhat left on their own because there are no rituals for this type of human loss. There are no funerals or memorial services. Friends and relatives, often misguided into thinking that mentioning the miscarriage will only be upsetting, are instead seen as uncaring in their silence. The grieving couple has only each other, and that may not be enough for the feelings of guilt and self-examining retrospection. And anger.

▶ Fast Forward

Miscarriage is a serious loss, unfairly unacknowledged by otherwise caring friends and family members.

After all, this isn't just some tissue that was discarded, like an appendix or a gallbladder. This is not just one of their parts. This was their son or daughter. There were dreams of seeing Little League events, helping with homework, attending dance recitals, walking down an aisle. And the whole sense of what might have been is lost to a clinical world of procedures, blood tests, and insurance forms.

As an obstetrician, I can assure any couple that their miscarriage is not just any clinical event. I've been delivering babies long enough to see some that I delivered wearing a mortarboard, and I waited in happy expectation during the early part of my career in anticipation of seeing that sort of thing happening. In a way I grieve with the parents too, because I know what is being lost in a miscarriage. I'm right there in the middle of it as well, putting it on a different level than the clinical protocols I employ to deal with it.

The science of in vitro fertilization (IVF) has brought about advances in our knowledge of conception and survival of the zygote and subsequent embryo. As mentioned before, we now know that there are many miscarriages that go undiagnosed, a fertilized egg unsuccessfully implanting or unable to do so because of severely distorted fusion of chromosomes. Such miscarriages are completely absorbed or fall away with what is seen as the routine menstrual flow. Taking this type of miscarriage into account, I've been careful to say that miscarriage happens in 20 percent of all *diagnosed* pregnancies, but total miscarriage risk is probably closer to 60–80 percent when the silent ones are considered.

Perhaps it is fortuitous that the majority of miscarriages go unnoticed, for we would be one bummed out species. Even the 20 percent is overbearing—just ask someone it's happened to. The more we learn about this the more we have to realize how special each person is. A couple who experiences a miscarriage really does know this. After all, it lands in their faces when the rug gets pulled out from under them.

It takes about three months before a couple can deal effectively with their loss. This is quite a requiem, which only underscores the importance of what has been lost. My advice for those who know such mourners is to ask them how they're doing. They really don't want to be alone in all of this. At the appropriate time they'll file this tragedy away for safekeeping and get on with the rest of their lives. Until then, let them share their grief with you.

A mathematician can count on his fingers, but that in no way reflects the beauty of mathematics. This word processor can lay down words at the application of certain keystrokes, but that in no way compares to the actual beauty of what is written. I manage the complication of miscarriage, but that doesn't reduce my feelings for what might have been. So I do not merely send them on their way with an invitation to return for the next try. Instead, I applaud them for going back into the world to once again play by the biological rules. They will have that baby not to replace that permanent little hole in the heart left by a miscarriage, but because they want a baby.

Babies and Daytime Emmys: Stress, Exercise, Sex, and the Risk of Miscarriage

Soap opera babies usually don't stand a chance. Miscarriages occur easily and frequently. I suppose the reason is that the loss of a baby is one of the most powerful misfortunes, and these programs are all about the human condition in all of its tragic splendor. *La condition humaine* meets *Les Miserables*. Thank goodness real pregnancy isn't like pregnancy on the daily dramas. An actress falls and she has a miscarriage. A character discovers that her husband is having an affair with her best friend's Tupperware distributor and the stress causes her to lose the pregnancy. Overworking may put her in the hospital for tests that take weeks of prime time daily viewing. There is no managed care on soap operas.

So just how tough is your baby anyway? First, we must consider that the human race has survived a big disadvantage in reproduction: we only have one at a time—usually (pending the absorbed twin controversy, coming up later in this chapter). The rest of nature guarantees the survival of the species by allowing multiple births, so that the most vulnerable of life, the infant, is exchangeable for the next that may survive where the first did not. This protection is taken to an extreme with insects, in which reproduction involves thousands of offspring in a very short time, so that even if most die during this vulnerable period, still there are many that do survive to keep the species going and ruin my backyard barbecue. Yet we have not only survived but thrived in spite of having only one at a time.

Having thumbs didn't hurt any.

Thumbs aside, your big compensation is your brain, which allows you to see the importance of protecting and raising your child. The human brain has also given you the field of pediatrics and modern medicine. You also have sense and foresee danger, so that your baby in your womb is well protected indeed since you yourself are smart enough to keep from personal harm. Your baby is secure as well, the pregnancy interaction between you and your child providing a safe haven. What all of this means is that it's tough to accidentally hurt your baby. Surely babies aren't invulnerable. If you were to try, it can be done. Alcohol, smoking, other drugs, and trauma can hurt your unborn—but isn't that where that brain comes in? Normal everyday activity, however, is not only harmless, but often helps the health of your baby as well.

▶ Fast Forward
Exercise and sex pose no danger to a normal pregnancy.

Patients often ask me if stress is hurting the baby. Only on the soap operas. And the thing to remember is that everyone has stress. Life is stress. It's a normal part of our lives. It's why we have adrenaline.

So it really is hard to hurt your baby by accident. Exercise especially is maligned unfairly, which is due in part to that soap opera mentality that pregnant women should merely glide along life on an air cushion without so much as a speed bump. All of the studies have shown conclusively that not only is exercise good for you and your baby, but it also decreases the likelihood of a C-section. The only warning is against overheating and dehydration. Aside from that, it seems all exercise is acceptable. Except kickboxing. You should stay away from that.

Many patients and their husbands ask me about the safety of intercourse during pregnancy. The only time you shouldn't have intercourse during pregnancy is in the delivery room. Please.

Of course, this is advice for normal pregnancies. High-risk pregnancy complicated by bleeding, premature labor, or infection has a completely different set of criteria, but generally all normal pregnancies are sex-worthy till the very end. Even orgasm, which is known to cause contractions of the uterus, seems harmless in normal pregnancies. A good rule of thumb is that you should avoid intercourse if it becomes uncomfortable; otherwise, sex is not a problem. With your spouse, that is. With others it is a problem.

I know that so far I'm saying all of the things you want to hear, but you also very much need to hear these things. Sex is important in a marriage. Exercise is important to the mother. But a baby is only important in a daytime TV drama if it moves the story line. Real people don't have story lines—they have lives. Just because you're pregnant doesn't mean you should stop living life as you know it. The simple joys of life are not only safe for baby, but good for maternal and marital well-being on many different levels.

Miscarriage Overview

The word *abortion* refers to any interruption of a pregnancy. In today's media, *abortion* is assumed to mean elective termination, but medically the word also refers to all of the types of spontaneous miscarriage.

Under the heading of abortion, there are several designations that are clinically important:

- Threatened abortion, threatened miscarriage: any bleeding in the first trimester until other innocent causes are ruled out. Serial hCG levels can determine well-being or danger. Ultrasound is also important in following such a condition.
- Missed abortion: a pregnancy that is no longer viable but hasn't been passed out of the body or caused any bleeding yet.
- Incomplete abortion, incomplete miscarriage: a spontaneous miscarriage that hasn't completely passed. This situation may lead to heavy bleeding and serious infection if some tissue were to remain in the uterus. A dilation and curettage (D&C) is warranted.
- Inevitable abortion, inevitable miscarriage: when the cervix begins to dilate, which is a sure sign of impending expulsion of products of conception from the uterus, but before actual expulsion has begun.
- Complete abortion, complete miscarriage: miscarriage in which the entire gestational sac, placental tissue, and fetus are expelled. No further treatment is necessary.
- Septic abortion, septic miscarriage: any type of miscarriage associated with an infection of remaining pregnancy tissue or of the uterus itself.
- Ectopic pregnancy: a pregnancy that implanted anywhere but the right place (the right place being the uterus). Most ectopics are in a fallopian tube, but they can be seen in the pelvis, ovary, and even the higher abdomen. Since almost all of them are in the tube, however, this makes diagnosis much easier because the tube has limited capacity for a growing process and soon will stretch enough to cause pain. The very unusual ectopic, in the pelvis for example, may get further along before symptoms

hint at trouble, making blood loss worse with surgical treatment. Non-surgical treatments are also available for some ectopics (see page 88).

- Molar pregnancy: types of conceptions spanning the gamut of looking nothing like a pregnancy to looking a lot like a normal pregnancy (incomplete mole). It is actually a tumor of pregnancy tissue, but usually only benign.

Threatened Miscarriage: Bleeding in Early Pregnancy

Most couples expect to get pregnant at some point and when they do for the first time, it suddenly dawns on them what a gamble pregnancy actually is. One of the most frightening things is to experience bleeding in the first part of the pregnancy. Termed "first trimester bleeding," it is any bleeding noted during the first twelve weeks, and it is one of the most common symptoms to send a woman to her obstetrician. And rightly so, because until a nonthreatening cause is identified, all first trimester bleeding is labeled "threatened miscarriage," or "threatened AB."

Let's look at the possible causes of bleeding in the first trimester unrelated to miscarriage.

Cervicitis

No bleeding in early pregnancy is to be considered normal—that's the bad news. But the good news is that most of the time it's caused by something fairly harmless. Cervicitis is a condition in which the delicate cells at the mouth of the womb (cervix) can bleed due to the mechanical action of intercourse or a Pap smear, the alteration of acidity in the vagina (pH), or the effects of infections on these cells.

- **Ectopy (ectropion).** With the hormonal changes of pregnancy, the fragile internal cells peek out a bit onto the external portion of the cervix, which is a harsher environment for them. Normally nestled more deeply away from sexual activity and the acidity of the vagina, now they can be battered both chemically and mechanically. They're easily damaged, causing bleeding. Of course, we're not talking about a whole lot of bleeding here—merely what is perceived as spotting. It must also be noted that these cells usually don't bleed with sex—usually there is a predisposing condition, like cervicitis. When these internal cervical cells are brought to a more external position, this is called ectopy. The damage they sustain is reversible and harmless.

- **Infection.** Often cervicitis is inflammation due to infection. Yeast can be the culprit, and a simple prescription or even over-the-counter cream can end this concern quickly. Bacterial vaginosis, *Gardnerella*, now thought to be the most common form of vaginitis, can also cause a coexisting cervicitis, so a microscopic evaluation is the best approach rather than just assuming it's yeast. Other infections are more worrisome. Sexually transmitted diseases (STDs) like gonorrhea, chlamydia, and trichomoniasis, for instance, can cause bleeding too. Some STD infections may be silent for years—there may have been an infection long before a couple even met each other. Knowing this can dispel any question of infidelity. Obtaining cultures for STDs has become standard in all pregnancies.
- **Pap smears.** Because your cervical cells can be delicate owing to ectopy or cervicitis, a Pap smear can be a mechanical irritation and cause some bleeding. This is harmless, the spotting being bright red the day of the Pap, perhaps brownish for a couple of days after.

Cervical Polyps
Harmless small polyps can cause bleeding. They are overgrowths of benign tissue, probably owing their existence to your estrogen production.

Subchorionic Hemorrhage
This sounds disastrous, but it usually turns out fine. There can be a small amount of bleeding between the membranes near the placenta and your uterine wall. Any bleeding is a hemorrhage, even a small amount. This is usually confined by the pregnancy tissues, some leaking of which is noticed vaginally as bleeding or, to a lesser extent, spotting. Serial ultrasounds will reveal a clot that doesn't increase in size but is seen to diminish over the weeks of the first trimester.

Shedding Decidual Tissue
Sometimes a small piece of uterine lining becomes loose and disintegrates through some unknown cause, causing spotting or the passing of tissue. It's

usually a hormonally stimulated collection of menstrual-like tissue that can often be confused with a miscarriage. No one knows why such a phenomenon occurs, but it is harmless. It's the passage of tissue for sure, so it will be very disturbing until the pathology report can ease everyone's mind by documenting that the specimen passed was not fetal. The stabilization of the lining of the uterus depends on estrogen and progesterone. In my practice such shedding of only decidual tissue has had no impact on whether a pregnancy would miscarry. The tissue is termed decidualized because of the pregnancy-like effect on it of estrogen.

Implantation Bleeding

In the past it's been thought that an egg eroding into the uterine lining would cause bleeding at the time because of a burrowing effect. Actually it's unknown whether there's any bleeding when this happens, and if so, it's probably too small an amount to notice. The idea that implantation causes bleeding persists because there are bleeding episodes for which no cause is ever identified and despite which the pregnancy goes on successfully to term. Such a mystery that starts off so menacingly but ends so well begs for an explanation that must include a natural process. Implantation makes sense under these criteria, but can't be proved. This may be a myth.

"Periods" During Pregnancy

Many women ask me about having regular periods during their pregnancies. They're concerned because Grandma or a cousin had periods every month during their pregnancies—and could that happen during this pregnancy?—making the last menstrual period (whichever one that was) screw up the due date. They swear on Bibles that these periods during pregnancy are true—that they really happened. It's false, all the swearing notwithstanding. Shedding one's layer of menstrual tissue is not compatible with life. The closest thing we have to this is shedding of decidual tissue. When Grandma swears that it happened, it's certainly the polite thing to listen with an open mind—just be sure to slam it shut by thinking about what's really going on in pregnancy. The cycling of hormones stops because a pregnancy causes the hormone levels to remain high. This is necessary for pregnancy to continue. There are no falls in the hormones, which is what causes a period, except right before labor. Most

> **Fast Forward**
>
> There are many reasons for bleeding in the first trimester, most of them harmless, so don't panic. True, miscarriage causes bleeding, but this can be ruled out or in with simple blood work and ultrasound. The other causes of first trimester bleeding often resolve and go on to be completely normal pregnancies.

likely, Grandma experienced a subchorionic hemorrhage, bleeding intermittently, misinterpreted as cyclic. That would explain her first trimester periods.

Although the above instances describe the causes of bleeding unrelated to miscarriage, still miscarriage should be ruled out if you have any bleeding at all. And when one considers that the cramping of a threatened miscarriage can feel exactly like the growing pains of a normal uterus, confusing everyone, it is fortunate that there are other tools to give you peace of mind.

Blood tests can prove that the pregnancy hormone is increasing as expected, which confirms a healthy pregnancy; ultrasound can demonstrate the physical well-being of a growing baby by showing a healthy heart rate or by ruling out an ectopic (tubal) pregnancy.

Miscarriage is a fact of life as we know it, and usually miscarriages begin with first trimester bleeding, but first trimester bleeding isn't always indicative of a miscarriage. Doctors always investigate first trimester bleeding until a cause can be determined, and usually there's a good outcome. So although first trimester bleeding can cause you a lot of anxiety and worry, your doctor can often find another—treatable—cause to blame it on.

But What If It Really Is Miscarriage?

Unfortunately, miscarriage can be a time-consuming event, and most couples wish to get it over with once they know for sure the pregnancy won't succeed. But your doctor will want to know such a thing with absolute certainty because he wouldn't want to intervene against a normal pregnancy. If there really is a miscarriage concern, your doctor is already on it. While looking for all of the other innocent reasons to explain away bleeding, blood work and ultrasound are done at the same time to find answers as soon as possible.

Ultrasound

If seeing is believing, then ultrasound can be an epiphany. There's nothing like seeing a normal fetal impression with a good fetal heart motion to reassure you when there are even the most troubling symptoms. And besides documenting the health of the fetus, ultrasounds can put another worry to bed—ectopic pregnancy. Seeing the pregnancy within the uterus itself will rule out a pregnancy in a tube or anywhere else, except in the rare occurrence of twins—one in the uterus and one in the tube.

✻A-FACTOR

I'd like to say that twins in which one is in the uterus and the other in the tube never happens, except that it happened once in my practice. But only once.

Ultrasound is also an excellent tool to follow any ongoing concern, like a subchorionic hemorrhage. Weekly serial ultrasounds can watch a blood clot shrink away, along with your worries.

If you've never had one before, a vaginal ultrasound will come as an awkward surprise to you since it uses a probe whose shape, designed to fit into your vagina, is no mystery. And on top of that, it's covered with a condom, which you probably thought had no other uses. It isn't painful, but you may be creeped out because you find the whole thing very icky at a time when you don't need anything else to bug you. So be warned. In early pregnancy, though, there's nothing like it to see very well into your pelvis. The older abdominal probes that slide on your abdomen have to see through your entire abdominal wall before getting to the pelvis. Since the back of your vagina is less than half an inch thick, it poses no barrier to a clear view of even the earliest pregnancies—it's like a picture window. What a vaginal ultrasound sees is weeks ahead of what an abdominal ultrasound can show you. It's really what is needed if you want ultrasound to address any miscarriage or ectopic concerns.

➤ Fast Forward

A vaginal probe ultrasound, although weird, is the best way to evaluate a miscarriage or ectopic worry. Its revelations are weeks ahead of what a regular abdominal ultrasound technique can show.

Blood Work

The hormone hCG, made by the placenta, rises and accumulates, plateauing around the end of the first trimester. By that time its levels possibly can reach the hundreds of thousands, but in early pregnancy the numbers are much smaller. This makes it possible to measure interval increases in this hormone. In early normal pregnancy the amount of hCG should double every two days or so. For example, an hCG of 1,800 should rise to about 3,500–4,000 over forty-eight hours. If it doesn't, but it's close, then another repeat sample two days after that will be helpful. If it does in fact double, then this is a good indication that everything is going fine. If it exceeds the doubling tendency, twins or molar pregnancy (Chapter 5) may be brewing, easily caught by ultrasound.

> **Fast Forward**
>
> Blood type and Rh are needed in case you're Rh-negative so that your doctor can prevent any immunization against your baby's blood, which can remain to attack future pregnancies. The pregnancy hormone hCG will rise in a predictable way and can indicate miscarriage, ectopic, or normal pregnancy. Progesterone levels are helpful, low being suspicious, high being reassuring.

Progesterone is maintained at high levels throughout the pregnancy. Although a pregnancy can be in trouble with a low progesterone level, most of the time the opposite is true: the progesterone is low because of a faulty pregnancy. There are absolute values that give obstetricians comfort (15–20 ng/ml). If the progesterone quantity were to come back low, this could indicate a problem even if the hCG is reassuring (usually the hCG will not be reassuring with an abnormally low progesterone). Borderline low progesterone levels may warrant progesterone supplementation, but really low values can be assumed to be because of the likelihood of miscarriage.

Your Rh type is a necessary item of information, but this was probably obtained with your initial blood work (see Chapter 2). If you're Rh-negative, you will need a RhoGam injection with any bleeding episode to prevent your blood from making antibodies to the baby's blood. This assumes that any bleeding involves mixing of the two to some extent.

Fast Forward

There's no such thing as an incomplete miscarriage that goes on to term, producing an abnormal baby. This simply does not happen.

Studies of the immune system, antinuclear antibody (ANA), antiphoso-lipid, lupus prep, and such, are usually reserved for women who have had recurrent miscarriages.

Time

Usually a threatened miscarriage will commit itself within days of the first bleeding. Some do linger, but eventually the truth will become evident. Either the cervix will open, making it an inevitable AB; tissue will pass, converting it to an incomplete AB; or the entire gestational sac will pass, a complete AB. Or it will go on to be a normal pregnancy.

Fast Forward

Miscarriage is an all-or-none problem. Either the pregnancy will miscarry or it will go on to be a successful pregnancy. Any threatened miscarriage that goes on to be a normal pregnancy was probably never a miscarriage risk in the first place.

Ultrasound, blood work to check levels of hCG and progesterone, and time are the three important diagnostic tests to determine whether first trimester bleeding is caused by an abnormal pregnancy destined to miscarry.

There's no such thing as an incomplete miscarriage that goes on to term. Patients sometimes fear that if they get over the hump of a threatened miscarriage, that what's left will result in a terribly abnormal baby at the end. This simply does not happen. Miscarriage is an all-or-none event. It'll either commit to miscarriage or commit to a normal pregnancy (barring any unrelated problems). You must remember what causes a miscarriage in the first place. An abnormal genetic conception will threaten as a miscarriage because it is incompatible with life sooner or later. But later is usually before the end of the first trimester.

Abnormalities like Down's syndrome and Trisomy 18 do make it down the line, but these are obviously haughtier abnormalities and don't usually present as a threatened miscarriage in the first trimester. Usually a miscarriage meant to be will present as such and then go on to ensue.

Therefore, a threatened miscarriage that proceeds on into the pregnancy, never miscarrying, was never a real threat in the first place. But since your doctor doesn't have that little whistling salt shaker Dr. McCoy used on *Star Trek*, every bleeding must be treated as a threatened miscarriage till proven otherwise. And for many, even for those in which it can't be proven otherwise, time will rule it out.

When the Verdict Is In: Treatment for Miscarriage

If a miscarriage occurs, it could be merciful and make itself obvious very quickly, allowing your doctor to effect closure quickly. Or it could torment you with equivocal blood work and ultrasounds too early to even identify a fetal pole that can be followed. As mentioned above, eventually a miscarriage will in fact miscarry. The pregnancy may die, but the tissue will not necessarily pass.

If the tissue doesn't pass (missed AB) or if it passes incompletely (incomplete AB), there is danger of bleeding and infection. The only type of intrauterine miscarriage that will escape a D&C is a complete miscarriage. Missed and incomplete miscarriages will require a little help in the way of a surgical scraping to remove the rest of the products of conception. The D&C (dilation and curettage) involves dilating the cervix for access if it hasn't already opened (inevitable AB) and scraping the inside of the uterus to dislodge any remaining pregnancy tissue. An anesthetic is required. An epidural or spinal may linger hours longer than the actual procedure, turning an outpatient surgery into an overnight stay, so the more quickly reversible general anesthetic is preferred. Some doctors merely use heavy sedation. The procedure is done under sterile technique and infection is rare unless it's there to begin with (septic AB).

Septic ABs are a particularly hazardous matter. They're rare, occurring with poor technique ("garage" abortions) or when bacteria have had time to colonize the tissue, as in cases in which a patient wanted to wait for an incomplete AB or inevitable AB to follow through spontaneously. It's also possible that a septic AB isn't the result of the miscarriage being infected, but a normal pregnancy being infected, actually causing the miscarriage. In other words, a septic AB may not be a complication of the miscarriage, but the miscarriage may be a complication of an infection. Treatment is the same. IV antibiotics in combination with a D&C will successfully manage such a complication that in generations past would have caused serious illness or even killed a woman. It can still be dangerous today, though, because a D&C can stir up the infection, possibly seeding the bacteria throughout the bloodstream. I am always a little nervous the night of a D&C for a septic AB, waiting for that temperature spike from the temporary sepsis I created with the manipulation of the tissue. But the D&C is necessary and the sepsis usually responds well to a full course of antibiotics. So a D&C for a septic AB would *not* be an outpatient procedure since several days of IV antibiotics are needed to completely eradicate the infection.

In a straightforward D&C for a miscarriage that isn't infected, a patient can be at normal activity the next day, although she may feel a little washed out by the anesthetic.

Modern equipment consists of a soft, plastic suction tube to retrieve the tissue, significantly reducing the amount of trauma to the uterine lining. This lining is resilient even with more aggressive scraping using the older metal scrapers (curettes), and internal scarring of the uterine cavity is rare. (Called synechiae, these bands of scar can wall off portions of the cavity, interfering with conception or fetal growth; they're discussed later in this chapter.)

Contrary to popular belief, a D&C is not always necessary to finish a miscarriage. There really is such a thing as a complete miscarriage (complete AB), and an obstetrician-gynecologist would serve her patient well by trying to avoid surgery for her patient if possible. Unfortunately, a D&C is often needed, but it can provide the patient with a definitive end to a sad chapter in her life, allowing her to plan for her next pregnancy.

Complications of D&C (Dilation and Curettage)

Infection

Since a D&C is an invasive procedure, there is always the risk of infection. This is rare. In fact, the most likely complication is not caused by the procedure itself: a bladder infection could occur because of the routine use of an in-and-out urinary catheter to empty the bladder before the procedure. This would haunt a patient within a week when she begins to complain of pressure or pain associated with urination. Antibiotic pills will treat this common complication.

> **A-FACTOR**
>
> Complications of D&C are rare. If there is an infection, more than likely it was there before the D&C.

Synechiae

Thankfully, the more serious complications are infrequent. The aforementioned infection of the uterus could cause scarring within the uterine chamber (the intrauterine cavity), such scarring stringing across from internal uterine wall to internal uterine wall. These synechiae can interfere with fertility if severe or can threaten miscarriage if mild.

> **A-FACTOR**
>
> The benefit of a needed D&C outweighs the risk of synechiae by light-years. Most obstetricians have never seen synechiae due to a D&C.

Perforation

If your doctor is properly trained, he should know how to use the curette to gently scrape your uterus without pushing the curette through its wall. But surprises can happen if your uterus is thinned out, as in a late first trimester D&C. Also, if there's an infection already, the tissue can be very mushy and won't provide the consistency that is normally felt—the accustomed resistance a doctor knows. But even if there's a perforation, an overnight stay for obser-

> **A-FACTOR**
>
> Perforations are probably rare. There are probably some "silent" perforations never noticed by a doctor, remaining unknown by virtue of the absence of any noted ill-effects.
>
> Any small hole will heal. I've only seen disastrous perforations through the blood supply of the uterus when I've inherited patients with botched abortions by untrained persons.

vation and antibiotics are all that's necessary. The observation is for bleeding and that will be obvious quickly, a stable blood count the next morning being plenty of assurance that a patient can go home with her antibiotics. A perforation toward the side of the uterus may injure the area of the blood supply to the uterus, but this would be immediately recognized with heavy bleeding during the D&C.

Fast Forward

Complications from a D&C to treat a miscarriage are very rare. The unlikely perforation will usually heal with no subsequent damage. Infections are probably there to begin with. Incomplete removal of products of conception will cause lingering bleeding but will usually resolve by itself with spontaneous passage. Synechiae are rare.

The benefits of a D&C, when indicated, far outweigh the risks of rarely seen complications.

Psychological Complications

If the clinical aspects of a miscarriage rudely eject you from the fairy-tale land of pregnancy and baby and rest-of-your-life-with-baby, the loss is all the more of a thud into cruel reality because of the unfriendliness of a surgical procedure. True, closure can be the best thing, but a D&C emphasizing what has happened is more than just a closure—it's a cave-in. It's something you have to do—you can't just mind your own business and miscarry; you have to go places and do things with other people. It's still better to get the whole painful crisis over with, but a D&C, although quick, is not an easy letdown. Then again, nothing would be. As mentioned before, it takes about three months to get over such a loss psychologically no matter how the miscarriage is addressed.

Incomplete Removal of the Products of Conception

"Products of conception" is a strange medical phrase that cowardly tiptoes around what's really happening in a miscarriage—the loss of a baby. Nevertheless, it is accurate. Since a D&C is a procedure guided mainly by a tactile sense instead of a visual approach, it's possible that some products of conception may be missed. If this were to occur, you may experience bleeding longer than the couple of days expected after a D&C. But the disruption by the D&C is usually enough to allow anything that's left to break away and pass spontaneously, thereby resolving the problem.

> **A-FACTOR**
> It is rare that a second D&C need be done to finish the task of emptying the uterus. That would be prompted only by an ultrasound indicating a lot of remaining tissue in association with continued bleeding.

Recurrent Miscarriage

If you were to suffer more than two miscarriages, it would be time to try to investigate why. Three miscarriages is the norm for suspicion of an abnormality, only because it really is possible to have two miscarriages in a row as a mere coincidence—albeit a bad coincidence. But when it happens a third time, it becomes obvious that a cause should be sought. Unfortunately, even when a full workup is done, a reason is only found in half of the cases. This is a very frustrating statistic for both you and your doctor.

Causes of recurrent miscarriage include:

- Genetic causes, either inherited along family lines or as associated specifically between husband and wife.
- Abnormalities of the anatomy, including developmental abnormalities of the uterus and tubes.
- Hormonal problems, like luteal phase defects in which not enough progesterone is produced to stabilize the early pregnancy.
- Chronic illness, like diabetes, lupus, etc., which increases the chances of miscarriage for each pregnancy, thereby increasing the total number of miscarriages, seen as recurring.
- Autoimmune disorders, like antiphospholipid syndrome (APS), which are found to be the cause of recurrent miscarriage in 5–10 percent of patients seeking a cause. APS is investigated by determining whether you have anticardiolipin antibody and lupus anticoagulant in your blood. Even in successful pregnancies, women with APS have an increased chance of pregnancy complications, like pregnancy-induced hypertension (preeclampsia).

Chronic uterine infection, although a cause of individual miscarriage, hasn't been shown to cause recurrent miscarriages.

If you and your husband have suffered recurrent miscarriages, you will most likely be referred to a geneticist, a perinatologist (maternal-fetal medicine specialist), and/or an infertility specialist (who might also be a reproductive endocrinologist). Chromosome studies on a miscarried fetus can also be useful.

Why wait for three miscarriages before a workup is indicated? What if you're in a hurry, money is no object, and two miscarriages have devastated you? I suppose there's no harm in beginning the investigation earlier, but this would only be warranted if there were a significant family history of miscarriage or genetic problems. Otherwise, it would be good that money is no object because it's going to be very expensive with little return: The odds of finding a problem after two miscarriages are less than the odds of just having two "random" miscarriages in a row.

5

Other Types of Pregnancy Loss

The loss of a baby for any reason prior to term is a miscarriage. The medical lexicographers will argue that if it's past the first trimester, fetal death is no longer called a miscarriage but instead called a fetal demise. These names are useful for a frame of clinical reference and I use them myself, but from the parents' point of view, it's still a miscarriage—a ravaging of their dreams. Intrauterine death, be it a miscarriage or a fetal demise, is a loss no matter which way a pregnancy goes astray. And ectopic pregnancy, molar pregnancies, and absorbed twins will rob a couple of their futures just as terribly as a conventional miscarriage.

Ectopic Pregnancy: Being in the Wrong Place at the Wrong Time

You have all of the necessary anatomy to house a normal pregnancy to term. Implantation of a fertilized egg in the uterus, however, depends on unencumbered transport along the fallopian tube (where fertilization took place). If there is scarring in your tube from a previous infection (chlamydia, gonorrhea, even tuberculosis of the pelvis), from endometriosis, or even from the bump where an old tubal ligation was rejoined together, the migration of the fertilized egg can get hung up before entering your uterus. This type of interference with normal transport can even happen for unknown reasons. It is not good.

Fast Forward

Ectopic pregnancy prime symptoms:

- Vaginal bleeding
- Pelvic pain

Ectopic pregnancy is when a pregnancy lodges in a tube or other site other than the uterus. It usually dies, causing bleeding as a symptom, often accompanied by severe pelvic pain. Ascertaining hCG levels and vaginal ultrasound is essential for early diagnosis. Treatment is usually by conservative surgery, aggressive surgery when there is hemorrhage, or chemotherapy to dissolve the ectopic.

An ectopic pregnancy is when a fertilized egg settles somewhere outside of your uterus. Places like your tubes, or even more unlikely, your abdomen, cannot accommodate a pregnancy like your uterus can. Your uterus is the specific organ with the ability to keep an expanding phenomenon like pregnancy self-contained until maturity of your baby. Your tube can't stretch to any great extent, and when it does it can cause pain or even burst, causing a hemorrhagic emergency. Commonly such a pregnancy dies in the tube. Surgical treatment now can be accomplished with a laparoscope, either by expressing the ectopic out of the tube (preferred) or by removing that portion of the tube that holds the ectopic (preferable only if this is a repeat ectopic in the same tube). The ectopic pregnancy can be expressed either from the opening of the end of the tube or by making a small slit above it. Unfortunately, when there is aggressive bleeding, conservative management could be unwise, and an incision may have to be made to handle the problem by conventional surgery.

In some cases a nonsurgical approach is appropriate that uses the chemotherapeutic (anticancer) agent methotrexate (MTX). This substance is fetocidal, leading to resorption.

As with all pregnancies and with all types of miscarriages, treatment for Rh-negative mothers (see Chapter 4) must include RhoGam to prevent immunological attack on subsequent babies. This is a shot of antibodies that will make your body's immune system think it has already responded to the baby's blood—seen as foreign—thereby preventing you from making anti-

A-FACTOR

With the national increase in STDs scarring up the works, ectopic pregnancies are common (one in one hundred pregnancies). But with modern obstetrics, severe complications should be very rare. Most of the time, they can be handled as out-patient laparoscopic surgery. Unfortunately, there's an increased chance of another ectopic either because of the surgical scarring of the tube to treat the first ectopic or because of the conditions that caused the first ectopic.

Alert! One of the biggest risks for ectopic pregnancy is the STD chlamydia. This infection is often silent, only to haunt a woman later with infertility or ectopic pregnancy. Any woman who is not in a monogamous relationship should have a chlamydia culture with each routine Pap smear. Tear this page out and give it to some party person you know.

bodies that can remain to attack a future pregnancy. The risk is only if your baby has Rh-positive blood (opposite of yours if you're Rh-negative). But in cases of miscarriage or ectopic, there is usually such little fetal tissue that the fetus's blood type isn't determined. Since RhoGam is harmless when given unnecessarily, the advice for RhoGam stands if you're Rh-negative. In other words, when in doubt, give RhoGam. Alternately, there is a blood test—the Kleinhauer-Betke test—that can see if your blood has fetal cells in it. The amount found is then used to formulate the amount of RhoGam given, if any.

Today, with early hCG (pregnancy hormone) measurements and vaginal ultrasound, it's becoming more commonplace to discover and treat early ectopics conservatively. Symptoms that can tip off an obstetrician include vaginal bleeding that is the result of hormone withdrawal when the ectopic dies. Since bleeding in early pregnancy usually prompts suspicion of a threatened miscarriage, ultrasound and hCG levels can further explore the suspicion of an ectopic pregnancy too.

The classic symptoms are most often (but not always) pelvic pain to one side (frequently on the side where the ectopic is) and vaginal bleeding during early pregnancy. But the presentation can be sneaky. I've brought pain-free patients to surgery with a belly full of blood, and I've seen many instances in which the pain was on the opposite side of the ectopic.

A structure stretched to its limits by an expanding pregnancy will ultimately rupture, tearing blood vessels that supply that structure—blood vessels that are already larger due to the pregnancy. If the ectopic ruptures, severe hemorrhage can result, causing a woman to suddenly collapse. Slowly increasing pain over several hours can indicate a bleeding tubal pregnancy. If the clinical situation is fuzzy and the patient is stable, blood work can usually demonstrate levels that can help establish the diagnosis. If there is ever any doubt, a diagnostic laparoscopy can be done to make the diagnosis certain. This is a handy tool, for it is otherwise safe with a normal pregnancy if an ectopic is ruled out by this method.

Often the internal bleeding is enough to cause a sizable collection of blood in the abdomen (*hemoperitoneum*). By laparoscopy or by a regular incision, the blood is evacuated, the bleeding sites secured, and the ectopic suctioned or scooped away. Sometimes the ectopic dies at such an early stage that no treatment is necessary.

An ectopic is just as tragic as a miscarriage, except the grieving is shorter—changed by worry because of the added danger an ectopic poses to the women's fertility and to her life. A potentially dangerous condition, ectopic pregnancy is nothing more than a pregnancy that didn't land in the uterus where it belongs.

If a woman has had one ectopic, she isn't automatically going to have another, even though the condition that provoked the first ectopic is still there. But she is at increased risk over those women without a previous ectopic history. A repeat ectopic on the same tube may warrant removal of that tube, though. Common sense prevails.

Molar Pregnancy: Abnormal Fertilization

Neoplasm means "new growth," and it is a medical word used to describe tumors. The words *neoplasm* and *tumor* are both general descriptions for any tissue growing "extra," be it a wart or brain cancer. So these terms are vague at best, because this is a wide range indeed. Any tissue in the human body, when it loses its ability to be specialized into the type of tissue it really is, can become neoplastic.

The only deviant growth that is not considered a neoplasm is a pregnancy. But pregnancy is not immune from developing its own neoplasm. If any tissue can undergo neoplastic transformation or deterioration, that includes the tissue of conception.

Gestational trophoblastic disease (GTD) is the medically correct term for hydatidiform mole, or a molar pregnancy. A cancerous fetus? Not exactly. We're talking about products of conception that become neoplastic. A molar pregnancy is the result of genetics gone bad because of a faulty fertilization. Molar pregnancy tissue is not of maternal origin and therefore, anatomically and psychologically, these tumors are probably the weirdest tumors that can be made in a woman's (or anyone's!) body. They are actual pregnancies, but there's abnormal fertilization, usually XX (female) or XY (male) chromosome matchings that are—and this is the strange part—all derived from the father. Very weird.

Fast Forward

In the United States and Europe, the odds of having a molar pregnancy are one in two thousand. Asian countries have increased odds. Americans and Europeans of Asian extraction assume the risk in the areas where they live, possibly indicating a dietary or environmental connection.

It gets weirder. A mole is a tumor. This means it has malignancy potential. Even in the benign state, it can metastasize to the lung and other organs, like the liver and brain. A D&C is used to evacuate this abnormal tissue from the uterus. Chemotherapy toxic to gestational tissue is used to treat the disease. There usually is no fetus, just swollen placental parts—a mass resembling grapelike clusters at the time of miscarriage, or looking like a whitish honeycomb-like a blur on the ultrasound.

The incidence of molar pregnancy is different in different parts of the world, which possibly adds a dietary or environmental preference to the mix. In the United States and Europe, it occurs in one in two thousand pregnancies.

Diagnosis of a molar pregnancy is made with ultrasound, but suspicion arises with the following symptoms:

- Vaginal bleeding
- Exaggerated common pregnancy symptoms, e.g., morning sickness progressing to hyperemesis
- Excessive amounts of hCG in blood tests. It must be remembered that gestational tissue is hCG-producing tissue, which is the basis for all of

our pregnancy tests, and gestational tissue out of control will make tons of the stuff.

- Difficulties of pregnancy that are usually associated with the third trimester, like pregnancy-induced hypertension
- Large cysts of the ovaries, called theca-lutein cysts, result from hormonal overstimulation from such a "hyper" pregnancy.
- In complete moles (moles in which there is no living fetus), the size of the uterus is often different from what the gestation warrants—smaller or larger.

Fast Forward

Molar pregnancies, the weirdest tumors of all, are rare chromosomal accidents. Almost always resulting in miscarriage of abnormal tissue, they can persist and may even be malignant. Caught early, another dazzling argument for early prenatal care, they can be cured and a woman can look forward to normal pregnancies afterward.

The treatment of a molar pregnancy depends on the severity of the disease. It can range from simple evacuation (with a D&C) all the way to chemotherapy with agents toxic to gestational tissue.

What about future pregnancy? Because hCG goes up both with pregnancy and also with failure of treatment of GTD, it is wise to wait until the hCG count has been zero for some time before attempting another pregnancy. Otherwise, there will be a great amount of confusion as to what's really happening—persistence of disease or a new normal pregnancy.

A molar pregnancy is in fact a miscarriage of sorts. It is just as tragic and sad. But like a miscarriage, it is more than likely a random event, with normal pregnancy expectations for the future.

Q & A—Miscarriage and Other Types of Pregnancy Loss

hCG Values

Question: My doctor is getting blood levels of hCG on me because of bleeding. Are there actual numbers that tell how far along in my pregnancy I am? Is she looking for something other than a miscarriage? So far the ultrasound hasn't been helpful.

Answer: Any pregnancy loss is a miscarriage, even if it's an ectopic pregnancy or a molar pregnancy. Your doctor is using hCG values because she hasn't seen anything yet on ultrasound to point her in any particular direction. She is looking, first of all, for a normal pregnancy in which the hCG values should double every other day. Also, there should be a normal-looking gestational sac when the hCG values are between 1,000 and 2,000 IU/l (International Units per liter). A fetal pole should be seen after 2,500. If a heartbeat isn't seen by the time the hCG reaches 5,000, this is compatible with a missed AB. Ectopics fall short of the doubling that is normally seen every thirty-six to forty-eight hours. Miscarriage can also fall short of the doubling, but still be seen to be increasing, keeping ectopic pregnancy still a possibility. A falling hCG isn't normal before ten weeks, although a slight falling can be seen when the hCG plateaus at the end of the first trimester.

Fast Forward

Normal pregnancy: a vaginal ultrasound should show a gestational sac when the hCG values are 1,000–2,000, a fetal pole between 2,500 and 5,000, and a fetal heart rate above 110 beats per minute at 5,000.

Abnormal pregnancy: hCG values will fail to approximately double every thirty-six to forty-eight hours or will actually fall.

hCG values: they are only meaningful up till ten weeks, when they can fall normally. But by then ultrasound should splendidly show a fetus.

Progression of ultrasound findings go hand in hand with rising hCG values, and sooner or later, both diagnostic approaches will agree on a conclusion. Until that time, either may point the way alone.

Exaggerated Grief in Miscarriage

Question: I have put off having babies for my career and have even resorted to abortion once. Now that I'm ready for children at the age of thirty-seven, I recently had a miscarriage a year ago and cannot get over the depression. Each month I don't get pregnant I sink lower. I blame myself for waiting to have children and wonder if I'll ever be able to do it.

Answer: Besides all of the false self-accusations about what you might have done wrong and the normal three-month episode of grief after a miscarriage, you have additional risk factors for prolonged miscarriage-related grief:

- First attempt at pregnancy under the nagging ticking of your biological clock. You blame yourself for waiting too long, and for increased time between your miscarriage and getting pregnant again. It's been a year and you're in more of a hurry than ever and feel regret over a previous abortion.
- You mention your abortion and your career and how they relate to each other—you are probably second-guessing the wisdom of terminating a pregnancy for a job when you now don't know whether you'll ever have children.

Fast Forward

The normal grief after miscarriage is about three months. This can become prolonged if you're under the gun of your biological clock, if your further attempts at pregnancy go unfulfilled, or if you've previously had an abortion. No one can turn back the clock, but an infertility doctor can put you on the fast track and even manage your depression. Thyroid conditions can aggravate depression, interfere with conception, and increase miscarriage chances.

It's true that the older you are, the less fertile you become. The clock becomes an incredible stress factor that significantly interferes with your ability to deal with the grief of your miscarriage in an appropriate way. The months that go by without a subsequent pregnancy torture you, and on top of that you fear that another pregnancy might end in miscarriage again. You may now regret the abortion, and as it applies to your situation now, it is regrettable. But the situation now is not the situation back then, and you made your decisions based on what was going on in your life at that time. So the abortion isn't really relevant to what you want now. Unfortunately, a previous abortion becomes much more psychodynamically disturbing in a woman who desperately wants a baby, and this will add significantly to any depression.

Going longer than six months without conception warrants a trip to the infertility doctor to put you on a fast track since you have nothing to gain in waiting. In the meantime, since you're being unfairly attacked by these other extraordinary influences, you might want to ask your infertility doctor what antidepressant you can use temporarily that won't interfere with such a fast track or a pregnancy. As an aside, I'd like to recommend that you get thyroid function studies done, because a third of all people with depression have thyroid problems, which can interfere with conception and increase the risk of miscarriage.

Absorbed Twin

Question: On early ultrasound I had two sacs and my doctor told me I had twins. Now there's only one sac and one baby. Was she wrong?

Answer: She may have been. Sometimes the yolk sac can be misinterpreted as a second gestational sac by inexperienced ultrasonographers. This is a sac that will become part of the umbilical cord and abdomen when it gets drawn into your baby. It makes fetal blood cells. Another mistake of inexperience is seeing the fetal head and the rest of the fetus and interpreting them as two different smaller structures instead of the larger single structure that is the whole fetus.

> **Fast Forward**
>
> Now that we use ultrasound routinely and early, we're seeing things that we've never had a clue about previously—like absorbed twins. In this unusual situation, the surviving twin will more than likely go on to experience a normal pregnancy.

But more than likely she knew what she was doing. With ultrasound part of mainstream obstetrics, we're beginning to realize that twin pregnancies happen more than we thought. No one knows what the final figure will be compared to the current official twin rate, but more and more investigators are beginning to report a phenomenon called the absorbed twin syndrome, in which one of the twins seems to dissolve away—an obvious missed AB of sorts that then gets reabsorbed. It may be the cause of some first trimester bleeding. For the most part, if the remaining twin looks great on ultrasound, you should expect a normal pregnancy thereafter.

We are only now appreciating the significance of absorbed twins. How many have gone undiagnosed for all the generations before ultrasound? Many other things, like subchorionic hemorrhage, are taken for granted when we were clueless about them before the days of ultrasound.

Safety of Intercourse with First Trimester Bleeding

Question: My doctor has diagnosed the cause of my first trimester bleeding as cervicitis, which he says is harmless. He has further instructed me to not have any intercourse. Why no sex if the cervicitis is harmless?

Answer: Just to avoid confusion. Cervicitis can resolve, either by itself or with creams if infectious. True, the delicate cells that bleed have nothing to do with your baby and won't hurt the pregnancy, but your doctor wants to avoid unnecessary first trimester bleeding workups from scratch if you have another episode of cervicitis-related bleeding. Remember, although a recurrence will probably be just another cervicitis episode, your doctor can't just blow it off as that. He must assume the worst each time, prompting unnecessary tests, expense, and time consumption. Make your life and his a lot easier by preventing a source of false alarms that would mandate another extensive investigation.

When to Attempt to Conceive Again After a Miscarriage

Question: How long should I wait to attempt conceiving after having suffered a miscarriage?

Answer: There is no universal agreement about whether it should be three months, six months, or not at all. I usually recommend three months— that is, after three normal, spontaneous periods. This might be a somewhat shorter period of time than the advice of other doctors, but I think the psychological aspect of your loss needs to be addressed too. The sooner you get pregnant again, the sooner you effect another type of closure. I recommend use of condoms during the wait, so as not to hormonally pollute the situation with birth control pills, which could delay the return of normal cycling. I also recommend staying on prenatal vitamins (with folic acid) during the three months in case you accidentally get pregnant before then. What then? Well, that's a *good* problem, I suppose, right?

Miscarriage and Pregnancy Between Two Sisters

Question: My sister and I were pregnant at the same time. She had a miscarriage and now that I'm starting to show, she's acting really distant. I know why, but will this ever end? We were so close before.

Answer: It doesn't matter whether you're twins, cousins, or just good friends. No matter what your relationship is, it's going to be weird because

Fast Forward

Friends or relatives with simultaneous pregnancies will have a peculiar test of their closeness if one of them miscarries. But if they're truly dear to each other, the one experiencing the loss—if she's not shunned to spare her feelings—will embrace the one who isn't.

you are so close. She won't be able to look at you and your pregnancy without wondering what might have been for her and her lost baby. Because you two shared your pregnancy with each other, it makes her loss all the more painful. She not only fantasized about all of the normal mother-and-baby things, she also looked forward to the two of you in the park with your babies, dueling baby showers, etc. You symbolize everything that is wrong with what she suffered. But sooner or later, she will come around. If she is genuinely close to you, she'll not only be glad that what happened to her didn't happen to you, but will celebrate your pregnancy and baby all the more. True, she'll always be reminded, but there's nothing you can do about that. The one mistake you shouldn't make is to assume she will be hurt by your including her in your pregnancy. Keep her included. She'll politely refuse until she's ready, and at that point she'll love you all the more for letting her share what's left between the two pregnancies—yours.

Look for other current questions and updates regarding pregnancy loss on BabyZone.com, by going to babyzone.com/features/expertsqa.

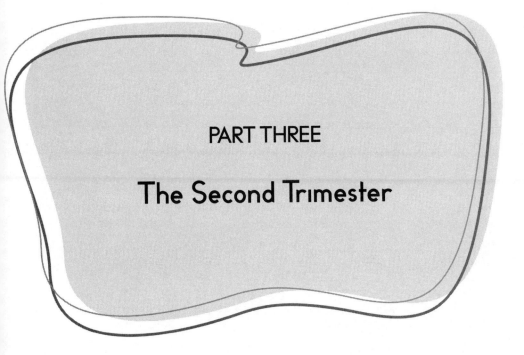

PART THREE

The Second Trimester

The Pause That Refreshes

If you were to map out nine calendar months, you would find that it counts out to approximately forty weeks. These forty weeks are what your obstetrician uses to date your pregnancy. Since pregnancy and fetal development represent a continuum toward the end result—your baby—there are many changes that occur on this long, strange trip.

At each stage of your pregnancy your growing baby is not the same baby he was weeks earlier. Different considerations and concerns mark the different portions of the entire pregnancy, and historically gestation has been divided into three main sections—the first, second, and third trimesters. While your first trimester was crucial for laying down the groundwork for the developing organs and for concerns over the possibility of miscarriage, and your third trimester will center on your baby attaining maturity and on the delivery process itself, your second trimester is a sort of reprieve during which your pregnancy can almost be enjoyed. Almost.

It is a very forgiving trimester; you're most likely to feel your best. It is a time when you have the chance and peace of mind to really learn about having your baby. Cramping and nausea of the first trimester go away and you can enjoy some time before the third trimester brings its own set of anxieties. (But then this is the *Anxious Parent's Guide to Pregnancy*, right?) This is the trimester when you will begin to feel your baby's movements, daily reassurance indeed. During this period you become somewhat accustomed to the challenges to your physiology, your physical complaints usually decline, and your visits to your doctor are mainly to make sure that you're still happy, alive, and pregnant. Of course this is an oversimplification.

Your obstetrician is actually doing a lot during these well-pregnancy visits. The fetal heart tones are assessed. The size of your baby is estimated and compared to the sizes recorded on previous visits to assure appropriate interval growth. Ultrasound is utilized to diagnose only a single baby versus twins (or more!). Your minor complaints are addressed, your doctor being especially sensitive to what might be a major problem presenting as a simpler symptom. Lab work is monitored to watch for anemia, urinary tract infections, or warnings of pregnancy-related illnesses, like pregnancy-induced hypertension (preeclampsia) and gestational diabetes.

In short, the second trimester is a regrouping of sorts and a springboard to the real business end of the pregnancy—the third trimester. It's the time when your body is finally promising a term pregnancy, retreating from the miscarriage scares of your first twelve weeks. Your pregnancy, from an obstetrical consideration, is finally betrothed to a delivery.

But not so fast, because it's not quite a done deal yet; there's still some fine print yet to be read in this contract.

Prenatal Care in the Second Trimester

Fundal height (the measurement from your pubic bone to the top of your uterus, as felt externally) and fetal heart tones will be recorded each visit, and intervals between visits will range anywhere from two to four weeks, depending on your doctor. The surveillance of your blood pressure, weight, and urine continues as well. The generalities of maternal and fetal health and appropriate fetal growth are observed. There are many self-help books on pregnancy, but each visit offers you a chance to add a perspective to the things you are reading. It is a good time for a free exchange of questions and answers addressing those things important to you as a prospective mother, and a caregiver's particular communicative skills will determine the quality of your education as it pertains to your particular pregnancy.

The Prenatal Record

The prenatal record is a synopsis of your entire pregnancy. It is a record of fields on a grid sheet that can portray sequentially the progressions of fundal

> ## A Typical Time Line for Prenatal Care
> ### *Second Trimester—Twelve to Twenty-four Weeks*
> - Visits every three to four weeks, much like the routine visits of the first trimester, except with the addition of listening for fetal heart tones
> - Between weeks fifteen and twenty, offering of alphafetoprotein screen (triple screen), determination of fetal growth by serial fundal height determinations, beginning prenatal classes at the hospital or by private instruction
> - Cervical cerclage optimal time is at fourteen weeks if threat of incompetent cervix. The second trimester is the best trimester in which to have any necessary surgery (gallbladder, for example).

heights, blood pressures, weights, urine tests, and documentation of fetal heart rate (FHR). There are also areas in which to record unique notes each visit and any complaints of swelling (edema).

This grid sheet is designed to flow down the page of the prenatal record so your doctor can see with a glimpse any trends worthy of concern. It is easy with this type of notation to see a steady rise in blood pressures or a sudden jump in weight. There are other parts of the record for going into more detail, especially if the necessary documentation warrants it, but this grid is the schematic from which your doctor will eyeball your pregnancy each visit. Even the newer electronic medical records endeavor to give the look and the feel of this grid sheet.

SAMPLE PRENATAL RECORD

Date	Gest. Age	Urine Protein/Glucose	Weight	Blood Pressure	Fundal Height	Edema	FHR	Complaints
4/7	15 wk	1+/Neg.	142	110/68	17 cm	0	168	fatigue
4/28	18	Neg./Neg.	144	112/60	19 cm	0	164	without complaint
5/19	21	trace/Neg.	148	108/72	22 cm	0	166	fatigue
etc.	etc.	etc./etc.	etc.	etc.	etc.	etc.	etc.	etc.

Gestational Age

The gestational age is recorded as the pregnancy progresses. Just as a downward scan can see any trends during the pregnancy, a scan horizontally will give a snapshot of each whole visit.

Urine Dipstick Tests

Protein and sugar (glucose) spilling into the urine are the most noteworthy indicators for the two most famous complications of pregnancy: pregnancy-induced hypertension (preeclampsia) and gestational diabetes (GD). These are usually graded as a 1+ to 4+ scale, or negative. It's not hard to get a positive glucose reading from your urine if you were naughty and had two donuts for breakfast. But enough sugar spilling into your urine to register on the dipstick is abnormal in the absence of any recent high-calorie crimes. Spilling sugar anytime during the second trimester may prompt an earlier screen in addition to the traditional twenty-six-week glucola test.

Weight—the Bump of the Second Trimester

Weight as a hot topic was discussed in Chapter 2, so I won't repeat the generalities. But a sudden jump beyond what can be explained by diet alone is usually the result of sudden fluid retention. Fluid is normal to some extent in pregnancy, but when accompanied by blood pressure increases and protein in the urine, it can be a sign of pregnancy-induced hypertension. (See "Complications Unique to Pregnancy," Chapter 20.)

The second trimester will have a sudden weight bump at around twenty weeks. Since delivery of the baby involves bleeding, your body will make extra blood (red blood cells and plasma) during the pregnancy to try to break even on the deal. The arithmetic won't be exact, but the extra blood will keep you out of dangerously anemic territory in the postpartum period. It is disproportionately produced during this midpregnancy phase, however, so at midpregnancy a six- to eight-pound weight gain between visits is not unusual. But take heart. You don't want to find yourself in a panic, figuring eight pounds every three weeks adding up to about sixty pounds before it's all over. Of course, you can only milk this extra blood explanation once, so if you gain six pounds every visit . . .

Blood Pressure

Blood pressure actually falls a little bit during this time because there's a self-indulgent expanding uterus. As the uterus increases in size, the less its ligaments support it. The ligaments ultimately fail altogether when the uterus is too big to fit in the pelvis. It lifts into the abdomen as an abdominal organ by the beginning of the second trimester. Blood flow from both legs merges into a larger blood vessel—the inferior vena cava, the main vein that drains your entire body below your heart. This is the same situation with blood *from* the heart in the aorta, splitting into smaller arteries for each leg. But arteries, and the aorta is the largest, have their own pulsatile force and can stand up fairly well to a weight sitting on top. The flow continues. Veins are a lot wimpier— they don't have the tough muscular shell that arteries do and they don't pulsate to blast their load onward. Blood flow through them is more of a negative-pressure-flow system, drawn up by the vacuumlike process created by the heart pumping it back out, further up.

What I'm talking about is a sizable weight. This isn't such a problem in the early second trimester, but by about weeks twenty-two to twenty-four, you will start to notice this effect. This is why your doctor will tell you to not sleep flat on your back. He's afraid that although the hypotension may go unnoticed in your sleep, the decreased blood flow to the uterus under less pressure will decrease nutrition and oxygenation to your baby. This is probably not the disaster it seems, otherwise there would be a lot of disasters about. But the mechanics of the physiology are rock solid and make sense. So do everybody a big favor, including your baby, and don't do it.

Depending on body shape, this particular effect may not present until the late third trimester. It's worse the bigger your baby gets. Ultrasound in late pregnancy with you lying flat on your back is often interrupted by feelings of nausea. The cure for this is flipping to one side.

Fundal Height

The fundal height is just that—the height of the fundus. The measurement will be larger as your uterus gets bigger. Your doctor will measure from the top of your pubic bone to the curve of the top of the uterus. It's generally measured in centimeters and is a crude diagnostic tool held over from the days before ultrasound, but it is still useful in large clinics where the same patient may not get the same doctor twice in a row for her prenatal visits. In those settings it provides some frame of reference for the continuity of the documentation throughout the pregnancy.

Relying on fundal height for assurance of appropriate fetal growth must take into account any explainable discrepancies. For instance, a third trimester baby who has dropped between the last visit and the current one may show a fundal height less than last visit! If a baby's turned sideways, as can happen in the second trimester, the fundal height can be unusually short for what's expected, since the greatest dimension then lies across the horizontal. A breech baby, usually sitting up high in your uterus, will yield a larger fundal height. These are all circumstances that can yield screwy fundal heights, so the due date is never revised based on a fundal height.

Generally, your pregnancy is halfway (about twenty weeks) when the fundal height is felt at your navel. For every finger's width above your navel the fundal height reaches, you can add a week. Likewise, below your navel you can subtract a week. But this relationship works well between weeks fifteen and twenty-five only. Before and after that this relationship goes out the window. It's not calculus.

Edema (Swelling)

Since all pregnant women have swelling to some extent, so will you. If you lived on the Moon or on Mars this wouldn't be a problem because a lot of the swelling is due to gravity. Of course, lack of a breathable atmosphere would make these unwise homestead choices anyway.

Back at 1G, your planet tugs at everything so that we won't go flying off into space. That applies to movable fluids within containers, and that container is you. But gravity works in concert with another effect because the weight of your occupied uterus can press on your vena cava to obstruct blood flow (drainage) back up to the heart. Such an obstruction backs up the works. When the fluids of your lower body can't balance out with the fluids in your upper body, your bottom half becomes overhydrated—flooded. You see this as swollen ankles. The swelling can also be fairly high up, even involving your wrists, giving you false carpal tunnel syndrome with tingling of your fingers.

Edema is normal, but it can also accompany pregnancy-induced hypertension. Swelling in the absence of hypertension, spilling protein, or jumpy reflexes is merely one of the Middle Trials of Pregnancy. It can continue and worsen, blossoming into a third trimester trial as well.

FHR (Fetal Heart Rate)

Many people think that a baby's blood circulation is directly connected to the mother's circulation. This is a myth. Many think that you can tell the gender of your baby by the count of the fetal heart rate per minute. Another myth. And there are some that think that Elvis is still alive. I'm sure about at least two of these.

The very fact that your own heart rate and your baby's heart rate are different is the proof that they're not connected. If they were, such opposing pulsatile forces would create a midpoint of turbulence, perhaps creating hem-

Fast Forward
Routine care in the second trimester:
- Visits every three to four weeks, much like the routine visits of the first trimester, except with the addition of listening for fetal heart tones
- Between weeks fifteen and twenty, offering of MSAFP screen (triple screen), determination of fetal growth by serial fundal height determinations, beginning prenatal classes at the hospital or by private instruction

Cervical cerclage optimal time is week fourteen if there's a threat of incompetent cervix. The second trimester is the best trimester in which to have any necessary surgery—gallbladder, etc. It is also a good time to have an abnormal Pap smear evaluated.

orrhoids for you the size of the wheelbarrow they'd have to be carried in. God, in His infinite wisdom, decided against such an arrangement. If we all knew how lucky we are, we'd all be in church every week, not just those in their last trimester.

The base of the placenta, slapped up against the inside wall of your uterus, is a separation, selectively filtering through oxygen and nutrition. These and other items are then distributed within the completely separate fetal circulation. Your baby's body is a solely owned subsidiary of you. Her heart beats independently, dependent on the factors unique to her. On the medical record, these rates are recorded. By term the FHR will be from 120 to 160. These are very fuzzy ranges and the FHR on the same baby can vary wildly as well, which is why you can't tell the gender from the FHR. (Otherwise, your doctor would have to explain why your daughter grew a penis since the last visit, after having lost it from the visit before that. And on and on. Penises don't disappear and then reappear. Men will be quick to point out their brazen opinion that penises are pretty amazing things, but a penis can't do that—with apologies to John Wayne Bobbitt.)

The FHR during the second trimester, especially before twenty-one weeks, can be irregular. Just as your baby's liver needs to mature to prevent jaundice and her lungs need to mature so as to breathe air, so too the electrical pathway of her little heart goes through maturation so as to correctly deliver the pulsations that'll drive the roughly two-and-one-half-billion heartbeats she'll have after birth. It's a quirk of normal maturation, but sometimes ultrasound views of the heart or Doppler audio will reveal a fetal cardiac arrhythmia that is absolutely terrifying. It happened to me. I once saw a twenty-week baby's heart stop cold for a moment, only to restart, the baby hopping around like nothing happened. These babies that give the second trimester cardiac frights almost always go on to have no problems at all. On the other hand, I had to take a long lunch after seeing what I saw that day.

If something like this were to happen, don't worry. Your developing baby doesn't have a heart condition; fetal echocardiography can document this for reassurance.

Reflexes and Other Miscellaneous Recordings

The prenatal record is a very personalized documentation, depending on your doctor. More than likely he has personalized it himself, having fields in the grid for things such as reflexes (hyperactivity of which is one of the signs of pregnancy-induced hypertension or preeclampsia), nausea (mainly a first trimester occurrence), contractions (to watch for troubling preterm labor patterns), and fetal movement.

Fetal movement (FM) is made redundant by recordings of the FHR, but reports of a change in the amount of movement would qualify for a special notation because your doctor is always on the lookout for decreased fetal movement as a sign of fetal jeopardy. This is different from a change in the *type* of movement, because as your baby gets bigger, you should expect the discrete kicks and flips to settle into more of a squirming and rotational quality—there's just less room for acrobatics.

Special Testing for the Second Trimester

Alphafetoprotein

Alphafetoprotein is a protein made by your baby's liver that gets into your own circulation in small amounts. It is a protein so unique to pregnancy tissue that it can even be used as a pregnancy test. Since it normally leaks into your circulation, the amount in you will rise steadily from conception until twenty weeks, when it levels off until falling after delivery. If your baby were to have a problem related to uncovered body parts (break in the skin), like in spina bifida or open-skull abnormalities, a lot more of the α-fetoprotein can leak into your system, giving you higher amounts on your blood test. Detecting these types of deformities was the original intent of this test.

> **A-FACTOR**
>
> A normal maternal serum alphafetoprotein (MSAFP) is reassuring, but an abnormal one isn't reliable. Inaccurate gestational age and normal variations of your baby and placenta may give a false positive. When abnormal, a Level 3 ultrasound and/or amniocentesis may be added to the pursuit of the truth.
>
> A high alphafetoprotein can be due to incorrect gestational age, multiple gestation, brain or spinal cord abnormalities, abdominal wall defects, kidney or bowel defects, and as a normal variation.
>
> A low alphafetoprotein can be due to incorrect gestational age, Down's syndrome, and as a normal variation.

The MSAFP of today, a simple blood test, can be performed as the triple screen. Instead of just alphafetoprotein, it measures two additional things, estriol and hCG. The additional components add accuracy and allow screening for Down's syndrome and other genetic problems. These are also compared with your maternal age to determine if they fall on the wrong sides of a bell curve. The center of the bell curve, the median, is the larger chunk of normal results. How far your results may stray from the median of the normal population, reported in multiples of median (*MOMs*) will determine how much extra risk you may have.

The MSAFP is an excellent screen, but a terrible test. By that I mean that although it yanks out of the general population those babies that need to be looked at more closely, it isn't very accurate in pointing correctly at abnormalities. Its best meaning is when it comes back normal. Even though this is no guarantee, it's an excellent reassurance. When it's abnormal, though, its results need to be discarded and better, more predictive tests need to be done: amniocentesis and ultrasound.

Since the amount of alphafetoprotein levels out after about twenty weeks, this screen is done during the fifteen- to twenty-week window of gestation. The gestational age needs to be accurate since normal values as applied to what is expected at one gestational age will look very abnormal when plotted against another inaccurate gestational age. In fact most of the abnormal α-fetoproteins are a result of improper dating of the pregnancy. Other things that can give an abnormal result for a normal pregnancy (false positive) are variations in the amount of α-fetoprotein made by your baby, variations in the rate of transfer from the baby's circulation to your own, and dilutional effects of your blood volume. Remember that there's a disproportionate surge in plasma as you near the twenty-week mark. Multiple gestations will increase the amounts in your own blood. Premature labor, pregnancy-induced hypertension, threatened miscarriage, and growth delay can also give falsely high α-fetoprotein levels.

Ultrasound

The point becomes moot when ultrasound, as the next step, indicts any faulty arithmetic. If a correction is made on the due date, your doctor may then end up with an appended, corrected α-fetoprotein result; if the ultrasound finds twins or other reasons to explain the bad result, amniocentesis (see below) may not be warranted.

An ultrasound for an abnormal α-fetoprotein is usually a Level 3 ultrasound, performed by a specialist in maternal-fetal medicine (perinatologist). Your regular obstetrician usually does Level 1 ultrasounds, which are general scans to check for body parts, normal proportions among them, normal interval growth, and other signs of well-being. The Level 3 is the top of the line in which very subtle aspects of your baby can be checked. Although ultrasound isn't the same as actually looking at the chromosomes from an amniocentesis, still two out of three Down's syndrome babies can be identified this way.

The alphafetoprotein screen's numbers, as applied to the weeks of gestation, give a Down's risk as compared to the risk you would normally have just being a certain age. Other measurements are non-age related, but are applied to straight risk based purely on the triple-screen numbers.

Amniocentesis

When the ultrasound is worrisome or if whatever reassurances the ultrasound provides aren't good enough, your doctor may recommend or you may want an amniocentesis. There is nothing magic about this procedure. It is simply the insertion of a needle through your skin into your uterus to retrieve amniotic fluid, done under sterile technique and with the guidance of ultrasound. Tests can be performed on the fluid, and cellular debris can provide tissue for chromosomal analysis. Ultrasound has made this test safe, as you can imagine.

The crown jewel of the amniocentesis investigation is the ability to culture fetal cells from which the chromosomes can be analyzed. This mapping, the *karyotype*, should be 46XX or 46XY, depending on whether you carry a girl or a boy, respectively. (Gender determination is 100 percent accurate with amniocentesis.)

Depending on the perinatologist, the complication rate is anywhere from 0.5 percent to 2 percent, or from one in two hundred cases to one in fifty. This poses a dilemma for the woman whose pregnancy was particularly hard earned through infertility treatments. No one wants to accept the risk of hurting a normal baby through infection, preterm labor, injury, or death from preterm delivery caused by an amniocentesis. There are some things that are no-brainers in obstetrics, but this isn't one of them. The decision to do an amnio is a weighing of quantitative risks with qualitative outcomes, comparing apples and oranges. More than likely you will be subjecting your child to a numerical risk that's greater than the risks suggested by MSAFP and ultrasound. In addition, the chance of damage from the amnio may be numerically higher than the chance of having a Down's syndrome child. Still, patients often opt for it because it gives them certain knowledge that the child does or does not carry the Down's syndrome karyotype.

A-FACTOR
Only 5 percent of MSAFP screens are abnormal. Of these, only 3–5 percent will be real problems. This gives the odds of three in a thousand babies. Don't panic with an abnormal MSAFP test.

This sort of discussion cuts deeply into profound sociological issues. The pro-life and pro-choice factions complicate matters even more with slogans and double-talk. Avoiding babies with serious abnormalities is a technological advancement and even hints at that dirty word *eugenics*, but it is the right of prospective parents who receive the bad news of such a diagnosis. To say that parents of such babies lead a life of regret is inaccurate, for there are joys in special children other parents will never have. (See "Having Special Children" in Chapter 22.)

The Psychological Toll of False Positives

A couple may be charmed through an uneventful first trimester, only to be thunderstruck by an abnormal triple-screen test. It's a given that you're going to anguish and suffer over an abnormal test that bears out a true abnormality, but what about those victims of the false positive? They are led on the worst-case scenario parade until the end when the final test simply says, "Never mind." And that's assuming they opt for the tests. All of these—triple screen, ultrasound, and amniocentesis—are optional. A couple who doesn't want the very small risk of the amnio or who is pro-life won't know the final outcome until that final test result is in—in the delivery room. They have over half their pregnancy to suffer through the unknown.

High Risk in the Second Trimester

In the second trimester problems that can make you high risk include all of the first trimester concerns, as well as a host of others.

Fast Forward

Things that will make your doctor consider you high risk in the second trimester:

- Incompetent cervix, increasing the risk of preterm delivery
- Bleeding (due to placental abruption or previa)*
- IUGR (Intrauterine Growth Restriction—a baby small for the corresponding gestational age)
- Gestational diabetes
- Pregnancy-induced hypertension
- Sporadic or noncompliant prenatal care
- Preterm labor*
- Kidney infection
- Premature rupture of membranes (or leaking)*
- Abdominal tenderness of the uterus (possible infection of the pregnancy)*

*Call your doctor for these!

Incompetent Cervix

Not all preterm deliveries are the result of preterm labor. If there's a weakness in your cervix, your baby might just slip on down into your vagina with delivery soon to follow. This is usually a problem of the second trimester, and second trimester babies don't have enough organ maturity to survive.

There are two risk factors that will alert your doctor to such a possibility: a history of a previous preterm delivery or previous premature dilation of your cervix, begun in the absence of labor; or an exam that demonstrates premature thinning, shortening, or dilation of your cervix.

The cervix is important in holding in the pregnancy and then in progressively dilating at term by yielding to the forces of labor. If there is a weakness of the circular tissues that provide the tensile strength of the cervix, it may yield prematurely, causing fear of a preterm baby to deal with. The cervix can weaken from previous traumatic delivery, previous rapid labor, previous destructive surgery for precancerous lesions, or due to heredity.

The structural tissue of the cervix doesn't repair itself very well, so if there's a history of a previous premature delivery, the diagnosis of incompetent cervix might be made. The treatment for this hasn't changed in generations. Bed rest and the unsophisticated technique of tying the cervix shut are still an effective way to manage this complication.

Called a cerclage, the surgical technique involves tying a piece of nonabsorbable tape around the cervix from a vaginal approach. There are variations on the way to do it, but essentially the outcome is the same—to keep the cervix from dilating. This is an out-patient procedure with a high success rate and a low complication rate.

Timing of a cerclage is important. The second trimester is the most tolerant time of the pregnancy for surgery. Surgery in the first trimester runs the risk of causing miscarriage or of being for nothing if there ensues a miscarriage. Surgery in the third trimester runs the risk of stimulating preterm labor. Whether it's a gallbladder, a carpal tunnel, a hernia that can't wait, or even a splenectomy, the second trimester is the safest time for surgery, short of waiting until after delivery. Cerclage is no exception. Most cerclages are done in the fourteenth or fifteenth week or pregnancy. It would be silly to put a patient through this before being out of miscarriage territory, and it's prudent to do it before any real contractions could possibly brew.

Bleeding

All of the harmless causes of bleeding described in "The Reality of Miscarriage" (Chapter 4) apply in the second trimester as well (but miscarriage in the second trimester, called fetal demise, is very unusual). The big bleeding worry in the second trimester is over something called placenta previa.

Placenta previa can be both a second and a third trimester problem. I've included it here because the second trimester is usually the time of first diagnosis.

> **Fast Forward**
>
> Bleeding in the second trimester can be due to placenta previa (low-lying placenta), which is at risk for abruption (separating, with resulting bleeding). Many cases can be managed conservatively, but for total previas, which cover the cervix—the way out for the baby—C-section is indicated.

The placenta is the vascular part of the pregnancy that adheres to the inside of your uterus, allowing nutrients and oxygen to pass through from the maternal side to the fetal side, then on through the umbilical arteries to your baby. Not only is it important for this structure to remain attached for the purpose of supplying your baby, but it is equally important that it not separate before delivery; such a tearing away (called placental *abruption*) could disrupt the vascular lining and cause blood loss from your baby as well as create a hemorrhagic incident for you.

Placenta *previa* is the positioning of the placenta in a way that blocks the cervix (the way out for your baby). Any thinning of the cervix—resulting in a loosening of the low-lying placenta's base of attachment—can lead to separation and with it, bleeding.

This is initially a second trimester problem because the cervix is so thick in the first trimester that a placenta previa is usually quiet. When the placenta covers the entire cervix, it is called a total previa. When only partially impinging on the area it is called a partial previa. Thankfully, total previas are rare, and most previas (previae) only encroach upon the edge of the cervical os (opening).

In early pregnancy partial previas are common because there just isn't a lot of surface area to the inside of the uterus, so any structure occupying the real estate there can commonly be positioned as a partial previa, or more likely, as a low-lying placenta. As the uterus grows, its upper part enlarges faster than the lower uterine segment, so a placenta lying over both areas will tend to grow away from the cervical os. We call this placental migration, but this is a misnomer. The placenta doesn't actually move; the tissue upon which it is embedded expands unevenly and it only appears to move up and away from the cervix. The result is a more safely positioned placenta, no matter what the illusion. When a low-lying placenta is seen in early or midpregnancy, chances are that it will be well out of the way by the time of the third trimester, essentially making it a nonissue. If a placenta is low-lying, even at the edge of the cervix, you can still deliver vaginally, your baby's head pressing against any part of your placenta that might want to bleed. (Although you can imagine the heightened sense of vigilance needed in such a labor.) When the previa is total, C-section will be mandatory. Ultrasound has given many life-saving warnings of placenta previa, and follow-up ultrasound has helped separate those women who continue in peril from those whose risk lessens over time.

When your placenta is low in your uterus, there are two problems. First, if it totally covers the way out for the baby (total previa), this roadblock may cause disaster should labor and delivery proceed. Second, the attachment down low is on thinner tissue of the uterus than the thicker, muscular layer higher up. Since the attachment is very vascular, after delivery when it separates, the lower uterine lining doesn't have enough muscle to contract and pinch off the bleeding openings that are left on the maternal side. This can lead to increased blood loss at delivery, but thanks to ultrasound, there is ample forewarning.

*A-FACTOR

A low-lying placenta in the first trimester or early second trimester will probably migrate up and away from the cervix, becoming a nonissue. A low-lying placenta in even the late second trimester may still have time to migrate, allowing for a vaginal delivery. A previa in the third trimester (the ones that persist are a tiny minority) is a cause for worry, because of the pending C-section delivery and the possibility for serious bleeding, which could jeopardize your pregnancy.

The biggest risk with a previa is abruption (separation of the placenta before delivery). The mechanical jostling from the baby and the thinning of the attached lower uterine segment cause this complication. (Abruption can also happen unrelated to previa, as in cocaine or cigarette use, diabetes, multiple gestation, hypertension, previous history of abruption, having had many babies, and with trauma such as car accidents.)

IUGR (Intrauterine Growth Restriction)

Almost all babies grow at about the same rate before twenty weeks, but after that variations due to genetics begin to alter this universal curve.

When there are problems that present as inadequate growth, all eyes turn to that turnstile of nourishment, the placenta. Healthy placentas grow healthy babies, but lousy placentas can seriously delay or even halt fetal growth. Diseases of the mother can impact the placenta by aging it prematurely or directly damaging it, both events that limit its ability to deliver the goods or whisk away the waste. Hypertension, pregnancy-induced hypertension, and diabetes are the famous villains. Certainly any woman with any of these conditions should have frequent ultrasounds to follow fetal growth curves and to look at the placenta.

If your doctor were to suspect that your baby is smaller than what he should be, the first thing that would happen is a re-ultrasound in a week or two. Ten different ultrasonographers will get ten different sets of measurements on the same baby, so no case of IUGR will be confirmed with only one ultrasound. But two suspicious sets of measurements, especially if the interval growth is less than expected or even absent, will be enough of a trend. Level 3

Fast Forward

All babies grow at about the same rate up until twenty weeks. After that, family characteristics (genetics) alter the normal growth curves into wider zones of normal variation. Intrauterine Growth Restriction (IUGR) is a falling away from even these widened zones of acceptability and is due to either bad genetics from the baby's end; bad nutrition to the baby from a faulty, aging, or diseased placenta; or maternal factors like disease, substance abuse, or toxic exposure.

ultrasound can examine the flow of blood within the placenta and umbilical cord. If there's an explainable cause, like hypertension, then the treatment really depends on the treatment of your hypertension. If there's no explainable cause or if in spite of adequate treatment of the cause there is no improvement in the growth, bed rest on your left side (keeping the weight of the uterus off of your vena cava), perhaps even hospitalization, and frequent ultrasounds and fetal heart rate testing will be done. If the inside environment—your uterus—proves to be more hostile than the outside environment—life as a premature baby—then delivery is common sense. In the home stretch of the third trimester, a baby can be rescued if an amniocentesis demonstrates lung maturity. In the second trimester your doctor's hands are tied due to the severe immaturity of your baby's lungs. The big contest is the race to maturity before a faulty incubator (again, your uterus) catches up with a struggling baby.

> **A-FACTOR**
> You can't make a diagnosis of IUGR from one ultrasound. There has to be a trend. Additionally, the gestational age must be right. But even if the dates are wrong, an interval growth should agree with the actual interval between the ultrasounds.

Gestational Diabetes

Almost 10 percent of pregnant women have a sneaky form of diabetes related to pregnancy, called gestational diabetes. Your pregnancy causes a certain amount of resistance to the beneficial effects of insulin, so it takes more to achieve its goal of handling sugar. Usually this isn't a problem, but if your insulin resistance reaches a certain threshold unique to your particular ability to handle sugar, you could be that one in ten women with gestational diabetes.

> **Fast Forward**
> Don't panic if you flunk your glucola screen (O'Sullivan screen)—that just means you can't yet be cleared and should have a real test—the three-hour glucose tolerance test (3GTT). Only 10 percent of pregnant women will be gestational diabetics during pregnancy, diagnosed with an abnormal 3GTT.

Unfortunately, neither extra insulin nor a higher sugar level are kind to tissue, and the placenta can get banged up enough to affect your baby. Besides macrosomia (large baby), fetal distress and even stillbirth are possibilities with any poorly controlled diabetes. Prenatal care prevents such disasters with an adequately monitored gestational diabetic pregnancy.

Is gestational diabetes as real as real diabetes as far as your baby is concerned? Yes, but it is a toned-down version. Because it is due to insulin resistance and not so much to insulin deficiency, eating a diet that doesn't call for much insulin usually works beautifully. A 2,200 calorie ADA (American Diabetic Association) diet is my standard. Of course, I hear my New Orleans Sugar Buster gurus gloating in the distance because what I'm talking about is a low-carbohydrate (sugar) diet. The diet isn't so much a decrease in calories but a shift in the types of things you eat. In fact most patients who follow it correctly find it difficult to eat everything on it every day. That's a good problem.

> **A-FACTOR**
> Gestational diabetes is almost always manageable with a low-sugar diet, which is a very reasonable amount of food.

Even when a patient has been compliant with the ADA diet, I've had to occasionally put someone on insulin. The insulin requirements were low and actually became unnecessary after delivery. These occasional patients were probably borderline diabetics—the real thing—to begin with, and it was just the pregnancy that tipped them over the fence during that time.

The O'Sullivan screen (glucola screen) is the screen your obstetrician will probably use as part of your routine care. Since the one in ten incidence of gestational diabetes means a lot of women, it's a test that makes sense for every single pregnancy on the planet. Although you're probably sure some people are not from this planet at all, you are; so your doctor will probably do this test at around weeks twenty-four to twenty-six. You'll drink a delicious (translation: sickeningly sweet) cola that contains fifty grams of glucose. Your pancreas will think you're crazy, but it should rise to the occasion by putting out insulin adequate to keep your blood sugar under a set pass-fail point by a one-hour mark. This test is a lot like the α-fetoprotein test in that if it's normal, you're most likely not diabetic; but if it's abnormal, the results are discarded in favor of a real test—in this case, the full 3-hour glucose tolerance test (3GTT). Gestational diabetes is dealt with in more detail in Chapter 20.

Pregnancy-Induced Hypertension

Of course, a rose is a rose, but *toxemia* is an obsolete word, a throwback to the days when diseases were the result of bad humors in the body. The term *preeclampsia* has fallen out of favor because of its pessimistic colorings. Eclampsia is the seizure that accompanies brain swelling with severe autoimmune reaction (rejection?) to the pregnancy; so *preeclampsia* was a word that wasn't unlike "Have you had your seizure yet?"

Pregnancy-induced hypertension is the current *nom du jour*. But even this term is lacking because it's possible to have it without actually demonstrating any hypertension.

The classical tetrad of pregnancy-induced hypertension, of which any single element or any combination may represent disease:

1. Hypertension (elevated blood pressure)
2. Proteinuria (spilling protein into the urine)
3. Edema (swelling)
4. Hyperreflexia (brisk reflexes, e.g., knee jerk)

Academically, we're now pursuing an autoimmune connection for pregnancy-induced hypertension, along the lines of the maternal organism still rejecting the fetal foreign body to some extent, in spite of decreased immune reaction in pregnancy. But immune reactions can be as varied as the persons doing the reacting, so there are many variations of pregnancy-induced hypertension, and your doctor will be sensitive to any red flags.

Early presentation in the second trimester is a sign that pregnancy-induced hypertension will become severe, and extremely close follow-up is mandatory. It is usually a phenomenon of the third trimester, as if your body is saying, "That's all I can stands—I can't stands no more!" But spinach won't help—the cure for this is delivery. The biggest suspense in obstetrics is the race to maturity for the baby before the hypertension becomes too dangerous for the mother. Although it rarely begins in the second trimester, it can, and it frequently happens with the non-time-related excess of pregnancy—

twins. Pregnancy-induced hypertension and its much more evil twin, HELLP syndrome, are dealt with in more detail in Chapter 20.

Preterm Labor

Preterm labor is mainly a third trimester problem. Every woman's uterus has its own threshold of tolerance for the size and weight of what it holds, and eventually labor will begin. This is somewhat oversimplified because labor is also the complex goings-on of hormones, biochemistry of the cervix, and uterine muscular activity and reactivity. But it is true that there may be some rumblings with "the load" by late second trimester. Most often it's a false labor pattern, but any rhythmic activity should be reported to your doctor.

Braxton-Hicks contractions, those irregular twangs that are strong enough to be noticeable, don't follow even the pattern of false labor and can begin as early as twenty weeks. These are harmless and were put into the system, it may seem, just to aggravate you.

Kidney and Bladder Infections

These are also more likely the further along you get but can occur at any point in pregnancy. As described above, the weight of your uterus, besides pressing on your vena cava, can also compress the tubes (ureters) that run urine from your kidneys down to your bladder. Like stepping on a garden hose, the tubes above the compression can distend into what are called physiologic hydroureters of pregnancy. But your body hates any standing fluids, be it in the ears or in your ureters. It is a fertile place for bacteria to collect and prosper. A kidney infection is different from a bladder infection in that your bladder is just a muscular pot to pee out of, but your kidney is an active, complex organ that has many functions besides filtering waste from your blood. It's difficult for antibiotics to get to (the end of the biochemical road), and the ones that can get to it with enough concentration are constantly being whisked away along with the waste. A kidney infection will put you into the hospital for a course of intravenous antibiotics.

Do all kidney infections begin with bladder infections that rise into the kidneys? No. It's possible to have just a bladder infection, just a kidney infection, even separate bladder and kidney infections with different bacteria.

The classic symptom of a kidney infection is left or right midback pain, tender to the touch. The diagnosis is made by seeing white blood cell lumps (pus), red blood cells, or bacteria in a urine sample. A catheterized specimen is least likely to be misleading, avoiding normal skin bacteria that might get swished into the sample with simple urinating. Antibiotics that are pregnancy-friendly are used until a culture report comes back. The culture is the actual bacteria grown from the urine sample and then tested against a host of antibiotics. If you had been prescribed an antibiotic the bacteria are resistant to, the culture will tell in enough time for you to be switched to some other prescription.

Kidney infection (called pyelonephritis) can get pretty rough. High fevers of 103 and 104 degrees are possible, and such temperatures can fry your red blood cells, causing a quickly progressing anemia. Usually the IV antibiotics can be stopped after the fever is gone, at which point you can switch to the pill form and leave the hospital.

Mere (mere?) bladder infections can be treated with oral antibiotics. Bladder infections are common in pregnancy, when swelling can pucker your urethral meatus (opening for urination) more to the outside world and its evils. Also, there are mechanical irritations from the baby against your bladder that, besides making you run to the bathroom frequently, could trigger a smoldering irritation ripe for infection should the opportunity arise. It's bad enough your bladder gets rapped by a penis from time to time. Your baby makes this an irritation on two fronts. You can have honeymoon cystitis coming and going! You will wonder why on Earth you were designed with so many important things jammed into one area.

For some reason women with bladder infections are more prone to preterm labor. If you were to show up at a labor and delivery unit with complaints of contractions, a urinalysis would be done to check for a urinary tract infection.

Premature Rupture (or Leaking) of Membranes—PROM

This topic is dealt with extensively in "Preterm Labor" in Chapter 20. The membranes keep amniotic fluid and baby in and infections out. If they rupture in the third trimester, it's a matter of how close to term you are. Often committing to a labor and a delivery will pose no danger to a mature baby. But when the membranes rupture earlier than fetal maturity, that is a dilemma of astronomical proportions. The further from maturity it happens, the more anguishing the dilemma.

Dilemma. Di-LEM-ma (noun). A difficult choice between two equally unsatisfactory alternatives.

Nowhere is there a better example of a dilemma than PROM remote from term: early delivery of a preterm baby versus delaying delivery with risk of infection for baby and mother. I include it here in that any unusual, liquidlike vaginal discharge should be reported to your doctor. It will probably be urine or a normal vaginal discharge of pregnancy that has had time to sit and liquefy a bit, but it can be impossible to tell these from leaking membranes.

Abdominal Tenderness of the Uterus

There are growing pains that can be felt on the skin (stretch marks felt before they're seen), in the uterus (with irregular contractions), and in the abdomen (the pushing away of other organs). But exquisite tenderness of the uterus is not normal and is the presenting symptom of an infection of the uterus or pregnancy (amnionitis). This is hardly a symptom that deserves its own exclusive airspace because an infection will present with irregular contractions, possibly PROM, fever, elevated white blood cell count, and other troubling hints.

The Middle Trials of Pregnancy: Other Second Trimester Considerations

Just because I said the second trimester is the most forgiving of the three doesn't mean it is without its own little woes. Beginning at twelve weeks your uterus is becoming too big to sit daintily in your pelvis. At some point, and it's usually in the transition between the first two trimesters, it pops up to assume status as an abdominal organ. In fact, it's finally able to be felt by your doctor, peeking over your pubic bone. Fetal heart tones can now be heard easily with a Doppler, and they'll usually be in about the 140 to 180 range. They'll generally get slower as the pregnancy progresses, which is a function of physics. (An elephant's heart beats about twelve times a minute; a mouse's heart beats more than two hundred times a minute.) Also, because your uterus is now a palpable (able to be felt) organ, it can be measured for fundal height recordings.

Fast Forward

The middle trials of pregnancy:

- Bladder spasm, urinary frequency (almost always)
- Urinary retention (rare)
- Ligament pain
  round ligament (almost always)
  uterosacral (rare)
  coccydynia (rare unless a recent injury to your tailbone)
- Sciatica (frequently)
- Swelling
  edema (always)
  varicose veins (frequently)
  hemorrhoids (more likely with bad habits)
- Stretch marks (frequently)
- Umbilical pain (rare)
- Adhesional pain (temporary—and only with adhesions)

Urinary Problems—Too Much or Too Little

With all of this progress comes the first fight between you and your baby. It's territorial, it's ugly, and it's over your bladder. Your baby will show no remorse over these problems, not even when he wants to borrow the car on his sixteenth birthday.

Bladder Spasm

Your bladder is not gifted; in fact, it is a particularly stupid organ. No offense to you, it's just that your bladder can't tell whether the pressure it wants to contract against is coming from inside or outside. Your uterus pushing on the outside of your bladder during the territorial dispute will make your bladder want to contract—it thinks it's full. We doctors call this *spastic bladder*, but you will call it crazy when you start running to the bathroom every ten minutes. And when you go, there will be just that squirt or two, and you'll be wondering what all the ruckus was about. Until ten minutes later when the urgency returns. By about fifteen weeks your uterus has risen above your bladder and you will get a break from this nuisance, only to have it return in the third trimester when your baby's head is big enough to poke your bladder again.

> **A-FACTOR**
> You're very likely to experience urinary frequency, but urinary retention is very rare.

Urinary Retention

This is the opposite problem. Instead of sweating it out over whether you'll make it to the bathroom in time, you are unable to urinate. This is because as the uterus makes the transition to becoming an abdominal organ, it can tug on the support under your sphincter, increasing the pressure needed to blow urine past it, opening it. Added to this mechanical dirty trick are the psychological pitfalls of trying too hard to initiate urination. (If you've ever been to a stadium bathroom and it's your turn and you know there's a line of people behind you waiting for you to do what you need to do—well, we've all been there, in the social throes of the dreaded sphincter-lock.) Frustration over the mechanical problem adds to the psychological hesitancy, and the combination of effects can grow worse.

Usually, sitting in a warm tub will help with the psychological delay. But sometimes no amount of force is enough to overcome the opening pressure needed to open your sphincter and a trip to the ER is necessary so that a catheter can cure you. True, no one wants that, but when you drain a liter of urine into all of those jugs, you don't care anything about those big eyes the ER nurses are making.

Urinary frequency episodes outnumber urinary retention episodes hundreds to one. Urinary retention requiring a catheter is very rare. It has happened in my practice twice in twenty years—each a doctor's wife, of course. Thankfully, urinary retention is very transient, the mechanical cause of it correcting itself within a week.

Ligament Pain

The menstrual-like cramps of the growing pains of the first trimester are replaced by the second trimester's ligament pains.

> **Fast Forward**
>
> Round ligament pain and uterosacral pain are harmless, but they can really hurt. Changing your position is the best treatment. If severe enough, physical therapy may be very helpful.

Round Ligament Pain

This is the most famous pain of midpregnancy. The round ligaments are two muscular and fibrous strips about a half-inch thick that run from the sides of your uterus, through your inguinal rings, and insert into the side walls of your vagina and inner thighs. They help hold your uterus in its correct anatomical position in the nonpregnant state. They're not so great a support for your uterus even when it's the size of a pear, so they really are useless when it grows with the pregnancy. But as your uterus grows, your round ligaments are stretched, pulling down the line, all the way through to your inguinal rings and even causing discomfort in your vagina and legs.

This pain is absolutely harmless, which is in distinct contrast to how it can stop you dead in your tracks when a round ligament twangs you. It usually hits you from just one side, even though you have right and left ligaments. This is because one of them is stretched more than the other with different positions. The uterus will flop to one side, strumming one of them in particular. Sometimes you might feel round ligament pain in bed, and simply lying on your other side will help. Other times it may strike when you assume a certain position, and shifting your position around further will give relief. (Complaint: "Doctor, it hurts when I go like that." Recommendation: "Well, then, don't go like that.") Besides a chancy stab at physical therapy, change in position is the only treatment.

Uterosacral Ligament Pain

These ligaments go from your internal (pelvic) cervix to your sacrum (over the tailbone). Like the round ligaments, they aren't the main support for the uterus, but a stretching of them will give you pain right above your tailbone.

Most doctors shrug off ligament complaints because of their innocent impact on the pregnancy. But if this seems uncompassionate, ask to be referred to a physical therapy group that is familiar with the trials of pregnancy. I get a fifty/fifty response from such referrals, but even a halfway chance of helping the pain is worth the visit if the pain is severe enough. Even without treatment, the changing anatomy of the pregnancy will allow this pain to abate over time.

> **A-FACTOR**
> You more than likely will experience round ligament pain to some extent. Uterosacral pain is less frequent—you may not have it at all.

Other Pains and Trials

Coccydynia

The coccyx is the tailbone, nothing more than a hinged joint. For the higher primates among us (you know who you are), almost everyone has broken it to some extent at some point in his or her life. Actually, *broke* is the wrong word. It's more like *snapped it back and forth* against its hinge. If you think back, you'll remember that time you saw stars when you fell on your behind one day, or you walked away from that horseback riding adventure walking more like a cowboy than when you started. For me, it was testing out the new "some assembly required" slide I had just finished putting together for my children. I had forgotten that I was about a hundred and fifty pounds heavier than the last time I had gone down a slide. Two hundred pounds makes quite a thud, I can assure you.

The problem with breaking your tailbone is that it never quite heals back all the way. The pain goes on for months and eventually goes away until some new stress yanks on it once again. Like pregnancy.

Coccydynia is the medical word to describe pain from the coccyx. There are no effective treatments for it, anti-inflammatories being on the no-no list during pregnancy. Tylenol isn't great for it, but it's better than nothing. Once again, physical therapy is the next step when coccydynia is ruining your life.

If you've been lucky enough to escape breaking your coccyx in your life, delivery may oblige you when your baby's head comes down the pike. It'll be

Fast Forward

Coccydynia (tailbone pain) results from an old injury being tugged on by the pregnancy. It can also occur during childbirth. The pain is self-limited and will go away eventually.

head versus tailbone, and head will win. I've delivered many babies when I've not only felt it snapping but even heard it. Mercifully, coccydynia will get lost in the shuffle of the regrouping of the postpartum period, so it's not usually a big complaint.

Sciatica

This isn't a pain involving ligaments, but an inflammation of an actual nerve, the sciatic. Unfortunately, it's a big nerve, and it runs from your outer buttocks down your back thigh. Both normal swelling around it and pressure from your baby's head against this nerve where it travels through your pelvis will give you a sharp pain along its course. Physical therapy is better for this than it is for ligament pain. Like ligament pain, sciatica is harmless and temporary.

Swelling

Swelling is a normal misery of pregnancy, beginning in the second trimester and lasting to the end. Normal physiologic alterations in handling salt and fluids and the mechanical compression of your uterus on your vena cava cause retained fluid and decreased clearance of fluid, respectively. If you eat half of a large pizza and then lie flat on your back, you'll swear you could see yourself bloating. (Don't do that.)

Swelling might also be a sign of pathology, as in pregnancy-induced hypertension, but disturbing trends can be caught by the serial nature of prenatal appointments.

Varicose Veins

Same problem, same cause. The system's all backed up. Veins that are backed up will distend.

Hemorrhoids

Same problem, same cause. Also, straining to have a bowel movement will make them swell even more, so you should avoid constipation by consuming lots of fluids and dietary fiber. Since the design of a toilet seat is such that there's a hole in the middle (thank goodness!), the only part of your rear end that isn't supported is the perianal area, hanging in dependent commitment to the task at hand. Circulation in the surrounding tissue is blunted by the pressure of the circular seat itself. This is a double whammy to cause the perianal varicose veins—what hemorrhoids are—to push out. The shorter the time on the toilet seat, otherwise brilliantly designed, the better. So don't read that whole *People* magazine.

All of the results of swelling—edema, varicose veins, and hemorrhoids—are best treated by avoidance of the causes. Elevating your legs above the level of your heart will help drain all of the fluid back into the system, but this is easier said than done for two reasons. First, if it all drains back into the system, you'll be peeing all night long. Second, elevating your legs above the level of your heart is a feat worthy of a contract from Cirque du Soleil, because you're not supposed to lie on your back, remember?

Umbilical Pain

Your navel is a hernia. It's the hole left over from your own umbilical cord. As the bulk of what's inside your abdomen expands against your abdomen, this normally small hole can enlarge into an umbilical hernia. Stress against its ringed fibrous border can hurt. This pain will usually plateau by the third trimester, then go away. If the hernia is really big and you end up having a C-section for some reason, it can be fixed at that time. If it's small, even if it hurts, leave it alone—the hernia will shrink after delivery and the pain will go away.

Adhesional Pain

Adhesions are internal scars, usually the result of previous surgery or infection. The body, in its dedication to walling off areas injurious to it, will leave a trail of bowel stuck to areas that were once inflamed from such events. Since the biggest problem with adhesions is the pain you will get when feces turn corners, stretching the bowel because it is tented up against something (adhesed) instead of flapping in the breeze, a colicky sensation can get to be pretty old. For although you may move your bowels in the outside world every one or two days, on the inside they're always moving. Adhesional pain happens even when you're doing nothing

Pregnancy is a great treatment for pelvic adhesions because the expansive phenomenon of a growing uterus will stretch adhesions until they snap. You will feel this over weeks, so the pain isn't severe—more like an occasional burning from time to time. And then it will stop. That's a good thing.

Abdominal Striae

The second trimester is the first time real expansion begins. Stretch marks begin, sometimes invisibly. Many things affect the tendency to stretch marks—genetics, skin quality, and sun exposure, among others. But it's important to realize just what is happening—you're expanding so fast that your skin doesn't have enough time to elasticize and survive the pulling, so tearing is the result. The biggest risk for stretch marks isn't how much weight you gain, but the speed at which you gain the weight. A woman who gains forty pounds evenly over her entire pregnancy may have fewer stretch marks than one who only gains thirty, but twelve of them were in her eighth month. Proper hydration, besides improving constipation, also can help with the skin's elasticity and diminish damage.

Not There Yet, But Getting Close

It used to be that twenty-eight weeks was considered the "time of viability," i.e., that gestational milestone after which a premature baby could survive. With the advent of neonatal ICUs, however, this time has been whittled down. Currently, twenty-five weekers are entertained as survivable. Less than that would put a baby into second trimester territory, but this is a zone that is hard to cross when talking about a baby surviving in the outside world.

The second trimester gives a pregnant woman a break, for the first and third trimesters provide much more intense worries. And if things go typically, she has the opportunity to rejoin the world for a brief time.

Q & A—The Second Trimester

Flying in Pregnancy

Question: Is a six-hour plane flight dangerous in pregnancy? I'm in my second trimester and don't have any problems. When's the safest time to fly?

Answer: Now. Long flights in the first trimester risk the worst-case scenario of having a miscarriage and bleeding heavily long before touchdown. And long flights in the third trimester would be dangerous for both you and your baby if there were preterm labor as a third trimester worst case scenario. But with adequate and reassuring prenatal care, the second trimester is the most stable time in pregnancy.

Most people are concerned with the air pressure of jets when flying during pregnancy, but in today's pressurized jet cabins, this is not a problem. What would concern me is the fact that you're flying for six hours. Unless you're flying from Tierra del Fuega to Terra Haute, I have to assume that you're flying over water, probably an ocean. The problem with this is that the only medical care on such a lengthy flight is what's available on the plane—almost nothing.

I've flown on most of the major airlines, and a jet is not a very good hospital, nor should it be. I've been the doctor when the loudspeaker has asked for one. It's not something I look forward to. The equipment is so lacking on some planes that I bring my own stethoscope when I fly. It would be bad enough taking a long flight over land, where a large city comes around about every hour and could be a pit stop for an ambulance to meet you. But over an ocean is pretty scary.

> **Fast Forward**
> When pregnant, don't take flights over oceans or go on trips from which you couldn't get to civilization in a hurry.

The same thing goes for overnight camping trips where rescue would require a long hike or paddling a long stretch of a river. Cruises to quaint islands will run you the risk of ending up in an island hospital where English goes nowhere.

Breast Masses in Pregnancy

Question: Is a small breast lump of concern in the fifth month of pregnancy, or is it a part of the normal pregnant breast?

Answer: Pregnancy is just the party the breasts have been waiting for all of their lives. Prolactin (the milk letdown hormone) rises and sometimes it's not unusual for lactation to begin even before delivery, which is weird but normal. Since the breasts are collections of glands that make milk, it's not unusual for a milk duct to get engorged during all of this stimulation. This happens frequently.

It's possible that a breast lesion, previously not felt, was pushed to a more prominent and noticeable status by thickening of the underlying breast tissue. Since it may be impossible to tell the difference, the criteria that make breast lumps suspicious apply just as much in pregnancy as when not pregnant.

The following signs will tell you if what you have is considered unsuspicious:

- Freely movable (cancers tend to invade and therefore feel stuck to the surrounding tissue)
- Painful, which usually means inflammation, not tumor. It is possible to get mastitis before actual breastfeeding begins.
- Vacillations of size (cysts related to milk production will change size with the ups and downs of the hormonal fluctuations. Bad cysts will stay the same size or grow bigger).
- Very round (malignancies are irregularly shaped)
- Small size (less than one centimeter is small)

Fast Forward

Breast lumps are common in pregnancy, but concerns should be based on standard protocols for breast lumps. Mammogram, if necessary, is safe, especially if an abdominal shield is used.

Usually an obstetrician, being also a gynecologist, can decide whether to be suspect of a lump that can be felt. If he is uncomfortable with making a diagnosis, then usually a second opinion from a general surgeon can help finalize the call. Putting a needle into a cyst to drain it can be both diagnostic and therapeutic—a lot of suspicion can be put to rest when clear or milky fluid is aspirated.

Chances are it's nothing. But we should respect the breasts, both for the life they will provide for your baby and for the disease they can present when cancerous. When in doubt, overreact. A mammogram usually involves less than ten mrads of X-ray exposure, 1/500 of the dose felt dangerous. And with an abdominal shield, the risk is even less.

New Eyeglasses

Question: My vision is blurry and my eyeglasses prescription is fairly recent. Should I get a new refraction done and new glasses or contacts?

Answer: Only if you don't mind a special pregnancy pair. The normal swelling in pregnancy is everywhere—not just in your ankles. It includes the cornea. Because it's a weak lens itself, swelling of the cornea can give you a temporary miscalculation for your prescription eyeglasses. Your eyes should return to their prepregnancy state after delivery.

Look for other current questions and updates regarding the second trimester on BabyZone.com, by going to babyzone.com/features/expertsqa.

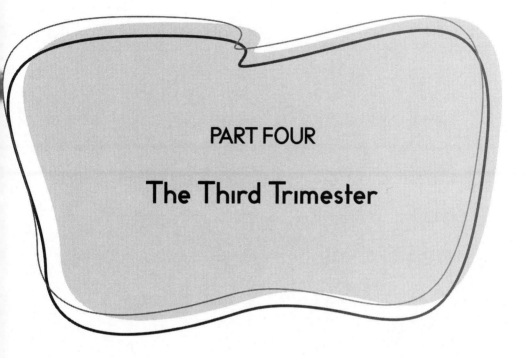

PART FOUR

The Third Trimester

8

Reaching Critical Mass

The third trimester is unfairly about a month longer than the previous two trimesters. Beginning at twenty-four weeks, this last part of pregnancy continues until delivery. In the last month of pregnancy, your baby gains at least half a pound a week—and that's just your baby. There's you too. You'll be wondering why you picked such an ungodly season to spend the last part of your pregnancy, and you'll wonder at what point you'll undergo gravitational collapse and begin fusion.

Prenatal Care in the Third Trimester

There are two main blood screens and one vaginal bacteria screen during the third trimester. The screen for gestational diabetes, the glucola (O'Sullivan) test, is done around twenty-six weeks. If you're Rh-negative, a blood antibody screen is done between then and twenty-eight weeks, some doctors combining the two around twenty-seven weeks so as to save your poor arm an extra blood drawing. At thirty-six weeks a vaginal culture for Group B ß-hemolytic streptococcus is performed. All three of these tests are detailed below.

The grid sheet of visit-by-visit documentation continues until term, but in the third trimester items like edema and reflexes assume greater importance in the watchfulness for pregnancy-induced hypertension. As I described in Chapter 6, those two items are part of the group of telltale signs for this disorder. The fundal height measurements are continued, with additional attention to too much or too little amniotic fluid—a sign of danger.

The timing of the visits in the third trimester is not the same from doctor to doctor, but generally you'll notice your visits getting closer together, adding further to any fixation on your pregnancy you may already have. From twenty-four to thirty weeks, your visits will be every two to three weeks; from thirty to thirty-five weeks, every two weeks; and from thirty-six onward, every week at least. At term, which is a particularly sensitive time and a famous tug-of-war between a baby that's still growing and a placenta that's starting to die, extra surveillance is necessary to assure fetal well-being until your delivery.

> **Fast Forward**
>
> Lab tests in the third trimester include the glucola screen if it hasn't been done yet, vaginal culture for Group B strep, antibody screen if you're Rh-negative, and a repeat of your blood count.
>
> Office visits continue to monitor weight, blood pressure, fetal heart rate, and fundal size, plus cervical checks and discussions about preferences of delivery, induction, etc.

At thirty-two weeks, your baby should have decided on a position for delivery, preferably head first. Obstetricians refer to this as *vertex*, and it is the normal presentation. Anything else is abnormal, although vaginal delivery doesn't absolutely depend on a vertex position. Some breech babies (buttocks first) can deliver vaginally with certain criteria met, but for the most part an abnormal "lie" will push your doctor into recommending a C-section. Some babies can be turned at thirty-six weeks so that they are vertex, but this is extra maneuvering and an intervention that requires your clear understanding of the risks versus benefits.

After thirty-seven weeks, your doctor may begin checking your cervix for changes that indicate impending labor. In the absence of any serious problems he won't do it before then because there's nothing in the exam that would make him want to intervene in a normal baby's gestation before lung maturity.

At forty-two weeks, two weeks after your due date watchful waiting for spontaneous labor becomes unwise, the complication rate becoming unac-

A Typical Time Line for Prenatal Care
Third Trimester—Twenty-four Weeks Through Delivery

- Twenty-four to thirty weeks: visits every two to three weeks
- At around twenty-six weeks: glucola screen for gestational diabetes.
- Thirty-two weeks: determination of fetal position—the "lie." This is the time a baby usually locks into position. A suspected breech baby at this time is a concern and warrants ultrasound.
- At around thirty-six weeks: Group B strep vaginal culture, attention to signs of preterm labor and institute monitoring if indicated.
- Thirty-six weeks: begin weekly visits or even more frequent if high risk, offer version (turning) of an abnormal position (breech) to normal position (vertex—head first).
- Thirty-seven to thirty-eight weeks: possibly begin weekly cervical checks.
- Thirty-nine weeks: offer induction if cervix is ripe and prospective parents are desirous.
- Forty weeks (term): begin postdates surveillance—more frequent visits, offering induction if cervix is ripe.
- Forty-one to forty-two weeks: postdate surveillance.
- Forty-two weeks: probable induction. Although most doctors differ somewhat as to which point indicates mandatory delivery, forty-two weeks seems to be a dividing line where further waiting begins unacceptable risks.
- Overall: heightened vigilance for diseases and complications unique to pregnancy.

ceptable. This is the time of necessary induction, as opposed to elective induction that can be offered after thirty-nine weeks.

Your body is gearing up for the big event, and if this is your first time, you'll suddenly find yourself in a panic about how clueless you are about what's to come.

For your obstetrician the third trimester is a shifting of one set of concerns for another. Besides problems that can spill over from the second trimester, such as placenta previa, hypertension, or suspicious ultrasound findings, the third trimester can open additional doors to new worrisome possibilities. But you're in the final stages of pregnancy, so the fact that your baby is approaching that magic moment called viability adds another option to any problems you may be having: delivery. Whereas before your doctor had to figure out a way for you and your baby to coexist with a problem, now you're heading into a time where bailing out is feasible under the right conditions.

Prematurity

There's a fuzzy line that marks the point at which a baby is considered deliverable with a certain degree of comfort. By degree of comfort I mean a situation in which you would have every reason to expect your baby to do fine—to go home with you from the hospital. This is usually sometime around or after thirty-seven weeks.

Your baby's lungs are important, for sure, but there are other considerations. His liver needs to mature, but this can fall a little short even at term. All you need do is walk past the nursery to know this from the ultraviolet lights a-blazin'. It's not a black light psychedelic love-in going on in there. The UV light is breaking up the bilirubin for those little livers that can't do it so well on their own yet. The retina of the eye doesn't fully mature until well after birth, which explains why your baby can't see well immediately. The immune system is still developing, which is why breast-feeding, thereby delivering your own protective antibodies, is such a good idea.

Your baby's central nervous system is still very primitive. The frontal lobes, seat of self-awareness and personality, aren't really locked in until about eighteen months, which means all of that goo-gooing and ooh-n-ahhing in baby's face actually has some value by stimulating pathways to and from her brain's frontal lobes. At birth the nerves along your baby's body aren't completely sheathed in a covering that helps transmit impulses at the right speed for agility or accurate pain perception, which is why some babies actually sleep through a circumcision.

But your baby's lungs are the deal breaker. Everything else can be tiptoed around. Ventilators? Yes, ventilators are a lifesaver, but it's like cutting diamonds with a jackhammer. Ventilators, even the miraculous ultrafrequency micropuff vents, beat up babies' lungs, so although it may be three steps forward, it's two steps backwards.

> **Fast Forward**
>
> Twenty-five weeks will get your baby to viability, the chance she will survive. Thirty-six to thirty-seven weeks marks maturity, the likelihood she will act like a term baby. Between twenty-five and thirty-six weeks is the span of prematurity, complications from delivery depending on how much earlier than thirty-six weeks the delivery takes place.

It is an anecdotal truism that babies seem to know when to come out. Be it thirty-seven weeks or forty-two, there is a consortium of processes, maternal as well as fetal, that conspire together to initiate the onset of labor. When there are problems that pose a conflict of interest between you and your baby, this consortium can be overridden by man-made decisions that take your baby's survival out of the path of known dangers, but into the uncertainty of prematurity. We call this obstetrics and it's not cheating.

Viability

Besides maturity, which is a nice milestone to achieve, there is the concept of viability. Viability is the time after which your baby can survive a premature delivery. If the comfort level of maturity resides in the zone between thirty-six and thirty-seven weeks, the earlier a baby is delivered prior to that time, the more risk to actual survival. Forget ventilators and bili-lights. There is a point in time before which a baby cannot and will not survive, no matter what miracles of technology are available.

Viability used to be twenty-eight weeks, so to say that the miracles of technology haven't had an impact is wrong. Babies as early as twenty-four weeks (sixteen weeks before term, twelve to thirteen weeks before lung maturity) have survived occasionally. Just one more week mature, the twenty-five-weekers are a quantum leap further along in survivability, and each week after that ups the success rate, with more surviving and less suffering serious complications.

But viability under any circumstances isn't necessarily a victory. The complications are serious indeed, including cerebral palsy, retardation, blindness, and the risk of eventual death anyway. The fact remains that your baby was meant to grow inside of you for at least thirty-six weeks, and prenatal care during the third trimester is focused on getting you and baby to that point.

Maturity

Thirty-six to thirty-seven weeks is a natural dividing point. Concerns of preterm labor are no longer important, preventing labor is no longer indicated, and orchestrating delivery is no longer chancy after having dodged a prenatal condition hostile to your baby during the premature period. Simply put, the premature part of the third trimester is that time wherein you don't want to deliver, and if you have to because of some overriding problem, you need to balance the timing between degrees of lung immaturity and the intrauterine danger to the baby. If your baby's lungs aren't mature, is the cruel, outside world going to be more dangerous to your baby with her bad lungs than some cruelty of the inside world which is prompting the delivery? After thirty-six weeks, we can save the day.

The *Lagniappe* Period of Pregnancy–
Laissez les bon temps roulez

The Cajun word *lagniappe*, when literally translated, means "something extra," and it is usually applied to the extra donut added to a dozen or that couple of pieces of candy thrown in after weighing the bag. Over the years it has come to mean anything nice that is extra and usually unexpected. Usually, if you've had a trouble-free and normal pregnancy up to thirty-six weeks, the rest of your pregnancy is *lagniappe*—the icing on the cake. Can we all relax at this point? Somewhat. I'd love to say things like "You're cruising, now" and "You have it made," but there's still the pregnancy there, so prenatal care is still important.

9

High Risk in the Third Trimester

The problematic concerns in the third trimester fall into two groups: those your doctor will notice and those you will notice yourself and should report to your doctor.

> **Fast Forward**
>
> Things that will make your doctor consider you high risk in the third trimester:
> - Inappropriate growth
> - Gestational diabetes
> - Positive Group B ß-hemolytic strep vaginal culture
> - Abnormal amount of amniotic fluid (too much = polyhydramnios; too little = oligohydramnios)
> - Decreased reactivity on nonstress test—the baby's heart rate does not accelerate after movement, which is the expected norm.
> - Abnormal positioning of the baby (breech, transverse, etc.). Your baby should lock into position by thirty-two weeks. Although she could still flip over again, that is the exception. Headfirst (vertex) by thirty-two weeks is what you want.

Inappropriate Growth

The reason your visits start to get closer in the third trimester is that you're building a bigger machine. More can happen in a shorter amount of time. The growth of your baby is watched closely, of course. If the size of your uterus seems inappropriate, your doctor will want to know why this is so. Too big or too small, too much amniotic fluid or too little, and abnormal positioning of your baby can all give the outward appearance of a fundal height that doesn't jive.

Gestational Diabetes

If you develop this, you'll be placed on a diabetic diet and your blood sugar will be evaluated every so often to make sure the values aren't creeping upward. Additionally, a blood test called an HbA1c can tell if your sugar's been out of whack for a couple of months; so if it's normal, you can be assured it was caught right at the beginning.

Group B β-Hemolytic Strep

This bacterium is a normal vaginal passenger in 10 percent of women. Occasionally, in transit, your baby can pick it up at delivery, and this can cause an infection for your newborn, which can become serious. It has been blamed for premature rupture of membranes (PROM) and preterm labor and delivery. It is otherwise a flimsy little germ, harmless to you. Vaginal culture for this is obtained at around thirty-six weeks.

Abnormal Amount of Amniotic Fluid

Polyhydramnios is too much amniotic fluid. Oligohydramnios is too little. Both are a concern. There are expected normal amounts of amniotic fluid, and it's easy via ultrasound to actually measure the amount. As seems obvious, the extra load of polyhydramnios will make you appear further along in your pregnancy, and the decreased volume associated with oligohydramnios will make it seem you're not as far along. Amniotic fluid abnormalities are a good argument for fundal height measurements, especially if you're being seen by a different doctor each time.

The load of pregnancy isn't just the baby. There's considerable weight and volume contributed by the placenta and the amniotic fluid. The amount of amniotic fluid has a certain range of normal values, the numbered score derived by adding up the centimeters of depth of four pockets of fluid seen on ultrasound. Some researchers feel one good pocket of three centimeters depth is enough to assume that there is adequate amniotic fluid around the rest of the baby. Either way, such a measurement of amniotic fluid is called the Amniotic Fluid Index (AFI), and it's one of the things that can be tested in a baby felt to be at risk.

The AFI is traditionally the addition of the observed four pockets of fluid, with the normal range from eight to about eighteen. There are fuzzy limits beyond these two extremes, but generally an AFI less than five to six is too little (*oligohydramnios*), and an AFI greater than twenty-four is too generous (*hydramnios* or *polyhydramnios*).

Most of the liquid in amniotic fluid is contributed by fetal urine. It shouldn't keep building indefinitely, otherwise they'd perch you up high and use you as a water tower for your community. The fluid also goes away, thank goodness, with a balance of production and elimination resulting in a stable amount.

Most of the fluid is recycled by your baby's swallowing it. Additionally, fluid is reabsorbed by the membranes and umbilical cord. The turnover is pretty fast—a couple of hours—so it's possible to have differing amounts of amniotic fluid from one day to the next, even from one hour to the next.

The AFI can be used to determine fetal well-being. A normal AFI is about twelve, but eight to eighteen is normal too. If there's an ample amount of fluid, then we can assume the baby's kidneys are functioning normally and indirectly assume the kidneys are being perfused normally, driven by a normal fetal blood pressure and normal heart activity—in other words, everything's working fine right on down the line. On the other hand, a low AFI at or near term may be an indication for delivery, either by induction or C-section, because it can be assumed that your baby isn't getting enough nutrition and/or oxygenation.

There can be anatomical abnormalities leading to oligo- or polyhydramnios too. Problems with the fetal bladder or kidneys causing a decrease in urine formation can lead to oligohydramnios. Alternately, problems that interfere with your baby's swallowing can lead to hindered recycling and the fluid can build up into a polyhydramnios. So when there's an abnormal amount of fluid, problems with both anatomy and physiology must be considered.

Decreased amounts of amniotic fluid also accompany rupture of membranes.

Decreased "Reactivity" on Nonstress Test

The nonstress test, also called a Fetal Activity Determination (FAD), is a non-invasive test in which your baby's heart rate is monitored and variations in rate recorded during times of fetal movement.

When you run around the block, your own heart begins to race. This is your body's way of speeding up the whole process of delivering more oxygenated blood to areas of increased need, your muscles. It's a good thing everything works together like this, or many of us would drop dead just chasing after that damn dog that got out again. In the same way, when a baby moves, which the mother marks on a fetal monitor, we should also see a corresponding rise in the fetal heart rate. This tells us that everything is pretty much working right in the baby too.

If the FAD is nonreactive (heart rate doesn't accelerate with movement like it's supposed to), your doctor will need to investigate further.

Unconventional Positions of Baby

The normal position for your baby is vertex (headfirst). The position before thirty-two weeks is of academic interest and shouldn't get undue attention because thirty-two weeks seems to be a dividing line after which your baby has only a minimal chance of changing position.

Babies like to seek the most comfortable position. You know this when you change sides in your sleep, only to have your baby fight back. The lower uterus has the most room since the upper uterus is partially occupied, typically, by the placenta. Since your baby's head is the biggest part of him, he usually will seek a headfirst position just because it's the most comfortable. Obstetricians call the position the baby assumes the *lie*.

Vertex lie is the most common. Frank breech is next, which is buttocks first. Then come the *footling* variations, single footling breech and double footling breech. Less frequent are the oblique lie babies and the instances of

---

✳A-FACTOR
If your baby is vertex by thirty-two weeks, you can pretty much relax; that will probably be the permanent arrangement until delivery.

transverse lie. The only babies that can deliver vaginally are the vertex and the frank breech. But even the frank breech vaginal delivery has some increased risk (see "Delivery," Chapter 16), so those of you with powers of telekinesis should will your baby into the vertex lie. The rest of you should just hope.

> **Fast Forward**
>
> *Version* is the process of turning a breech baby to vertex position. It has some risk and only works half the time, but if it's successful, you just might save yourself a C-section.

Since anything other than vertex means a planned C-section or at least an offered C-section (with frank breech, which would be a wise choice, by the way), abnormal lie after thirty-two weeks will put you into a different type of mode as far as your prenatal care goes. If the C-section is the plan, there may not be any need to do cervical checks. You can either be scheduled a week before your due date or be allowed to go into labor in the hopes that your baby might spontaneously move to vertex, calling off the C-section and saving everyone a lot of trouble. But usually your baby won't accommodate you, and the trouble is in doing a C-section in the middle of the night. And I'm talking about your trouble, not your doctor's, because statistics show that any surgeries done at ungodly hours increase the risk of complications and infection.

Under certain conditions, a breech baby can be turned to vertex. This is called version, and it's successful half the time. It must be done at thirty-six weeks, because any later makes your baby too big to push around to vertex, and any earlier would be meddling with immature lungs should this maneuver cause fetal distress. It is done under ultrasound guidance and while listening to the fetal heart tones so that the whole process can be called off should the heart tones crash at midmaneuver. For this same reason it should be done in the hospital with a C-section room open, ready, and reserved for your baby. Although all of these preparations sound scary, I've never had a version go that bad. I've had to stop, but the heart tones have responded favorably to my merely backing off.

Offering version is something that should neither be discouraged nor encouraged—just offered. Because there's a risk, many parents decline, philosophizing that their baby must be breech for a reason. This is superstitious and fatalistic, but I can't argue with a couple who don't want to create any risks for their child.

Decreased Fetal Movement

The third trimester will see your baby's movements convert from wild flips into squirming and readjusting movements. Not that he won't try the acrobatics from time to time. It's just that there's less room. A decrease in the robustness of movement isn't a concern, but the frequency of movement shouldn't change.

> **Fast Forward**
>
> There's a big difference between decreased amount of movement and changes in the types of movement. The gradual transition of kicks into more squirmlike behavior doesn't mean a decrease in the amount of movement and isn't a concern. A decrease in the actual number of movements is and should be reported.

A simple test you can do before calling your doctor is to lay on your left side after eating lunch or supper and then see how long it takes your baby to move ten times. The books say if it takes longer than four hours, this is troubling. I've always told my patients two hours, just to be safe. In practice, it'll probably take ten minutes. I refuse to believe recent studies that indicate children don't go hyper after a sugar load. This simple test at home will prove the relationship to you when your baby goes ballistic after a hefty supper.

This test is called the baby count test. Its reliability is close to that of a nonstress test done in your doctor's office, except that it's free. The paranoid (not that there's anything wrong with that) will do it every evening until they deliver, and as a doctor, I'm just fine with that.

Moving babies are good babies. If there really is a decrease in the amount of movement, this could be due to a baby that's doing poorly. A sick baby will use all of his energy just to grow and will tip off a doctor by decreased movement. Also, some genetic disorders, like Trisomy 18, involve decreased muscle tone and will therefore result in decreased movement. Report all decreased movement to your doctor.

Abdominal Tenderness

There are growing pains and there can even be adhesional pains as your uterus expands. But a diffuse tenderness to touch (pressing on your uterus) isn't normal. Unfortunately, there can be confusion caused by tenderness of your abdominal muscles as you begin to walk a little differently because of your pregnancy load, using muscles you've never used before. Your doctor can tell the difference. If it's just muscle aches, this is harmless. If it's your uterus that's tender, this could represent amnionitis (infection inside your uterus). But usually amnionitis is accompanied by very obvious events, like blatant rupture of membranes, fever, and even preterm labor. So abdominal tenderness is probably just harmless muscle aches or ligament pain till proven otherwise.

Contractions Coming More Than Four an Hour

Preterm labor is a very big deal, and I deal extensively with it later. But I talk about it here because it's on the list of things your doctor should worry about and/or things you should report to your doctor.

> *A-FACTOR
> Even as many as four contractions an hour won't usually create any cervical change.

Making a diagnosis of preterm labor involves ruling out false labor and the harmless, sporadic Braxton-Hicks contractions, which can begin as early as twenty weeks. There is a continuum from false labor to true labor. Since labor is defined as a change in your cervix (a yielding to forces), every woman has a point at which uterine contractions can make the transition to cervix-changing forces. But less than four contractions an hour won't do it. In fact most women don't have more than ten a day before the real thing kicks in. Use four contractions an hour as your criteria. More than four an hour should be reported to your doctor.

Bleeding

Once again, bleeding in pregnancy is abnormal till proven otherwise. Besides the scary things like placenta previa, spotting or bleeding may represent a changing of your cervix as it thins. This is called bloody show and would be a preterm labor concern.

> **Fast Forward**
> As always, any bleeding should be reported when it happens. This shouldn't wait until the next office day, even if it means going to the ER, which admittedly is a real drag.

Other causes of bleeding are bacterial vaginosis and yeast infections. Even though they're still considered harmless, they can cause bleeding. Bacterial vaginosis has been suspected of increasing the risk of preterm labor, so your doctor will treat it with cream or suppositories, but the link to preterm labor has never been proven.

Your doctor will begin doing vaginal exams as you near term, and spotting after a cervical check is common and harmless. Report it anyway, but be a sport and try to do it before office hours are over.

Any Sudden, Sharp Pain That Doesn't Go Away

You're walking in the mall, right, minding your own business, when all of a sudden you double over and your Momma freaks out and calls 911 on the cell phone. And then ten seconds later you're perfectly fine.

Your pregnancy will play these stupid little jokes on you, and your doctor will never know what caused these attacks most of the time. But such episodes should be reported as they could possibly indicate a kidney stone, bladder spasm (indicative of an infection), or even an impending placental separation (abruption). But if it goes away in ten seconds, it's not a 911 event. Nor is it something you need to beep your doctor over if it's the middle of the night. Report it during regular office hours. But if the pain doesn't go away, you should contact your doctor or report to the emergency room of your doctor's hospital.

Colic, much like your baby may get after delivery, can happen with all of the crowding going on inside your abdomen. Gas and intestinal contents have to maul their way through tighter turns. It is harmless. Pain from a kidney infection, however, isn't. A stone's pain may go away momentarily, but it will be back. Bladder spasm can happen because of infection or just because your

> **A-FACTOR**
> Things that can cause sudden debilitating pain:
> - Bowel or gastric colic (You'll probably have a few instances, but it's harmless.)
> - Bladder spasm (Infection needs to be ruled out. If it's not due to infection, it's probably your baby poking you and is harmless.)
> - Renal colic, from a stone (Unusual, but serious.)

baby's head is rubbing it through the uterine wall. If it's your baby, it's harmless. If it's an infection, it needs to be treated.

Leaking Amniotic Fluid

Not good, of course. The problem is that you won't be able to tell whether it's urine or amniotic fluid. If you're typical, you'll swear on a stack of Bibles (Korans acceptable) that you surely can tell the difference. Believe me, you really can't. The distortion to the anatomical supports of all of your sphincters is significant. And urine doesn't always smell like urine.

Your doctor can tell the difference with simple testing. It will require an office visit (or after-hours hospital visit), but this is information that shouldn't wait. If you truly are leaking fluid out, you may be taking bacteria in, setting you and your baby up for a nasty infection that could change everything.

Since premature rupture of membranes (PROM)—and leaking counts— is a condition associated with preterm labor, it is covered thoroughly in the "Preterm Labor" section of Chapter 20. (It is also an event that would make your doctor want to treat you for Group B strep.)

Burning with Urination

This is the classic symptom of a bladder infection. Infection stimulates a lot of processes in the human body, and one of them is a certain trigger-happy tendency toward labor. The reason a bladder infection is so famous as a cause of preterm labor is that it's so much better at instigating it than any other infection; and it happens so frequently in pregnancy.

Bladder infections in pregnancy can be very sneaky. The classic and most frequent symptom, as mentioned above, is burning—called dysuria. The next most frequent sign is blood-tinged urine due to cystitis (inflamed bladder tissue).

After that, there are a host of other signs and symptoms that may not be as obvious. Bladder pressure and frequency of urination, although associated with urinary tract infection, are also par for the course just with pregnancy and may be blown off by both you and your doctor. There is also a sizable percentage of bladder infections with absolutely no symptoms, diagnosed only as part of the workup for preterm labor.

The bottom line is that if your bladder goes "Boo!" you should have your urine evaluated.

Emotional Abnormalities

Pregnancy is a stress that may fully bring out borderline psychiatric conditions. The whole science of pregnancy-related neuroses, psychoses, and postpartum depression is poorly understood, but these conditions can be quite dangerous, especially if you're acting in such a way as to pose a danger to yourself or others or if you're thinking thoughts so strange that they upset you. Pregnancy can be a stressful challenge to a still-maturing relationship between two people, so don't assume or be convinced by others that your reactions are necessarily pathological when they might just be ups and downs of an inexperienced married couple.

When indicated for real depression, the newer antidepressants are quite safe, especially in the third trimester.

Nausea and Vomiting

Nausea in the third trimester can't be looked at as the typical morning sickness of the first trimester. This late in pregnancy nausea may be a warning that there are more serious things afoot. Hepatitis, gallbladder disease, and a variation of pregnancy-induced hypertension called *HELLP* (see Chapter 20) can push you into an early delivery in the third trimester. You need your liver, and if your liver is deteriorating because of your pregnancy, everybody—you and your baby—will be better off with a delivery. Nausea and vomiting in the

Fast Forward

What you should call your doctor about in the third trimester:

- Decreased fetal movement. Expect a change to more squirminglike movements, but the actual number shouldn't decrease.
- Abdominal tenderness. Report any tenderness of your uterus (painful to the touch).
- Contractions coming more than four per hour. Actually, report more than ten per day. It's nowhere close to four per hour, but it will tip your doctor off that your uterus may be irritable.
- Bleeding. Report any bleeding to your doctor (as always).
- Any sudden, sharp pain that doesn't go away. This could be anything from harmless ligament pain to a kidney stone.
- Leakage of fluid vaginally. Rupture of membranes is a very serious complication. Let your doctor determine the difference between this and the harmless liquefying of normal vaginal discharge or urine.
- Burning with urination. Even a simple bladder infection could provoke preterm labor, not to mention risk a more serious kidney infection.
- Emotional abnormalities. Pregnancy is a stress that may fully bring out borderline psychiatric conditions. Most women who cross a line into psychiatric pathology will have warnings. Report any feelings that you know "aren't like you."
- Nausea and/or vomiting. Not the typical morning sickness of the first trimester, this being late in pregnancy, other more serious problems may be the cause. An ultrasound of the gallbladder will rule out gallstones (cholelithiasis); liver function studies with blood tests will say whether your liver is ailing; and other enzymes will rule out problems with your pancreas. If all of this is normal, then you've got nausea that's unexplained but harmless.
- Right upper quadrant pain or right-sided back pain. This pain is more specific to the liver and a little more ominous because the diagnosis is less in doubt. It's possible that a kidney infection can radiate toward your right flank, but usually this diagnosis is obvious with fevers and abnormal urine analysis.
- Leg pain. This is probably just leg cramps, but thrombophlebitis (inflammation of a vein) can be dangerous. Any continuous sensitivity of your leg muscles, especially your calves, should be reported.

third trimester, unrelated to eating that stale donut you now regret, will plant a big, ugly red flag into your liver for all to see.

An ultrasound of the gallbladder will rule out gallstones (*cholethiasis*); liver function studies with blood tests will say whether your liver is ailing, and other enzyme studies will rule out problems with your pancreas. If all of this is normal, then you've got nausea that's unexplained but harmless. And even though throwing up is no fun, neither are the other causes, so relish being a mystery.

Right Upper Quadrant Pain or Right-Sided Back Pain

The same applies as in nausea. But this symptom is more specific to the liver and a little more ominous because the diagnosis will be less in doubt. It's possible that a kidney infection can radiate pain toward your right flank, but usually this diagnosis is obvious with fevers and an abnormal urine analysis.

Leg Pain

Any continuous sensitivity of your leg muscles, especially your calves, should be reported. Thrombophlebitis is an inflammation of the deep veins, which could possibly cause dangerous blood clots that are able to travel to your lungs. This is different from mere leg cramps, which are sporadic: the pain of thrombophlebitis is continuous. Pain with walking qualifies as continuous pain.

Fetal Surveillance in High-Risk Pregnancies

In Chapter 9, "High Risk in the Third Trimester," I described the problems that can put you into the high-risk category. What if your pregnancy is one of the ones that are considered high risk? Will your doctor's management of your pregnancy change? How will your doctor watch your baby and you in order to get the most out of the pregnancy before anything bad happens?

Let me reassure you. As I mentioned earlier, your doctor will adjust his prenatal care plan to fit your unique risk factors. Also, in the last twenty years many simple tests have been developed and employed in the mainstream of medicine to determine fetal well-being, and your doctor will use all that are appropriate to your risk factors. A baby with a genetic condition that poses danger in and of itself is watched for appropriate growth and signs of distress. A baby who is compromised by a condition you yourself have developed can be watched the same way. The diagnostic tests by which your doctor can determine whether to continue your pregnancy are designed not only to watch your baby but also you.

Frequent Visits

Your doctor can't go wrong by overwatching you. In certain high-risk situations, being seen twice a week is better than being seen only once. Your doctor will know how fast things could change with a particular condition and schedule appointments accordingly.

Ultrasound

Ultrasound is still the best way to look at your baby and determine fetal well-being. Results of the nonstress test and ultrasound are combined to produce the reliable "Biophysical Profile" of your baby.

Nonstress Test

If you were to run around the block, your heart rate would increase. This is your body's way of dealing with the extra demands of the exertion—faster pulse means more oxygen to your working muscles. It's a good thing everything works together like this, or many of us would drop dead just chasing after that dog that got out again. In the same way, when a baby moves, which the mother marks on a fetal monitor, there should also be a corresponding rise in the fetal heart rate. This tells us that everything is pretty much working right in the baby too. Your baby's movements are her exertion, and your doctor expects to see a rise in her heart rate. This test requires no needles—just a belt to listen to and graph your baby's heart rate. You will mark the strip every time your baby moves by pushing a little button. If there are accompanying heart rate accelerations, at least twice in forty minutes, you can reasonably assume fetal well-being. Done repeatedly, this is a great way to watch your baby. Its accuracy, however, isn't good if it's abnormal. In these instances, the Contraction Stress Test is used (see pages 158–159).

> **Fast Forward**
> The combination of ultrasound evaluation and the nonstress test makes up the Biophysical Profile, the most sensitive noninvasive evaluation your baby can have.

Biophysical Profile (Peek-a-Boo, We See You!)

A generation ago women were seen by obstetricians as just sort of getting pregnant and just sort of having a baby nine months later. Most of them, anyway. Occasionally a disaster would strike and due to the lack of meaningful ways to observe the baby, these disasters would often come as a complete surprise. Certainly an astute obstetrician of the time could pick up on some warning signals, such as questionable growth (assessed by means of the size of the prospective mother's abdomen), irregular fetal heart beat (heard with that very strange-looking horn device), or abnormal position (determined by grasping and feeling the abdomen according to certain described maneuvers). The mother's condition was easier to check, but the baby's evaluation was a hide-and-seek affair, the obstetrician getting only insightful glances through the noninvasive techniques of the time.

▶ Fast Forward

The components of the Biophysical Profile with corresponding scores:

1. AFI. The amniotic fluid index is a measurement of four pockets of fluid in one dimension. The sum of the four numbers should be 8–12. Less would represent decreased fluid, possibly a sign of jeopardy; more would mean too much, a problem of fetal development.

2. Fetal movement, as seen on ultrasound.

3. Fetal tone, as seen on ultrasound.

4. Fetal breathing movements, another sensitive indicator of fetal well-being. The fetus doesn't really breathe in the sense that he exchanges air, but the chest walls move, going through the motions.

5. Nonstress test. Test items 1–4 are done via ultrasound. The NST is performed as described earlier.

Each component can have a score of 0, 1, or 2. A perfect score would be 10 out of 10. A score of 8 or greater would probably be a stable pregnancy; 6 or 7 would probably indicate the pregnancy must be very closely observed; 5 or less probably would indicate an induced delivery or C-section.

Fast forward to the present. The cost of a doctor's diligent care has increased tenfold, but the modern obstetrical abilities have multiplied exponentially into the priceless range. After all, how much is a healthy baby worth? Today we actually see the baby by ultrasound. Guesses at appropriate growth are eliminated and replaced by exact measurements, upon which are based timing for crucial diagnostic tests and parameters of maturity. Also, the baby's position, still most frequently determined by physical exam, is confirmed.

Amniotic fluid, a normal amount being one of the most crucial determinations of fetal well-being, can be measured. Fetal movement, tone, and even breathinglike movements can be directly observed, visually assuring a mother-to-be of her baby's good health.

Another test, the nonstress test (NST)—also called Fetal Activity Determination (FAD)—makes use of the valuable relationship between fetal movement and fetal heart rate, as described earlier.

The combined results of the ultrasound exam and the NST are referred to as a Biophysical Profile. Scores are assigned by adding up all of the criteria met (observed). Over the years many researchers have exhaustively tabulated what all of these results mean. When all of the normal ultrasound items are found and the nonstress test is normal, their statistics have demonstrated that a baby has a 99 percent or better chance of another week's worth of fetal well-being ahead. So doing these evaluations once or twice a week on high-risk mothers has immeasurably increased the value of prenatal care (priceless) as compared to a generation ago. We get the earliest of warning signals that allow us to intervene if necessary, and all of this information comes without a single needle, drug, or tear. The price of steak has gone up just as much as the rise in the cost of prenatal care, but a generation later we're still getting the same steak.

Baby Counts

This is the do-it-yourself nonstress test. After you eat lunch or supper (that is, after a calorie loading), lie down on you left side and see how long it takes your baby to move ten times. The books say if it takes longer than four hours, call your doctor. I've always cut that in half, telling my patients if it were to take longer than two hours, go to the hospital. With a good, healthy baby, it'll probably take less than twenty minutes. You can do this every single day in the last two months of your pregnancy.

Contraction Stress Test (CST)

This is the best of the tests. If the Biophysical Profile is the best noninvasive test, then this is the only test that's better. No test is as accurate in determining your baby's health as this. In this technique, done in a hospital, actual contractions are stimulated with Pitocin (oxytocin) or via nipple stimulation (see next item) until you are experiencing three rhythmic contractions every ten minutes.

Contractions are the greatest challenge to your baby's well-being. When your uterus contracts, the area of exchange for nutrients and oxygen is decreased. If your baby has borderline capabilities to withstand stress, this test will show funky heart rates with your contractions. A deceleration in two out of every three contractions is considered abnormal, and your baby certainly won't tolerate hours of labor. Your doctor will be talking C-section. And rightfully so.

Since a contraction stress test (CST) involves an IV and an initiation of labor, albeit temporarily, it's a much bigger deal than a nonstress test (NST). For this reason it is usually reserved for instances in which the NST doesn't show the expected accelerations with fetal movement or in cases of suspected serious fetal jeopardy.

After a stress test is complete, all that need be done is to disconnect the drip. Usually the contractions will fizzle out in less than an hour. If they don't, that's a good problem. Seldom is a CST needed before maturity of your baby, so if the contractions continue, your doctor will run with that and allow your spontaneous labor to continue (unless the CST was abnormal).

Nipple Stimulation Tests

(Husbands, read this entire section before getting any self-gratifying ideas.)

Breast-feeding, besides providing nourishment for your newborn baby, also helps you survive delivery by stimulating contractions so that your uterus will shrink and there will be less internal surface area to bleed. You will know this phenomenon as the unwelcome experience of afterbirth pains. We use this reflex to our advantage by conducting CSTs via nipple squeezing instead of a drip. It's the same test.

For those who may be tempted to try the ol' T-twister at home to bring on labor, do know that the reflex can produce more potent contractions than your own labor might, possibly stressing your baby when he otherwise would tolerate normal labor just fine. Nipple stimulation tests are done in the hospital for this very reason. There your baby can be monitored appropriately. Don't try this at home.

Trial of Labor (Prolonged Stress Test)

When the crystal ball looks particularly cloudy, the Bishop's score borderline, and your chances at a successful induction iffy, your doctor may offer you a "prolonged CST," that is, a contraction stress test that keeps on going. In this way, if your cervix changes, the whole process can be labeled an induction; if it doesn't, you can be sent home with the best CST in the world—hours long and not just the few minutes of the usual in-and-out CST. You won't find this in any of the other books, because it's a nudge-nudge wink-wink affair that hopes to get you delivered without committing you to a C-section if the induction doesn't take.

Artificial Rupture of Membranes (AROM)

This is done in the hospital so that the fluid can be evaluated for meconium or blood. Needless to say this is a procedure done when you're already committed to delivery for a medical problem or done during labor to make it more efficient (see the Birthing Understanding, pages 179–186).

Other Considerations Near Your Due Date

Lumping together a number of decisions under Other Considerations is a real cop-out. These concerns are important enough to warrant whole chapters. Because they are decisions that should be made between you and your doctor, I list here the pertinent points of each. Some I will discuss in length later in the chapters on labor or delivery, but I list them here because the third trimester is the time to think about them.

Elective Induction

See Chapter 13 for a complete discussion. Suffice it for now to say that every pregnancy is different, and every pregnancy that ends in an elective induction has reasons unique to it. Necessity, prudence, and even convenience all have their corresponding criteria that make elective induction proper.

Repeat C-Section Versus VBAC

It used to be said, "Once a C-section, always a C-section." Then came the studies that proved that worry over uterine rupture of the previous incision site was mere paranoia and that under special criteria women could labor safely with a previous C-section. There are pros and cons to just giving in to a scheduled repeat C-section or to attempting VBAC (Vaginal Birth After Cesarean). The bottom line is that in the financially driven frenzy to bring down C-section rates, VBAC has been championed as completely safe, which it isn't. There is still a 1 percent chance of rupture.

Maternal Choice C-Section

This is discussed in "Controversies in Obstetrics" in Chapter 22. There has been talk that vaginal delivery, although great for the natural experience that it is, is terrible for your bladder support, possibly pushing you into bladder surgery for incontinence in the future. Fecal incontinence is also seen as a complication resulting from vaginal deliveries, too. When all of the possible future costs and surgery to correct urinary or fecal incontinence are added to the vaginal delivery, the risk versus benefit of having a C-section is about the same as a vaginal delivery. Controversial? You bet! But it should be a woman's right to choose how she has her baby.

C-Section-Hysterectomy

There are women who have a hysterectomy in their future. If you want no more children, severely incapacitating periods between pregnancies, precancerous changes, and large fibroids could be reasons to consider having a hysterectomy now instead of later on. This is especially true if you're going to have a repeat C-section anyway. Another candidate would be someone wanting to have permanent sterilization via a tubal ligation with these conditions. Why have two surgeries when you can have one?

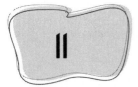

II

The Terminal Trials of Pregnancy

The terminal trials of pregnancy, those of the third trimester, besides including and perhaps embellishing upon all of the ones of the second trimester, include unique additions:

- False labor
- PUP rash
- Back pain (the pride of pregnancy)
- Shortness of breath
- Paresthesia, including carpal tunnel
- "The Wait"
- Nesting frenzy (mainly for husbands)

The Victor Hugo Index: Who Was Victor Hugo and What Does He Have to Do with Pregnancy?

My dad, the late Dr. John DiLeo, a thoracic surgeon, used to refer to anyone who was being a first-class whiny baby as a *Misérable*. *Les Misérables*, the classic by Victor Hugo, was his favorite book, so he lifted the title and would throw it around to hold up a mirror to his children's misbehavior at times. How much misbehavior? That's none of your business, but I myself was one of four children and, being in the middle, was a *Misérable* more than my fair share. Now I've got four of my own and when there's any aimless complaining or whining, the fingers of accusation from the others point out this *Misérable* or that *Misérable* or even the whole bunch of *Misérables*.

Taking it one step further and trying to add a little class, I now present the Victor Hugo Index (VHI), that relative scale of miserableness:

1+ Victor Hugo Index: A little aggravated

2+ Victor Hugo Index: Plenty aggravated

3+ Victor Hugo Index: Really miserable and letting you know it

4+ Victor Hugo Index: Obnoxiously miserable and letting everyone know in no uncertain terms just how unacceptable it is

False Labor: The Frequent Flier Club

The differences between false labor and the real thing are explained in Chapter 14. False labor is the little labor that thought it could, but couldn't. The psychological toll, however, can get pricey. First of all, here you are with a mature baby, prenatal classes are over, and you're ready for the final exam. And then . . . contractions . . . wonderful contractions. The suitcase has been packed for days if this is your first baby (there aren't any suitcases for the other babies). You hop in the car and you and your husband, whom we shall call Mr. Right, haul on down to the hospital.

Fast Forward

False labor is a real drag and can take a psychological toll on you when you feel you've paid your dues and are ready to have your baby. But you can't deliver via false labor, so you'll be sent home as a "false alarm." This is common, so don't be embarrassed, and . . . it's better to have a hundred false alarms than to hold out and deliver in your car.

The fact that you can still hop should be a tip-off because once you're on the monitor your nurse is not impressed. You'll get an exam and the examiner, be it your nurse, doctor, or midwife, will not be impressed. You get sent home if after an hour your cervix doesn't change, and you are offered some sedation to calm the false labor down, like some nice parting gift from a game show. And then you feel pretty stupid. This is a Victor Hugo Index of 1+.

It happens again, but this time the contractions are harder. "Surely," you say to yourself, but three hours later you're back at home sporting a Victor Hugo Index of 2+.

It happens again, but this time you're not going to be stupid about it—you're going to sit it out. So you suffer with these little sissy contractions, which aren't really that bad, until you realize that they're beginning to eat away at your patience threshold like any good Chinese water torture. You make it to your next doctor's visit without going to the hospital yet again, but you find you have a need to let her have it good.

"When, oh, when? I'm having contractions. The baby's ready. The room's ready. I go to the hospital and they send me home. And my husband has the gall to complain. Well, I'm the one who's suffering, not him. I'm the one who's ready. What did he do, really? All he did was have an orgasm. Yeah, he really had it rough. So when, oh, when?"

Your husband is now Mr. Wrong.

Your doctor looks at you and says nothing, simply because there's nothing she can say to make this any better. She does the exam and you could slap her for responding with that frown on her face, meaning there's been no change in your cervix.

Now you're at Victor Hugo Index 3+. "See you next week," she tells you.

"Next week?" you ask, as if this foolishness should last even another day.

Two days later, in the middle of the night, you walk into Labor and Delivery, holding your lower abdomen. Surely this must be it. These lousy, miserable contractions are really starting to hurt. The nurses start referring to your pregnancy as being on the Frequent Flier program. And then there's still no cervical change!

Victor Hugo Index of 4+, which in most NATO-block countries is equivalent to DefCon Delta.

False labor is one of the most exasperating miseries of pregnancy, especially if this is your first baby and you don't know what to really expect, even though you've read the books and gone to the classes.

You might be able to find the humor in all of this in about ten years, but right now it really is torture. Like your doctor's silence, there are no printed words to make it any better, except that it's not truly a false labor from a functional standpoint. All of those seemingly ineffective contractions really are doing something, and many feel that it's the beginning of a continuum that will eventually result in the real thing. So take heart. And don't go crazy. And go ahead—tell your husband he's insensitive. If he's a smart man, he'll just shut up.

Pregnancy Rules for Husbands

Rule #4: If you think you're aggravated about these false alarms, you're not a millionth as aggravated as your wife. Listen to me closely: you're not aggravated. Not at all. Ever. And watch your body language and facial expressions—you're being studied. And whatever you do, even if Notre Dame is attempting a 60-yard winning field goal with two seconds to go, do not—DO NOT—suggest she drive herself to the hospital and call if it's the real thing.

Puerperal Urticaria of Pregnancy (PUP)

This is an itchy rash that can affect your arms, legs, chest, abdomen, and back. The rash consists of patches of small speckles. There are some who feel it is an allergic reaction to your baby's sloughed skin cells that somehow got into your circulation, got deposited at the end of an arteriole, and then invoked an immune response. It is harmless. If severe, you can take a steroid dose-pack, but that's only if you feel like you're in the movie Killer Fleas. Victor Hugo Index of 1–2 +.

Back Pain

Your posture tends to slink back a bit, shoving your belly out at the world. It's the in-your-face posture, what used to be called the "pride" of pregnancy. But

---

Fast Forward

Your posture will change to accommodate the shifting of your center of gravity as you near term, stressing infrequently used muscles that can strain.

you're not doing it to show off—it's the way you have to stand if you're going to remain standing at all, because your center of gravity has shifted. Your lower back takes the brunt of this shift of stresses, and you'll be using muscles that you've never used before to compensate. Victor Hugo Index of 2 +.

Shortness of Breath

As your fundal height increases, the closer the top of your uterus is to your diaphragm. Your diaphragm is the floor of your chest, and it moves down, creating the negative pressure that sucks air into your lungs. It's how you and I both breathe. Well, near term, it's more how I breathe than you do, because your uterus crowding upward means less downward space for your diaphragm to act as a bellows. But you have to breathe, right? Right.

> **Fast Forward**
> Shortness of breath is another of those things that come from cramming two people into the space of one.

Now you're beginning to use what are called the accessory breathing muscles. These are the intercostal muscles between your ribs, acting to assist the limited diaphragm by spreading your ribs out, adding to the negative pressure needed for lung inflation. But every time you use something you've never really used before, your body thinks you're crazy and responds with pain brought about by the mild inflammation of stressing the usually unstressed muscles. Your chest may hurt.

> **A-FACTOR**
> True hypoxia (oxygen deprivation) doesn't happen unless you have pulmonary disease to begin with.

Lying down will make shortness of breath worse because of simple gravity—you're allowing the heavy uterus to fall back (or up, when reclining), further imposing on the diaphragm's space. This is why you will find it more comfortable to sleep slightly upright with a few pillows under your back. Victor Hugo Index of 1–2 +.

Paresthesia

Steven Wright, one of my favorite comedians, said, "I hate it when my leg falls asleep during the day. That means it'll probably be up all night long."

When your nerves go completely dead, as with novocaine, it's called anesthesia. When they're not completely numb but are acting a little goofy, it's called paresthesia. Getting the proverbial pins and needles is a paresthesia.

> **A-FACTOR**
> Swelling around your nerves can give you tingling and numbness, but if the circulation's fine, it's harmless.

A famous pregnancy paresthesia site is the leg, and it's usually the right leg, because our old friend the vena cava, shifted slightly to the right, splits, but the right-sided blood vessels are more of a target for the weight of your uterus than the left. This is also why you may notice swelling is a little worse on the right side too. Victor Hugo Index of 2+.

The Wait: Expecting the Expected Date of Delivery

This is the opposite of the false labor, Frequent Flier aggravation. You approach your due date and nothing—I mean nothing—is happening. Your doctor checks your cervix and nothing, again. And then the due date finally comes and you're not delivered. You wish you had something—anything—happening, and you envy those women with at least false labor. Victor Hugo Index of 3–4+.

I've always felt that a "due month" was more useful than a "due date." The due date, the center of the bell curve, is seldom the actual day of delivery. Every baby has his own clock. The due date is what applies to the gestational expectations for the whole human race. It can become irksome to have that day slip away undelivered if you're in that half of women who deliver sometime after the due date. Or to have the next day slip away too. Or the next day. And on and on.

The problem with the expected date of delivery (the EDD, or due date) is that the expectations for this date are too high, and the disappointment is too bitter when nothing happens. What can be done?

You can be induced if you're expecting a vaginal delivery and you're at least thirty-nine weeks. If you're a repeat C-section, you can schedule the C-section anytime at or after thirty-nine weeks. But if you hit a 4+ Victor Hugo Index before thirty-nine weeks with no medical reason to induce, you're out of luck. Also, if you're philosophically opposed to induction you'll have to make an intellectual decision on whether to forego your position.

Pregnancy is a self-resolving situation, and you can take some comfort in the fact that sooner or later you will in fact deliver.

Time to Get Busy

The Nesting Frenzy

In the deepest Fairy Godmother recesses of every obstetrician's mind is the fantasy that there are certain yet-to-be-discovered hormones that affect behavior.

I've been the doctor involved in private adoptions and noticed what I thought were too many instances in which a previously infertile newly adoptive mother turns up pregnant soon after cradling her new baby for some length of time. For lack of a better term, I've always called the undiscovered, fanciful hormone PregNog. Gives it sort of a holiday flavor.

And then there's Frenzitol, that other mystery hormone that drives you to get the house in order while it inhibits the onset of true labor until everything's ready. The nesting frenzy is a terminal trial of pregnancy, but for your husband. The moving of furniture, the cleaning, the new bed sheets and comforters, the fresh paint—you will seem to be a little too insistent for his liking. And he'll be clueless about the need for such urgency.

Pregnancy Rules for Husbands

Rule #5: With pregnancy, the house is no longer yours. Not even half of it. None of it is yours. Accept it. The only reason you still command the remote is because of her gracious generosity.

Is there such a thing as a Victor Hugo Index of 5+? Yes, but it's an imaginary category because it's the scale that would be used if men had babies.

Questions You Forgot to Ask Before the Eleventh Hour

Now that you're rapidly approaching term, it's time to get busy with making some decisions. If there are any questions you may have regarding how your doctor will do things, now is the time to ask them and to straighten out any misunderstandings because this is your last chance. The time not to try to iron these things out is during labor.

There are a few questions you may not have thought about.

Does Your Doctor Deliver All of His Own Patients?

No doctor does this, and you have no special protection from being on the receiving end of the ol' switcheroo. But a lot of doctors really do try to deliver all of their own patients, only getting call coverage for social commitments that are mandatory, like weddings, vacations, or that $20 million ticket to ride with the Russians to the Space Station. Alternately, there are actually doctors that deliver none of their own patients, like the big shot tip-of-the-large-group-practice pyramid. And there are all of the types of involvements in between. Here's the gamut:

Doctors Who Deliver None of Their Patients

These doctors are, as mentioned above, either the head of a big group, delegating all of the work to junior partners, or part of a clinic that has no affiliation with a hospital or birthing center. The latter group generally turns their patients over to other doctors sometime in the early third trimester.

Doctors Who Deliver Most of Their Patients

These doctors are in a call group with other doctors, but will generally request the labor unit call them for their own patients even when they're not on call, unless they're doing something they can't get out of.

Doctors Who Enforce Their Own Off Time

These doctors are in a call group, but after hours only deliver their patients when it's their night on call. Most doctors fall into either this group or the one that delivers most of their patients. But even if your own doctor is in this group, there's still a greater than 50 percent chance you'll get your own doctor, because these doctors usually are responsible for their own patients during the daytime, probably nighttime too, and use their call coverage just for the weekends.

Doctors Who Deliver All of Their Patients

These doctors, as attractive as they may seem to your own needs, are the crazy doctors. They don't do anything else in life, and they're always really tired. Most doctors fall into the middle two groups, which means there is a chance another doctor may attend your delivery. Financially speaking, there is an incentive for your doctor to deliver you, for if he doesn't, he's going to be writing some other doctor a check.

Who Are the Doctors Who Cover for Your Doctor?

This is an important question, but not for the reasons you might think. Your first consideration is over whether the doctors covering are any good. You need to assume they're at least as good as your own doctor. They are. Your doctor wouldn't pick a bum. (Unless he himself is a bum, but you picked him!)

That's not the problem. True, they may not be as charming and wonderfully sweet as your carefully hand-picked choice, but your doctor's not going to be looking for trouble by swearing allegiance to a jerk who doesn't know anything. The real problem is whether coverage might be with a doctor that you've been to before. Let's face it, you were probably going to another doctor before finding Dr. Wonderful. If your doctor is off on the big day and Dr. I-Still-Owe-Money-To or Dr. I-Left-You-Because-You're-a-Big-Jerk-and-I-Told-You-So walks in, this is the type of awkwardness that will ruin even the most carefully scripted delivery method you've gone to all of the classes to pull off.

Find out who all of the covering doctors are. If there's one who's a deal breaker, tell your doctor. Perhaps she'll get another doctor to cover a weekend if it's that important. Your doctor should want to please you and will usually try anything reasonable to give you peace of mind.

Don't beg her to be on call just for you on her time off. This is unfair. The divorce rate in obstetrics is high for a reason, so grant your doctor the right to have some off time. Just discuss it beforehand so that everyone is happy. And don't flip out over not getting your doctor. The real brains behind your pregnancy is the prenatal care—getting you to the point of delivery. Nurses, after all, do all of the monitoring; Dr. Wonderful shows up if there's a problem, during a few interval evaluations, and for the delivery. And you're the one doing the delivering!

Which flows into the next question: How do you want to have your baby?

This is where knowledge is power.

Prenatal Classes: Lamaze or Bradley?

Whether you want to have the most natural experience you can or want your epidural drip to begin ten weeks before your delivery, the information picked up at prenatal classes is extremely useful. In the Introduction I made some statements about prenatal classes that may seem unfair. OK, the instructors for prenatal classes really are kind of geeky, but after all, the geeks run the world, don't they? And yes, you really will wonder for the life of you why someone would choose to do this as a vocation. Well, someone's got to do it. And of course these instructors feel that their way is the ideal way to have a baby, singing their songs of political correctness. And yes, most of them probably drive Volvos. But I love this stuff.

What I love about prenatal instruction is that pregnancy and delivery is a wonder and a gift and of ultimate importance. Anything that teaches you about it is a major investment in yourself, and anyone who does the teaching makes for everyone a major investment toward the human condition. We're all mammals. Our superior brains, however, allow us to appreciate the significance of birth and the birthing process, and nothing short of the actual delivery is better for appreciating the philosophy of reproduction than the study of its physical aspects in prenatal classes.

Enter Dr. Ferdinand Lamaze and his psychoprophylactic method and Dr. Robert A. Bradley and his husband-coached approach to childbirth. Enter the dozens of variations on the two. These instructive lessons do a marvelous job in explaining what's going on and what you can expect of labor and delivery. They are family-oriented in that they involve the father. They are beautiful in that they focus on the grace and splendor of reproduction.

But they're also a pain in the neck because you have to go back to school, get thrown into a fuzzy subject you have no perspective about, with cheerleading teachers who drill you like you're at an Up With People publicity workshop.

For the record, I like the Bradley method. I like Lamaze. I would prefer every woman be focused on her body and her delivery of her child. I only have one caveat: it's not for everyone.

This is true, even if Drs. Lamaze and Bradley themselves were to come back from the dead and serenade you into the right breathing patterns. And this is also true, no matter what an instructor tells you. And it's even true for some people who are absolutely convinced they can have a natural childbirth. Alternately, a person who just knows she could never do it is cheating herself on the front end if she otherwise would have liked to have tried.

The difference between Lamaze and Bradley is that Lamaze is based on self-hypnotic exercises that distract you from your pain—a Vulcan would make an excellent Lamaze laborer; the Bradley technique relies on more of a mammalian discipline, using natural breathing to achieve synchrony with your body, leading to relaxation.

Whether you're Mrs. Spock in naturally detached anesthesia or want the Vulcan nerve pinch of an epidural, it's important once again to state that it's not how you have the baby—it's how you raise the baby.

I personally prefer the Bradley method, even if the instructors seem to be a little more militant than the Lamaze instructors about insisting on refusing all of the "unnecessary" interventions. Perhaps this is because Lamaze is usually taught by the Labor and Delivery nurses on staff at the hospital, staffed by—guess who?—the doctors, who order all of those unnecessary interventions. Also, Bradley is a for-profit outfit, and there's no better way to champion your livelihood than by embracing it as superior. And it is superior. It's just not for all women.

Every woman has a different set of pain nerves and every woman feels labor differently. It makes no difference whether they're college graduates or they're mentally retarded. Across the board, in every conceivable type of individual, there are some who can pursue a natural approach without difficulty and others who will be climbing the walls at two centimeters dilation.

Natural childbirth—like anything in medicine—when it works, it works great; when it doesn't, it's a disaster. If you can have a life-changing experience by participating successfully in your delivery on every level, you can just as easily have a really bad experience if unsuccessful. These instructors are sure of themselves and what they teach, but this is sometimes corrupted into a one-size-fits-all approach to the beauty of natural birth. Look around at everyone's shoes. They're all different sizes.

The same goes for pain perception. Pain is perceived in your head, so methods that allow you to deal with labor pain by training your head are absolutely the correct approach. And even if your head has its limits, still the knowledge of how to breathe and knowing the finer points of the different methods of childbirth are practical for seeing the big picture, even if you have your own particular plan on approaching childbirth. Even if you have an epidural that accidentally slams you, knowledge from prenatal classes will allow you to push using muscles you can't even feel. It's weird, but it's doable. When a dentist numbs your jaw, you can still open your mouth.

Also, since obstetrics is a field where the bottom can drop out at any time (no pun intended), it would be nice to have a knowledge of possible emergencies so you're not clueless when everyone's running around like chickens with their heads cut off. This will not likely happen, but knowing about such things will make everything smoother for your doctor, your nurses, and others, which will then translate into a better chance of successful countermeasures. Prenatal classes are a good education into all of the possibilities.

So although some teachers often use these classes as a vehicle for their particular political agendas, the medical information is good. It's your baby and you can have it any way you want. If naturally is that way, your obstetrician will support you 100 percent. If you change your mind, you're not a wuss—the real test is in raising the baby. On the other hand, if you really are a self-proclaimed wuss and know it ahead of time, do what's needed to make your delivery a pleasant experience, even if it requires the "unnecessary interventions."

The thing to remember is that ultimately the method of birth is unimportant. C'mon, everyone sing along: it's not how you have the baby, it's how you raise the baby.

When Should You Go to the Hospital?

Ask your doctor about his criteria. Does he want you to call him first? Does he want you to just go and let the nurses call him instead? How far apart should the contractions be before he would have you get on the road? (See Chapter 14.)

What Are Your Doctor's Quirks When it Comes to Labor and Delivery?

Every doctor has her own style. Her technique has been honed by a combination of book knowledge and experience over the years on what works best for her. It's probably why you chose her in the first place. Still, it's good to know just what might go down here. Will she cut an automatic episiotomy? Will she refuse to cut one? Will she pop your water bag? Is this necessary? What about induction? Many people see the birthing contract as the answer to all of these questions.

Should You Get a Birthing Contract?

The birthing contract is the darling of the self-help self-appointed experts on pregnancy and of the online parenting sites. But the birthing contract presents a love-hate relationship in prenatal care: patients love them, doctors hate them.

A contract? A contract is a legally enforceable binding agreement. Who thinks up these things? You choose your doctor, you trust your doctor, you like your doctor . . . and then you hand him a manifesto designed by a non-doctor, from somewhere-who-knows-where. Asking him to enter into an agreement is an insult to the doctor-patient relationship.

So am I down on birthing contracts? No, not unless you really do consider it a binding agreement. Lately, its title has been softened a bit to birthing plan, but don't be fooled—your doctor isn't.

This isn't a house you're building. No architect gives you a scale model of your child, based on blueprints and cost estimates for every nail. Your body is a dynamic physiologic entity with a complex yet-to-be-determined fate. Things come up. You're not paying your doctor to just be a warm body present at your delivery. You're paying him to act in any situation that may come up. This is where you get your money's worth. And things will come up.

The one person whose hands you don't want to tie is the one who could make the difference in the quality of life for your offspring for the next eighty years. To take advantage of all that obstetrics has to offer, you must allow your doctor to use good judgment.

You should take the time to make a birthing "understanding." Not a contract, not a plan, but an acknowledgment of what your preferences are that also serves as an educational tool for you.

There's nothing wrong with asking your doctor to try to avoid an epi-siotomy if she can, to explain why she might want to pop your water bag, or to accept that you would like to try a natural delivery but want to be able to go with an epidural should you prove to be a poor candidate for this type of delivery. There's nothing wrong with asking that you not have an enema upon admission. Shaving your pubic hair, scalp electrode monitors, ability to walk around—all of these things are reasonable in a birthing understanding that should be a list of understood preferences.

But any promises will have your doctor examining you with crossed fingers, for if your doctor feels your baby may be in jeopardy and wants to attach a scalp electrode in spite of your preference to the contrary, you need to back off and let the person who trained for this save the day. If you need a C-section, I would think you will have chosen a doctor you feel comfortable with to make such a decision. You wouldn't call in an arbitrator to negotiate the points of your birthing contract at such a time.

Birthing contracts are constructed by well-meaning couples who care about the whole process of labor and delivery, and that is a good thing. But they must avoid the idea, propagated by meddling political correctness gurus, that you can march into your doctor-patient relationship insistent on the way things must be done. You might as well deliver at home, which is a sore sub-ject. Many pregnancy books use the birthing contract (plan) as an "Us vs. Them" statement about the doctor-patient relationship. For the record, the doctor-patient relationship is sacred to your doctor, as much an integral fiber to medicine as any oath taken. In many ways the practice of medicine is still the noble profession, in spite of your doctor's demotion to the position of a mere provider by those thieving bastards, the insurance companies.

Which brings me to another point: why is there no birthing contract with your insurer? Deciding what they'll pay for is a deceitful way of indicating how your doctor should practice medicine. You may not be able to afford what your doctor wants if they won't cover it. Shouldn't you have a say in what some third-party insurer deems necessary? I can't understand why a patient would whip out a birth contract for her doctor whom she trusts, but blindly accept the arrangement her insurance company says is good enough for her baby—like they really care.

How About a Birthing Understanding?

Below is a list of typical questions my patients have asked me over the years, along with my typical responses. Please know that you may have your own unique questions and that these responses are mine, not a universal answer sheet.

> **Fast Forward**
>
> A birthing understanding is a kinder, gentler overture to your doctor, serving as an educational device for you. The difference between a birthing contract and a birthing understanding is that the birthing contract challenges your doctor's judgment, but a birthing understanding allows you to partner with him.

Typical Questions and Answers from a Birthing Understanding

Will I need an episiotomy? Can I get by without one? Maybe and maybe not. I don't do automatic episiotomies. I can't tell if you'll need one until the very moment when I should cut one. I will only cut one if it looks like you're going to tear. And you have the right to refuse the episiotomy. But a bad tear is a lot harder to recover from than a cleanly cut episiotomy. I make this statement in a clear challenge to what you might read in other books. Whether you see the area of vaginal delivery as a playing field or a battleground, I've seen all types of events and all types of recoveries. On the other hand, if it looks like you're not going to tear, I won't cut one because it's a lot less work for me and a much smoother recovery for you if I don't.

Will I need to be shaved? No. Automatic shaving and enemas went out with the Ford Pinto. Shaving was once thought to protect you from infection that might complicate episiotomies, vaginal tears, or even your baby. We now know that any bacteria unique to hair aren't a particular threat, especially with the routine antiseptic cleansing done at the time of delivery.

Also, there is something particularly immunologic about this whole area. Consider this: there is damage to the vaginal tissue with every delivery. There doesn't have to be a laceration or episiotomy—there's enough damage from the extreme pressures of your baby's head against this delicate tissue. So with the milking of feces or bacteria from your rectum that accompanies the bulldozing effect of delivery against your rectum, why aren't there more infections? If there's one place and one situation in which the amount of infection to damaged tissue is so much less than it should be, it's your perineum (vaginal floor and tissue down to your rectum) during a delivery. If you rubbed feces or rectal bacteria into even a brush burn on your arm (and I'm not advocating this), it would probably get infected. When you consider how seemingly invulnerable the perineal and vaginal tissues are to infection during such a gumbo of exposure to bacteria, it's hard to worry about pubic hair with a straight face.

Will I need an enema? Same answer. Enemas have never been shown to stop infection. In fact, the many trips to the bathroom associated with the watery expulsion of the enema may pose more of an infection risk, especially if your water bag has broken or has been broken, allowing a route in for bacteria.

Will you pop my water bag? I'd prefer you didn't. The "water bag" is the collection of fetal membranes (chorioamnion) that holds in the amniotic fluid and keeps bacteria out. In fact, this is the reasoning behind induction at term if the water bag pops: so that delivery can be accomplished before any chance of serious infection. This question, however, refers to the procedure of artificially popping the membranes (amniotomy), instead of allowing them to burst spontaneously. The routine use of amniotomy is for the purpose of jump-starting an induction or enhancing the progress of a labor. It is felt that this flimsy bag won't make as good a dilating wedge against your cervix as your baby's hard head. Studies have shown that any increase in the efficiency of labor is when amniotomy is performed before you're six centimeters dilated.

When is amniotomy indicated and not just a trick to speed up labor? First of all, sometimes speeding up labor is a really good idea. If your labor begins to slow, this can pose some hazards for your baby (lengthier labors are lengthier ordeals) or for you (increased chances of needing a C-section). Besides Pitocin, amniotomy is a useful tool in the mix of remedies. Second, if there's any doubt about your baby's status, amniotomy is very useful. A nonreassuring heart rate can be directly monitored with a scalp electrode, only possible with direct access to your baby's scalp. Examination of the amniotic fluid at amniotomy can be diagnostic of fetal distress (meconium). Bloody amniotic fluid could be the first warning about placental abruption. Foul-smelling fluid will indicate infection. Amniotomy isn't just a pop and a splash, but a true diagnostic tool when indicated.

I'd like to avoid a scalp electrode. The scalp electrode is a very flimsy attachment of a very shallow corkscrew metal, the depth of which won't go any further than the needle you use on the dead skin around a splinter in your finger. Like anything in medicine, if used properly, it really poses no danger to your baby. But if you're upset about the little pinch it causes, you're going to be even more upset if you were to need an unnecessary C-section. The noninvasive ultrasound monitor on your abdomen that records the fetal heart rate also picks up bowel sounds, fetal movements, and even the sudden abdominal crunches that accompany coughs and sneezes. Do you really want your doctor to make a decision about a C-section for fetal distress based on a recording that includes bowel sounds?

The scalp electrode tells no lies. What you see is what you have. It is an actual EKG of your baby's heart. In fact, this was even one of my questions on my oral board exam. I was given a hypothetical situation in which there was a nonreassuring heart rate recording on a fetal monitor.

"What's the first thing you do?" asked my inquisitor. I wondered, should I prepare for immediate emergency C-section? Should I tighten all sphinters and say a "Hail Mary"?

"I perform an amniotomy and apply an internal scalp electrode," I answered. He looked at me with a poker face for the longest time.

"Next question," he announced, with no indication as to whether my answer was right or wrong. It was right. Oral boards—ya gotta love 'em, right?

I don't want to be strapped down to a monitor the whole time. I'd like to be able to walk around. This type of thinking is crucial to the success of Lamaze or the Bradley method. All of those wires and tubes are the encumbrances that are so symbolic of a distortion of the natural process of labor and delivery. But all of this stuff isn't just a collection of balls and chains used for the tortures of dungeon pregnabondage. They are useful devices that represent the advances in obstetrics over the generations. Since labor and delivery is a natural process, not everyone will benefit from them. But the ones who will, really will. The nice thing about delivering in a hospital or a properly accredited birthing center is that you can have the natural freedom to roam, but if bad situations arise, you can take advantage of all of those tubes and wires.

The minimum monitoring necessary by standards of the American College of Obstetricians and Gynecologists is determination of a reassuring fetal heart rate by stethoscope or monitor at least every five minutes, or more frequently if indicated. Internal monitoring with a scalp electrode is indicated if there are any questions about the well-being of your baby.

Can I skip the IV? Pregnancy is a condition where you can be completely normal one moment and have a bleeding emergency the next. Although this is unlikely, the IV can be lifesaving, allowing your doctor to administer drugs, fluids, and, if needed, emergency transfusion. If you're afraid you might get some medicine through the IV, a compromise is a heparin lock, the IV tubing that remains in your vein but is capped, ready to use in an emergency. (Not having at least a heparin lock is dangerous. It's not easy to try to find a vein for an IV when someone is undergoing cardiovascular collapse. Been there, done that, hated it.) Short of using an IV for mere hydration if needed, the rest of your labor can proceed naturally with a heparin lock. It is not attached to any other tubing, so you're not flitting any tubes about every time you move your arms. You can walk about without that flagpole they hang the bags on.

I'd like to avoid a C-section unless it's absolutely necessary. Wouldn't we all? Think about what you're saying here. Of course you shouldn't have a C-section unless it's necessary. Absolutely. A good deal of the literature your doctor reads deals with ways to avoid C-section and when they need to be done. Also, there's a thing called peer review. If your doctor is doing unnecessary C-sections, she will soon be called before a disciplinary committee at her hospital to explain her actions.

The indications for C-section are:

- Fetal distress in which a C-section would be a more timely delivery than a vaginal delivery.
- Vaginal bleeding that is a danger to you or your baby, as in placental abruption.
- Failure to progress in labor, such that successful delivery probably won't occur, presenting a danger to an unborn baby. There are criteria for a failure to progress as well.
- Malpresentation of your baby, as in breech or transverse lie, risking severe trauma to your baby should vaginal delivery be attempted or forced.

- Infection, in which C-section would be more timely than awaiting a vaginal delivery. Of course, operating through an infection poses slightly more risk to the mother, so the timeliness of both types of delivery should be weighed along with the severity of the consequences for each scenario.
- Previous C-section, if you were to refuse VBAC (Vaginal Birth After Cesarean), which is your right.
- Maternal Choice C-section, which is also your right as a woman. (See Chapter 22.) This should not be considered an unnecessary C-section.

Who can I have in my room? Family? My children? A doula? Another birthing assistant? And what if it's a C-section? This is an illustration of how there need not be a conflict between a natural approach to childbirth and modern obstetrics. Having a birthing assistant (midwife, doula, or others) should be very helpful as long as the obstetrical decisions (interventions) are called by the obstetrician according to a birthing understanding. No obstetrician should have a problem with a birthing assistant that helps you through your labor. But there would be a big problem if there were an argument between your doctor and birthing assistant, either overtly or via mind games. By this time you trust your doctor. So should your birthing assistant. This understanding should be crystal clear before going to the hospital. A smart birthing assistant will take a back seat in the medical decision making. She can still be very helpful no matter how the delivery goes.

What about others? Family? It's common—even recommended—for the father to be there for you, of course. Often your mother may find herself there, either by your request or her meddling. Keep in mind that this is a very personal thing between your husband and you. Having a child is your love brought to fruition. Cheerleaders, your posse, and persons who might pass out may take away from this moment. Evaluate this life experience before you go into it, set the rules for visitors, and both of you stick to it. If you're afraid to hurt someone's feelings, ask your doctor to be the bad guy in asking that they leave. Better yet, ask the nurse. They love all of that authority stuff.

Fast Forward
Children in the delivery room are a really bad idea.

I think having children in the delivery room is a bad idea. I'm not talking about your twenty-two-year-old daughter who has already had a baby herself. I'm talking about your eight- or ten-year-old. The stick figures she may see in the pages of her health book are nothing like the graphic true-life brouhaha she would witness here. The forces of labor and delivery are such that even I'm amazed at how it transpires successfully, much less a wide-eyed, astounded little girl. It's not that she couldn't handle getting grossed out, but this should not be your young daughter's first hands-on introduction to sex, in this case the end result. Seeing this process could be very damaging to how she perceives sex and intimacy in the future. Sexual abuse, for instance, rewires a child's brain forever, with the amount of psychological damage far out of proportion to the physical harm done. Ask anyone who was abused as a child. Seeing childbirth isn't sexual abuse, but you are stirring the gumbo before it's ready. Additionally, even with the best of breathing techniques, there will be the grimaces, huffing and puffing, and generally visible unpleasantness on the face of someone she loves and will worry over. A mix of fear and polluting her sexual being with such a distortion of the anatomy right in front of her may not be good for her. And that's if everything goes well.

Can my husband cut the cord or assist in the delivery? When comedian Bobcat Goldthwait was asked if he wanted to cut the cord during his wife's delivery, he asked, "Isn't there someone here more qualified?"

In my opinion anything that doesn't interfere with your health or your baby's health should be your decision. The cord's job is over. If your husband wants to whack the cord, great. I've even had an American Indian cut a segment of the cord and pray over it in a corner of the room. None of this will impact your safety or your baby's health. If this sole criterion is met, then you should be able to do anything you want. Assisting in delivery is another matter. I myself would have no problem with your husband gowning up and gloving so that he can put his hands over mine to feel my pulling on your baby to assist delivery. The problem, however, would rest with the hospital. This would pose a legal liability—although I trust how much pulling is going on, I'm the one doing it. But in such a situation the hospital is responsible for allowing Dad and me to be practicing medicine together, so unfortunately this can't be done. Dad can cut the cord, you can breast-feed immediately—leave the rest of the thrills for raising your baby. That's the important part.

Can we take video or pictures? This wouldn't bother me, but some hospitals have a policy against video in that it's a medium too prone to misinterpretation should something go wrong. Again, they have a responsibility to avoid unnecessary legal liability. Take for instance a friend of mine, an excellent obstetrician who attended a delivery that was going well. The atmosphere was jovial and celebratory, and both parents looked forward to every ensuing minute. The infant went on to have an infection in the nursery, became very ill, but eventually did well. The parents sued the doctor, and their lawyer spent no less than twenty minutes in the deposition grilling the doctor on how he wasn't taking the delivery seriously, based on the light banter on the videotape. In medicine, when things go well, they go great; when they go badly, they can go very badly. The retrospectroscope in the hands of a lawyer can add more blame than is justified, as in the case of my friend. He felt he was being sued for having a personality. Ironically, this is probably what attracted this patient to him in the first place.

In any event, video doesn't interfere with your health or your baby's health, so it's OK with me. But the hospital may have its own rules, so if this is important to you, ask the nurses during your prenatal visit there. Also there may be an anesthesiologist involved who has veto power over video. These things should be settled beforehand. Still pictures are probably fine with everyone.

There's yet another consideration. Is the graphic video of your delivery going to be something you're going to watch over and over? Are you going to show your in-laws and neighbors? In today's world where video cameras are almost disposable, it's tempting to record your life in every detail, from the entire wedding ceremony that no one will want to watch in its entirety to every dance recital in the years to come. The expecting couple has a tendency to dissociate themselves from the delivery, as if the blood and mucus and swelling of your labia are not really you. "That's some other person and not li'l ol' me." And sure enough, you'll probably be restored close to normal again by the time anyone sees the video. But it really is you. And it's your external genitalia flapping around for all to see. And it's personal. All of this suddenly will dawn on you as the tape begins for your trampy niece's deadbeat boyfriend to guffaw over. What I recommend, if there's video, is to tape the goings on of faces only, strategic shots of the newborn that miss the NC-17 poses, and following the baby to the nurse's evaluation and back to you thereafter. If you want a memory, this is the one you want—not one Sam Peckinpah would shoot.

Can I breast-feed immediately? May the baby stay with me and not be whisked away? Once again, as long as it doesn't interfere with your baby's health, this should be the preference. In fact, breast-feeding immediately after delivery is a good thing, triggering the reflex that helps contract your uterus, decreasing the bleeding that accompanies the immediate postpartum period. Also, your baby's been through a rough time, being shoved out of her little 98.6-degree puddle into the blinding light and 72-degree world. Suckling is the tenderness that more than makes up for that. If you took that portion of your baby's brain that was responsible for accepting the stimulation around her mouth and face, you would find that she dedicates a largely disproportionate amount of brain to it as compared to the rest of her body. Feed her mind by allowing her to feed on you. There's nothing more beautiful and unifying. Let Dad take the pictures—you two have much more important things to do.

But what if immediate breast-feeding were to interfere with your baby's well-being? I'm talking about distress at the hands of a low blood sugar level or poor ability to tolerate the sudden change in temperature from the 98.6 to room temperature. Sometimes a baby can crash, which is completely reversible and harmless if the cause is recognized and addressed. But a baby that is sputtering needs to be stabilized before occluding the mouth and nose with your breast. This is just common sense. Generally, if the delivery nurse knows you want to breast-feed right away, she will make that happen unless there really is a problem.

Will you tell me what medicines I'm getting before I get them? Of course. Unless there's an emergency that prevents a civilized discussion of what's going on, you should have a relationship with your doctor in which explanations are part of the process of giving any medicines.

And then there's my question for my patient: *If a true emergency arises, do you trust me to do anything—I mean anything—to save your life or your baby's well-being?* The Right Answer: Of course.

Then we have a deal!

Induction

So, What About Induction?

To hear some talk about it, induction is a dirty word. In truth, there really is no greater meddling into a natural process than induction, but you don't have to wash your mouth out with Betadine just yet. Induction is a legitimate procedure that is important when indicated, as it is in the following circumstances.

Postdates

If you're at forty-two weeks (two weeks past your due date), your baby will keep trying to grow but the placenta is dying. At some point the nutrients and oxygen for your baby are going to fall short. This will make for a more hazardous spontaneous labor and an increased risk of fetal distress, and such melodramas result in emergency C-sections.

Diabetes

Diabetic babies get very big and suffer fetal distress more readily. Once again, induction will allow a labor under controlled circumstances and under an eye watchful for distress. Also, the smaller your baby is, the less likely you'll need a C-section. Induction may allow you a vaginal delivery as contrasted to the C-section you may have needed a week later while waiting for spontaneous labor. The majority of women, in spite of this increased risk, do just fine, delivering vaginally with no problems at all. But if you're a self-admitted big coward (and there's nothing wrong with that), you may want to take your doctor up on the offer. And if you're a li'l bitty thing and your husband's a big galoot, likewise.

Pregnancy Complications
There are complications in pregnancy in which your baby is better being outside than inside.

Rupture of Membranes
This is what's commonly referred to as "your water bag popping." If fluid can leak out, bacteria can invade, causing infection. And infection isn't limited to bacteria. Genital herpes, if you have an active lesion, can put your baby at risk with ruptured membranes.

Need to Change Incubator
You are your baby's incubator. There are some maternal problems that won't get better until you deliver (kidney problems, gallbladder disease, etc.). If your baby is mature (thirty-seven weeks or beyond) and the incubator gets sick, it might be time to change incubators.

False Labor Torture
"TBP" means tired of being pregnant. Although that's a flippant medical slang, there are difficult situations in which painful contractions can be unrelenting for weeks, but with not enough of a cervical change to call it labor. This can cause confusion as to when to go to the hospital. Every woman has her breaking point, and an elective induction may prove more healthy for your psychiatric health than risky for you or your baby.

When You Shouldn't Have an Induction
- Electively before thirty-nine weeks
- Electively after thirty-nine weeks if you don't want it
- If your baby's tolerance to labor is compromised (abnormal nonstress test or stress test)
- If there's any reason to avoid a vaginal delivery (breech or other abnormal lie, placenta previa, etc.)

With a history of a previous C-section, vaginal birth after cesarean (VBAC) has a higher complication rate when induced, so special care must be taken in considering it. A previous classical C-section (midline uterine incision) or low vertical incision (same, but on the lower uterine segment) is an absolute contraindication for induction, however. These are the types of incisions on your uterus that can separate during labor, risking your baby's life and even yours.

Criteria for Induction

If you're going to have your baby via elective induction, there are certain criteria that need to be met. First of all, the success of an induction relies on two things—the inducibility of the cervix and the efficiency of the labor.

The cervix has to be inducible—it's got to be *gimme*. We use something called a Bishop's score to determine the readiness of a cervix to yield to the forces of induction. This is a numerical score that adds up factors such as dilation, thinning, whether the cervix is lined up with the birth canal (anterior), and where your baby's head is positioned. The higher the score, the more likely the success of a planned induction. The lower the score, the more likely an induction will fail, leading to a C-section. How urgent it is that your baby be delivered can overcome the objections of even a low Bishop's score, so if there's a medical need for delivery, it would be nice to have a good score, but you may need to start your engines regardless.

Pros and Cons of Elective Induction

We're not talking about an induction that's medically necessary here, but one purely for convenience, assuming you're thirty-nine weeks or beyond and you have a favorable Bishop's score and no reason to forbid a vaginal delivery.

Convenience

Many women's lives will be so much more uncomplicated if they can slip a delivery between school semesters or during leave time. Other women have the same time constraints on family coming to town to help out. Others may want to finish their pregnancies so they can hold their babies and love them. None of these considerations are frivolous if you have no philosophical objections to induction. You might not get flowers from the Bradley folks after, but you're an adult capable of making intelligent decisions.

Comfort
If you're four foot eleven inches tall and have an eight-pound baby, you're not going to be breathing very well near the end. This is just one example. Painful varicose veins, unremitting false labor, and stomach upset are others.

Safety for Your Baby
One of the most stressful times for your baby is during labor. If your baby is in a borderline condition, this may be just the extra amount of challenge to send her into fetal distress. What better place to have such a thing happen than in a hospital under controlled circumstances.

Increased Risk of C-section
Sometimes an induced labor never quite picks up the steam that a thundering spontaneous labor will, and at the end of a long day you can find yourself with a choice of going home undelivered or throwing up your hands and giving in to the C-section. You shouldn't accept an elective induction unless you're willing to be a good sport—you could end up with a C-section.

Excommunication from the Church of Natural Processes
So much for that beautiful experience the childbirth instructors preach. Spontaneous onset of labor is one of the hallmarks to these delivering philosophies. But let's think about this. Do you really need to junk everything you've learned in your Lamaze or Bradley prenatal classes? Induction, done correctly, shouldn't exceed the normal physiologic levels of what a spontaneous labor should be. If that's the case, why couldn't you still employ your breathing techniques and make use of your husband and birthing assistance?

Many doctors, once your own labor mechanism has kicked in, turn down the induction drips, often discontinuing them altogether. This can still be natural childbirth, but with a jump-start.

The Home Stretch

The last few weeks of your pregnancy will be your doctor's opportunity to gauge how quickly you're approaching impending delivery. This is done by checking your cervix during a vaginal exam. During this time he will evaluate you as to whether it might be prudent to offer an induction if there are problems with the pregnancy. If you've had the perfect Barbie and Ken pregnancy, you're fine to go your merry way until labor develops, you pop your baby out, and you and your husband live happily ever after. But if you're like everyone else, the pros and cons of induction will be discussed with you. Also, a technique called "stripping the membranes" will be offered to you. Your doctor will discuss what will be done past your due date if you're still undelivered. Your weekly visits may change to twice weekly.

Stripping the Membranes

All of those cervical checks help ripen the cervix. There are biochemicals in the cervix and associated with the membranes that are factors in the initiation of labor. One technique used in the course of a regular exam is called "stripping the membranes."

Labor is a very complicated cooperation of many factors—fetal, maternal, hormonal, and mechanical. One thing alone won't necessarily push you into labor, including stripping the membranes. This is a pelvic exam in which your doctor will feel around just inside your cervix where the membranes ("water bag") are attached to its rim. By running an examining finger around the inside of your cervix, he can separate the amniotic sac from where it's stuck there, which theoretically allows the bridging molecules that stick the membranes to the inside rim of the cervix to break—all at a molecular level, mind you—and so be released and then converted into prostaglandins, which are powerful stimulants of labor.

You would think that one time and Wham-Bam-Labor, Ma'am! But it doesn't actually work that faithfully. Usually it'll help irritate things just a bit so that an induction will "take" better. Repeated strippings may be performed before spontaneous labor develops, but then no one knows whether this is a coincidence or the result of finally enough stripping. My books say you can expect labor within three days after stripping, but I've found this very inconsistent.

Once frowned upon, today stripping is done frequently at or near term so that spontaneous labor can be conjured up before your baby gets bigger than need be. Your baby will grow by half a pound or more a week in the last month, so the difference between a thirty-nine–week baby and a forty-two–week baby may involve up to 1½ to 2 pounds more of a baby for your pelvis to negotiate during labor. Vaginal Birth After Cesarean (VBAC) candidates may agree to the rationale for stripping membranes, considering it less meddling than the C-section it is meant to prevent. Yes, it's meddling. But so are antibiotics, ventilators, IVs, or anything else we've come up with since the witch doctor days. It's a practical decision made by your doctor that is part of the individualization of your care.

Does stripping the membranes violate the Bradley Method or Lamaze ideology? Well, it's certainly unnatural. But if it allows spontaneous labor to ensue in which you can then employ these methods, is that really cheating? Just call yourself a follower of the Bradley Method, *Reformed*.

Normal Cervical Changes Near Term Prior to Delivery

If this is your first baby, your cervix will thin out before it dilates. If you've had several babies, your cervix will dilate before it thins out, remaining slightly thick. There are also varying degrees of mingling of these properties. I've found that thinning of the cervix and its lining up in the same axis of exit along the birth canal gives me the best predictor of impending labor or who might more than likely successfully undergo induction.

Q & A—the Third Trimester

"Front" Pain

Question: I am in my thirty-second week and getting sharp pains directly behind my pubic bone that are constant and accompanied by a lot of pressure, but no back pain. Is this labor? I can't stand up without experiencing this pain.

> **Fast Forward**
> Causes of lower, midline pain near your pubic bone are bladder infections or separation of the pubic bones (*pubis diastasis*). Pubis diastasis is harmless but can be incapacitating.

Answer: Again, from the "Terminal Trials of Pregnancy" Department, this particular pain sounds like what's called *symphysis pubis diastasis*. Translated, this means that the joint between the two central pubic bones is opening a little. Two hormones, progesterone and relaxin, rise in pregnancy to relax this joint as well as other joints. (Progesterone relaxes the bowels too, causing the famous constipation of pregnancy.) This opening up of the pelvic ring results in a larger circumference for the baby to pass through. The pelvis is a ring structure, and if you open a ring in front, it's going to have to crimp in the back. Don't be surprised if the payback crimping in you is a pain at the sacroiliac joints on either side of your lower middle back. Sometimes you just don't know whether you're getting clobbered coming or going.

Diastasis can occasionally be very severe. I had a patient once who even needed traction! But the pain is almost always harmless to you, and certainly harmless to the baby. Physical therapists can work wonders while we obstetricians tell you with a wink that the cure for this is delivery—but you're not laughing. Insurance should pay for a visit to the physical therapist, so ask your OB to write a prescription for it.

Urinary tract infections can be pretty sneaky in pregnancy, so any midline pain should invite a urinalysis or urine culture. An exam of your cervix to check for premature dilatation, although unlikely, can be prudent as well.

Leg Cramps and Leg Pain

Question: I have leg cramps, especially at night. My doctor has increased my calcium intake, but this hasn't helped. Are these cramps dangerous?

Answer: Thrombophlebitis and blood clots in your legs can be life threatening, so report all leg pain to your doctor. However, mere leg cramps are a famous "trial of pregnancy" and they are distinctly different from thrombophlebitis. They range anywhere from a fleeting muscular pulling all the way to hopping around in agony like a big idiot (been there, done that—I feel your pain).

Pregnancy Rules for Husbands

Rule #6: This isn't funny. Don't laugh when you see your wife dancing around the bedroom at three in the morning.

There are many factors that can contribute to the increased tendency toward leg cramps in pregnancy, and there is no agreement among doctors as to which factors are the more important causes. Among them are:

• Pressure of the baby's head on the nerves of the pelvis can fire off the leg muscles.

- Alterations in calcium and magnesium, not only because of the altered physiology of pregnancy, but also because of alterations in circulation due to swelling and changes in blood volume.
- Increased exertion on muscles due to changes in weight and center of gravity later in pregnancy. In other words, your leg muscles do just fine when nonpregnant, but prove to be out of shape with the increased physical demands of pregnancy.

Fast Forward

Leg cramps are harmless.

Inflammation/infection of the deep leg veins of your calves, called thrombophlebitis, is an obstetrical emergency requiring hospitalization because of the risk of blood clots that can travel to your lungs.

Leg cramps are very common. Thrombophlebitis, however, is very uncommon. Because of its seriousness, however, any leg pain should be reported to your doctor.

Remedies for leg cramps have been dismal failures. Massaging the cramps is the most immediate remedy, but that can be like chasing your own tail. Taking extra calcium in supplements sounds like a good idea, but this is probably voodoo. In my practice these remedies have fallen short of any meaningful relief. What I have seen work the best is continued exercise to keep the leg muscles in shape, but this assumes good exercise and toned muscles before pregnancy too. The good news is that the phenomenon is harmless in spite of the severity. Now you know everything I know about leg cramps in pregnancy, which is pretty sad. But here's the most important thing: report all leg pain to your doctor because leg pain may be something more serious if it's not just common cramps.

Thrombophlebitis (the biggie that you need to call your doctor about). Leg cramps may be harmless, but it is crucial to differentiate this pain from the pain of thrombophlebitis, which is an inflammation of the deep veins of the legs—usually the calves. Thrombophlebitis is an emergency and a very big deal because deep leg veins so inflamed can develop blood clots that can fling off toward your lungs and suddenly endanger your life. Now before there is a flood of hysteria about leg cramps possibly being thrombophlebitis, please know that there is a simple method of distinguishing between the two. With sporadic leg cramps, the legs should not hurt when there is not a cramp. Squeezing the calf muscles shouldn't be painful in between these episodes. But causing pain by squeezing the calf muscles at any time would be very disturbing. The treatment for thrombophlebitis involves anticoagulants (blood thinners), which are medicines that decrease the blood's ability to clot. The management of the doses of the anticoagulants can be quite tricky, so it is necessary to hospitalize such patients for a while.

On the one hand we have leg cramps, which are an inconvenience at worst; on the other we have thrombophlebitis, which is extremely dangerous if not diagnosed and treated. If a simple squeeze of the calf muscles leaves any doubt, ultrasound can look at the deep leg veins to see if there are any clots.

Varicose veins are *not* dangerous, and they are *not* thrombophlebitis. Varicose veins are a problem with gravity and the weight of the baby on the drainage of superficial veins back up toward the heart. Varicose veins are mere engorgements of these structures and have nothing to do with clots in the deep veins of the legs. Although they can hurt, they aren't the danger that the deep blood clots are. Because they are a result of partial obstruction of their drainage, wearing those nasty grandma stockings can help keep them compressed. There are specialty girdles that are sold that can help all the way up to the vagina if you were to suffer from varicose veins in the vaginal labia.

Lactation Before Delivery

Question: It's still a month before my due date and I've started dripping milk from my nipples. Is this weird? Does this mean the baby's coming?

Answer: No, it's quite normal. It does not portend imminent labor. Ignore it if you can. (Easier said than done.)

Induction Versus Labor at Thirty-Seven Weeks

Question: I'm thirty-seven weeks and my doctor says my cervix is ripe. He said he would not stop my labor if it came on its own, but he won't induce me. What's the difference? Why is he afraid to induce me but isn't afraid for me to have a baby now with regular labor? It's the same baby.

Answer: It may be the same baby, but it's not the same process. Induction, as any good Lamaze aficionado will tell you, is meddling. There exists a double standard of when it's acceptable to allow delivery and it is this: thirty-six to thirty-seven weeks for spontaneous labor; thirty-nine weeks or more for elective induction.

Since labor is a result of numerous actions and reactions within your body, its spontaneous onset is respected at the point there is likely lung maturity. But since lung maturity is spread out over a bell curve, this means that some babies may not have mature lungs until even thirty-nine weeks. Spontaneous labor is forgivable since lung maturity itself possibly plays a role in stimulating it. Elective induction before thirty-nine weeks, on the other hand, ignores the variability of the timing of lung maturity and can result in a baby needing breathing support. For this reason the legitimacy of induction is established at a point so far to the friendly side of the bell curve as to minimize the possibility of respiratory distress—and that point is thirty-nine weeks.

If you were to go into labor at thirty-seven weeks and your baby were to need a little oxygen, at least it was a natural process that led to this; induction at thirty-seven weeks that were to lead to your baby needing respiratory support would be blameworthy after the fact and regretted by both you and your doctor. I don't need to tell you how your lawyer would feel about the whole thing.

Indicated induction, however, doesn't follow the thirty-nine–week mandate since there is a medical problem that may endanger you or your baby (or both).

Mucus Plug

Question: After today's thirty-nine-week appointment, I lost my mucus plug. Should I call my doctor?

Answer: No. Your cervix is a mucus-producing structure, plugged by the glob of mucus it has produced. This is a barrier of sorts, but it becomes less important at the end of pregnancy because of its tendency to fall out with vaginal exams or even spontaneously with the natural thinning and dilation of your cervix. A vaginal exam can dislodge it; normal changes of the cervix will

Fast Forward
The mucus plug is not important. If it falls out, it's not important. F'geddabout it!

loosen it. Don't worry; you'll make a new plug. If it fell out all by itself, delivery isn't imminent. All it means is that there have been the normal changes of your cervix.

This shouldn't be confused with leaking of amniotic fluid, which will be watery as opposed to the gelatinous nature of your mucus plug. Leakage of fluid should be reported immediately. If you don't know the difference, call to be safe.

Look for other current questions and updates regarding the third trimester on BabyZone.com, by going to babyzone.com/features/expertsqa.

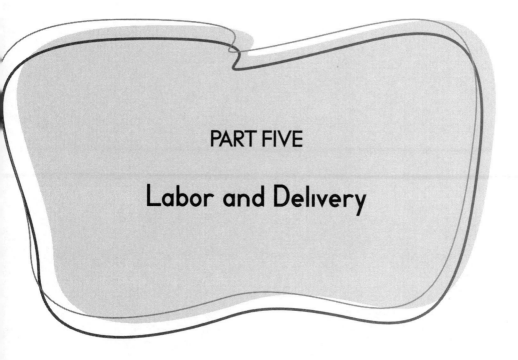

PART FIVE

Labor and Delivery

Labor

Causes of Labor

What causes labor? For the answer to this question, we're still at the mercy of Dr. Hellifino. When a woman goes into labor, a baby is pushed away from her and toward the outside world. Lucky for everyone there is an opening at one end of her womb to allow the baby exit toward those who await him.

Of course, you're not unreasonable in wanting to know just who the hell thought up this little arrangement. In that silly argument over whether God is a man or a woman . . . well . . . let's not go there.

Resentment aside, you have some things going for you. First of all, your uterus, normally a little pear of an organ you wouldn't even notice except for those sincere monthly reminders, has an amazing capacity to expand and, just as amazing, the ability to push someone out of you once he has worn out his welcome. The pushing is done with muscular contractions against your cervix, which yields by opening. That's what happens in labor. Why it happens probably depends on many things. Currently there are two main theories to explain why labor happens and why it happens when it does.

Pregnancy Retreat

In this theory, pregnancy is maintained by endocrine (glandular) and biochemical processes. After a signal, either from your baby or by a consortium of effects within you—or by both—whatever processes that were in place to maintain the pregnancy no longer do such a good job, and it's time to pack the bags as your body decides it's time to retreat from pregnancy.

> **Fast Forward**
> We still don't know what causes labor.

Uretonin Theory

This theory implies that your uterus becomes more sensitive to the things that make it contract as chemicals called uretonins (hormones that effect your uterus) increase in number.

Both of these trends in labor explanations are open-minded about a fetal signal of some sort. There's a lot of biochemistry going on—in you, in your baby, and between the two of you. The science is always growing, any detailed description taking up whole books. Suffice it to say, your thyroid, pituitary, hypothalamus, and adrenal glands probably play a role; your baby's lungs, adrenals, and brain probably do too. That liaison, the placenta, may also control the timing. There may be many factors collaborating to initiate labor, but the interesting thing is that not all of them need play a part, some of them just enough to begin the process until the others catch up. As far as knowing exactly what causes labor in the way of an official flow sheet, we're still tap dancing on stage waiting for the next act to show up.

And Baby Makes . . . a Lot

The initiation of labor is complex, but you shouldn't forget that final reminder, the size of your baby. There is no doubt that your uterus contracts. You've been experiencing Braxton-Hicks contractions (see page 205) and false labor enough to serve as the poster child for abstinence in a sex-education class. But as you approach the real thing—real labor—your uterus becomes more sensitive to stimuli. One of those stimuli is the sheer bulk of what your uterus is carrying. This is an instance in medicine where I can truthfully say that size does matter.

Your uterus is a reluctant host. It would rather just mind its own business, longing for the day you go into menopause. Fortunately, your uterus is not the boss of you, although you may have argued that point during some past periods from Hell that you find hard to forget. The rest of your body has plans for your uterus from time to time (from pregnancy to pregnancy), and your uterus only begrudgingly obliges. It doesn't like to be occupied by anything, be it menstrual tissue with the cramps that work to expel it, an IUD (the two happiest days in your contraceptive life are the day you get it in and the day you get it out), or a baby. Trespassers are always prosecuted, and in the case of pregnancy that involves expulsion via labor. At some point.

But your uterus is accommodating for a while. Sooner or later, in spite of any biochemical signals or lack of them, your uterus will be stretched enough to want to contract against your baby to push him out. After all, your baby is a *foreign body*, thanks to Dad's DNA contribution. The mechanical reality is that your uterus has a breaking point. This is one reason a woman with twins has such an increased tendency toward premature labor—her uterus thinks her twenty-eight–week twins are a term single baby. In the Uretonin Theory of labor, alteration in the size of the uterus may play a role in making it more sensitive.

The biochemistry of your pregnancy changes when your baby is mature. Taking all of the above into account, it's tempting to think that your pregnancy has its own mysterious clock, as if your baby knows when it's time to come out. This fatalism doesn't always hold up in the case of prematurity, but at term we have the luxury of giving in to such sentimentality. Since the majority of the human race delivers babies around the same gestational time, the clock makes a good metaphor. The timing of how long we need in our mothers is set like a mainspring in our DNA.

How to Tell Real Labor

If the irritability of your uterus were the sole factor of when you were to go into labor, there would be a smooth continuum, the muscle fibers of your uterus contracting with increasing intensity. The forces would begin humbly with the cramping of the first trimester that represents growing pains, gain strength as the disorganized contractions called Braxton-Hicks, then organize rhythmically into false labor, then channel all of the vector forces against your cervix until a consummate intersection of force and timing of the contractions developed into latent labor, progressing into real labor. Such a crescendo would make for one miserable pregnancy.

Thankfully, the cramps of growing pains back off once your uterus is big enough to become an abdominal organ; the Braxton-Hicks contractions are sissy contractions—a mere bother; and false labor may come, but it also goes away. And believe it or not, there are many women who feel no contractions until active labor presents itself as suddenly as switching on a light. Most women fall between the light bulb and the crescendo with varying degrees of uterine activity that are sometimes so subtly different as to be very confusing. Read on.

Fast Forward

The continuum of uterine irritability that leads to real labor and subsequent delivery:

Growing pains—cramps that are a reaction to something (someone!) in your uterus. Usually an early pregnancy symptom, they ease up after twelve weeks when your uterus pops up out of the pelvis to become an abdominal organ.

Braxton-Hicks contractions—sissy contractions

- Irregular
- Nonrhythmical
- Painless

False labor—enough to make you miserable

- Irregular
- Not rhythmic
- Doesn't get stronger over time
- Pain usually in lower abdomen
- Can be sedated away, using such agents as Seconal, Demerol, Brethine, etc.
- *No change in cervix!*

True Labor ("Wait a minute! I didn't bargain for this!")

- Regular pattern
- Intervals between contractions get shorter
- Intensity gets stronger over time
- Pain over entire abdomen and even back
- Cannot be sedated away
- *Changes in the cervix including dilation (opening), effacement (thinning), and position (moving anterior—in line with birth canal)*

Growing Pains

These are a first trimester problem, so forget them till next pregnancy.

Braxton-Hicks Contractions

These are described academically as tightenings of your uterus that are not uncomfortable and that do not cause a change in the cervix. *Williams Obstetrics*, the Bible of my field (published by McGraw-Hill, parent company to my own publisher, I'm proud to say), describes them as "irregular, nonrhythmical, and painless." The typical sufferer of Braxton-Hicks contractions will say, "Every once in a while, I will have a tightening in my abdomen, which, if you touch my abdomen, you can feel hardening with your hand. Sometimes it is only on one side or just down low; sometimes it is my whole abdomen."

Generally Braxton-Hicks contractions are seen after twenty weeks, but there can be a little play in this range, so feeling them as early as nineteen weeks is quite possible. Since the uterus is muscular, it probably contracts during the entire pregnancy, as soon as the baby grows enough to enlarge it, but these contractions are imperceptible.

Braxton-Hicks contractions are great for sympathy. They can be felt by others besides yourself—like your doting husband at the mall. I recommend stopping dead in your tracks, assuming that Lady of Fatima expression on your face, and placing your husband's hand on your belly. Sure it's horribly painful, you assure him, but you'll maintain that stiff upper lip because that's just the type of woman you are, deserving of any expenditure at the Donna Karan store in front of you. Buy anything. He won't have a clue it could never fit you now. Those returned items can build quite a store credit for those thinner times after your pregnancy.

False Labor

False labor is a prelude to true labor, so it is uncomfortable. These contractions usually occur in the last couple weeks of pregnancy and can be quite

---

Pregnancy Rules for Husbands

Rule # 7: Always, always acknowledge the pain and suffering your wife must be going through when she has you feel her contractions. And look around you—surely there must be something you can buy nearby to mercifully distract her from her suffering.

painful. Have all of your mall trickery done by then. But the diagnosis of real labor isn't made unless there's a change in your cervix, as determined by a vaginal exam.

True Labor

True labor, on the other hand, involves a regular pattern, with the space between the contractions getting shorter and the intensity getting stronger over time. The pain is over the entire abdomen and can involve severe back discomfort. The definitive property of real labor is that it will effect a change in your cervix, beginning the process that will result in delivery of your baby. The change from Braxton-Hicks to false labor to true labor represents a sporadic continuum, with more and more biochemistry playing a part in the approach to the real thing. Probably the mere mechanical irritation of an expanding pregnancy plays the most part with Braxton-Hicks, but the full maternal-fetal-biochemical process stimulates the contraction mechanisms that lead to real labor. It is the unevenness of these processes that gives you lengthy breaks from an otherwise continuous process.

Latent Phase of Labor—"Ladies, Start Your Engines"

Latent labor is really a part of true labor, which won't noticeably change your cervix but is more difficult to sedate away than false labor. It's the idling of the motor—still going at a couple of thousand RPMs, but before you actually run through the gears. Your uterus sees the yellow light and awaits the green. In the background the tissue that is responsible for the toughness of your cervix is weakening and preparing to yield.

Methods of Induction

There are generally two ways to start an induction of labor. The old standby is to use Pitocin (oxytocin), a chemical identical to what is made in your own pituitary gland for natural labor. The advantage of Pitocin is that it has a very short half-life, and if there are side effects it can be shut off and out of your system within minutes.

Prostaglandin, another substance that takes part in active natural labor, is also being used more frequently. It's given by either vaginal suppository or by mouth, but the problem with these methods is that once absorbed, you're stuck with its effects, good or bad, until it wears off. Currently it is best used to ripen the cervix in those people needing to deliver but in whom the cervix isn't quite ready. Often doctors will ripen the cervix with a prostaglandin suppository, then augment the labor with an IV transition from prostaglandin to Pitocin. Alternately, some use the prostaglandins the whole way.

Lately there has been a protocol in which prostaglandin pills (by mouth) have been used to effect labor. I've seen good results with this, but it is not in common use as of yet.

The types of contractions caused by Pitocin have three qualities—they have rhythm, intensity, and staying power enough to generate a vector force out (pressing baby's head against the cervix). The prostaglandin contractions are shorter, but peak much higher and more suddenly. You can actually see the difference on a monitor. Of course, natural labor is a complex affair, involving the right natural mix of both of these (and probably more!) substances.

Why Don't Contractions Other Than True Labor Change the Cervix?

You would think that even a collection of weak contractions, over time and if there were enough of them, would do something to the cervix. But the cervix is made up of fibrous tissue and some muscular tissue, which provide a resiliency from even frequent bouts of false labor. Also, since the third trimester uterus is shaped like an inverted urn, the muscular waves of contraction need to be rhythmic in themselves, with all of the forces adding up to one net vector force outward toward the cervix. If the vector forces are in disarray, there's nothing more than a shimmying, perhaps hurting as much as a regular contraction, but not pushing out in one direction.

The Nuisance of Other Types of Labor Before the Real Thing

False labor may not happen at all. If you're typical, though, you'll have at least a few runs of contractions for a few hours at a time. Only your own concern will govern whether you'll go to the hospital for evaluation, but false alarms are not to be considered hysterics. As tidy as I've made the different types of labor seem, sometimes the distinctions among them can be a bit blurred. When in doubt, go to the hospital or call your doctor. As an obstetrician I can tell you I'd rather you have a hundred false alarms than have your baby delivered in your car. If you would just take the time to get a mental picture of that, you should have no qualms about running to the hospital. But that's just me. Ask your doctor about her criteria for after-hours. Also, ask if you should call her first or just go to the hospital. Some doctors want to know beforehand that there's action brewing before springing $100 for the kids to see a movie; others would rather the first contact be from a nurse at the hospital so they can be apprised of contractions, blood pressure, fetal heart rate, and so on, instead of your own subjective appraisal of what's going on. Of course, if it's during office hours, call the office first.

Besides the false alarm of false labor, there is also the sometimes very trying latent phase of labor. It can typically last as long as twelve to twenty-four hours, and you won't believe your ears when the nurse tells you there's been no change in your cervix and that you should go home. This is the famous scene where you see women walking the halls of the hospital, under the delusion that this will help convert the contractions to true labor or resolve the latent phase of labor. The results of walking are so mixed that I can't tell any difference between the walkers and the parkers.

One thing that does seem to help is hydration. This is especially true with false labor, and I think it definitely helps with latent phase too. A few glasses of water seem to do more than following all of those colored stripes on the hospital's floors.

Fast Forward

In latent phase of labor, I don't see any difference between those who walk the halls and those who lie in bed. Walking is probably a myth at worst, a distraction at best.

Stages of Real Labor

In 1978 Dr. Emanuel Friedman presented his famous manifesto on labor. His landmark descriptions simplified the way obstetricians assess the potential for success of labor. He described three stages of labor, but it was his revolutionary thinking about the first stage that is still used today.

Stage One: Latent phase and active phase of labor, ending when the cervix is ten centimeters dilated.

Stage Two: That time from ten centimeters dilation until delivery. This is your pushing phase, your last chance for your husband to holler that he "don't know nothin' 'bout birthin' no babies."

Stage Three: From delivery to the expulsion of the placenta.

Other stages:

Stage Four: A medical slang term to mean from delivery of the placenta until the end of the postpartum period (puerperium), usually anywhere from six to twelve weeks.

Stage Five (as described by DiLeo): From the end of stage four until the time your child graduates from college and is out of the house.

Fast Forward

Stage One: Latent phase plus active labor phase until the cervix is ten centimeters dilated

Stage Two: From complete dilation until delivery of your baby

Stage Three: From delivery of your baby until expulsion of the placenta

Stage Four: Thereafter

First Stage of Labor

This is made up of a latent phase continuing on through an active phase, involving the dilation of your cervix up to ten centimeters, the size that your baby's head should be able to pass through. During the active phase, your cervix should dilate at about one to two centimeters an hour, depending on how many babies you've had, how big your baby is, etc. The "Friedman Curve" is the crossing of the lines on a graph, one line going down to represent progressive descent of your baby's head toward the outside world, called station, the other line going up to represent the progressive dilation of the cervix to ten centimeters. Wherever they cross on the page, they each should be changing over time so that they crisscross and don't flatten out, which would mean lack of progress on one of these two measurements.

Station

The whole mechanism of delivering a child, of course, involves the actual exit of the baby through your pelvis. Station is a traditional reference that has developed through generations of obstetricians. It is used to document on the record how far the head of the baby has descended toward delivery. In discussing a laboring situation, nurses and doctors must be able to convey information in a way that can be universally understood.

Station is based on how far down the head has dropped in relation to two bony prominences (called the ischial spines) that mark the midpelvis (halfway out). In a pelvic exam the examiner can feel where these spines protrude from the pelvic sidewalls. Then, the position of the "presenting part," i.e., that part of the baby (hopefully, the top of the head) that will be the first to deliver, is felt as compared to the ischial spines. If the very top of the head is at the ischial spines, it's called a zero station. And for every centimeter distance from the spines, either above or below, the presenting part can be said to be anywhere between −3 and +3.

For instance, −3 is three centimeters above the ischial spines (three centimeters higher up in your pelvis than the spines), and +3 is three centimeters below the ischial spines, and, well, you better call the doctor because that baby's about to deliver! A +3 station shows the baby's scalp on the perineum (at the opening of the vagina).

Besides graphing the progress of cervical dilation, the Friedman Curve also records descent of your baby's head by noting station. With normal labors progressing to delivery, the station starts at the upper left of the graph and over time is marked toward the lower right, while the dilation begins at zero at the lower left and rises to ten over time at the upper right hand corner of the graph. In this way, there should be an X on the graph. Significant distortion of this X will indicate either a problem in the descent of the baby's head or in the dilation, and such graphic aberrations are used to question the likelihood of a successful vaginal delivery.

Usually when the baby "drops" (locks in) during the third trimester of pregnancy, this signifies the attainment of a zero station. This is a good sign for pending delivery. Its quaint term is *lightening*, and you will notice when it happens because it's a lot easier to breathe, but at the expense of your baby pushing a lot more on your bladder.

The Friedman Curve

The implication of Friedman's Curve is enormous because it became possible to recognize abnormal labor patterns bad enough to require a C-section. Before this, obstetricians relied on the rhythm of labor and the intensity of the contractions, which Friedman showed were very inexact in diagnosing an abnormal labor.

But just as Friedman took us out of the dark ages (dark ages being previous to 1978), his famous curve has been overused, resulting in an increase of the C-section rate since that time. For this reason midwives usually condemn the Friedman Curve as a diagnostic tool upon which to base the need for C-section. They say that doctors don't take into account alterations and pauses in the Curve's progress due to the lack of positioning that lying flat in bed prevents. True, some doctors don't, but most really do. The midwives' trick of flipping from side to side to get the Curve going again is common sense to most obstetricians who recognize gravity as an important tool for persuading your baby to seek the most comfortable position—a position that changes as labor progresses, those changes allowing the labor to progress.

▶ Fast Forward

The Friedman Curve is a graphic representation of the progress of both cervical dilation and descent of your baby's head, the two things that are the most important in judging whether a labor is going well or not. Abnormal labors are easy to see when applied to the expected curve.

In normal labors the curve can look screwy for many reasons, so this diagnostic device is just a guideline that must take into account other factors, like epidurals, lack of changing positions in bed, etc.

Not being able to move about is also why midwives condemn epidurals, by the way. But your doctor will readily agree with me that fighting the pain when Lamaze isn't working can hold up descent of your baby—that the good relaxation that comes with an epidural will sometimes bring about the vaginal delivery that flinching and tensing hold off. Each delivery is a unique event, and neither graphs from Friedman nor militant nonintrusion from midwifery fits all.

Obstetrics is easy after a point because when you're in active labor, you're either going to have your baby vaginally or not. Barring the need for C-section because of fetal distress or reasons unrelated to labor, if you're going to need a C-section, sooner or later a faulty labor will become obvious. This wasn't so obvious before the graphic representation of labor by Friedman.

Types of Abnormal Labor

If you keep dilating, you still may not deliver. But if your baby keeps descending, sooner or later you will dilate. This seems strange, but as related as descent of baby and dilation of cervix are, you still can have one without the other. If it's the cervix that is hesitant in dilation, it ultimately will dilate as long as there continues descent of your baby. But with dilation or not, your baby must descend into and through your birth canal. (*Birth canal* is a layman's term usually meant to vaguely encompass your pelvis, cervix, and vagina.)

The most common presentation of abnormal labor, though, is a combination of the two. There will be slowing or stopping of both cervical dilation and descent to some extent. You may stop dilating at eight centimeters, with your baby never having entered your pelvis; you may not have progressed beyond four centimeters, your baby's head wedged in low against your pubic bone. Whatever the presentation, if your cervical dilation and/or descent of your baby haven't resulted in a delivery within about eight hours or so of active labor, something is wrong. Don't worry, your doctor will be ahead of this point of no return by several hours, seeing the subtle warning signals long before you prove him right.

When there is abnormal labor, several things may happen:

1. The labor may revert back to normal just as mysteriously, resulting in a normal vaginal delivery. This is when flipping positions can come in handy. The passage of your baby through your pelvis involves negotiating a few turns here and there, so position and gravity have been known to make the most dysfunctional labor glow in the sweet smell of success.

2. The labor may continue to the complete dilation of the second stage, and assisted vaginal delivery (forceps, vacuum extractor, or pushing on your fundus by an assistant) may accomplish that which was doubtful, saving you a C-section. The baby may be just big enough to make a tight fit, your pelvis just small enough to make the exit cramped, or your uterus just pooped out enough not to be able to muster enough force to close out the match. A certain position of your baby's head, facing straight down or straight up, and sitting on the floor of your vagina, make these assisted deliveries possible. Assisted deliveries involve using a vacuum extractor, which is a suction cup that is applied to your baby's scalp to help pull her out, or forceps, which are safe when used correctly (like anything in medicine). "Fundal pressure" is the non-elegant method of an assistant pushing your abdomen downward so as to push your baby outward. It's crude and many doctors fear it because sometimes such a necessary maneuver to effect delivery may be a warning of impending shoulder dystocia, as described in Chapter 17. I'll have more to share on these methods later.

3. Alternately, there may be no way you can have this baby from below. Here we're talking about a C-section. Depending on your attitude about such things, this may be a legitimate second choice or the worst thing in the world. Keep in mind: it's not how you have the baby, it's how you raise the baby. But by this time, a C-section isn't a philosophical exercise, but a medical necessity, even if it requires you make a leap of faith in your doctor's judgment. Also keep this in mind: your doctor doesn't want a baby with problems—for many reasons. Everyone is on the same side here.

No Labor (What's It Going to Take?)

Now that I've talked about real labor and abnormal labor, what happens when nothing—absolutely nothing—happens. The fact that you're a human being expected to go into labor at some predictable point is not reassuring when you don't. Thirty-seven-week babies will have as much as a five-week head start in the stroller parade. You will feel certain that they are mocking you. At what point will your doctor intervene if your normal labor seems to rest at one extreme of the bell curve? It can be like waiting to role doubles to get out of jail while everyone else is snatching up Boardwalk and Park Place and all the greens. Forty-two weeks is the point of reckoning.

At forty-two weeks, the placenta starts aging, but your baby keeps growing. Your baby's needs may exceed the placenta's ability to deliver the goods, so most doctors want to induce if there hasn't been spontaneous labor by this time. If your cervix isn't ripe for induction during this time, the chances of a vaginal delivery decrease because your baby is even bigger than he was on the "due date."

We now have prostaglandin (like the very powerful chemical your body makes as part of labor) that we can give as a vaginal suppository or as a pill, and that does a very good job of ripening your cervix in such cases. This technique of induction has done much to turn the C-section rate around in the "42+" crowd.

With a ripe cervix a traditional Pitocin drip can be used until your own mechanism takes over. The prostaglandin can also be used, but currently it's favored more for the unripe-cervix postdate pregnancy.

Not Enough Labor (Half-Fast Labor)

Some women make the transition between latent phase and active labor, dilating well until things seem to peter out, a situation called suboptimal or hypotonic labor. We don't know why this happens, but we have what we call augmentation of labor, in which your doctor will hang a Pitocin drip to supplement the action up to a point he feels is effective labor. This can be done with Lamaze or Bradley methods, in that you're only brought up to the point at which labor is considered normal.

Too Much Labor (As If Just Enough Labor Weren't Enough)– Tetanic Contractions

The strength and rate of contractions is unique for each pregnancy. The typical effective labor involves contractions coming from every one to four minutes, and each contraction lasting forty to sixty seconds. When your uterus contracts, there is a temporary decrease of oxygen exchange between your and your baby's circulations. Babies are tough and they can take this for the few hundred times until delivery because of the recovery in between the contractions. But if a contraction were to last an unusually long amount of time—a tetanic (or hypertonic) contraction—your baby's reserve could be compromised, leading to fetal distress. As kids we've all played the game to see how long we can hold our breath. Some babies, it turns out, can go longer

Fast Forward

Signs of abnormal labor:

- Lack of cervical dilation
- Lack of descent of your baby's head
- Suboptimal (hypotonic) labor (Requires augmentation)
- Hypertonic (tetanic) contractions (Mandates discontinuing any contraction-causing agents—induction, augmentation, etc. May lead to fetal distress.)
- Precipitous labor (May indicate infection)
- Postdates (No labor after forty-two weeks)

than others. A tetanic contraction is almost always a temporary event, with your baby recovering completely afterward. It is also usually associated with induction or augmentation, the simple solution being to turn off the Pitocin, which clears from your circulation very quickly.

The difficulty with such tetanic contractions isn't that they happen at all, but why they happen. Like most transient events in labor and delivery, the answer will probably not be found. But one (your doctor) must wonder why your uterus was so sensitive as to respond like that. Could there be other signs of infection of the uterus (amnionitis) that could pose a danger to you and your baby if ignored? Rest assured that your doctor won't ignore signs of amnionitis.

Fast Forward

All C-sections due to failure to progress result from dysfunctional labors, but not all dysfunctional labors result in failure to progress and C-section. There are numerous positional tricks and manipulations of Pitocin that can get a labor back on track.

Precipitous Labor

There are those lightning-fast labors that will blow Friedman out of the water. Two centimeters at ten o'clock and complete by ten after, with delivery by 10:12, fifteen minutes after arriving at the hospital. These are very rare with first babies but tend to happen with women who have had either precipitous

labors or lots of babies before. Amnionitis can cause a labor to be particularly fast.

Except for amnionitis, which is an effect on a particular labor, most other
precipitous labors come with some degree of warning. A simple history of the
obstetrical past can give the clues necessary to offer an induction so that such
a delivery can best be managed under controlled circumstances. Once again,
you're invited to conjure up that mental picture of a delivery in your car.

Labor—What It Means for You in the Real World

All of the above is about as interesting as cataloging birds (with apologies to
pregnant ornithologists everywhere). But what does it mean to you? When is
it time to pack your bags?

As you approach your due date, you can become apprehensive about when
you should go to the hospital to have your baby. The timing of going to the
hospital varies. Certainly a high-risk patient needs to go with any unusual
occurrence. A normal pregnant mother need only go, however, when it
appears labor is for real. How do you tell?

Fast Forward

The best time to go to the hospital is when the contractions satisfy the criteria
for real labor or real concern:
- Rhythmic, coming like clockwork
- Increasing in intensity
- Durations between them get shorter
- When there are warning signals that must be checked out—bleeding,
  leakage of fluid, or decreased fetal movement
Forget about losing your mucus plug. That doesn't mean anything.

Labor is defined by obstetricians as a change in the dilatation and thinning out of the cervix, determined by an exam. There are many false alarms,
especially in first timers, when what seem like real contractions fizzle out when
monitored in the hospital. The truth is that it's hard to tell the real thing without a hospital evaluation.

The onset of labor usually develops gradually. Although the contractions of early labor, also called latent phase of labor, don't do much in the way of dilating the mouth of the womb, they do thin it out and cause the baby's head to descend against it so that active labor will have a yielding target when the real forces begin.

To act as a dilating wedge against the cervix, the infant's head must push against it with a rhythmic force. Not only must the force be sufficient, but the rhythm must be unremitting. A battering ram is a crude yet accurate metaphor. If contractions are irregular, coming first every twelve minutes, then every two, then every sixteen, the rhythm is ineffective. Onset of real labor is more likely with contractions every eight minutes like clockwork, even though this is a longer interval than the two minutes that were part of the disorganized sequence I described first. Therefore, a clockwork rhythm is a better signal for going to the hospital.

Bleeding is never considered normal, except a little spotting after an exam. You should report any bleeding or go to the hospital when it occurs. Luckily, this is a sign of imminent labor, as a dilating cervix sometimes disrupts tiny blood vessels within it. Loss of the mucus plug doesn't count.

Rupture of amniotic membranes (popping of the water bag) is another mandatory reason to check in with your doctor. If fluid can come out, bacteria can get in, and it's only a matter of time before infection can jeopardize you and your baby. Leaking of fluid carries the same importance. Spontaneous active labor usually begins when this happens, and most deliveries, inductions and otherwise, beat out most infections that may develop.

What Will Make the Difference Between Your Having a Vaginal Delivery or a C-Section? The Three Ps of Labor

In spite of what you've heard, most women still have vaginal deliveries. (Fine print: The rest have C-sections.) What makes the difference between these two groups? The best way for me to explain it is to think of a snappy little maxim I learned on my very first OB-GYN rounds on Labor and Delivery at (formerly) Charity Hospital. A staff obstetrician reiterated once again, according to tradition, the concept of the three *P*s: Power, Passenger, and Passageway. Basically, this means the force of labor, the size and position of the baby, and the size of the birth canal.

Your Power

Your labor must develop as a series of rhythmic contractions such that a net vector force is in one direction—toward the cervix—and the way out for your baby. Irregular contractions and false labor may become strong enough to become very uncomfortable, but they don't exert enough of an organized force in one direction to push your baby downward and out against your cervix. Your baby's head cannot act as an effective dilating wedge to accomplish dilation, the criterion used to define the beginning of real (active) labor. In other words, false labor doesn't generate enough "ramming" power to start the necessary actions in your cervix that lead to delivery.

On the other hand, the force of labor may no longer be enough at the end of a long labor. Your uterus may become fatigued. The Power needs to be enough to do the job until delivery, and when it can't, cesarean delivery may be the only way.

Your Passenger

The size and position of your baby are crucial factors in assuring a vaginal delivery. Obviously, if your baby is just too big, you and your doctor are up against the laws of physics. The proof is in the labor, however, and everyone deserves an attempt at a vaginal delivery, no matter how big the baby is estimated to be. The laws of physics, though, help point the way: either your baby's going to fit through or not. And if not, your doctor will know sooner or later. There will be an obvious slowdown in progress. If it's not the Power or the Passageway, he will know then that it's the Passenger.

> **A-FACTOR**
> Good news! Most women have vaginal deliveries.

Position of your Passenger can affect success also. His head can be angled such that the widest part is pitted against the narrowest Passageway of the bones of your pelvis.

Your Passageway

When your Power is good enough (adequate active labor) and your Passenger is not unduly large, the only other peril to a vaginal delivery is your birth canal. The pelvis, with it's hollowed out bony architecture, is the most important part. Soft tissue can elasticize to accommodate your baby, but bone will effectively stop her, causing head compression and possibly fetal distress. When the Power pushes the Passenger against a too small Passageway, your labor progress will stop.

Fast Forward

Whether you're able to pass your baby vaginally or will require a C-section depends on the power of the labor, the size of your baby, and your pelvic bone measurements. Luckily, our species has done well with this arrangement, but when the laws of physics are against you, you can't use a square peg with a round hole.

Time is the best test of labor. Your baby's going to deliver vaginally or not, and sooner or later the truth will be known. Although the concept of the three *P*s is simplistic, it applies when for some reason there's no baby after a time. All your obstetrician need do is go through the three *P*s checklist. This only takes three fingers to count, which is fortunate, for the other seven are used to count the other things we worry about. But that is another chapter.

15

Pain Relief in Labor

"Lamaze is for the birds!"
—ANONYMOUS, ABOUT A JILLION TIMES

Living with It or Through It—the Philosophy of Pain Relief and Labor

Childbirth is a natural event. Because of this, many feel that it should be natural all the way, including no pain relief. To this end, techniques like the Lamaze and Bradley methods have done a lot to help women who so choose to get through the experience as The Experience. But there are those who really can't do it without a lot of suffering, and it's impossible to predict who these will be because we're all different.

Perhaps everyone's pain nerves are different in abundance or distribution. Perhaps different people are more sensitive to different types of pain than others: pressure pain of the baby's head coming down the pelvis, stretching pain of the baby distending soft tissues as descent takes place, bone pain of the baby's skull rubbing against the expectant mother's pubic bone, contracting pain of the uterus itself. There are many ways pain can contribute to the general discomforts of labor and delivery. Each individual woman is unique in the way all of these causes of pain gang up on her.

> **Fast Forward**
> All women feel labor differently, so if you feel the discomfort is unacceptable, you should be able to have pain relief (sedation, epidural, etc.) if you want it—medically as well as ethically.

Natural childbirth techniques, frequently successful, cannot always eliminate that one type of pain a woman may be most sensitive to. Let's be fair. Natural childbirth is an ideal for a natural process. But let's not forget that not too long ago dying in childbirth was a natural part of this also. Now I'm not saying that the pain of labor can cause death. What I'm saying is that if we're willing to eliminate the "natural" mortality rates associated with childbearing, isn't it acceptable to eliminate the natural pain in those who feel they can't tolerate it? Because something's natural, does that make a more comfortable experience off limits for the woman who would prefer some of the modern methods available, like analgesics and epidurals? The woman who feels she needs something will be the first to tell you her relief is not off limits.

As an obstetrician I can tell you that all I care about is getting a healthy baby and a healthy mother out of all this. Everything else should be the expectant parents' decision—natural or otherwise. There are certain guidelines expected of me to get to my goal, and as far as I'm concerned, the parents are the boss for everything else. Natural birthing methods are a wonderful idea for some (or even most) women. For others it may be a terrible idea. Yet many who have put in a good faith effort to try it have a lot of pressure on them to try longer than they should. Political correctness has no place in the labor and delivery suite. Methods of labor relief, natural or otherwise, should be made—like voting—behind the private curtain of a parent's wishes. The delivery of one's child should be a memorable event, not an ordeal. Forgive me for saying it again, but it's not how you have the baby, it's how you raise the baby.

Relief Is on the Way

Thank God it's today! Would you have liked to have had a baby in 1902? Back then, as compared to today, a hundred times more women died from pregnancy. Back then, the marrying age was much younger. My grandmother was

> **Fast Forward**
>
> Today's pain relief options for labor include sedation, epidural anesthesia, spinal anesthetics, pudendal nerve blocks, local anesthetic, and combinations of these.

married at the respectable age of 15. This means that pregnancy occurred at a much younger age too.

It's not a particularly bad thing that teenagers had babies; physiologically that might be the best time to do it. But humanly and sociologically, there's a considerable downside. In 1902 young women had little education. And certainly there weren't the Lamaze or Bradley organizations available to them. And there were no real anesthetics to relieve the pain. You're mixing 1902's lack of medicines, antibiotics, and analgesics with adolescent, uneducated women. If you were a woman back then, this was your lot. It's much better now.

Sedation

There are many pain relievers (analgesics) available today. They are most effective given by shot or by IV. In labor, since you benefit from the presence of an IV anyway, there's no reason to be an eight-hour pincushion. Today, we've added agents such as Stadol to the narcotics Demerol and morphine, which are time honored for their safety.

Epidural Anesthetics

If the skin on your back is numbed prior to using the larger needle of the epidural, it's well tolerated. Even for big crybabies. (I'm a big crybaby—big crybabies rule!)

Epidurals have been around for more than twenty years now, and adequate training has turned this once exotic remedy into a smooth maneuver of pain relief. Additionally, time has allowed many blessings on epidurals; the one-time slug that made the lower half of your body absolutely dead is now a sophisticated continuous application of just enough medicine to relieve the pain but not so much that you can't push or move. And the advances continue.

Basically, medicine is delivered through a needle into a space just short of your actual spinal canal. There the medicine seeps in, numbing all of the body

Back at Charity Hospital . . .

Two medical schools shared Charity Hospital—Tulane and Louisiana State University (LSU). I myself trained through LSU, thank you. The head of the LSU Department of Obstetrics and Gynecology at the time was Dr. Abe Mickal, a wonderful educator who had this thing about women suffering: it was not to be. The typical Charity Hospital laboring patient was of a socioeconomic group that interfered with things like good nutrition and consistent prenatal care, so certainly prenatal classes were out of the question. Since weeks of prenatal instruction on how to deal with labor weren't part of the patient's résumé, IV sedation was the likely substitute.

Dr. Mickal wasn't anti–natural childbirth, he was anti-suffering. These patients were not the stuff of "the beauty of natural childbirth." It was often said that you could hear the difference between the Tulane and LSU sides of the labor wards at Charity Hospital back then. I'm not saying that women suffered needlessly or were hollering death throes on the Tulane side, but it surely was strangely quiet on the LSU side. Especially when the man himself let it be known he was on his way to make rounds. You could see the wave of anger in his face if he heard anyone suffering. If a patient suffered, the resident on the labor ward was sure to be suffering soon too.

Two years later, the anesthesia department was amply supplied enough to administer epidurals to *all* of the women who could benefit from them. I'm not saying that Dr. Mickal was responsible for that—the times a'changin' did that—but I am saying that a generation of southern physicians were trained with the highest sensitivity to those who are suffering. This is possibly the late Dr. Mickal's greatest legacy.

segments supplied by the nerves. The spot for placement is well below any part of the actual spinal column, so even an inadvertent spinal anesthetic, caused by the needle advancing too far, won't damage your spine. That's the good news.

The bad news is that if this were to happen, or if the medicine were to rise in the epidural space too high, a lot of things could stop working. You could stop breathing for one. But before you warn your anesthesiologists about

> **Fast Forward**
> With epidurals, the anesthesia rolls downhill, bathing with numbing medicine the nerves that travel downward. The technique has been refined over the years and is easily tolerated.

lawsuits and such, know that there's no better place in the world to have a complication from an epidural than with an anesthesiologist breathing down your neck. Anesthesiologists have equipment, they have supplies, and they know what to do with it. And the whole epidural is monitored as if this could happen every time. Back to good news: it hardly ever happens. I would venture to say that without epidurals there would be more women jumping out of windows, threatening to take their lousy no-good sperm-donor husbands with them, than women who suffer this very rare complication. This rant may sound extreme, but I use it to emphasize how much suffering has been eliminated with that invention known as the epidural.

Most commonly, complications that occur with epidurals involve lowered blood pressure, which is possibly also due to repositioning a pregnant patient flat on her back immediately after administering the epidural, and we all know what that big fundus does to blood returning to the heart when it's sitting on top of the vena cava.

Complications include the aforementioned hypotension, of which nausea is a tip-off, and accidentally doing a spinal anesthetic if the needle goes too far in. An accidental spinal has the same complications as an epidural going too high, so the anesthesiologist is ready for that too. A hole in the covering over your spine can cause headaches later, but this is easily—and instantly— cured by injecting a few cc's of your own blood into the epidural space, effectively sealing the hole.

If all goes well, you might think it would be time to take out the deck of cards and wait for the whole thing to blow over, but here's the surprise. Elimination of pain is best celebrated by enjoying the birth experience. It's amazing how much you can get out of a delivery without the distraction that agony can provide (assuming you're the agony type, in which case you will definitely sign up for the epidural). You can enjoy the experience of bonding with your

A-FACTOR

Complications from epidurals are rare and well controlled. Since the whole procedure of putting one in involves monitoring for and standing ready to manage such complications, epidurals are seldom dangerous although they can be unpleasant. The most common complication is an accidental spinal anesthetic, causing headaches later. The headaches can be cured instantly with a "blood patch," which involves injecting a little of your own blood into the epidural space, sealing the hole.

Stories of paralysis and permanent back trouble are myths or left over from the early days when epidurals weren't quite as slick as they are today.

husband. You can thrill to the first sight of your baby. You can focus. And the medicine in an epidural doesn't effect the baby, which eliminates a major concern for the drug-free, natural childbirth enthusiasts.

With all of the bad press that epidurals have gotten from those who teach birthing techniques that rely on self-control and focusing, the irony is that women who benefit from an epidural will be able to focus unbelievably on a major life event that would have otherwise been wasted behind the din of suffering, exasperation, and the unknown. I've seen beautiful natural childbirth, but I've also seen the beauty of a pain-free delivery. It doesn't suck.

Spinal Anesthetic (Saddle Block)

This is what began the whole revolution of what is called regional anesthesia. Before regional anesthesia, women were treated to something called twilight sleep, which was such a dizzying affair that it would justify any woman's claim that her baby was switched at birth were he to knock over the glass of milk for the third time in one meal. Twilight sleep was close to a general anesthetic. I myself was born this way. My mom drifted off into the twilight zone and I was pulled with forceps toward that signpost up ahead. If you think the natural childbirth enthusiasts hate regional anesthesia, the thought of the old twilight sleep is enough to have them scream *pregnacide*.

The spinal anesthetic, medicine injected into the spinal canal fluid, was administered so low as to numb up only your bottom—that area that would make contact with a saddle. Hence its name, saddle block. But since it was a spinal anesthetic, it was replaced universally with the epidural to cut down on the inevitable headaches. Today, spinals are used for repeat C-sections, and here is an excellent niche for them. Epidurals can be a little spotty sometimes, which can be acceptable for labor, but a "hot spot" during surgery won't do. The newer needles now used in spinals are so thin that headaches are increasingly uncommon.

New Concoctions

Today there are a number of hybrid approaches to pain relief, seeking the ideal result of total pain relief with minimal effect on your ability to move or push. The newer "walking epidurals" incorporate a limited spinal anesthetic with an epidural adjunct. Continuous epidural drips have replaced the whammies of drugs previously given at intervals.

Pudendal Block

This is truly a local nerve block; anesthetic is injected toward the back of the vagina on either side to numb the pudendal nerves. This will give anesthesia to the area around your vagina and anus, which will cover you for repair of an episiotomy (a what?) or vaginal tear. Pudendal blocks can be a bit iffy, sometimes giving relief to one side only. In these cases a local anesthetic is also used.

Local Anesthetic

Given right before delivery, this is Xylocaine injected right into the stretched portion of the midline tissue between your vagina and anus, for coverage in case of a repair. It's the least obtrusive, but also the least effective. In fact it's usually administered at the time of maximum stretch of your perineum before your baby's head crowns, and it's unlikely you would feel any tears beyond the massive twang that your baby's head will provide for you. All of this applies if you're going natural. Those of you in the epidural club need not bother with this melodrama.

Choosing the Way to Give Birth

What happens during delivery of your baby—that moment that stands as the Big Bang of life as you'll know it forever—depends on your labor and the ways you and your doctor have dealt with it.

Natural Delivery

This is a very efficient way to have a baby because the urge to push becomes reflexive during the second stage of labor. Even if you skipped that important Lamaze class to go see Eric Clapton in concert (reasonable), your body will help you know what to do. It will almost seem automatic.

Assuming you wanted it this way and have actually pulled it off, this can be a magic moment in your life. There is a catharsis with the release of your child into the world, not only a physical release that dissipates all of the pent-up pressures of your entire pregnancy and labor, but also a profound meta-physical explosion of hopes and dreams that joyfully announce the first moment of the rest of your life as it was meant to be. The philosophical ram-ifications are as enormous as the weight of the door you swing open with the birth of your child. Even if you've been numbed up to your halo (you do have one, don't you?), you can still experience this intellectual unfastening of all of your life's promises, but the physical release is an emphasis all its own. No wonder the natural childbirth advocates go crazy over all of this. They're absolutely right. Did I mention, though, that it's not for everyone?

Natural Delivery with Local Sedation or Pudendal Block

This delivery isn't much different from a natural drugless approach because the local anesthetic is given only as needed to address a vaginal cut (epi-siotomy) or tear. You still pretty much experience the whole natural encounter.

Delivery with Sedation

Although this may be an old-style method of delivery, there are some posi-tive points. You're not so zonked that you'll be amnesic of the whole event, but there's enough relief to help you through the difficult moments. Believe me, you'll know there's something important happening. This borderline approach may be the best of both worlds in which you feel enough to claim the experience, but the peaks of intolerance have been blunted enough to get you through it without regret. Sedation is a muddying of your mind, but it won't be strong enough to prevent your pushing your baby out and knowing it (a good thing).

Delivery with Regional Anesthesia

Part of the skill of the anesthesiologist-obstetrician team is knowing how an epidural may truly interfere with labor and delivery. It used to be said that epidurals cause C-sections. Obstetricians steadfastly refused to believe this. I know, because I was one of them.

One day I read a study about how giving a patient an epidural before five centimeters tripled her chances of a C-section. The rationale was that there are muscles that help guide your baby's head correctly into your pelvis. Before five centimeters, the head will come down sloppily if those muscles are relaxed by way of an epidural. Even with a small head and a big pelvis, if your baby's head were askew, it would be like trying to get your car out of your garage sideways.

Today the studies have fine-tuned their caveat from five centimeters to the criteria that your baby's head be past the midportion of your pelvis. Pretty much the same thing.

▶ **Fast Forward**

If you can hold out for your epidural (with sedation) until you hit five centimeters or your baby's head has reached your midpelvis (0 Station), you significantly decrease your chances of having a C-section.

Newer concoctions, like the "walking" epidural, don't seem to unfavorably impact on your C-section chances, even when given before five centimeters.

So we obstetricians take our tails and place them meekly between our legs and admit that the natural childbirth champions had a point. But we're quick to smugly point out that they didn't even know why, while they chanted antiepidural slogans with as much to back it up as droning on about evolution and the Bible.

Where You Deliver Is Part of How You Deliver

A by-product of hospitals competing for your business is the *LDR* room. It means that you Labor, Deliver, and Recover in the same room. Sometimes referred to as a birthing room, it is decorated with a warm homey touch. The bed you labor in can do all kinds of gyrations to convert into a delivery bed, then back into a regular bed. It used to be that you labored in the labor area, were moved to the delivery room, then moved again to the postpartum floor. Now you can do all of the labor, delivery, and immediate recovery in one room. If it's an *LDRP* room, you also do the postpartum stay there too. Smaller hospitals and the hospitals of one-hospital towns may not have the accommodations to compete with this quaint arrangement, but they don't have to compete either.

Certainly it's worth a trip to the hospital you're going to use to case the joint. All of the big hospitals are about the same, but scoping out the view takes one more unknown away from this whole process.

Some Thoughts That Come to Mind When You've Seen a Zillion of These

One of the things that makes my authorship of a pregnancy book different is that I've been there. OK, maybe not a zillion times, but a few thousand. The other books and the natural childbirth educators approach your pregnancy and delivery on the front end, with the desired result deemed a cinch at the end. It's as if the right approach will guarantee the right destiny. Your doctor, on the other hand, will approach your delivery—not on the front end—but with his knowledge of all of the back ends (figuratively speaking, of course) that he has experienced in the numerous deliveries of his career. He wants a good outcome for the rest of your baby's life.

The benefits of natural delivery cited are true, but pregnancy is a condition that can take a bad turn suddenly and without warning. The "intrusive" obstetrical care that is so maligned by the naturalists has some very important advantages.

For instance, say you're Dr. Lamaze's granddaughter. You've made him proud and gotten to ten centimeters without any narcotics or epidural help. You're really into this and you're beginning your pushing, your baby's coming down fine, and everyone's checking the battery status on their minicams. Suddenly, your baby's heart tones start to slow down with each push, but they recover with each break between contractions too. After a while, however, your baby's heart rate becomes a little sluggish in recovering until it stays slower than it should be. You don't need a C-section because your baby is right there—you just can't push her out. Your doctor calls for either forceps or a vacuum extractor.

Suddenly the beauty of natural delivery becomes very unimportant when your baby's life or intellectual potential is at stake. Forceps can deliver your baby straightaway, but forceps technique needs anesthesia. You don't have any.

Now your doctor will do what's necessary, but it surely would be helpful if you had some anesthesia—even a touch. A pudendal block won't be quite enough.

Just a doctor's thoughts—a doctor who's been out there in the real world.

> ▶ **Fast Forward**
>
> If you want your doctor to be ready for anything—even the really rare complications—you should have an epidural of some sort to provide an anesthesia route in. You would be covering yourself for the complications that are in fact really rare.

The Perfect Approach

Is there such a thing? No. So the big question is: What would I do, or how would I want my wife to do it? Or my daughter? (By the way, she shouldn't even be thinking about such things yet.)

If she wanted to wuss out and just get the job done, I'd recommend she have an elective induction at or after thirty-nine weeks (assuming the cervix was ripe), have an epidural, and shop online until time to replace her tray into its upright position and begin pushing. If she wanted to take the Earth Mother route, I'd recommend a walking epidural—that limited epidural that minimally impacts on movement—and let it wear off if natural childbirth was her goal. At least that way she'd have an anesthetic-line in should some assisted techniques prove necessary. But this is just at the DiLeo house, not that there would ever be a home delivery there. (More on that in "Controversies in Obstetrics" in Chapter 22.)

If you're dead set against any intervention, even prudent, temporary measures that will alter the natural event the least, then you are taking somewhat of a chance. Small, admittedly. Kind of like not buckling your seatbelt when you're just going to return *Father of the Bride II* to Blockbuster down the road (which—I'm sure—will be sporting a late fee).

Your doctor, as I said, wants a good baby and a good Mom out of all of this. She's thinking that if something goes awry, she would like to be ready to act. A totally natural approach makes it a little harder for her. Wouldn't you want to make it as easy as you can in case things were to go off kilter?

Second Stage of Labor

Labor expends a lot of energy, hence its name. By the time you've reached complete dilation, which is the entrance into the second stage, you've burned enough calories to make Richard Simmons cry "Uncle!" (I pause as I muster a mental picture of Richard Simmons in labor.)

But now your contractions do something a little extra. Besides pushing your baby outward, the shape of your uterus changes so that it straightens your baby's spine. It's like telling your baby, "Stand up straight!" (Remember that line—more than likely you will utter it a few more times in the upcoming years.) This straightening causes your baby to "stand up straight" an extra four inches; that extra tallness aids her descent into your pelvis.

Labor is also aided by certain helper tactics. Specifically, I'm talking about the addition of your abdominal muscles to the effort—what is called bearing down, or pushing. This adds a considerable force to effect delivery, and the loss of such abilities with anesthetics is the "I-told-you-so" of the natural childbirth proponents. But with a little imagination, I propose that even if you're numbed out from your nipples down, you can invoke bearing down forces anyway. After all, it's your brain that initiates the volition of contracting such muscles. If your suffering has been answered by the godsend of an epidural, is an assisted delivery as much a defeat as a vaginal delivery in which you undergo unacceptable suffering?

Let me put your conscience at ease: No. Make your calls as the time and the labor progress. Don't suffer unacceptably because of what might happen. You're not bucking womanhood, but politics.

16

Delivery

The Moment We've All Been Waiting For

The command is "Push!" You use the same muscles you would use to force a bowel movement. Distasteful but accurate. Even if your epidural has numbed you too much, you're accomplished enough at having a bowel movement to will these muscles into action even without feeling them. Back at Charity Hospital, I remember hearing "Don't push!" just as often, because frequently patients would land there with no prenatal care and completely dilated, flailing and yelling about the baby coming. A hall of patients would clear very quickly when this happened. We didn't know what was coming our way—head first, breech, twins, prematurity. It was like waiting for Pete Sampras's serve and not being Andre Agassi.

Under your controlled circumstances, however, your baby's most likely head position is face down. This makes for your easiest delivery because his head can pivot up once past your pubic bone—pivoting right out. This position is called occiput anterior (back of the head is up, face is down, or OA). Occiput posterior (back of the head is down, face is up, or OP) is also usually deliverable, but it's like adding another pound on your baby because the nape of his neck can't flex up past your pubic bone like in OA. Instead, your baby's head has to come straight out. Without the pivot that allows a certain mass to "sneak" out with more negotiable slack, the full dimensions of the head come out, and at this point it brakes for no one. Occiput transverse (OT), in which your baby's face is facing to the right or left, won't usually deliver. Interestingly, your baby's head spends considerable time in the OT position higher up your birth canal before spontaneously rotating as it descends. Persistent OT, however, is a major cause of C-sections.

So your baby's head is out—and you'll know this—prompting your doctor or midwife to suction out her nostrils and throat. Sure she could probably get by without this, but why make things hard? Especially with breathing. I'm also not a big fan of waiting to clamp the cord until all pulsations stop because, if the baby is held above the height of your intact placenta, blood may congest into the placenta, causing anemia in your baby; and if held below, blood can congest in your baby, causing a cardiac overload. So if you're going to immediately breast-feed, at least clamp the cord. You don't have to actually cut it—merely close the gates.

I am a really big fan of immediately breast-feeding, even if you don't plan on officially doing it. Be a sport and let Junior or Missy latch on. Besides a wonderful experience somewhere in that immature little brain, it's a break for your doctor because suckling will stimulate contractions that will expel the placenta sooner and cut down on your blood loss. And who knows, that maternal wave of mammalian imperative may flow through you, causing an epiphany revealing the good sense in breast-feeding.

By the way, if you don't breast-feed, be prepared to get the stink eye from the lactation czar, whose only job is to instruct you on how to do it. I like breast-feeding and I strongly recommend it, but once again it's how you raise the baby that's important. If you do breast-feed, the lactation nurse is a godsend. There's a whole science behind it—it's more than just having nipples. (If you don't breast-feed and would like to be spared the lectures and disapproval, have your baby on a Friday. Chances are your lactation nurse specialist will be off until Monday because it's a cushy job.)

After delivery, the placenta will usually deliver spontaneously, assisted by some gentle traction on the cord. After this, your doctor will check for tears that might need repair or will repair an episiotomy if one was done.

The Position of the Unknown Baby—What Is It and How Does It Get That Way?

Your baby's head is the largest part of his body, so when he delivers headfirst, it usually follows that, well, the rest of him follows. But there are many variations from the standard headfirst descent, like breech, transverse, shoulder-first, etc. Even among the headfirst deliveries, the face can be pointing down, up, sideways, or even face-first. It's these little surprises that keep an obstetrician or midwife on alert with each seemingly routine delivery. In the head-first category, the shape of the mother's pelvis can determine which way the head is placed.

The most common way is facedown—OA—and this allows the easiest measurement to clear the pelvis. If the face is down, you may well ask, what exactly is up, or anterior? The occiput is the back of your baby's head, and all references to head position are based on where the back of the head is. So if the back of the head is anterior or up, it follows that the face is posterior—down.

The OA position is especially helpful because the back of the head can pivot up against the pubic bone, allowing the chin's appearance to finish the delivery of the full head. You do this very thing every time you slip on a narrow-neck sweater.

Face-up, OP (back of the head down), is a more difficult delivery because your baby can't flex his head on exit. It's like delivering a baby that's a pound bigger. It's not impossible, but it's more difficult to push with effectiveness, and the pushing stage of labor can last longer than usual. If the head is side-ways, OT, then the rotation necessary for delivery is incomplete. The head can usually be gently rotated by the obstetrician to face down (OA) for a normal delivery.

Asynclitism is a word that describes a headfirst position wherein the head is tilted to the right or left from the midline, similar to the position you would sport if you had a stiff neck. Many people feel that an epidural given before the head has descended well into the pelvis causes the maternal muscles that normally guide the head down correctly to get relaxed, resulting in a sloppy, unguided descent. It's a hard positioning to work with and, as discussed before, can lead to the need for a C-section.

And then, after all of the headfirst positions, there's every other way.

Breech refers to feet- or buttocks-first presentation. This is a real thinking obstetrician's dilemma because, as mentioned above, the largest part of the baby is the head. So delivery of the feet or buttocks creates a scenario wherein larger and larger parts of the baby have yet to prove the ability to clear the pelvis. In other words, if the head won't fit out in a headfirst baby, delivery can be effected via second-choice—the C-section. But in a breech delivery, if the head won't fit out, the rest of the baby already has. The cord is out as well and is compressed in the birth canal on its way up to the placenta. This is such an emergency that most obstetricians feel that a breech presentation should always be delivered by C-section.

Lately the medical literature has offered studies in what criteria have been established by which to allow a vaginal delivery of a breech baby. Some brave obstetricians (not me if I can help it) are doing vaginal deliveries of breech babies, but this isn't acceptable unless the baby is estimated to be at least a pound less than a mother's previous largest baby, the baby is a frank breech, and the maternal pelvic measurements are generous. Not as an obstetrician, but as a father who knows what an obstetrician knows, my unofficial recommendation is that all breeches should be delivered by C-section, criteria notwithstanding. This is based on findings that indicate the "soft" neurological signs, like dyslexia, attention-deficit disorder, and behavioral disorders, might be increased by vaginal deliveries of breech babies. The studies are ink on paper, but you have to raise your child all of his life. Is this really something important enough to champion?

But why do some babies come out head first (vertex presentation) and some breech? Your baby tends to seek the most comfortable position inside your uterus. If his largest part is his head, then over time he will fidget (oh, how he will fidget) and maneuver around until his head gravitates to the largest space. That most generous space is the lower uterine space. And usually at thirty-two weeks this position will stick.

When it happens that the lower uterus is not the biggest space, breech and other less likely presentations occur. For instance, a low-lying placenta or placenta previa can occupy enough space down low so that the biggest space is up high. Also, congenital abnormalities can make other parts of the baby the biggest part, such part becoming the lowermost presenting part.

In a frank breech, the buttocks are first. In a footling breech, one or both feet are first—the single footling breech and the double footling breech. The difference depends on whether the knees are bent or not. In both, the hips are flexed, but if the knees are straight, then the lower legs, along with the thighs, are bent over the baby's abdomen, resulting in the frank breech. If the knees are bent, then the feet are positioned back toward the cervix and the outside world.

Thankfully, most breeches are in the frank position. Occasionally I'll encounter a baby that's in a crazy position, like transverse (whole body sideways) or shoulder-first. C-section is the safest way to address this malpresentation; this is common sense when the unified vector forces of labor don't push a headfirst baby outward, but instead crunch a baby that's not pointing straight down.

I'll Answer the Rest of Your Delivery Questions Now

The rest of the chapter addresses common questions that go along with the actual delivery process.

What's the Deal on Episiotomy? When an Irresistible Force Meets an Immovable Object

Episiotomy has been referred to as everything from rational obstetrics to genital mutilation. The simplest way to describe it is as a tidy, doctor-inflicted cut performed to replace the not-so-tidy tear that seems imminent at the time of delivery. It's as unnatural as any elective surgery. Most folks, to be sure, prefer not to be cut for any reason. But just because it's unnatural doesn't mean it's unjustified. It is actually a helpful procedure, along with the other unnatural aspects of labor and delivery—epidurals, IVs, etc. An episiotomy involves making a vertical incision in the tissue between the floor of the vagina and the rectum, thereby increasing the circumference of the exit for the baby's head at the time of delivery. It is painless when done under an epidural, local anesthetic, or pudendal (nerve) block. Even without an anesthetic, feeling it is lost when done at the very time of crowning, the skin pulled so taut as to eliminate a lot of the sensation from the cut. With an episiotomy, the circle of tissue that is the outlet for the baby is made larger and the chance of tearing less.

Since it is easier to repair a surgical incision than a traumatic tear, the decision to cut an episiotomy is made at the last moment when it looks like there may be tearing without one. In this way, it should be looked at as preventative. But it only prevents superficial tears. An episiotomy—an increase in circumference of just the vaginal outlet—won't prevent deep tears if the force of the delivery (due to a large head, forceps, or precipitous expulsion) exceeds the elasticity of the tissues of the pelvis. Something will have to give, and it's usually the baby's head that wins.

Tissue elasticity is an amazing thing. I think, under ideal circumstances, that your vaginal tissues could easily do without an episiotomy and still not sustain any tears. But only under ideal circumstances.

This ideal is easy to miss in all of the excitement of the labor reaching its climax, the inherent rate of expulsion of your baby's head ignoring any elasticity criteria, stretching your outer tissues too quickly for them to adequately elasticize. Even with a controlling hand from your doctor, all it takes is a little jerk in your baby's pivotal maneuver to spring a breach in your tissue.

In spite of what you've heard at prenatal classes and what you've read in the other books, your doctor would rather not cut an episiotomy because sewing it back together is more work for her. But she surely would prefer to repair a clean cut than a tattered disarray of layers of tissue.

Tattered disarray of layers of tissue? What the heck is this all about? Up to now there's just been talk of being pregnant, having labor, and having babies. No one ever said anything about tattered disarrays of layers of tissue. Especially there. Especially on you!

Don't flip out. Most of the time when you think of mucous membranes, you're thinking about boogers and snot and all kinds of other unsavory substances. And certainly, since you're a lady, these things have about as much to do with you as unicorns. But mucus is an important part of your life and your body, and if you doubt this, wait till your baby comes home—you haven't seen anything yet! The importance of mucus and the tissue that makes it is that it is a very forgiving type of tissue. Everything heals so much better when there's mucus around, which is probably not a result of the mucus, but of the type of tissue that makes mucus.

Your vagina is a mucous organ, just like your nose. In fact, if you were to compare vaginal wall and nasal tissue under the microscope, they would look the same. It is a benefit to our survival as a species that evolution has decided to birth us through mucous tissue. It makes more births possible because even the most extensive tearing seems to heal up just fine, layers lining up right, edges lining up right, everything regrouping back the way it should. After all, there was no suture hundreds and thousands of years ago.

Now let's talk about tidiness. Sure you'll heal, but when the tissues are helped back with suture (absorbable, thank God), you get a great head start. Also, open tissues, while awaiting spontaneous closure, can be exposed to the possibility of infection. It pays to take advantage of the sutures your doctor will use if there's a tear or an episiotomy. Fear of infection, though, isn't that big a fear. There's something about the immunology of the area that seems to protect it more from infection than anywhere else. All of the mucous mem-

> **Fast Forward**
>
> An episiotomy is a cut into the edge of the vaginal floor, increasing the circumference of the outlet for your baby's head. It's done to prevent superficial tears. It won't prevent deep tears. It's not necessary, but it's easier to recover from a clean episiotomy than a ragged tear.
>
> In order of ease of recovery:
>
> No episiotomy, no tears—*is easier than* small episiotomy, no tears—*is easier than* no episiotomy, but tears—*is easier than* large tears with or without episiotomy.

branes share this characteristic, which is probably why they heal so well. You can cut your arm and then go swimming in a chlorinated pool, and you'll see at least a superficial infection. If you bite your tongue, it heals very well in your mouth, one of the dirtiest places on you, especially if you're Andrew Dice Clay. Drag feces and blood through the tears of the vagina and most of the time the worst effects are only aesthetic sensibilities.

You may well ask, *What if I don't have an episiotomy and I need one?*

Then you might tear. But the only advantage to an episiotomy is in preventing superficial tears, which are easy to fix and the recovery isn't too rough.

You may well ask, *What if I have an episiotomy and didn't need one?*

Then you got one for nothing, but this is a retrospective through a crystal ball, so don't even go there.

You may well ask, *Won't an episiotomy start a glitch in my tissue that can then more easily tear further?*

Perhaps, but it's your baby's head that will do the actual further damage.

Some espouse never cutting an episiotomy. Although this philosophy won't cause deep tears, the superficial ones can increase the time of recovery by a few weeks. The gamble here, of course, is whether or not a patient will get away with nothing needing repair. It is tempting, but it is certain that a surgical repair of a straight incision hurts less and heals faster than a disarray of tissue split in several different directions.

You may well ask, *What's the best approach?*

Leave it up to your obstetrician—that's why you chose your doctor. Of course, discuss the issue ahead of time so that both of you are clear on a common plan. But keep in mind that your doctor doesn't do episiotomies if clearly not needed. They're included in the global fee, so there's no financial incentive, and it's more work to repair one than not repair one. So if it looks like the baby will deliver without unreasonable stretching and risk, your doctor will gladly skip the episiotomy. If it looks as if there may be some trauma, an episiotomy—the smallest necessary—will be used for your benefit.

Absorbable suture means you don't need the stitches removed. The unique immunology of the area means infection is rare. Since this area ultimately heals so well, even when there was tearing, it's often difficult to tell a woman's had one by exam. Thinning of the floor of the vagina, if seen later, is from the passage of the baby, not from the decision to do an episiotomy or not.

One must remember that childbirth is an amazing phenomenon of physics, pushing a body's capacity to the max. Compared to the actual delivery, episiotomy can be thought of as an inconvenience or an advantage, depending on what could have happened with or without it. But it is a secondary consideration when an irresistible force—the baby—meets an immovable object—you.

What's the Deal on Vaginal Tears?

The deeper tears, even tears into your rectum, can be repaired and repaired well. It's a part of the specialty of obstetrics. Once all of the swelling is gone and things are healed, there is seldom anything noticeable about the area other than what you're supposed to notice. You may walk like a cowboy (cowgirl?) for a while, but you'll do fine. True, there are infections that jeopardize the repair, but these are extremely rare, as explained above.

Lately there has been evidence that vaginal deliveries stretch the muscular layers around the rectum and vagina so much that this is the cause of incontinence and pelvic relaxation, repairable only with surgery. This has been used to fuel the argument for "maternal choice" C-section. I'm officially neutral on this, but I feel strongly that a woman has the right, barring any undue risks, to choose how to have her baby.

What's the Deal on the "Husband Stitch"?

I can't tell you how many times, while suturing the vaginal tissue right after a delivery, a husband has said to me, "Hey, Doc, how 'bout putting in that extra stitch?" And then he shoots me that little mischievous grin that I'm supposed to share, because after all I'm in the club.

Except for me, of course, men can be such jerks sometimes. But in all fairness, they just get a little goofy with life events that move them.

For the record, the husband's stitch is a myth.

In fact, there's so much swelling going on that all your doctor can do to put things right is to do it correctly. There's no extra stitch. Even if a plastic repair, eliminating redundant, stretched out tissue were requested, the distortion to the anatomy would make this unwise for two reasons. First of all, what might look symmetrical now won't after all of the swelling goes back down. Second, in pregnancy, everything bleeds more, so adding more surgery beyond what is necessary is foolish.

"Oh, yeah, the extra stitch," I say. "That'll be extra." And then there's an uncomfortable pause, broken when the new mom slaps the crap out of him. This is her way of saying that if it were his balls that had gotten torn, fine tuning things would be the last thing on his mind.

Pregnancy Rules for Husbands

Rule #8: During that holy and profound experience of witnessing the first few precious moments of your child's life, your wife will never forget that all you were worried about was how you might feel even better when getting laid. If sex has anything to do with pregnancy, this may be an only child. Don't do this.

What's the Deal on Forceps?

Smoothly shaped and curved, obstetrical forceps are thin metal pulling tools used to help a baby's head toward delivery. Many people fear them, and patients tend to have a negative reaction when they are considered. But they have been responsible for saving many babies' lives, especially when delivery is prudent during fetal distress. As far as safety goes, they aren't different than any other medical tool, technique, or drug: Used incorrectly, they can cause serious harm; used correctly, they actually provide a gentler delivery for a baby's head than no forceps at all. There are ways of checking for correct application, and when the criteria aren't met, a forceps delivery should not occur. Simple. But when criteria are met, the forceps are handy for effecting a timely delivery when a sudden urgency presents, as in fetal distress, or when delivery can't be spontaneous, as in stage two failure to progress.

Proper placement provides a halo of metal around the baby's skull, protecting it. All of the force is applied at the cheekbones. In this way, the baby's brain is not subjected to the compression-decompression forces that the vaginal sidewalls exert against it as the head descends. All of the force is spread over the metal halo. So why wouldn't we want forceps on all deliveries?

In spite of my making the pressure of the birth canal sound difficult on a little unborn head, we're actually designed to take it pretty well. Most of us began our lives escaping this vise on our own, without the use of halos, metal or otherwise. In fact, this is the advantage of the skull bones not being solidly fused together yet, so that they can mold into shapes as the delivery ensues. Another reason forceps aren't used on everyone is because they can sometimes be more traumatic to vaginal tissue than a spontaneous delivery, causing an extension of an episiotomy. Additionally, extra lacerations occasionally can result too, delaying recovery for a new mother. Clearly, forceps are indicated when rapid delivery is necessary in an emergency. And they are fairly gentle when used at the lowest possible descent point of the baby's head (low outlet forceps), mercifully shortening the end of an exhausting labor.

Alternatives to the necessary use of forceps include C- section or vacuum extractor. The vacuum extractor involves a suction device that is applied to the baby's scalp so that the obstetrician can gently tug outward. The advantages of the vacuum extractor are that it can be used safely slightly higher than what's allowed with forceps, and it allows for the spontaneous rotation of the descending head as delivery takes place.

What's the Deal on the Vacuum Extractor?

Think of the vacuum extractor as a kinder, gentler version of forceps. A soft suction cup is applied to the top of your baby's head. It has a safety feature that allows it to pop off if too much traction is used, so it's not as effective as forceps in delivering a stubborn baby. But it's easier on you.

Complications from vacuum are related to scalp damage, but if used according to criteria, this is rare. There are guidelines on how many times a doctor should apply it and for how long.

What's the Deal on Fetal Distress?

No matter how you say it, you just can't make fetal distress sound good. It's a crucially important consideration and it's a paranoia that pits all of the natural childbirth proponents against all of the methods of interventional obstetrics. As I said before, those who champion nonintervention look at labor and delivery on the front end. Your doctor carries a brain with him that is his own particular legacy of obstetrics—what can go wrong and ways to catch it and deal with it. Just as in lectures on sexually transmitted diseases in which we say that when you have unprotected sex with someone, it's like having sex with everyone they've had sex with, when you deliver under the management of a doctor you're being assessed for every complication he's ever seen. This isn't to say that the older doctors are better at what they do, because 99 percent of the serious complications for a doctor happened during training.

Fetal distress is such a big deal, of course, because of what's at stake—the rest of your child's life. The field of obstetrics has gotten very proficient at picking up signs of it, but there are many fuzzy warnings as well as false alarms that still make delivering babies as much an art as a science. This art often runs covertly in your doctor's mind alongside your innocent mere expectations of a natural outcome from a natural event.

Studies have shown that when the minimal standards of surveillance during labor are followed, the complications are minimal too. What are the minimal standards of surveillance? According to the American College of Obstetricians and Gynecologists, it's recommended that your baby's heart rate be recorded at least every thirty minutes during stage one of labor (up to ten centimeters) and every fifteen minutes during stage two. It's mandatory that the timing of listening for the heart rate is immediately after a contraction because a contraction is the most stressful time for the baby. If the fetal heart rate is consistently less than 110 beats/minute, continuous monitoring is necessary. If the heart rate is less than 100, fetal distress is likely.

I myself am a big sissy coward. As long as you're not doing anything else anyway that day, as long as you're content to just lie there, I'd rather you have continuous monitoring. The minimal standards are fairly reliable, but they're embraced a little too firmly by some midwives as the maximum standards necessary if you're seeking the quintessential beautiful event.

What isn't beautiful, though, is bringing your child to specialists throughout childhood because of the quest for this beauty, and this is the thing on your doctor's mind until delivery. True, some doctors go overboard, insisting on continuous monitoring, no walking, and other dictatorial policies. At worst, this policy denies you your beautiful experience. But the opposite extreme may put your baby at risk. By the time you get to this point, however, you and your doctor should have worked out how things will go.

17

Complications

What Could Go Wrong?

This is a section I'd like you to read and then forget because I'm listing weird, uncommon things that probably won't happen. I include them here so that in the unlikely event that you experience one of these complications you'll have a vague recollection of my saying something about it and can look it up again. So, blur your eyes so that the spaces between the words become white snakes on the page . . . you're getting sleepy . . . you're not worried at all. . . .

Shoulder Dystocia—When a Baby Throws a Shoulder Block

This is when your baby's shoulder girth is too large, causing your baby to be stuck in the middle of delivery, the head out but the shoulders wedged in. In this position a sort of point of no return has been reached: the umbilical cord is compressed by the chest and shoulders of your undelivered baby, and with the chest compressed by the vaginal walls, the lungs can't expand to move air.

Back in the olden days—that is, just a few years ago—shoulder dystocia frequently resulted in injury to the infant due to the delay in effecting delivery. Nerve paralysis of the arm from frantic pulling and brain damage or subtle outcomes of oxygen deprivation could follow a difficult birth that involved this complication.

After traction in different directions, complicated corkscrew maneuvers were next in the sequence of attempts to finish the delivery. The clock would keep ticking. The baby's clavicle, a flimsy bone in the shoulder, would give way either by accident or by design so as to make a collapsible escape for the respective shoulder. The scene was tense for all of the right reasons.

Now we use a technique called the McRoberts maneuver. In this technique, the woman's thighs are flexed far back onto her abdomen. Additionally, an assistant applies pressure downward right above the pubic bone. The maneuver of the thighs causes the pelvic ring to tilt upward to provoke release of the shoulder, and increases the expulsive pressure within the uterus. The pressure on the baby's shoulder from above the mother's pubic bone forces the shoulder out toward the doctor who is pulling with an additional force. Most often these babies are delivered within a moment of recognizing the problem. In my experience, even the meanest shoulder dystocias tend to just fall right out with the McRoberts maneuver combined with pressing down above the pubic bone.

The technique was named after Dr. William McRoberts Jr., who popularized it, and it's hard to give credit to this maneuver to the extent that it deserves. How many injuries or even deaths have been prevented would be impossible to tabulate. I suppose the Nobel people are a little too upscale to consider rewarding something that is a variation on yanking, but when you consider the quality of life it has meant all over the world since 1983, its revelation seems no less miraculous than vitamins. This uncomplicated technique is a powerful reminder that for all of its intricate biochemical processes and miraculous genetic unfolding, birth is still a process of mechanical simplicity.

Shoulder dystocia is a risk factor for every baby over about eight and a half pounds. Your obstetrician knows that the chances of it occurring are increased with a history of previous shoulder dystocia, a history of large babies, or diabetes. Since the head is thought to be the largest part to deliver, with the rest of the baby supposed to follow thereafter, shoulder dystocia often comes as a surprise. But there are subtle signs that can tip off your doctor. Slow progress of labor should caution him not to help the head out with forceps. This may in fact invite a shoulder dystocia, and no vaginal delivery at all would be preferable. A C-section, although second choice, is better than the victory of a vaginal delivery at the expense of your child's health.

The McRoberts maneuver works well. There can still be a broken clavicle from time to time, often found incidentally after delivery and which heals well, but the laws of physics are used to advantage to prevent terrible outcomes in what used to be one of the most feared complications of childbearing. It won't guarantee an injury-free delivery, but it decreases the chances of injury because it will usually guarantee a delivery.

Uterine Atony

The prefix *a-* means without. The word *tonus* refers to muscle tone. *Atonus*, or *atony*, is when your uterus fails to contract down after having your baby. Typically what happens is that after your baby is delivered, your uterus will contract to expel the placenta. When your uterus is completely emptied, the contractions continue and cause a clamping down around the bleeding openings that had placed your own circulation adjacent to the placenta. This is all a strategy for our species to survive—birthing and living to tell the tale. This reflex is helped to a great extent by breast-feeding, and the contractions you will feel with suckling are the famous afterbirth pains. You don't have to like them but you should be grateful for them.

When labor has been unusually long such that the muscle tissue of your uterus is pooped out or when your baby is so big that your uterus is stretched too thin, the afterbirth contractions can be weak. Since the vascular bed upon which the placenta sat isn't constricted enough by your weak—your atonic—uterus, bleeding can be brisk. Luckily, we know about such things and can take the steps to minimize the blood loss. Merely massaging your uterus usually works. Pitocin drip, the same stuff used for inductions, will also strengthen the efforts of your uterus. Prostaglandin by vaginal suppository or IV is another powerful stimulant for contractions. If your uterus remains boggy, surgery may be necessary to tie off the blood vessels to reduce the bleeding. This hardly ever happens, so it's not something to worry over as part of your thinking on delivery.

Uterine Inversion

If the placenta were too firmly attached to the inside of your uterus, removing the placenta could drag the uterus inside out. Conditions like this in which the placenta actually grows into your uterus are very rare. They're called placenta accreta, increta, and percreta, these designations referring to the various depths of invasion of the placenta.

There are two reasons that this is dangerous. First, if your uterus is inverted—pulled inside out—the lining over it is stretched. There's a weird reflex of nerves from this lining that can result in a severe drop of blood pressure. Second, when the placenta doesn't just cleave away cleanly, the area bleeds profusely. Resolution of this problem involves separating the placenta away as much as possible and then reinserting your uterus back into its anatomically normal position. This is a little rough, but if you've had an epidural you're covered.

Sometimes there's no placental accreta, just too overzealous a pull on the cord to remove the placenta before it's really separated or a floppy uterus from a prolonged labor that inverts too easily. I'm inclined to think that either there's some unusual placental tenacity there or the uterus is so atonic that it inverts with even the usual amount of traction on the cord.

Cord Breakage When Trying to Remove the Placenta

Typically the insertion of the umbilical cord is fairly strong, but sometimes the individual vessels of the cord may start to fan out just above the insertion into the placenta. This weakens the base and the filmy tissue can tear away with the normal traction applied to the cord that helps to express the placenta. Oops.

It happens, but it's no big deal. Unless your placenta finds the exit on its own, your doctor will have to reach inside your uterus to find and gently pull it out. It's not a pretty sight, but it's not dangerous.

Retained Products of Conception: Retained Placenta

Depending on how a placenta is attached, there may be some parts of it that remain attached even when the rest comes out and looks complete. This will cause prolonged bleeding. An ultrasound can make the diagnosis. If it's a big enough chunk, it can be delivered spontaneously with Pitocin, but if the placental fragments are smaller, you may need a D&C. Most of the cases of retained placenta are incidental findings in which a patient would call her doctor and ask what that chunk of tissue was that fell out, and then the problem's over.

Failure to Progress

If in the course of your labor you go two hours without a change in your cervix or descent of your baby's head (three hours with an epidural), you've met the criteria for the diagnosis of "failure to progress." This is grounds for a C-section. If your baby isn't complaining with fetal distress, you can afford to wait beyond these criteria because sometimes surprises happen. But even if you were to start moving again, there are the worries of shoulder dystocia, too short a cord, and the fetal distress beginning again.

Fetal Distress

This means what it says. The fetal heart rate in a happy baby will exhibit no prolonged drops in the heart rate (decelerations) and will maintain a good beat-to-beat (BTB) variability, i.e., small fluctuations in the heart rate from moment to moment that indicate your baby is compensating for everything from moment to moment—a sign of fetal well-being. Drops in the fetal heart rate, with or without a loss of the BTB variability, bear closer watching.

There are two types of fetal distress (my designations):

- Mere complaining. In this type your baby's heart tones will go down with contractions, but they recover nicely after each one. And the timing of the decelerations follows the rise and fall of the contractions. These are called early decelerations, and the BTB variability remains good. We see complaining with failure to progress. You'd complain too if someone pushed your head up against a pubic bone for hours.
- Real fetal jeopardy. In this type there is real compromise in your baby's ability to tolerate the labor. Whereas the early decelerations of mere complaining resolve themselves along with the relaxation of the contraction, in real fetal jeopardy, the recovery of the heart rate doesn't happen until after the contraction (late decelerations). Loss of BTB variability indicates added jeopardy. This signifies that your baby is no longer accommodating to the stress of your labor. Unless a rapid labor allows you a rapid vaginal delivery, you need a C-section.

Meconium

Meconium is baby's expulsion of intestinal content into the amniotic fluid. It is made up of fetal hair (lanugo), sloughed skin, bile, and inflammatory elements. There are two schools of thought.

Fast Forward

Complications in labor include:

- Shoulder dystocia—rare
- Uterine atony—rare
- Uterine inversion—very rare
- Cord breakage—rare
- Retained placental fragments—rare
- Failure to progress
- Fetal distress—late decelerations, loss of beat-to-beat variability, or meconium
- Meconium
- Amnionitis—rare
- Bleeding—rare

The first school of thought: If an unborn baby were to need oxygen for some reason, either not enough was being offered from the umbilical cord or the placenta, or if a fetal condition were to require more oxygen than what was available, he might try to gasp for breath. This involves a sudden depression of his diaphragm, which is the way you and I breathe, also. This sudden movement can squeeze his intestinal tract, causing some bowel contents to be expelled into the amniotic fluid. Because he didn't have that Whopper you now regret having had, his bowel contents are the mucuslike cellular debris listed above.

A-FACTOR

Failure to progress and fetal distress are the most common indications for C-section. One of these usually occurs in about one in eight labors. The other complications are extremely rare.

The second school of thought: The latest ideas suggest that because the meconium is irritating, it may cause inflammation of the surfaces of the umbilical cord and fetal vessels, and diminish the amount of Wharton's jelly, the thick substance that helps protect the umbilical vessels from crimping. Such inflammation of the fetal vessels could cause fetal distress as a result of decreased oxygenation. In other words, the meconium isn't because of fetal distress, it's the cause of fetal distress.

Regardless of the significance, meconium can be a big deal for a couple of reasons. First of all, we don't like to see it because it means something has been or is happening that indicates a disturbance in the pregnancy that could jeopardize baby's health. Second, when he's born, his first breath and inhalation may suck some of that mucuslike substance into his lungs, which is very irritating to the lung tissue and can cause a serious lung inflammation. Ventilators are sometimes needed in such cases.

Forewarned is forearmed. One of the handy things about having your water bag popped while in labor is that the fluid can be observed. Meconium is a very obvious, greenish material and is easily identified. This alerts your attendant, doctor, or midwife to suction out his throat and nostrils carefully before even that first breath to remove the meconium.

No one likes to see meconium, and its presence requires a close eye on the labor, including continuous monitoring, preferably with an internal monitor. Signs of late decelerations or loss of good BTB variability will tip your doctor over toward C-section. But I've seen countless meconium labors that have progressed on like nothing's happened, resulting in completely normal vaginal births and babies. The second school of thought could change everything and prompt clinicians to effect delivery the fastest way possible (C-section), since this theory implies on-going damage to the placenta when meconium is noted, and not just a concern over your baby's first breath.

A recent technique called amnioinfusion is a means of using a thin tube of fluid to irrigate around your laboring baby to prevent the compression on the umbilical cord with ruptured membranes or to dilute the meconium.

Amnionitis

Infection around your baby while in labor will both jeopardize him as well as speed up your labor, which shows much wisdom on the part of your body. In fact the labor becomes so efficient that it's often hard to get a C-section together before a vaginal delivery intervenes. Such babies are examined very carefully for signs of infection and placed on antibiotics if warranted. They usually do well, but Group B ß-hemolytic strep is still a killer, so if there are any possibilities, a pediatrician will err on the side of giving antibiotics rather than withholding them.

Bleeding

The same conditions apply as in amnionitis. Serious bleeding at term requires a C-section unless a vaginal delivery beats it out.

Now, when I count to three you'll awaken, refreshed, with the understanding that things can go wrong, but they probably won't happen to you, and if they do, your doctor will know just what to do, and you, your husband, and child will live happily ever after, and you'll tell all of your pregnant friends that this is the book that changed your life. One . . . two . . . three!

What's the Deal on C-Sections?

Fetal distress, failure to progress, breech presentation, herpes lesions . . . let's make a deal. And behind door number two is C-section.

Most think the cesarean section was named after the way Julius Caesar was delivered, but this is a myth. His mom had a vaginal delivery because a C-section patient in those troubled times didn't survive. (History has many references to his mother after his birth.)

C-section—it's the thing that is sure to cause esophageal reflux in any Bradley instructor. If you're a Gaea Earth mother, fountain of nature, you'll feel at first like a C-section is the Anti-birth and has ruined your life. But then you'll hold that beautiful baby and all else will pale in comparison. In other words, when it comes to the C-section, you'll get over it. Besides, you'll have a chance at a vaginal delivery for the next one (called VBAC—vaginal delivery after cesarean).

And if you're a rockadelic modern now-a-go-go woman, you were over the whole C-section thing by the first trimester. Your doctor, whether you have a vaginal delivery or C-section, will feel his job is done when everything turns out well. But he won't do a C-section to get on the greens. It's not a golf thing. Besides, it's mostly dentists who play golf.

Besides the philosophical battle over C-section that is waged between the naturalists and the pragmatists, there is the issue of recovery. It is in fact a surgery, so it takes longer to recover from than an uncomplicated vaginal delivery. The thing you won't read in the other books, however, is that a complicated vaginal delivery is harder to recover from than an uncomplicated C-section. This means that heroism to pursue a vaginal birth, besides creating risk for your child, has a point of diminishing returns for you.

Indications for C-section are:

- Failure to progress
- Fetal distress
- Herpes outbreak—a fresh herpes lesion can shed virus to your baby through the traditional vaginal route, making C-section the obvious preventative method for travel.
- Infection—amnionitis, infection around the baby, is particularly dangerous and time may be important. If vaginal delivery isn't imminent, prompt delivery can be effected by C-section.
- Abnormal presentation—breech, transverse, and oblique (every other angle) positions, and multiple gestation (twins, triplets, etc.) are best delivered without the constraints of the birth canal.
- Previous C-section—unless you seek VBAC, merely scheduling a repeat C-section is legitimate and should be your right. You or your doctor may decline VBAC because what happened last time to prompt Cesarean delivery is likely to recur.
- Maternal choice—we hear all of this talk today of reproductive choice, but it deals only with babies that are less than an inch long. What about term babies? If you had a choice in whether you were going to have this baby at all, shouldn't you have a choice in how you want your baby delivered? Why are Planned Parenthood groups so strangely silent about that?

What's the Deal on C-Section Rates?

The situation—or as some call it—the crisis—of C-section rates is a real bogus issue. It all started off as a monetary crisis when doctors and hospitals were paid more for C-sections than vaginal deliveries. And those that had the most to lose were those mercenary misogynists, the insurance companies. Then the medical specialties got into the act with unofficial rumblings of hurting women unnecessarily—after all, it was surgery and by golly there was just too much of it going on.

It is interesting that the rise in the C-section rate coincided with the changes in rate of two other things: the rise in the rate of elective breast augmentation—yes, with surgery; and the rise in malpractice claims by patients who sued because a C-section wasn't done.

There didn't seem to be a breast augmentation crisis. This might have been because insurance company executives liked big breasts, but it was probably because insurance companies don't pay for plastic surgery. Another reason it wasn't a crisis was because with today's antibiotics and surgical techniques elective surgery isn't all that unreasonable. As far as malpractice claims, I've never heard of anyone suing her doctor because she did a C-section—only the opposite. Could it be that being heroic for a vaginal delivery with warning signals increases the risk of bad outcomes? In this light, if your doctor is practicing legally defensive medicine, she isn't in conflict with your best interests.

Consider this: your obstetrician has incredible pressure on her to bring her C-section rate down, yet there better be the best of outcomes. She has to go to peer review meetings during which she'll be notified if her C-section rate falls out of the normal. Yet the malpractice engines keep churning. Unfortunately, most people have been convinced that if they don't have a perfect baby, someone must be at fault and someone must pay. If your labor goes swimmingly, you should expect a vaginal delivery. But I'm proud to say, as doctors interested in what's best for you and your baby, I and I'm sure your doctor will shuck any thoughts of C-section rates if there is any suspicion of fetal distress going on.

What's the Deal on VBAC (Vaginal Birth After Cesarean)?

I certainly don't mean to say a C-section is no big deal. And some people find the extra concerns of surgery unacceptable enough to refuse another one. This thinking fell right into the C-section rate pseudo-crisis, fueled even more when studies indicated it was safe to have a vaginal delivery after a previous C-section.

Frightened by our C-section rate red flags, we doctors began doing VBACs. Insurance companies loved it and sponsored many seminars on how this was the way to go for women, as if they really cared about them and not the fiscal year's bottom line. And then we obstetricians out in the trenches began seeing complications. And we compared notes with our fellow obstetricians and discovered that they too were seeing complications. And not just little complications, but things like rupture of the uterus, babies with problems, and the like.

I think that for a time, hopefully by accident, the complication rate of VBAC was being underreported. Now you're talking about hurting women!

Now that a lot of the statistics have been sorted out, the complication risk is one out of a hundred. That's not bad, unless of course you're the one out of the hundred. For this reason most obstetricians don't push for VBAC anymore, but don't discourage it either. It's considered a legitimate choice, but one you make—not your insurance company.

There are certain criteria that need be met for VBAC to be a realistic option for you. First of all, the statistics aren't good if your first C-section happened in a labor in which you got up to six or seven centimeters dilation. This means that you probably had an adequate trial of labor and it portends poorly for your chances of being able to pull it off on your next try. Secondly, the scar on your uterus (not your abdomen) must be a horizontal scar because this is the one that heals strongly enough to withstand a labor. A vertical scar is a weak scar and prone to rupture. And it goes without saying that you shouldn't have a VBAC if there are conditions making a vaginal delivery at all risky, like breech, twins, or placenta previa.

Like all things in medicine, when a VBAC goes well, it goes great; when it doesn't, it can go very badly. So before choosing VBAC, a VBAC really has to choose you—you have to be a good candidate. If so, great! Full speed ahead. If you're not a good candidate, have the crummy C-section, get a good baby, and get over it, because chances are good you might not have been able to get a healthy baby without it.

The best candidates for VBAC are women who had never had an adequate trial of labor: babies that were delivered by section before any labor, like breech or herpes conditions; fetal distress that cut an otherwise excellent labor short; aborted inductions because of pregnancy-induced hypertension or other maternal disease. The worst candidates are those that had an adequate trial of labor but failed to deliver vaginally. And women with a vertical scar on the uterus are noncandidates. For the record, 60 percent of VBACs succeed. This isn't bad for a condition that once earned the slogan, "Once a C-section, always a C-section." But the 40 percent failure rate (need for repeat section) should prompt you to be a good sport about accepting C-section should any warning signals arise.

Recovery from Delivery

Real women give birth and then are back in the fields later that afternoon, right? Maybe on Mars.

It may be a natural event, but it's a doozy. There are massive changes that come about, shifting you from the maternal incubator to the parental caretaker. Just the fluid shifts are enough to make you a bit unsteady for a few days after. Hormonal changes are also afoot, not the least of which is the preparation for breast-feeding.

Your uterus is still enlarged, and the raw surface where the placenta was will ooze for a while. *Lochia* is the term for the bloody-serous vaginal discharge originating from your uterus. Within a few days the bright red lochia rubra will convert into the lochia alba, or whitish discharge, but some women can have intermittent bright, red bleeding for up to six weeks.

If there's a problem related to bleeding, it's usually due to infection, retained placenta, or subinvolution (meaning your uterus doesn't contract down well, remaining boggy). An infection will be accompanied by pain. Retained placenta will bring increased bleeding over time. These are usually minor problems if dealt with quickly, but they can become major problems if you wait to report them.

If you had an episiotomy that was small, recovery is quick, usually within a week or so. If you had a large episiotomy or a bad tear, you may not be comfortable for six weeks. Hot soaks are the best thing for such a convalescence, the radiant heat of the water mobilizing all of your best healing abilities. If you smoke, healing will be delayed since nicotine is a famous vasoconstrictor that limits the amount of oxygenation that gets to the site of injury. Your doctor will recheck all of this in about a month and lift the ban on intercourse at that time if all is well.

If you had a C-section, the acute recovery is more difficult, but your bottom will feel fine. When the discomfort of the incision wears off, you'll feel better more quickly than a woman who had a tough vaginal delivery. Postoperative complications include bladder infections (easy to treat) or incisional infection.

Whether you have a C-section or a vaginal delivery, the lochia is about the same. It's a mess, so have a stash of the mega-maxi-jumbo industrial-strength pads ready for when you get home.

What's the Deal on Induction?

The philosophical ramifications of induction of labor were discussed in the section on the third trimester. Here it's appropriate to deal with the nuts and bolts.

Induction of labor is any process that initiates labor before it might spontaneously begin. It may seem unnatural, but it is a completely legitimate technique that is often necessary to bring a pregnancy to a happy conclusion when medical complications might make continuing a pregnancy dangerous to yourself or your baby.

An elective induction, although not the natural way to have things go, is quite acceptable if you're within one week of your due date and your cervix is ripe. Your doctor could agree to an induction if the cervical criteria are right and you're within that time window.

As to the questions of whether inductions are harder labors than natural labors, the answer is that if an induction, for either medical reasons or personal reasons, is done with a good Bishop's score and within a week of the due date or beyond, it should be no more intense than a natural labor. Indeed, your own natural contraction mechanism usually takes over in these cases, allowing your doctor to turn the drip down or even off altogether. On the other hand, an elective induction without an inviting Bishop's score is a bad idea, as it is liable to be a long drawn-out affair, with the shadow of C-section looming if the war against the laws of physics is lost.

What's the Deal on Saving and Storing Cord Blood?

Is the belly button really the end of the line for the umbilical cord? One of the newest items of interest in obstetrics is umbilical cord blood retrieval of stem cells at birth. This isn't the fetal stem cells that are so controversial in the abortion debates, but stem cells collected very easily from the umbilical cord that remains attached to the placenta (afterbirth) after the cord has been cut and the baby no longer connected. Long considered a waste by-product of the whole pregnancy and delivery process, this "waste" began to rise in interest when cancer specialists, called oncologists, partnered with immunological and transplant doctors in claiming that the blood from a baby's umbilical cord at birth, if stored properly, could be used as a bone marrow transplant if the baby (or a family member) were to need enough cancer treatment radiation such that it would destroy the bone marrow.

The bone marrow is where all of the blood elements are made: red blood cells (oxygen-carrying cells), white blood cells (infection-fighting cells), and platelets (clotting elements). The blood of the umbilical cord at birth is rich in what are called stem cells—cells that can transform into any of the three types of blood cells mentioned above.

When your baby is born, her blood is quite different from the blood of an adult. There is a different type of hemoglobin altogether, which is gradually replaced during her first year with the adult blood type. And there is a much greater concentration of stem cells. Therefore, tapping this source will yield a very rich collection for storage.

This has become such an exciting development in the normally two unrelated fields of obstetrics and donor/recipient graft rejection that a whole new industry has sprung up to provide this service. And the prices of storage have plummeted significantly such that anyone can afford it.

Is this storage a type of insurance for cancer? Really now, ask the critics, what are the chances? If you took even the hundred dollars or so a year over several years and compared (via apples and oranges method) the cost to the chances of actually needing the cord blood, the financial risk may not match the medical benefit. Or so they say.

But it really is an apples to oranges comparison because if you're the person to benefit from it, it doesn't matter that you're a rarity. At worst, it's a reasonably priced luxury. At best, it's a lifesaver.

But let's throw a few cantaloupes into the apples and oranges mix, too. If even a family member of the baby who had cord blood stored needs it, there's still twice the chance the match will assure acceptance over rejection when compared with a match from outside the family. So depending on the number of family members, the odds on your "investment" yielding a benefit can go up dramatically.

There is also the matter of simplicity. Collecting cord blood in case someone might need it one day is quite different from waiting to get bone marrow after finding out there is a need. One of the startling contrasts in comparing cord blood retrieval to bone marrow retrieval is that in cord blood at birth, the retrieval is painless, inexpensive, and involves absolutely no risk. Add to that the increased survivability from stem cell donations to family members and suddenly the critics' objections begin to get a little wispy.

I could name a lot of unnecessary things that cost a whole lot more than what it costs to store cord blood, and I suppose we must all take inventory as to what's important in this life. But we all agree that life itself is important to us, and cord blood storage adds another advantage to surviving the slings and arrows of outrageous fortune. More information is available through the Cord Blood Registry at 1-800-588-6377 or at www.cordblood.com.

Q & A–Labor and Delivery

Each Labor Gets Faster

Question: Each labor for me has come faster and faster. My last one was twenty-eight minutes. I'd like to get pregnant again, but I'm scared. Should I be?

Answer: The first thing I would recommend is a careful review by your doctor(s) to determine whether you had prematurely dilated before going into those light-speed labors. If so, it may be that you have an incompetent cervix. If not, then, yes, you have really fast labors and the next one is likely to be the same.

In my patients who have a similar history, I begin checking for cervical dilatation a few weeks before the usual times, at about thirty-two weeks. I will also do checks at twenty, twenty-four, and twenty-eight weeks, just to further reassure myself there's no incompetent cervix. Assuming the cervix is closed until the actual labor, I would find it prudent to do an elective induction for many reasons—not the least being that you don't want to have your baby in the car! There's no better way to trash the new minivan.

Fast labors have a higher risk of placental abruption, so an induction would allow things to proceed in a more controlled way, with a whole hospital wrapped around you should some problems due to rapid delivery develop.

As far as your being scared of what might happen, you should base your decision about having another baby or not on whether you want another baby, not on what might happen. Leave that worrying to your doctor.

Umbilical Cord and Stillbirth

Question: My friend was due about the same time as me, but she had a stillbirth near term because the umbilical cord was too tight. How could this happen? My doctor says I will go into labor any day now. Is there any way to avoid this?

Answer: Since so much depends on that lifeline called the umbilical cord, it's a wonder it isn't our greatest worry in obstetrics. But there are many safeguards that protect this structure.

First of all it's long enough to not get yanked with undue traction. Second, the blood vessels within it, two arteries and a vein, are cushioned by a gel called Wharton's Jelly, which can keep these vessels from getting crimped even when there's a knot in the cord. True knots in the cord are unusual, but most end up causing no problems because of Wharton's Jelly. There are exceptions, and these exceptions are real tragedies because when the umbilical cord stops providing oxygen and exchange of nutrients, the baby will die.

"Too tight" a cord is probably just an expression simplifying what happened to that baby. If it was too short, which is rare, the biggest complication is placental abruption, in which any movement of the baby can yank on the cord's insertion point on the placenta, causing the placenta to pull away, leading to bleeding. Also, at delivery, a too short cord could put such tension on the blood vessels within it that it would be compromised, showing on a monitor as fetal distress.

More than likely the cord was wrapped around the baby's neck several times. Wrapped around once is actually quite common (20 percent) and only shows as a mild, intermittent, recovering distress on the monitor. It is called a nuchal cord, and it can cause some real distress when it wraps around twice or more, making the length of the cord short enough to cause undue tension. I once had a patient laboring fine until the heart tones crashed. On doing an emergency C-section, I found the baby had a nuchal cord times four (that is, wrapped around the baby's neck four times). In residency, I once knew of a patient who had a nuchal cord times seven! But this was probably because this baby had an abnormally long umbilical cord.

Ultrasound can sometimes show a nuchal cord, but a preemptive C-section for this is overreaction, and operative deliveries are usually recommended only for *complications* of nuchal cord (fetal distress) and not just a nuchal cord itself. And in today's managed care climate, where everything is being done to bring down the C-section rate, a single nuchal cord hasn't yet earned preemptive C-section status.

Sometimes there is a stillbirth for absolutely no discernable reason. Further investigation may reveal a listeria infection or subtle genetic abnormality. Other times there will be no reason, and this can be so frustrating that a doctor will use his or her best guess, looking at the cord as the most likely culprit—but it is a guess—a good guess, but a guess. Don't let this rare but tragic event discourage you in how you think about pregnancy. In most cases everything is fine. In the rest, many of them have problems that can be addressed. Unfortunately, the notoriety of bad outcomes for the few crowds out the news of all of the good outcomes.

Traveling Late in Pregnancy

Question: I know I'm not supposed to travel at thirty-seven weeks, but I must. What information should I bring with me should I go into labor out of town?

Answer: You're right, you shouldn't travel this late in pregnancy, but I can certainly see where a death in the family or similar life event might mandate your presence.

Any new doctor would want to know your age, how many babies you've had and how, any allergies, medical conditions, or troubling symptoms. You could provide this history yourself. It would be helpful to know blood type, due date and whether it was determined by ultrasound, and whether there were any specific concerns your doctor had been following you for.

Bad Tears with a Previous Pregnancy, the Likelihood of a Repeat Bad Experience, and Types of Episiotomies

Question: With my last baby I had a midline episiotomy, but still tore badly. What are the chances of a tear with the next delivery?

Answer: All an episiotomy does is prevent the superficial tears. Deeper tears are usually the result of a large baby or the skin of the perineum not having enough time to slowly elasticize.

I prefer the midline method of episiotomy because the tissue is thinner there—therefore, less tissue trauma, less bulk to heal, less pain. The downside is that if it extends with a large baby, it'll tear right into the rectum. This can be fixed right there, though. The alternative is a right or left mediolateral episiotomy, in which the cut is made from the center of the floor of the vagina down an angle, on either side of the rectum. This will spare the rectum, maybe, but a tear can shred in many planes through much thicker tissue than the midline would have. It can be messy. A midline is much easier to recover from than a mediolateral, and a midline with an extension tear into the rectum is easier to recover from than a mediolateral with extension tears along irregular paths into all of that thicker lateral tissue.

If you've had a bad tear previously, the chances of the same thing happening are less since the tissues of the vagina and perineum have already been elasticized once. But that's in a perfect world where it's assumed that all other parameters are the same—same doctor, same type of episiotomy, same size and position of baby, same type of labor, etc. No two pregnancies are alike, however, so I'm afraid it's going to be "I don't know." Generally, the more babies one has, the less likely the prudence (notice I didn't say necessity) of an episiotomy.

I do know this: most obstetricians—myself included—love to get by without an episiotomy at all. But I'm not afraid to cut one if I can see it's the only thing holding the head back without nasty tearing. It's a last-second call. But in my practice I cut no automatic episiotomies. It would be a good idea to discuss with your doctor the policy on episiotomy—are they automatic, are they midline or mediolateral, are they with quickly dissolving suture or delayed absorbing suture, etc.?

Sutures Used in Episiotomy. There are three main types of suture used in episiotomy: quickly dissolving—usually chromic, which dissolves in about two weeks and usually softens during this time; delayed dissolving—usually a polyglycolic or polyglactic suture—which dissolves over about six to eight weeks or longer, but can stiffen and give a sticking sensation sometimes; and permanent (nonabsorbing) suture—used when there is an infection and previous episiotomy repair breakdowns. (I don't use this. So far, anyway.)

Look for other current questions and updates regarding delivery on Baby-Zone.com, by going to babyzone.com/features/expertsqa.

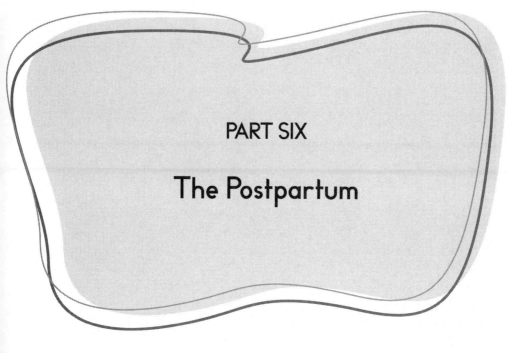

PART SIX

The Postpartum

The Puerperum

After the birth of your baby, either by vaginal delivery or by C-section, many changes take place to get you back into the nonpregnant state. There are dynamic fluid shifts that can take up to two weeks to equilibrate, resulting in prolonged swelling for some time after delivery. Your ankles will be the last to find this out. Your uterus, within hours of delivery, is already less than half the size it was while pregnant. Lochia, the normal postpartum bleeding, can last up to a month to six weeks. It's a result of processes that do more than just shed tissue or blood, but ready your uterus to go again sometime in the future. You are thinking, some long, long time in the future. Perhaps even in a galaxy far, far away.

Breast-feeding (beginning on page 279), besides providing perfect nutrition for your baby, is also ingeniously integrated into our survival as a species because it helps to stimulate contractions of your uterus, decreasing the amount of bleeding from it. Nipple stimulation evokes a response from the pituitary gland in the brain to release oxytocin (the same stuff used to induce or augment labor). With each breast-feeding, there is an initial "crunch" of a uterine contraction, the so-called afterbirth pains, or afterpains. Therefore, breast-feeding and afterbirth pains have an evolutionary survival function, helping to limit blood loss from the uterus after delivery.

The Background Goings-On

Immediately after delivery, nursery personnel tend to the needs of your baby. This is the period known as the third stage of labor, between delivery and the expulsion of your placenta. Assuming there's no problem with her breathing, your baby's biggest risk is temperature regulation. She will be dried off so that evaporation on her skin won't chill her. Remember that she has just gone from 98.6 degrees to room temperature. If she has trouble regulating her temperature, she could suffer distress. This is an elementary rule of newborn care. Other things that can cause a newborn distress are meconium aspiration and low blood sugar (if you were diabetic, the high flow of sugar getting cut off abruptly when the cord is cut). Again, this is all elementary, and nursery personnel and your doctor know all of this. If you've arranged for cord blood storage, cord blood will be obtained in special vials.

> **Fast Forward**
>
> The third stage of labor begins right after your baby's delivery and ends with the delivery of the placenta. While that's going on, your baby will be dried to avoid cold exposure, suctioned, with special emphasis if there is meconium, and examined for well-being with a crude but practical barometer called the APGAR score.

The APGAR Score

Dr. Virginia Apgar was an anesthesiologist who developed the APGAR score in 1952, which is the standard barometer of newborn well-being one minute and five minutes after delivery. Each of the letters in the word APGAR stands for a particular observation and a one- or two-point number is assigned. The *A* is Appearance (pink is good, blue isn't); *P* is Pulse (heart rate, which should be above one hundred); *G* is for Grimace (reflex irritability); the second *A* is for Activity (floppy babies flunk this one); and *R* is for Respirations (crybabies win here). With five parameters and a possible score of 0–2 on each, a good APGAR is considered anything above 7.

Troubled babies will usually have low APGARs. But a score of 1–3 at one minute may not be meaningful if the five-minute APGAR is normal. A persistent low APGAR at five minutes is worrisome. Scores of 4–6 are considered borderline, and 7–10 is considered normal.

The score is not a crucial predictor for which babies will have problems in later life, so care must be used in treating it as a generalized quick appraisal. But it's easy and has the eloquent beauty of demonstrating the progress of your baby from his first minute to the next five-minute interval. A baby usually "grows" into the APGAR between the one-minute and five-minute scores. The usual routine is to record both, for example, a 7/9 and a 9/10. The 9/10 is the typical score for a baby doing great. You won't see 10/10 APGARs given, except in children of lawyers.

Perhaps there should be a *DILEO* score . . . yeah, that's the ticket. A *DILEO* score would include the following areas.

Defiance: whether your baby bites your doctor's finger when its used to open the mouth for suctioning, with an extra half point for peeing on your doctor.

Interest: whether your baby is interested in life as we know it by showing robust activity. Kicking and screaming at the new world order portends well.

Love organ: how well your baby's heart is beating. (I know this is an ambiguous Hallmark valentine connection at best, but I was stumped on *L*. Dads shouldn't be tempted to record the DILEO score off the scale because of what they feel the love organ is.)

Exhaling: respiratory effort. If you're exhaling, you've got to be inhaling. (Unless you're Bill Clinton.)

Off-color?: whether your baby is nice and pink or off-color.

The Placenta Has Left the Building

Powerful contractions after your delivery diminish the area under which the placenta is attached, buckling it, which leads to separation. These contractions, called afterpains, continue after delivery of the placenta in order to control the bleeding from the inside of your uterus. In this way big bleeding openings of blood vessels become narrow openings, effectively minimizing

Fast Forward
Baby leaves, placenta leaves, you recover, then you leave.

the amount of blood loss. For your further protection, you've been building up extra blood throughout your pregnancy.

The placenta then wants to separate and, like Elvis, leave the building. Your doctor will grasp the cut cord that is dangling from you and put some gentle traction on it. This speeds up the process, which is good. You want everything to be finished so that the room can be tidied, you can be tidied, and you can have a chance to bask in your motherhood.

The Magic Moment

But there's more to the postpartum period than hormones and tissue and lactation. The birth of the family begins the instant you and your husband share the room with your child. Even if you're not going to be breast-feeding, I recommend you have your baby breast-feed at least right then. You are maternal, and you can embrace your baby who was only your passenger moments earlier.

In a way the delivery melee is like your wedding reception. There are a lot of goings-on all centered on you and then the party's over. Soon (a few minutes later if you breast-feed) the extra relatives usually go skipping off with your baby to the nursery, and the personnel dedicated to the infant are also gone. You and your husband are left with your doctor and a nurse, and it gets really quiet. If your husband has a chance to go off with the baby parade, I recommend that he not. I recommend that he stay with you.

Remember this moment, for this is a magical moment in your life together as husband and wife. Never does a shared smile between lovers mean as much as during this moment. It is a time when you and your husband share the same body, pressing just as philosophically close as passionate intercourse is physically close.

The ancient philosopher Philo said that God is a hermaphrodite creature, made up of man and woman together, and that this longing for togetherness creates the attraction between the two. And now you have a begotten son or daughter to complete the metaphor.

The recent firestorm of burned calories, dehydration, and any pain medicines that now go unopposed closes in on you and you doze in and out. Batten down the hatches, for this is the final calm before the floodgates open and the torrent of the rest of your life goes crashing along the nooks and crannies of its path.

Do indeed savor this moment with your husband, for it really is just a moment. There will be other life moments to be sure, but you only get this one once.

Soon your doctor leaves, and the remaining nurse, for lack of a better description, prepares to hose you down. After all of the soiled linens or barrier drapes are bagged, the instruments taken away, and your bed reconstituted to its predelivery splendor, your dignity is finally restored.

Your Own Parade—Who Are These People?

The slick hospital marketing that has resulted in LDR and LDRP rooms has made for a more comfortable experience. The waiting room where husbands pace the floor is an anachronism as relevant today as dragons are. The modern room makes for an excellent receiving room for well-wishers, but an unsupervised train of visitors can make you crazy. It will seem as if the world is beating a path to your hospital room door. You're not feeling your best and you know you're not looking your best. I recommend that you police it on the sneak. Tell the nurses how many people you want coming through, which relatives aren't welcome, and when to turn off incoming calls. They have a lot of experience in doing it discreetly, and you remain innocent.

A-FACTOR

So much is written about birthing plans and labor preferences. A lot of couples put a lot of emphasis on the delivery, but they should also plan for the moments after delivery as a special time between husband and wife.

There will be plenty enough time for the fans to cheer you and your baby later. Let the labor nurses know your preferences about visitors during this special time. Have them police the whole scene so that if anyone's offended, you're not the bad guy.

The Recovery

From a Vaginal Delivery

Certainly the peculiarities of your delivery will determine how easily you recover from it. If you had a spontaneous vaginal delivery, recovery isn't much more than a dull thud at the end of your pregnancy. Episiotomy or vaginal tears may add some sharp edges to that dull thud, but you'll be up and about within a few hours. If you had an epidural, the catheter in your back is usually removed soon after delivery.

From a C-Section

Recovery from a C-section is another story. This is truly an abdominal operation, so you have the extra burden of your abdominal wall tenderness. Also, your bowels are great, big wimps and they shut down if you even look at them the wrong way. Surgery does more than that and they take their nice sweet time getting back on line. This will delay any meals you're anxious to begin because if you put in before you're putting out, you're going to expand with gas pain.

Gas pain is the worst pain in a surgical recovery. When severe and associated with abdominal distention, it's called *ileus*. Ileus is even worse than the incisional pain. At least if you lie still, the incisional pain won't hurt, but gas pain will come after you, even if you're minding your own business. What I have found to work best is to withhold any type of food until there are good bowel sounds all over the abdomen, heard with a stethoscope, and there is no abdominal distension or unusual tenderness. You'll only wait an extra half a day or so before eating, but the pain of starvation is preferable to gas pain. If you can skip that step, things won't be so bad.

The latest studies have indicated that there is no difference in recovery whether food is withheld or given immediately. I've tried it all kinds of ways, and you just can't go wrong waiting for good bowel sounds.

The inherent risks of any abdominal surgery, including C-section, are infection and bleeding. The return of bowel function is a very good sign because if there is internal postoperative bleeding or infection, the bowels will not work properly. So if you're passing gas (since you're a lady, we know you really don't do that), then there can't be a lot wrong going on.

Fever after surgery is always a worry. If it happens the next day, it's usually due to your not expanding your lungs enough because it hurts to do that. If it's within a few days, a fever is most likely due to a bladder infection. If it's three to five days postop, it might be an incisional infection. (Doctors will call an incisional infection a wound infection, but that has always sounded masochistic to me. I don't use that term. The rough-and-tough "I'll-cut-on-anything" general surgeons would call me a wimp for my sensitivity.)

Your doctor is looking for all of these problems so if one occurs it will be nipped in the bud. You won't notice such keen observation because you'll be casually pressed on your abdomen and prodded nonchalantly in the midst of pleasantries like, "So how's that big boy (girl)!" or, "Wow, you don't even look like you were ever pregnant." Your doctor is always multitasking. Don't be fooled by the glib demeanor—your doctor's working.

Lochia–How Much Bleeding Is Normal After Having a Baby?

At first this sounds like a simple question; actually, it's a question that entails the entire postpartum period—that six weeks we obstetricians call the puerperum. The uterus is not only ingeniously designed to accept, then carry, and then expel a pregnancy; it is also designed to do it over and over again. After the placenta comes out, the uterus undergoes a process called involution, or shrinking. This is important because the site on the inside of the uterus where the placenta was attached is rich in blood vessels. Shrinking of this site reduces the amount of surface area that can bleed.

Involution happens quickly. There is bleeding, however, and it's bright red for a couple of days (lochia rubra); by two weeks the weeping effect doesn't have enough blood mixed with it to keep it red, and a pale discharge is noted (lochia alba). Generally, bleeding should get less and less over time, but there can be some bursts of activity for up to a month. Most of the substantial bleeding, however, should be over within a few days. Any irregular bleeding after a month is more than likely a result of the body trying to regroup hormonally. Breast-feeding will delay this regrouping even longer, which aids (but doesn't guarantee) birth control.

The placental implantation site doesn't just scar over during involution, otherwise its surface area would be a dead zone for future implantations of fertilized eggs. What actually happens is that its bed is separated and falls away as part of the lochia. The tissue underneath it heals and pushes it away, not unlike a scab that finally falls off.

Any bleeding that's more than a heavy period should be reported to your doctor. Keep in mind, though, that a large clot is only the sudden passage of a clump of partially clotted blood that's been collecting for some time. What you're seeing could be a whole night's collection, with your sudden vertical position upon rising allowing gravity to cause it to fall out. Recurrent clots, however, are not normal and should be reported to your doctor.

Causes of continued abnormal bleeding include subinvolution (inadequate shrinking of the vascular placental site, described below), retained placental tissue, or infection.

✳A-FACTOR

Infection of your uterus, endometritis, is well treated with antibiotics. It is rare in private practice. It can be dangerous if not treated, but your doctor is trained to catch it because it's one of the famous things to evaluate for. It was in his Obstetrics 101 class. He'll spot it fast.

Complications in Recovery

Puerperal Fever

Any fever greater than 100.6 degrees twice within six hours is called febrile morbidity, a fancy way of saying that something's up. Besides decreased lung effort, bladder infection, or incisional infection, your doctor will watch you for endometritis, or infection of your uterus. The cause of this is usually infection before delivery, and like draining a boil, the emptying of the infection via delivery will usually resolve this. But if the fever lingers and your uterus remains tender, IV antibiotics may be necessary.

Subinvolution

If there is incomplete involution of the placental site, it can bleed because it hasn't shrunk. This is called subinvolution. Whether there is subinvolution or

▶ Back at Charity Hospital

Puerperal fever is an old term. When I was at Charity Hospital, a reorganizing of medical records occurred that necessitated a clearing out of different records stashed here and there. One such book I saw in a corner, covered with dust, was the *Record of Births at Charity Hospital, June 19, 1852, to February 17, 1891*. I spent many on-call nights looking through it, fascinated by the fact that it spanned the recorded births during the Civil War. It was literally a chamber of horrors, for most births at that time were home births, only complicated cases going on to the hospital. The names recorded were all first-generation Irish, German, and Italian immigrants. Under the Comments for each delivery, the beautiful calligraphy of the nuns was in stark contrast to the horrors that were recorded. Most of the deaths were from puerperal fever. Today we have antibiotics, so such a complication would earn merely an extra paragraph in the discharge summary dictation.

I asked the medical records night shift custodian what they were going to do with that book and the others like it stacked so carelessly in the corner. "Probably just throw them away," she said. I thought to myself, I might just have to steal that book. It was a don't ask, don't tell moment.

whether retained placental tissue or infection is causing the prolonged bleeding, it used to be thought that a quick D&C was indicated, but now a more conservative mind-set has evolved: A D&C may traumatize the lining, jeopardizing subsequent implantation. Also, a piece of placenta might have caused the bleeding and would probably be washed away with the sudden bleeding episode, curing itself. Lately, ultrasound has been used to great advantage to indicate the need for D&C (when placental-like impressions are seen on the scan).

Tenderness with or without fever is never normal (not to be confused with cramping, or afterbirth pain). Inflammation can delay the normal healing and involution processes, resulting in bleeding. In this case antibiotics for the infection and medicines to contract the uterus are indicated.

With infection a D&C can do nothing more than seed the bloodstream with the infection. Eating my words, in any of these conditions a D&C could still be necessary if heavy bleeding continues in spite of the above management. Also, clotting studies should be considered since bleeding could be due

Fast Forward

The typical puerperum is marked by lochia rubra for a few days, growing paler as the lochia alba by ten to fourteen days. Bleeding can occur off and on for up to six weeks. An occasional clot is forgivable, but recurrent large clots or significant bleeding after the first few days should prompt an evaluation by your doctor.

to problems with the normal ability of the blood to clot and not because of subinvolution.

Blood Loss

Whether you have a vaginal delivery or a C-section, there's going to be some bleeding. If there are complications such that the bleeding is excessive, you might need to have a transfusion. But before you call 911 to have a Jehovah's Witness rushed to your bedside, understand that for the most part blood is safe. It is checked over, under, around, and through. In fact, even if your own husband wanted to donate for you, the blood bank would still put it through all of the tests for HIV, syphilis, hepatitis, and so on.

Of course they're still going to get you to sign that paper that says you could just plain die. This is because you never can tell when hepatitis Z will get discovered, but it probably won't be the day you need blood. And you will really need the blood if your doctor offers it because it's not given as just a good idea anymore. Giving it as a good idea is a bad idea, but withholding it when you really need it is a worse idea. Your tissue needs oxygen to heal, and it's your blood that delivers it to the tissues. If you're running on empty, this sets you up for delayed convalescence and a weakened resistance to infection.

Fast Forward

Complications after delivery include fever (infection), bleeding from subinvolution, retained placental tissue, or infection.

What are the criteria used to give blood? It used to be that if you lost a lot you got it. Now, no matter how low your blood count, your doctor won't generally transfuse unless you're battling a major infection or you have symptoms of acute anemia, like low blood pressure, a rapid pulse, or dizziness upon standing.

We doctors hate giving blood. You won't get it unless you really need it. And if you do, you can be sure that you're the rare case indeed. Doctors who give blood too much are usually investigated by hospital committees as to why.

> **A-FACTOR**
> You would have to cross a certain threshold of severity of fever or bleeding for it to be serious enough for IV antibiotics or transfusion, and that threshold is rarely crossed. When it is, modern postpartum care is astute in catching it early.

Infection

If you have a vaginal delivery, you could have an infection in the area of epi-siotomy or vaginal tear repair. Usually antibiotics by mouth will do the trick nicely. A C-section is at risk of an abdominal incisional infection. Superficial ones respond well to oral antibiotics, but deeper ones may have to be drained and treated with IV antibiotics, delaying your departure from the hospital. Both types of delivery can develop endometritis, which is an infection of the uterus and can be quite serious. In private practice, however, such infections are extremely rare. (At Charity Hospital almost half of the patients who had C-sections ended up in the septic ward. In fact, we referred to the C-section post-op ward as pre-Septic. But the indigent fall victim to poor nutrition and compromised healing. Some drop in without prenatal care, prone to many complications. The best protection from a complication is good nutrition and the vigilant appraisals that prenatal care affords.)

Urinary Tract Infections

It's hard to get through a hospital experience without a catheter up your blad-der. But in spite of a nearly 10 percent chance of developing a bladder infection from them, the benefits of catheters far outweigh the risk. Urine output is a crucial measurement that all is well in you after an experience like child-birth. Because of the distortion to your anatomy while you reconstitute, you may have trouble urinating. After a C-section a catheter is necessary to record your urinary output hourly until the next morning. Just as the fetal well-being of your baby can be determined by evaluation of the amount of amniotic fluid (largely made up of fetal urine), so too your well-being is assessed. If you can get by without a catheter with a vaginal delivery, that's the best way to go. But if you could benefit from one, it's usually worth it. Nevertheless, any burning with urination or frequency or urgency of urination should prompt a call to your doctor to rule out a bladder infection. It is also noteworthy that just having been pregnant and just having delivered make you prone to bladder infection, even when no catheter was used.

Even though a bladder infection is no big deal in the cosmic scale of things, it can be very uncomfortable, so it's best to nip it in the bud. Since most antibiotics take a day to start working, the sooner the better.

Postpartum Depression

Having a baby is like going on that dream vacation to Europe. It's wonderful, but it's also terrible in that it's a lot of work, you're living out of a suitcase, you don't feel great, and you're the one doing all of the packing and unpacking. There will certainly be an undercurrent of strain between you and your husband at some point in your hospital stay. This is normal. Focusing on what you two have produced will far outshine the fact that he had the unmitigated gall to go to work for a couple of hours the next day.

> **A-FACTOR**
> Postpartum depression is normal and temporary. Being bummed out is one thing, but thinking malevolent thoughts is another. If postpartum depression has you thinking weird thoughts of hurting your baby, this is an emergency—report it immediately and without fail. True psychosis is rare and gives plenty of warning.

But you will have the wherewithal to let it all ride. Your hormones will make you pay first with a few good cries, but then your spirits will lift just as mysteriously as they collapsed.

Blaming the baby for how you feel is not normal, however. Neither are thoughts of regret, anger, or fantasies of hurting the baby or yourself. When your thoughts turn really nasty, report this to your doctor immediately. We still don't know why postpartum blues (depression) sometimes will turn into psychosis. But there will be warning signals. And you'll know you're not your-self—sort of like an out-of-body experience. If your conscience tips you off that there are bad vibes in your head, this is a psychiatric emergency. You don't want to be on the front page of the newspaper, and no matter how nice, sweet, and religious you are, you have no special protection making you immune from the trappings of a psychosis.

Thrombophlebitis

Just as feared as it is before delivery, thrombophlebitis (inflammation of the deep leg veins that could generate a blood clot) is a serious complication requiring anticoagulants (blood thinners). But since your baby is out, you can get by with oral anticoagulants instead of the shots or IV needed before delivery.

19

Breast-Feeding and Other Postpartum Concerns

The Mammalian Art of Breast-Feeding

Because we're mammals, we have retained several physical characteristics that are pinnacles of evolution. None is as nurturing to our kind, however, as breast-feeding. Besides the obvious immunological superiority over formula, there are also the bonding, affection, and warmth of the maternal-newborn exchange that snuggling in this way affords.

Your infant's face, where most nerve sensitivity is centered, is surrounded by your motherly bosom—a physical act of love. And from this act of love, life flows, literally. The lactating breast answers your child's mouth, satisfying the void that the suckling fills.

The best fed are breast-fed, it is really true. The incidence of diarrhea, respiratory infections, other infections, bowel disorders, and possibly things like sudden infant death syndrome are lower with breast-fed babies. There is definitely an immunologic benefit.

> **Fast Forward**
> During breast-feeding, keep yourself well hydrated and continue your prenatal vitamins.

If you're committed to breast-feeding, you will be disappointed if it doesn't work out. Although true breast-feeding failure can happen, it is rare. Most failure occurs because of pain and impatience with or worries over the amount of flow. There are many hormones and processes necessary for milk letdown, so as a new mother you should grant a grace period after the birth for the process to engage. And you'll be relieved to know that nutritional deprivation for the baby need not be a concern because a full-term infant has a few days of food supply on board, so any success is extra during this time. Within a couple of days of delivery, any further concerns over your baby's nutritional needs can be addressed by your pediatrician.

▶ Fast Forward

Colostrum begins by postpartum day two or sooner (even before delivery), and dilutes out to the usual milk over the next month. The colostrum has maternal antibodies that make it superior to formula.

The precursor of the more dilute milk, colostrum is an immunological protection for the baby, providing maternal antibodies that provide an edge in fighting infection. It is also rich in minerals, protein, and fat. It's almost always produced by the second day after delivery and then will last up to a week, slowly converting to milk over the next month. Full flow from your breasts may take up to three or four days after delivery, so during this time you should relax while the interaction between your infant and your breast is fine-tuned.

The mechanics of breast-feeding are basically this: each breast can be drained in around ten minutes, the highest fat in the last part. Once a rhythm is established, most breast-feeding schedules are punctuated by feedings every two to four hours. You should drink a lot of fluids during this dehydrating action, and you can judge the adequacy of hydration and nutrition of your baby by expecting six or seven wet diapers a day. With patience and determi-

✳ A-FACTOR

True breast-feeding failure is rare, usually due to impatience or employment. Late bloomer infants have a couple of days of starvation-proof nutrition already on board, so don't panic if it takes a little while to jive.

nation, most breast-feeding attempts end in a satisfying maternal-infant nurturing experience. But just dabbling in it is not enough.

Supplementing with bottles will often fail because your baby might from then on prefer the easier draw of the artificial nipple. For this reason, stopping temporarily because of infection of the breast (mastitis) will often cause a permanent end to breast-feeding. In such situations, it is recommended that you continue breast-feeding in spite of the infection. It is safe for your baby because the infection probably originated from the normal bacteria in your baby's own mouth.

Minimenopause

When you're breast-feeding, your estrogen plunges and your normal cycles are suspended, not unlike a hint of what menopause will be like. Decreased hormones can lead to headaches, moodiness (although it's always your husband's fault—and hold your ground on this), and dryness of the vagina. A dry vagina interferes with lubrication with sex, but this can be overcome with adjusted foreplay or KY Jelly. Urinary incontinence might also be a problem because besides the distortion of your anatomy that isn't back to normal yet, the thinness of the dryer vaginal tissues means less support under your urinary sphincter, which normally is tucked nicely to keep you dry. Kegel exercises can help with this, but it's not a magic bullet. (Kegel exercises involve tightening the muscles you would use to stop urinating in midstream.) Sometimes the vaginal tissue gets thin enough to become irritated (atrophic vaginitis).

> **A-FACTOR**
> During breast-feeding, your body thinks you are a breast-feeding maniac, and the rest of your hormones crash. But you won't shrivel up like you've been sucked dry by The Fly, so take heart that it's temporary.

Your doctor will have semi-helpful suggestions for all of these problems, but the true cure comes when you stop breast-feeding and start your cycling again. The good news is that you won't get all of these side effects, and in fact you may get none. La Leche League International has a lot of helpful suggestions at its website, www.llli.org.

Care of Your Breasts

The fact that your breasts and nipples were made to do what they do makes them fairly easy to care for. Simple cleaning of the nipple area (areola) with mild soap and water should be done before and after breast-feeding. Because your milk is rich in carbohydrates, yeast can easily flourish there, so you should pay careful attention to any signs of irritation or fissures. These irritations can easily get infected with bacteria, leading to mastitis that can involve the milk duct system. Occasionally even abscesses form. These are easy to treat because most bacterial breast infections are sensitive to even the older antibiotics. Nipple shields are useful when the areola is tender.

Your breasts will weigh more during lactation, so a good support bra will not only help with breast pain, but with back pain too. Most breast engorgement will peak after the first five days, but pain from engorged breasts can last as long as two weeks.

> **Fast Forward**
>
> Keep your breasts and nipple areas clean, and when not nursing, as dry as you can. Problems like fissures and inverted nipples warrant only common sense remedies, but La Leche League International has information on these and anything else you might want to know. Except working at Hooters. They frown on working there. In fact, they're in denial that such places even exist.
>
> Today we don't use any medicines to dry up the breasts. The drug Parlodel isn't used routinely anymore because of a very slight risk of serious complications. But it can be used if the benefit outweighs the risk.

If you're not breast-feeding, you need do nothing but bind your breasts with a tighter bra. Unfortunately, stopping the works isn't like flipping a switch. Your body, quite happy with millions of years of mammary gland evolution, won't let you get away that easy. Therefore, if engorgement pain continues, try ice packs. Do not pump the breasts to eliminate the engorgement because the reflex of emptying will cause more filling to come back with a vengeance. Some have used cabbage leaves, citing lactation suppression properties. I've seen mixed results with this, and I wonder if the milk letdown didn't decrease on its own.

Bromocryptine (Parlodel) is used to lower prolactin levels, but today it's only used for benign prolactin-producing tumors. It used to be prescribed to

> **Fast Forward**
>
> Breast-feeding pros:
>
> - Better for your baby's immune system
> - Optimal nutrition
> - Tidy and convenient
> - Bonding
> - Pregnancy less likely
> - Very inexpensive—in fact, free
>
> Breast-feeding cons:
>
> - Leaves Dad out, unless he volunteers his own nipples at times (marriage's best kept secret). Everyone agrees—it's just not the same.
> - Infections (mastitis)—not a reason to decide against breast-feeding. They're easy to handle.
> - Pain and engorgement. The engorgement peaks and then goes in less than a week, so it's not a big deal.
> - Social anxiety. Do you really want the leaf-blower guy gawking at you? (And don't leaf-blower guys always sort of look like the rapper Eminem?) In spite of the geeks a'gawkin', discretion is an easy art.
> - Being tied down. This is a *psuedo*con—thinking breast-feeding will keep you tied down. Why did you get pregnant? Life isn't one big date, right?
> - You can still get pregnant.
> - You're in a sort of twisted menopausal state with low estrogen, causing dryness of your vagina and a personal attack on your sex drive.
>
> The verdict: Despite any cons, justifiable or supposed, breast-feeding is still better than not breast-feeding.

women who weren't breast-feeding, but this use was stopped when it mixed badly (stroke, death) with those who had pregnancy-induced hypertension, not uncommon in pregnancy. Such bromocryptine complications are extremely rare—I've never seen one—so if you suffer from engorgement, all the other remedies fail, and you haven't had hypertension, ask your doctor about using bromocryptine.

Like nutrition, there's no way I can do breast-feeding justice in this small section. Whole books are available on it. The famous one—and my favorite—is La Leche League International's *The Womanly Art of Breast-Feeding*. There's a lot of weird stuff and political correctness in their literature (for example, the "family bed"), but the medical info is right on target.

The Evasive Art of Not Breast-Feeding

Indeed, you and your breast-feeding child constitute a different mammal altogether, a unique unit of togetherness. So with all of this beauty, free for the asking, why do so many women choose to forego it by bottle-feeding?

First of all, few women get proper instruction in the art, either from their own mothers or from their doctors. Everyone is so busy frantically preparing for the new baby that no one is preparing for the actual feeding. Instruction is sparse at best, with most advice consisting of nothing more than let the baby latch on and then hope the whole deal takes. Work is the other enemy of breast-feeding. Employment has expectations, none of which include a twenty- to thirty-minute break every two to four hours for breast-feeding. Failure outright is the final disappointment sending new parents to the grocery to anguish over iron, soy, and concentrate.

Fast Forward

Bottle-feeding pros:

- Anyone can do it.
- Allows Dad to bond and have special time with baby.
- Won't affect your child's rank in class as compared to breast-fed children.
- You don't have to expose yourself (unless you hold the bottle with your cleavage).
- Sex will be better for you because there's estrogen back in your personal formula when you use processed formula. (Estrogen is usually decreased substantially while breast-feeding.)

Bottle-feeding cons:

- Is expensive.
- There are two microwave liabilities: (1) Those bottles can explode (usually at 3:00 AM), and (2) You need to check the temperature because there's no 98.6-degree setting on the microwave. You can seriously scald your baby's throat.

Then again, maybe you just don't want to do it. Maybe you did it after a previous pregnancy and have decided to bottle-feed for this one. Maybe you just want this whole pregnancy thing to be over with. In forgoing breast-feeding, you've endured the scorn of the Lactation Czar at the hospital. Every excuse you came up with, she had an answer for. Perhaps you finally just told her you don't want to "because!" So there.

Now what do you do? You have this whole dairy industry churning away in your chest. Not that that's bad, because you have a pair of breasts that could make even Billy Graham do a double take. But you don't want big wet spots on your blouse because if you don't have an adequate supply of nipple shields, you'll be snagged into a college bar to compete in the wet T-shirt contest. Also, as big as your breasts are, when they're sore, they're sore big. And then there's the worry that if you don't breast-feed, your child could end up on a bell tower one day, strafing everyone with brown shoes.

The fact is that modern formula is pretty close to your breast milk. The big companies have spent fortunes to get it that way and have the research to back it up. The only thing formula can't match is the immunologic benefit, the antibodies that breast milk has. On a human note, what you're giving up is the breast-feeding cuddling, but that's not important because you will have cuddling down pat at every other opportunity. What is important, so some say, is that you're giving up your baby's appetite relief being associated with this cuddling, a rush of complex satisfactions on many levels. There's the whole some-of-me-is-in-you that has been used from the time that Christ said, "Take this and eat" to the *grokking* of Robert Heinlein's science fiction classic, *Stranger in a Strange Land*.

There may be a point there, but I don't think declining breast-feeding is on the same level as rejecting Christ. It's an interesting historical note that La Leche League International took its name from a shrine dedicated by the Spanish New World explorers to "Nuestra Senora de la Leche y Buen Parto," translated "Our Lady of Happy Delivery and Plentiful Milk."

Anyway, I defy anyone to show me who was breast-fed or bottle-fed by how they turned out as an adult. Unless, of course, that particular adult is still breast-feeding.

Don't laugh. How long is too long? When your child can unbutton your blouse—that's too long. When he asks you why one of your breasts seems to be a little larger than the other—that's too long. When he suggests that he should try other women's breasts—that's way too long.

But back to your ruining your child's life by shirking your breast-feeding duties. There is one huge advantage to formula: Dad gets to share in the feeding. This may seem like it's just a break for Mom, but as a father I can tell you that one of my greatest joys in life has been the very private time I've spent in the wee hours of the morning, just my baby and me. It was a reflective time for me. Sure I was tired, but the dozing in and out with my baby in my arms was all part of the mystique. At 3:00 A.M. there's nothing else to do but be with your baby and dream of the future. Speaking selfishly, this has meant so much to me with all four of my children that breast-feeding seems unfair to fathers.

> **Pregnancy Rules for Husbands**
> **Rule #9:** Do this. You'll never have this moment again with your child. I wish I could make this recommendation a whole chapter long because that's how much it meant to me.

As an afterthought, I have to warn the new dads who want to strike that Kodak moment pose by holding your naked baby to your naked chest. It's nice and all dads do this. But if your baby is hungry, you'll have a mouth hunting your hairy nipple like a heat-seeking missile. It's absolutely startling, this rooting reflex. Baby's mouth will circle its prey and then latch on for a most un-Dadly experience. This happens in every fatherhood, although no man admits to it. It's one of marriage's best kept secrets. It's a feeling that's plenty weird and boy! will your baby get pissed off when there's no flow. Better have Mom ready.

What's a Good Excuse Not to Breast-Feed?

Included in all of the good reasons to not breast-feed are all the things you don't want, like active, untreated tuberculosis, positive HIV or AIDS, illicit drug abuse, other medications (check with your pediatrician, not your obstetrician), and breast cancer. Breast-feeding isn't wise if you have cold sores because this is a herpes infection that can cause serious complications in your baby, especially if younger than one month.

Tandem nursing, in which you breast-feed your baby and an older child at the same time, and which is championed by La Leche League, makes me nervous. This implies that breast-feeding continues while pregnant again. Nipple stimulation is a powerful stimulant for uterine contractions, and anyone at risk for preterm labor (which could conceivably include all pregnant women) should not nurse while pregnant. This is controversial, but that's my opinion.

Smoking isn't good with breast-feeding. Smoking isn't good for anything, except for the manufacturers of postoperative chest tubes. When the nicotine gets into you, it definitely gets into your baby. But I think that if you're not breast-feeding only because you smoke, then the Philip Morris people should honor you with its *Smoking Industry Mother of the Year* award. And that goes for Dad, too. Think of it as heroin, Dad. Would you really say, "Oh my wife got off heroin because she's breast-feeding, but I still enjoy shooting up every day. Of course, she makes me go outside"? And if you smoke while breast-feeding, well, now, there's a Norman Rockwell scene if ever I saw one!

Regarding smoking . . . angrier sentiments to follow.

Disadvantages of Breast-Feeding

Mastitis

There are two types of infections, fungal and bacterial. Fungus likes moist, warm environments, so the slobbering on your nipples makes you a set up. If you merely keep the nipples dry when not breast-feeding, however, this won't occur as easily. Thrush (yeast in your baby's mouth) can spread as a fungal infection, too, and it could require treating both of you, which is easily done. The tissue ravaged by yeast can become secondarily infected with bacteria, and then you have a real mess on your hands (well, not on your hands). Whether a bacterial infection is a secondary invader associated with yeast or all by itself, it's usually from your baby's mouth, so breast-feeding is not only safe, but recommended as being continued so that you don't add engorgement to your symptoms.

The human body doesn't like standing fluids, be it in the middle ear or in the breast. Bacterial infections tend to develop. If the flow in the breast is sluggish in one area, then a bacterial mastitis can happen. Antibiotics almost always resolve this problem.

Prolonged Galactorrhea

This is a case of turning on the tap, but then not being able to stop the leak afterward. Prolactin is the milk letdown hormone. If it's elevated, as it is in breast-feeding, you of course have milk letdown, which allows you to breast-feed. It's possible your breasts can occasionally leak or milk can be expressed if the nipples are squeezed for years after you stop breast-feeding. One of two things is happening: either you've continued with large amounts of prolactin; or your breasts have remained exquisitely sensitive to normal amounts of pro-lactin. It's usually the latter and it isn't rare. In fact this condition has been used in the past to nurse children of women who were indisposed to doing it. Wet nurses, as they're called, made up an honorable profession that took the well-qualified nanny and added one extra talent, the ability to breast-feed. These were usually well-educated women—they just didn't hire boobs to do this job. (Sorry, I couldn't pass that line up.) Aristocratic women and royalty were favorite employers of such wet childcare. Even King Tut had one, Lady Maia, who because of her delicate responsibilities to the great king had her own royal tomb.

Social Anxiety

If your name is Cloud, and you're the free-spirit child of free-love baby boomers, you may not have a problem "whippin' one out" and nursing. But there's nothing like breast-feeding in public to blur the lines between nudity, nature, and exposure. I call it decent exposure, but there are many who feel it is indecent exposure, and you might fear the glares of adults or the snick-ers of children that you know are out there. Or you just might not want strangers looking at your breast. I don't even like that, and I'm a guy.

Historically, though, there's not quite anything as beautiful as an infant suckling from a mother's breast. Rembrandt knew it. So did Michelangelo. I don't think, then, that the bus driver is qualified to decry your act of beauty on the downtown route.

But there are ways of doing it discreetly, and I don't think you're selling out if you meet discretion half way. Even though you have every right to shout back at those stares, "Why don't you take a picture—it'll last longer," there's no reason to give anyone a show beyond what is necessary to get the job done.

Make life easy for yourself. La Leche League International has information on discreet breast-feeding in public. You really can do it without being the Coochie Coochie girl.

Being Tied Down

Not really. An infant who is breast-feeding is the easiest infant to haul around. You don't need all of the extra paraphernalia that *EMA*s (extra-mammary activities) require. If you're breast-feeding, just a couple of extra diapers and a pack of wipes and you're good to go. Even to a movie, believe it or not. A newborn is only going to squawk when hungry and there you are, ready to squelch the squawk.

Delay in Mammogram

Not really. If you need a mammogram, you can get one while breast-feeding. The radiation, about 1/100 of that of a chest X ray, won't turn your baby into the Amazing Colossal Woman or Radioactive Boy. The only problem is that mammograms are designed to be over-read, and your extra bulk provides a lot more tissue to yield false alarms and interferes with getting a good picture. If you really need one, get it right after emptying the milk load via breast-feeding. If there's a significant worry over something going on in your breasts, perhaps you should discontinue breast-feeding to pursue it.

Pregnancy

I list this as a complication only for those who still think it's impossible to get pregnant while lactating. It's hard, which helped our species space our children, but it's not impossible. If you add condoms, you've got a pretty good double whammy against conceiving. But this still doesn't make it impossible. If that's an issue with you, see the next paragraph.

Contraception While Breast-Feeding

Breast-feeding will stimulate some of your hormones but diminish others, thereby disrupting your menstrual cycle such that ovulation is infrequent and the lining of your uterus isn't very receptive should an egg ovulate and become

Fast Forward

When breast-feeding, what you can take and when you can take it:

- The minipill—two to three weeks postpartum
- The regular birth control pill (low-dose versions)—six weeks postpartum
- Depo-Provera—six weeks postpartum
- Abstinence—as long as you want (Tell your husband anything—he'll buy it.)

fertilized. This has provided a survival tactic of evolution so that a woman need not be wrapped up in the serious medical swings of a subsequent pregnancy before the last baby has had a chance to graduate away from the maternal shadow. But it can happen. And it can happen to you.

Generally, if you're not having periods while breast-feeding, then you're probably not ovulating regularly, either. However, if you're menstruating monthly, you're probably ovulating as well, and this is the situation that will render you fertile. (Even nonmenstruating women can fire off an egg, so no rules are absolute.)

Used correctly, condoms, along with breast-feeding, have worked well to prevent pregnancy for my patients. Condoms are overly maligned because their failure rate takes into account horny kids in the back of cars. In motivated people (and breast-feeding women are motivated people), condoms are usually used correctly.

I once had a 16-year-old new patient tell me she was sexually active, so I asked her if she used protection. She was using condoms, and when I pressed her, she assured me that she knew how to use them correctly. When I did the vaginal/speculum exam to perform a Pap smear, I found two condoms in her vagina. When it comes to the vagina, what goes in must come out, and this young lady broke the Law of Vaginas. This is why condoms get a raw deal in the statistics. I would like to see what the failure rate for condoms is overall compared to the failure rate in married women with a history of a previous pregnancy.

Used correctly, you shouldn't fear the uncertainty of the condom while breast-feeding. But if you do, breast-feeding doesn't cut you off from some of the traditional pharmaceutical methods:

✳A-FACTOR
If you were to get pregnant while exposed to the hormonal content of prescription contraceptives, there isn't any worrisome risk to your next baby. (Next baby? Yikes!)

Depo-Provera

This is a shot of progesterone you get every three months. You can get it while breast-feeding after your baby is six weeks old. It may interfere with losing weight as rapidly as you would like.

The Minipill

This is the progesterone-only pill (POP). It's missing the estrogen that the conventional combination birth control pill has. But it's effective, although it's contraceptive ability could be enhanced by the typically nonovulation nature of breast-feeding. You can start this when your baby is two to three weeks old.

The Combination Oral Contraceptive

This is the real birth control pill, chock full of estrogen and progesterone. It works extremely well, of course, even when you're not breast-feeding. Low-dose combination pills can be started after six weeks. This has always made me a little nervous, but the literature supports its safety, so I guess I'm just being a dad about it and not a doctor.

If you're daring enough to read the literature that comes with these prescriptions, usually printed on what seems like old fax paper and in a font size only discernable to the Incredible Shrinking Man, you'll be startled to find out that there is some amount of bad-mouthing going on about exposure to these hormones in pregnancy, should you get pregnant. First of all, you probably won't. Second, hormonal risk to developing babies from these particular hormones is theoretical at best and hasn't been documented. Don't sweat this.

Cosmetic Concerns

Your breasts will change. You love them now, but they'll begin underachieving after you stop your breast-feeding. There's no doubt that the pendulous nature of the breasts makes any increased weight within them cause more noticeable flaccidity later on. In other words, the bigger they are, the harder they'll fall later. What your breasts end up looking like, though, won't be because you breast-fed, but because you were pregnant at all. Remember, they were big before they were ever open for business.

Other Postpartum Concerns

When Can Sex Resume?

Usually after six weeks of healing (even with a bad tear) your vagina will be ready to receive visitors. Only one, of course—I think that's the understanding. If there were no lacerations or episiotomy, you can even begin sooner, as early as four weeks. Your doctor will "clear" you for sex, as if you're a 747 being cleared for take off. But a GYN exam is not the same thing as sex, in spite of all the overused comments I hear at every high school reunion.

> **Fast Forward**
>
> You can generally resume intercourse four to six weeks after delivery. Even if your doctor "clears" you, postpone it if it hurts because the exam is no substitute for the mechanics of sex. Also, wait for the right time. Sexual lovemaking should be just that—a reestablishment of intimacy, not just bobbing for climax.

No exam can predict how well you tolerate the rhythmic, persistent mechanical nature of intercourse. It really comes down to your comfort. If sex hurts, back off for another week or two, in spite of what your doctor tells you.

Also, I recommend you not resume until you get horny again. A baby crying can wreck the mood faster than seeing a mouse run across the bed. And you're tired. And you're worried about the next day. And you're dry. And you haven't used your vagina, except as an exit, for a while.

Don't worry, there won't be severe tire damage by allowing your husband to go in opposite to the way the baby came out. But stack the deck in your favor by waiting for everything—physical as well as psychological—to be favorable for an enjoyable experience. You may get a pout from your husband worthy of a 4+ on the Victor Hugo scale, but your vagina is for both of you, not just him. (Your sex organs are connected to your brain, but his aren't.)

Some women complain that they have lost the ability to have an orgasm after delivery. This is probably due to the psychological concerns stated above, but it can also be due to the distortion to the anatomy. Almost always it's a temporary problem.

What About Birth Control?

The methods of contraception are touched upon under breast-feeding, above. Basically, the choices are the same, except that if you're not breast-feeding, you need not worry about possible exposure of your baby to pharmaceuticals, so you can start immediately. Besides the birth control pill (combination estrogen/progesterone oral contraceptive), the minipill (progesterone only pill), Depo-Provera shot, and condoms, there is also the newer monthly combination estrogen/progesterone injection. Norplant (time-released progesterone in under-the-skin capsules) is now almost extinct due to litigation over its inconvenient but harmless side effects.

A diaphragm is a bad idea in the early postpartum period because it won't fit well after the distorting influences of your recent delivery. Even when you feel you're completely back to normal, you will need to be refitted in case there's been a change in the shape of your vagina.

Your doctor won't discuss these options until your final postpartum checkup, and that's OK because you're not supposed to be having intercourse until cleared anyway.

What About Circumcision?

The volatile nature of circumcision is discussed in detail in the section "Controversies in Obstetrics" in Chapter 22. I include it here only to discuss the timing. It's best done after twenty-four hours, so that your pediatrician has had a chance to check your baby. Waiting any longer allows your son to better develop the sheathing over his nerves that will better carry pain sensation. But the window, from purely a private practice experience, is still several days. Today, use of topical anesthetic creams is urged, but I haven't seen convincing results. Some babies holler, some don't. And they all fall back asleep immediately after. The only anesthetic that will completely numb the area involves

Fast Forward

It doesn't matter who does the circumcision—your obstetrician, the pediatrician, or your rabbi.

sticking needles into skin all around the glans, but I think this is crazy and more of a production than what's involved in circumcision.

If a circumcision is done, it will likely be done either by your obstetrician or the pediatrician. The obstetrician lays claim on the procedure because it has been a traditional part of the global delivery process. The pediatrician lays claim to it because, after all, your baby is now his patient. It's a friendly turf battle of sorts, but it really doesn't matter—they both do a good job. More than likely, the obstetrician will do it because your doctor is already paying crazy malpractice insurance premiums that include surgery, and many pediatricians don't want to pay so much for the privilege to do the procedure we all love to hate.

What About Tub Baths?

The great hypocrisy is that you're told to avoid tub baths, but if you have an infection from an episiotomy, you're urged to soak in warm water. The bottom line is that baths are fine, otherwise they wouldn't be recommended with infection. The vagina is what is called a potential space. For you men out there, this doesn't mean that it has a great potential, but that it's not a space unless something actually occupies it. Otherwise, its walls, floor, and ceiling collapse together. Water won't get in unless you open the lips of your vagina and swoosh it in. That would be bad, cause infections, and warrant the admonitions. But that won't happen accidentally, so tub baths are fine. Keep in mind that tub baths make you more prone to bladder infections, though.

What About Driving?

You can drive as soon as you're not dizzy. The fluid shifts and anemia that can accompany delivery may make you a little unsteady for a few days. But if you don't suffer from that, driving's fine. For C-sections the above applies, but add that you should also be able to wear a seat belt without discomfort. Why go through all of the trouble of having a baby if you're not going to wear a seat belt?

What About Stairs?

Any activity, including stair climbing, if it doesn't hurt or easily fatigue you, is OK. Even after a C-section. If you listen to your Grandma, she'll have you "lying in" for six weeks. Get as active as your body lets you. Those who join the land of the living fastest, heal the fastest.

What About Scissors?

Don't run with them. But now that you are a parent, you already know that.

The Cosmetic Aspects of Childbirth (by Elizabeth Kinsley, M.D., plastic surgeon)

Congratulations! You've successfully navigated fertility, pregnancy, and childbirth, and now have a beautiful baby. Unfortunately, you now have your grandmother's breasts, and the bigger they were, the farther they fell. You look at yourself and feel you have enough extra skin on your belly to start your own skin graft donor business, not to mention thighs that have more dimples than a Miss Teen USA pageant and veins that resemble a New York City road map. It sounds awful, but don't throw those bikinis away just yet. There is help, and it's called plastic surgery.

Everyone is different, but unless you were born with genes like my sister-in-law, the ex-cheerleader "Abdomin-izer" model, you probably have some areas of concern. The amount of weight gained during pregnancy, as well as the physical condition you were in prior to pregnancy, plays a big part in how you will look afterward. And then there is the professional help. This is offered as a brief guide to some of the plastic surgery procedures that can correct or minimize the effects of childbearing.

Melasma

This is the medical term for the pigmentation changes in the skin that occur during pregnancy. A result of hormones running amok, melasma can leave your skin looking sun damaged and splotchy. It is possible to bleach these spots (à la a famous moonwalking pop singer) with various creams. The effective agent is hydroquinone, which will fade the spots over several weeks to months. This should not be used while nursing. If that is unsuccessful, the next step is a chemical peel, which will usually result in a more even skin tone. It is important to see a physician for treatment of melasma, as over-the-counter products do not contain the appropriate strength of the active ingredients.

Spider Veins

So named for the weblike appearance of tiny veins, spider veins occur mostly over your legs. There are basically two methods of treating this condition, lasers and injections. Both are slightly uncomfortable and neither will eradicate the veins altogether, but you will notice a significant improvement in the appearance of your legs after treatment. Both methods require several sessions and about six weeks for noticeable results. I prefer injecting the veins with a sclerosing agent that causes them to scar down and eventually fade because the results are more predictable.

Breasts

Whether you breast-feed or not, there is a good chance your breasts will not look like they did before you were pregnant. Weight gain and engorgement stretches the skin of the breast and afterward results in a breast that appears deflated and sometimes sagging.

"Not a good look," you will murmur to yourself.

Correction of the breasts depends on how much the breasts have dropped, a condition known as ptosis. If your nipples are at approximately the same position on your chest, you may need a simple augmentation. If your nipples are pointing south, however, correction may involve a breast lift (mastopexy).

Breast augmentation is performed as an outpatient procedure. Saline-filled implants are placed beneath the chest muscle or under the breast tissue, with the more natural result being when placed under the chest muscle.

Pregnancy Rules for Husbands

Rule #10: If your wife asks you whether she needs plastic surgery and if you've not finished your family yet, tell her, "Of course not." If you've finished your family, tell her, "You're perfect for me, but you do whatever makes you feel better. You deserve it." Stupid husbands will ask about how much plastic surgery costs—and after everything you've been through!

Abdomen

Liposuction is a sculpting procedure, not just a debulking. It's best that you lose your pregnancy weight first so that you can get the best result. Abdomino- plasty (the "tummy tuck") is a much bigger procedure and is more of a recu- peration investment.

Plastic surgery isn't magic. You've got to meet it halfway by attaining a reasonable return to your prepregnancy weight. Also, and this is the most important thing, you really should wait until you're finished having babies before getting the bigger procedures, unless you're spacing your babies widely and can't live with the way you look for the interval.

Q & A–Postpartum

Conehead Babies

Question: I was in labor for a long time but then needed a C-section. My baby's head is shaped like a cone. I've heard that C-section babies' heads are round. Is this normal for him?

Answer: Your baby's head wasn't shaped like a cone, but like the inside of your pelvis. This is where he got hung up, either because you were too small, he was too big, or one of many other reasons. Nevertheless, he was stopped in his tracks.

Because the bones of his skull aren't fused, so as to allow for growth, his head was able to "mold" during your labor. This often works successfully to allow a vaginal delivery. His head will reshape to round within a couple of days. Fret not, you don't have a little conehead baby.

How Many C-Sections?

Question: How many C-sections is it safe to have? I've heard three, but I want a fourth child.

Answer: There is no general answer for this. It all depends on how your uterus has fared with the previous C-sections. Unfortunately, inspection at the time of the last C-section is the best thing we have to go by.

For your particular case, I'd ask your doctor to review the operative dic- tation about anything unusual or worrisome about your lower uterine segment that last time around. Based on that, she should be able to give you a general idea as to the safety of a fourth pregnancy and C-section. You won't get any guarantees, though, because there are cases of uterine rupture even with no previous C-sections. But your information should be good enough to make your decision.

Breast-Feeding with a History of Hepatitis B

Question: I had hepatitis B and I want to breast-feed. Can I?

Answer: You can breast-feed if your baby has been immunized. Ask your pediatrician about the baby's immunization to hepatitis B.

Rubella Vaccine

Question: Can I get the rubella vaccine if I'm breast-feeding?

Answer: Yes. The American College of Obstetricians and Gynecologists (ACOG) recommends all women who haven't had rubella be vaccinated in the immediate postpartum time, whether they're breast-feeding or not. The biggest risk to a baby is one week before conception to four weeks gestation. No risk to babies in the postpartum period has been documented to justify putting your next baby in peril.

Postpartum Tubal Ligation

Question: I just had my baby yesterday, but my doctor refuses to do a postpartum tubal ligation. Wouldn't it be easier if he did it while I was in the hospital already?

Answer: Tubals can be a touchy subject. This is something that should have been discussed long before delivery. A doctor may have religious reasons for not doing it. Or he may believe in the controversial "post-tubal syndrome" (see "Controversies in Obstetrics" in Chapter 22), as a medical reason to avoid the procedure. You're right in that it would make sense from a logistical point of view to take care of it while you're trapped in the hospital anyway, but I'll share with you my own reasons for not doing postpartum tubal ligations.

The riskiest time in your baby's life is the first week. In fact, neonatal mortality rates are defined based on the number of neonatal deaths during this time. With a tubal you're burning your bridges while your baby is extremely young, before she climbs out of the shadow of vicious statistics. And no matter how much you don't want another child—no matter what—you still can't predict how you'll feel being sterile with a baby experiencing complications. My secondary advice is to get your baby home, make sure she hits all of the milestones, and then after a year burn your bridges if you must.

If your husband is reading this over your shoulder, close the book and use some excuse like you have to go to the bathroom and go there with the book.

OK, you're there? Private? Good. My primary advice is if you're seeking permanent sterilization, wait as I explained above, then do it via vasectomy. There's no alleged post-tubal ligation syndrome to worry about, it's cheaper, and for a vasectomy the doctor doesn't have to enter a major body cavity, although you would never be able to convince a man that his scrotum isn't a major body cavity of major importance.

If you're having a C-section/tubal ligation, this makes my argument less attractive because your doctor is already there—in your major body cavity. But the fear of neonatal complications applies here too and it makes just as much sense to wait.

A tubal ligation is a legitimate procedure, but a vasectomy is the least the callous brute can do after all you've been through. You may now return to where you were reading before. But tear this page out.

Spacing Babies

Question: Is the perfect spacing of siblings for sociological reasons every two years? And is there a medical rationale to what the best interval span is to assure complete recovery between pregnancies?

Answer: There is no perfect spacing for sociological reasons. Environment, quality of parenting, a moral basis for teaching civilized behavior, religion, and economic status all play a role. I've known many people from all types of spacing practices, and I've never been able to detect a trend between the princes and the stinkers. If spacing them too close together were sociologically detrimental, then all twins would be jerks. Do what's right based on your medical recovery, financial status, desire for time with your baby, and your age.

Medically, it's just as fuzzy, although recently there has been suspicion that the preterm labor risk is greater if you conceive within a year of your previous delivery. C-section adds a structural fear into the recovery picture because it's assumed the incision through the lower uterine segment should have time to heal adequately before being stretched again with a subsequent pregnancy. Most obstetricians like to see at least two years between cesarean deliveries, but this is an intuitive assumption.

Look for other current questions and updates regarding postpartum issues on BabyZone.com, by going to babyzone.com/features/expertsqa.

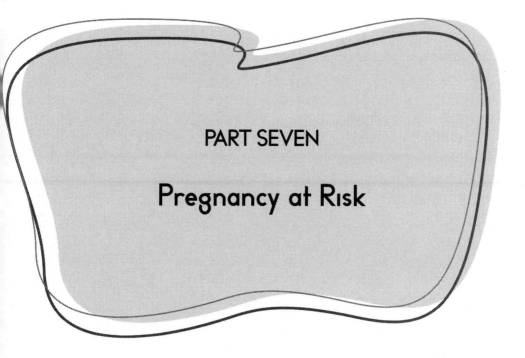

PART SEVEN

Pregnancy at Risk

20

Complications Unique to Pregnancy

The main premise of this book—even the title—is to allay anxiety, so it is with some misgiving that I begrudgingly include this chapter and the following one, describing in greater detail those conditions that could put you and your baby at risk. Although complications can arise in pregnancy, for the most part they can be spotted and addressed—but there will be the exceptions that can blindside a doctor. Thankfully, these are rare, and since no such book is complete without them, I hold my nose and include them.

At best, these chapters will demonstrate what your doctor, the thinking obstetrician, considers with each and every pregnancy, one eyebrow raised in anticipation for warnings that are otherwise missed by a couple enjoying their pregnancy. At worst, you might end up using this part of the book to look up a particular condition that complicates your pregnancy. If so, this discussion will give you a perspective on such complications and not just a sterile list of all things bad.

Preterm Labor

Prenatal care is the clearinghouse—the air-traffic-control tower to clear the runway for incoming arrivals—premature or otherwise.

Of all the concerns an obstetrician has, prematurity is the most fearsome. The repercussions of preterm delivery are so staggering that the damage cannot be truly assessed: seventy or eighty years of a human being's quality of life, severely altered, plus the emotional suffering to parents and siblings, not to mention the shocking economic costs to an entire family's financial security and to the community itself—it is overwhelming. In fact, with so much riding on it, prenatal care to identify premature labor is one of the most important developments in the twentieth century.

Although many of these children end up just fine, we see the others that have been afflicted by the unfair penalty of premature labor. We may indeed have the appropriate compassion for them, but it is a passing sympathy. To those who live the problem, however, the upheaval in their lives happens every day. This is the powerful thought of your obstetrician when faced with a premature labor.

As the lesser of two evils, there are many reasons why premature labor must sometimes proceed. Major provocations for delivery are premature separation of the placenta (abruption), infection, overload from twins or triplets, and pregnancy-induced hypertension (preeclampsia). There are also numerous other causes, less likely, that cannot be helped.

Although we still don't know all of the reasons patients may experience preterm labor, there are nevertheless many things that we do know can provoke it:

- Infection of the uterus or pregnancy (amnionitis), frequently with Group B β strep
- Multiple fetuses—twins, triplets, etc., which cause the uterus to reach critical mass earlier, at which time it tries to expel the contents like it would a term single pregnancy
- Incompetent cervix in which the structural integrity of the cervix cannot be maintained in a tightly closed condition (Dilation may invoke several neurological and chemical reflexes that may provoke labor to continue the process.)
- Bleeding within the uterus, usually caused by abruption of the placenta (premature separation of the afterbirth)
- Vaginal infections (still not conclusively proven) like yeast, bacterial vaginosis, etc.—infections usually inconsequential in the nonpregnant
- Urinary tract infections—bladder or kidney
- Other systemic infections, like pneumonia, peritonitis, appendicitis, etc.
- Previous history of preterm labor with prior pregnancy
- The largest category: unknown reasons

Management of preterm labor (PTL) is a serious challenge for any obstetrician. Many times the cause of contractions before term is never found. Also, often even the most rhythmic, persistent contractions seem to do no harm at all, resulting in unnecessary overtreatment. The problem is that doctors frequently don't know when they're overtreating, and if we get a baby to term we'll never know whether we were overreacting or not. But then again, we'd rather have a good mystery than a bad "known."

We're cowards. And if we've spun a few extra wheels unnecessarily to get a healthy baby, so be it. The truth is we really don't know the risk of false labor in preterm situations. It might not be as harmless as it is at term. If there's rhythm to the contractions preterm, we go running for the ounce of prevention. Another point of confusion is what is actually happening inside the uterus. To effectively push a baby against the cervix as a dilating wedge, there must be a net vector force in one direction—out. There can in fact be seemingly powerful contractions, but with all of the vector forces going in different directions so that the net force is not organized in one direction. There's just aimless contracting going on, and the cervix doesn't change. But in keeping with the same cowardice, we don't know when those vector forces will finally organize into one direction.

There is currently a silent war being waged between those in academics and those in private practice over diagnostics and therapies of PTL. A lot of the methods described in this book for testing for and dealing with complications are very expensive, and in the cost-containment mind-set of managed care there must be justification for spending this money to save just a few extra babies.

Just a few extra babies? I won't even go there, because to me every baby is priceless, even if it costs as much as a B-2 bomber. But unfortunately, these are the times we live in. Modern medicine with all of its expensive new improvements *is* very expensive, and study after study tries to determine what is the best way to spread it all around to do the most good with the least amount of financial liability. It's a terrible situation, but it may be the only way to really provide good care across the board.

Meanwhile, we in private practice are not obligated to live the philosophy of cost containment. Our patients are not the faceless population of a study. They are faces we will see again and again, and we have a responsibility to these individual faces because each one represents a unique doctor-patient relationship.

If your doctor is overreacting, then it's better than underreacting. The ideal formula is: Slight Overreaction + Common Sense + Judgment = Correct Management for the Individual.

Sometimes a premature labor may develop for no apparent reason, and an in-depth workup rules out all of the identifiable causes. As unsettling as it is for the cause to remain unknown, still it gives your doctor sanction to use one or more of the several medications that have proven effective in managing contractions. Even if treatment fails, gaining an extra week or two of maturity for your baby can sometimes make all the difference in the world.

Medication Used in Preterm Labor

Medicines that decrease the strength of uterine contractions are called tocolytics. Using them is called tocolytic therapy. The most popular tocolytics are:

Magnesium Sulfate

This is a muscle relaxant, given by IV. Its historical use was to prevent seizures due to preeclampsia (pregnancy-induced hypertension). It is still the dominant preventative in such cases, but its ability to relax muscles, including uterine muscle, has made it a first-choice drug for halting preterm labor. It's dangerous if its levels get too high because it can also relax your breathing muscles, which you would complain about vehemently were you able to voice anything at all. Its incredible safety record, however, stems from the ability to measure it in your bloodstream so that such levels don't occur. For this reason, management of magnesium sulfate is very simple and, done correctly, very safe.

Accompanying magnesium sulfate therapy is hydration, since the medicine must be given along with the fluids of an IV. Since hydration alone may lessen contractions, magnesium sulfate has a sneaky secondary effect to decrease uterine activity.

Nifedipine (Procardia)

This is a blood pressure medicine that acts to lower hypertension by relaxing the muscular layer surrounding your arteries. It blocks calcium at the molecular level in these muscles, causing the relaxation. The uterus goes along for the ride, too, getting nice and relaxed. The advantages of Procardia are that it can be taken in pill form as an outpatient and it also is available in a once-a-day dose. Caution should be used when mixing it with magnesium sulfate since it could possibly heighten the hypotensive effect.

Terbutaline (Brethine)

Terbutaline is an asthma medicine that relaxes the muscular tone of your bronchi to treat bronchospasm as is often seen in asthma. It will relax your uterus, too, thereby quieting preterm labor. It will also stimulate your heart to beat faster, and the rapid pulse becomes a good indicator that you're getting enough of the medicine.

Even if you were taking what's considered frequent doses of terbutaline, if contractions were to start before the next dose were due and your heart rate were less than a hundred per minute, it would be safe to take the next dose earlier. Usually an adequate blood level of terbutaline is associated with a heart rate of at least 110. Yes, it will make you feel really crummy, just like palpitations do, but it's harmless and worth all the trouble to keep your immature baby undelivered.

The combination of terbutaline to stop contractions and steroids to help jump-start the maturity of your baby's lungs could lead to the bad combination of fast heart rate with fluid retention. Such a combination can lead to fluid in the lungs, called pulmonary edema, which is as debilitating as pneumonia. Don't freak out if you are given this drug combination; your doctor knows all about this famous side effect. If you need it, you will get it. It's worth the risk. But if pulmonary edema were to start, all the tricks go back into the bag—you would not be a candidate for continued terbutaline at that point.

Because terbutaline kicks in with a sudden heart-racing effect, there have been efforts to make its administration smoother, which of course would affect a smoother tocolytic control of preterm labor. To this end, there is now a terbutaline pump ("T-pump") that administers the drug through a little catheter needle into your leg and that you can wear like a holster at home. There are companies that provide 24/7 support via toll-free numbers to help monitor the dosages and contractions.

Matria is one company providing such monitoring, and it also provides home nursing management of hyperemesis in the first trimester, pregnancy-induced hypertension, and gestational diabetes.

Newer Agents

There still isn't the perfect drug for preterm labor. No doubt there will be a slew of them within ten years, but for now we use mostly magnesium sulfate, nifedipine, and terbutaline.

If there's a good reason to have your baby, tocolytic therapy isn't good for you. Bleeding, infection, and other causes of preterm labor that wouldn't get better until delivery may pose considerable risk if tocolytics are used. The real success to controlling preterm labor is when your doctor can get another week or two out of your pregnancy. If it's easy to stop and goes on to term, it may be that it really wasn't preterm labor, but just a false labor.

Just having contractions does not mean preterm labor. Contractions have to be organized enough to cause a net vector force outward, causing thinning and dilation of the cervix (same as real labor). Contractions usually begin after twenty weeks in normal pregnancies. It's just that they're so mild they're not usually even felt, much less cause damage.

When Is Labor Preterm? Does Gender Influence How Babies Do in Preterm Deliveries?

Preterm labor is any labor before thirty-six to thirty-seven weeks (or term). Efforts to stop preterm labor are only as heroic as the distance is from lung maturity. A preterm labor at thirty-five weeks and five days won't be as aggressively managed as one at twenty-eight weeks. Thirty-four to thirty-six weeks deserves definite intervention. Thirty-two to thirty-four weeks deserves aggressive intervention. In fact, any preterm labor before thirty-four weeks requires the most dramatic intervention, including steroids.

We don't know why, but girls do better with immature lungs than boys. And white girls do better than African-American girls. The order of coping is: white girls cope better than black girls who cope better than white boys who cope better than black boys.

Modern Developments to Fight Complications of Prematurity
Steroids

Steroids are used to help mature a preterm baby's lungs. These drugs, which are given to you and get to your baby through the placenta, won't grow mature lungs, but will lessen the severity of immature lungs. These aren't generally given after thirty-four weeks because this is a borderline gestational age for the good steroids might do, and the risk of the steroids outweighs the benefit.

It used to be thought that the beneficial effects of steroid treatment lasted only a week and that it should be repeated weekly. Current thinking challenges the one-week effectiveness limitation, and many—including me—feel steroids bestow their blessings upon a baby's lungs for weeks. With the increased risk of pulmonary edema and the uncertainty of how long steroids may be effective, repeated doses are no longer recommended unless there's a serious fear of imminent delivery. There's no doubt that steroid treatment has been a lifesaver for countless babies over the last twenty years.

Tocolytics
These were described in the preceding section of this chapter.

Neonatology
A neonatologist is a pediatrician who does extra training (a fellowship) to treat high-risk newborn babies. If your baby were to be premature, this is the doctor who would be directing the management. Many medical specialties boast of situations in which lives are saved, but all of the other specialties combined can't outshine what a neonatologist does in a Level III nursery every single day. It is truly a specialty close to godliness. And these guys never get a fruitcake at Christmas.

Level III Nursery (Neonatal Intensive Care Unit, or NICU)
As specialized as a neonatologist is for newborns over and beyond what a pediatrician does, so also a Level III NICU is over the regular knock-on-the-glass well-baby nursery. (By the way, please don't knock on the glass.)

To be designated as Level III, all neonatal surgical specialties have to be on the staff of the hospital, and the nursery itself has to have the equipment to treat even the smallest babies. Twenty-four- and twenty-five-week babies are now surviving when they didn't ten years ago, and one wonders how much lower that bottom line will go. Right now it's a very fine line, the other side of which is the gestational age range considered legitimate to abort. Forget the philosophical fight over whether abortion is right or wrong because the next biggest fight will be over the later gestational ages that can be aborted overlapping into the earlier gestational ages that can survive.

Even medium-size hospitals are equipped to handle very small babies. They're labeled by the slang medical term Level II½. All they might be missing is the capability to do neonatal cardiovascular surgery or neurosurgery, for which premature babies can be transported to a larger regional center with a full-fledged Level III nursery.

Home Uterine Activity (Antenatal) Monitoring (HUAM)– Your Baby Goes Online

Home uterine monitoring is a technique wherein you wear a belt that contains a pressure-sensitive button that is discriminating enough to record uterine contractions. This information is recorded into a small electronic device. A telephone can then be laid on the recorder, a toll-free number dialed, and with a push of a button all of the information is transmitted within a few moments. Nurses at a central location have computer software that interprets the results and can allow them to call your doctor if there are any troubling data.

The studies have shown that unless you're carrying twins (or more) this advance warning system doesn't improve the outcome for the population as a whole. Your insurance company, of course, doesn't want to pay for this expensive service. They won't care if you're the one out of a hundred whom HUAM would have really helped.

The reason the population as a whole doesn't seem to have a generalized improvement in the prevention of preterm delivery with the use of HUAM is because there is often a misdiagnosis—or more accurately, an overdiagnosis—of preterm labor. Just because you're having contractions doesn't mean you're in preterm labor. The same criteria apply as in real labor—a physical change indicative of moving the baby out of you.

Home uterine monitoring is considered legitimate and efficacious if there are complaints of contractions and there is a history of preterm labor with previous pregnancies or there is a change in the cervix as determined by a patient's doctor. Since this is a noninvasive test that poses no risk, it's hard to argue against using home uterine monitoring in such cases. Also, it may be prudent to monitor patients in this way who have fibroids in the uterus, abnormalities of the architecture of the uterus, and hyperthyroidism or arrhythmias that use medicines that might provoke contractions. All multiple-gestation pregnancies are an indication for home uterine monitoring.

Used scrupulously, HUAM is an aid in buying more time for a pregnancy. It won't get you all the way to your due date, but in any maturing baby every day counts. The downside to HUAM is that it will condition you to fixate on every little tightening, perhaps increasing your anxiety and heightening fears of pending labor. Such fixations tend to put you through a lot of extra medical protocols when you go running to the hospital with every errant false labor pattern.

How Should Your Preterm Baby Be Delivered?

If a preterm labor were to complicate your pregnancy, your doctor must answer two questions:

First, is your baby better off inside of you or outside?

Second, if the answer is outside, is your child best delivered vaginally or by C-section?

The cause of your premature labor may be straightforward, and answering these two questions can be easy. It is the outcome that may prove difficult, so your doctor must answer these questions as early as possible. The first question's answer is usually that your baby is better off outside if the cause of the preterm labor is known—abruption, infection, etc. It's the preterm labors that are technically for unknown causes that do best with tocolysis and other preterm labor measures because all of the things that would weigh against continuing the pregnancy have already been ruled out.

If your baby's better off in, full speed ahead with treatment to ward off delivery. If your baby's better off out, your doctor will consider whether there's time for steroids to take effect—usually within twenty-four hours. If so, your doctor will delay as long as it takes to get the most benefit from them, all the while watching your baby very closely. If there isn't time for steroids, and delivery should be effected immediately as an emergency, then the fastest route should be used if the situation is unstable (translation, C-section if the whole thing is going from bad to worse, as with bleeding). If you're stable, a vaginal delivery can be attempted.

Picking the Right Dentist

In the beginning of the book, I discussed picking the right obstetrician, the right hospital, and so on. But I saved the dentist for now.

> **Fast Forward**
>
> Is your baby better off inside of you or outside?
>
> If inside, and continued pregnancy isn't dangerous, you'll be treated to stop the preterm labor. If outside, is your child best delivered vaginally or by C-section?
>
> If you're stable, allowing a vaginal delivery via induction is acceptable. If your or your baby's condition is worsening, C-section is the most expedient method of delivery.

The dentist? Hot off the press are studies that say if you have bad gum disease then you have a fivefold increase in the risk of preterm labor. The first time I heard this, I thought surely this related to the type of people who would not brush and floss regularly—or at all. Certainly someone in that group is more likely to have bad nutrition and forego prenatal care, thus putting her at risk for all complications, including preterm labor. But the new studies claim to have corrected any bias based on socioeconomic level.

What this means is that anyone with dental problems is at high risk for preterm labor, so adding a dental visit before conception may be just as important as a check-up of everything else. And yes, you should continue flossing.

Incompetent Cervix and the Mechanical Aspects of Premature Delivery

Your cervix—that circular, muscular, and fibrous purse-string opening—typically holds tight until contractions cause enough force to push your baby's head against it as a successful dilating wedge. When it finally gives way and opens, you have entered what is called real labor. But if there is a weakness in its structural integrity, it can fall open without the usual necessary forces. Any cervix having a mechanical weakness that diminishes its ability to hold in a pregnancy to term is called an incompetent cervix.

Actual labor at term is a complex mechanism that falls into place like so many tumblers in a lock. We are designed with a clock that ideally lines up the chemical and physiological tumblers after a baby is mature enough to survive. But if your cervix is weak, gravity alone can be enough to allow even a premature baby's weight to cause it to dilate. The gate is open, so to speak, and your baby can follow, unfettered, into the outside world. The earlier before term this happens, the worse off for your baby of course.

Causes of Incompetent Cervix

The causes of weakness in the cervix are:

- Damage to its structural integrity. Previous traumatic delivery that shreds the cervix. This can occur with precipitous delivery or melodramatic life-saving forceps delivery. Also, when a C-section is done in the second stage of labor when dilation is at ten centimeters, the cervix is paper thin and delivery of a baby's head that is socked in can cause a cervical tear. Treatment of precancerous lesions of the cervix can sometimes, though rarely, result in weakening of the cervix. With the early diagnosis of these lesions, more and more young women and adolescents are having them destroyed by freezing (office cryosurgery) or burning (laser).

- Congenital weakness, which is extremely rare except in cases like the DES debacle, in which estrogen was given to women with threatened miscarriage. The estrogen didn't work to prevent those miscarriages anyway, but the female babies that went to term had alterations of their own fetal genital development, including incompetent cervix. DES was given in the fifties, but with those women's daughters having premature babies, this mistake took a toll for three generations. Now it's 2002, and it's over, except for those babies, now in their twenties and thirties, who carry handicaps that their prematurity caused.

Aggressive Treatment for Incompetent Cervix–Cerclage

Whether a baby is born prematurely because of preterm labor or because of an incompetent cervix, the result is the same—it's too soon for the baby to do well without neonatal intervention. Premature labor is a warning in itself, but an incompetent cervix is a surprise in a first baby. (For second babies doctors are on it.) Certainly if there is a history of cervical treatment involving cryo or laser, your doctor will be prompted to check your cervix at the initial exam and again at the beginning of the second trimester. If it is unduly short, the treatment is surgical, and the second trimester is conveniently qualified to be the best trimester in which to have surgery.

The surgery, called cerclage, is actually a simple matter of inserting a nooselike tape around the perimeter of your cervix to keep it closed. At the appropriate time it can be snipped to allow delivery. It is done vaginally and usually works well. If the compromise to the cervix is so profound that there's nothing left into which to sink the cerclage, thereby eliminating the benefit of this surgery, prolonged bed rest, even in a hospital, may be necessary for months.

In such cases there is another way out. The usual cerclage placement is from a vaginal approach, but when there's nothing left of the cervix to work with, a surgical abdominal approach is possible that can purse string the portion of the cervix that extends internally past the wall that is the back of the vagina (on the inside of the pelvis). Called an internal cerclage, it involves an abdominal incision and is best done before conception rather than after because any surgery done during pregnancy, especially abdominal, is fraught with problem bleeding due to the extra blood vessel development that accompanies pregnancy.

With an internal cerclage, the trick is to predict, before they even become pregnant, which patients won't do well with a second trimester vaginal-approach cerclage, so that the internal one can be done before pregnancy.

Internal cerclage has other problems. Because it's placed via an operation from within the abdomen, it closes off the vaginal birth route. This means that since the cerclage is internal, your doctor can't later snip it vaginally and thus delivery must be by C-section. And although the cerclage can be left in for subsequent pregnancies, we're also talking about subsequent C-sections for them, too. Few obstetricians have actually done them at all, and although it's a simple procedure, doctors may be uncomfortable with learning to do it on one of their own patients. Even in my practice, I've done less than five in twenty years. It's a simple operation actually, but it is nevertheless an operation.

Unlike the permanence of the internal cerclage, the vaginal cerclage is done when you're already pregnant and is designed to be removed near the end of each pregnancy—a mere office procedure—allowing a vaginal delivery soon thereafter in the hospital. It is structurally more risky as success rates go. The internal cerclage is a better cerclage, but you're talking a surgery to put it in, a C-section for each baby thereafter, and astute predictive abilities that may not be possible without a crystal ball.

Although it's somewhat barbaric to think of preventing premature delivery by "tying the sack" closed," a cerclage is a lifesaver and an intuitively obvious solution to the problem of incompetent cervix.

Conservative Treatment for Incompetent Cervix–Bed Rest (Horizontal Pregnancies Take Their Toll on Upstanding Women)

Because most people actually crave a little extra time in bed, it wouldn't necessarily seem that you could have too much of a good thing. Not many specialties can prescribe bed rest with a straight face, but I happen to practice one of them.

Whether it's due to a failed cerclage, a case wherein cerclage is unwise, placental bleeding, or preterm labor, often an obstetrician must put the prospective mother at rest. Denying gravity its role by taking the weight of your baby off of your cervix can be helpful in prolonging pregnancy. Since it's easy, risk-free, and blatant common sense, you would think that such a simple method of treatment would be well accepted.

Unfortunately, life goes on around you when you're socked away at bed rest, spitefully dramatizing the stark contrast between your forced inactivity and the hustle and bustle just out of your reach. If you're the main provider, your income falls. There may be children that need to be fed or who insist on being held, chores that can't be ignored, and emergencies and mishaps that pop up one or two rooms away in any household. When you're at bed rest, you're just one ill-timed lurch away from taking action.

Bed rest is hard. Your doctor will understand perfectly what she is asking you to endure when she hands down this sentence. You may not have parents or in-laws to help out in a pinch. Your husband may have to travel in his work, leaving the other head of the household—you—on your own to manage the home from a horizontal position. Often, the best intended therapy of bed rest becomes impossible to carry out at home and hospitalization might be required for enforcement. It's a tough thing when you're the matriarch.

The biggest risk of bed rest in pregnancy is psychiatric. Hormones can accentuate feelings of helplessness when you are lying ridiculously impotent in bed—the clock ticking outside of your room. You will notice the clock because you're not distracted enough to keep from watching it. Anger is easy when you see something handled differently from the way you like to do it. If the bed rest is in a hospital, there are also the never-ending surprises of blood tests and the daily nuisances of monitors and hospital noise. Depression is easily come by.

And then there is the uncertainty. Rarely will your obstetrician know exactly when a pardon will be handed down, allowing you to resume your upright life. If the bed rest is substantially long, physical therapy can be helpful to reinforce range of motion with passive movements and exercises.

Being put to bed for a complication of pregnancy is one of the most grueling therapies in medicine. Will the little darling appreciate it? Of course not. How you sacrificed won't come up when you are asked to lend your offspring the car years later. But is it worth it? Of course it is, for reasons that transcend philosophical differences over car use, tongue-piercings, and your children's choice of friends.

Premature Rupture of Membranes (PROM)

The sac surrounding your developing baby, the amniotic sac, performs many functions. Besides holding your baby in, it keeps infection out. It also plays a part in the turnover and reabsorption of the fluid, mostly contributed to by your baby's urine. Additionally, the pressure within this fluid collection has a role in development of the baby's lungs. The amniotic sac is made up of the membranes commonly called the "bag of water." All in all, it's a pretty important structure. So when it pops before your baby is mature, there can be danger to both you and your baby because if fluid can leak out, infection can creep in.

Anytime the membranes rupture before the onset of labor, obstetricians refer to this as premature rupture of membranes, or PROM. It is thought that infection or impending active labor, or both, probably provoke it. (PROM resulting in complications of premature birth has sometimes been associated with Group B strep.) When PROM does happen, labor usually develops spontaneously, which is dangerous to the premature but probably prudent for a term baby. In many of these cases the infection that caused the membranes to rupture probably causes the irritation that provokes labor. Infection is no good for a baby, lung disease and meningitis being prime fears in such a situation. And if the membranes rupture unrelated to infection, there is then a route in for bacteria. Obviously, premature rupture of membranes or even leaking membranes is considered a situation that must be addressed without fail.

If rupture of the membranes happens during the mature, later part of the pregnancy and labor doesn't spontaneously ensue, then labor can be induced so as to effect delivery before any infection can set in. This is because the clock is ticking after rupture of the membranes, the onset of infection of your baby in many cases dependent on time of exposure. This infection can also be injurious to you, possibly endangering your uterus.

There are flow sheets that obstetricians follow to manage these cases. Below is one example of a flow sheet, but there are subtle variations from doctor to doctor. The fact that the American College of Obstetricians and Gynecologists has changed protocols for PROM many times over the last two decades underscores the fact that we still don't have the perfect management answers.

PROM Management
Term
If you're past thirty-seven to forty weeks, induction of labor is wise if labor doesn't develop spontaneously. Most obstetricians were trained to set the timer for twenty-four hours after PROM, moving to C-section if vaginal delivery had not occurred. Although the twenty-four–hour rule is not etched in stone, infection becomes more likely the longer it takes. Also, it is recommended that the pelvic exams be kept to a minimum as this may drag in infection. If your baby is at or near term and you're a repeat C-section (you've decided against VBAC), plans can be made to perform a repeat C-section soon after the PROM.

Premature, Before Thirty-Two Weeks
If you suffer PROM before thirty-two to thirty-four weeks (before six to eight weeks prior to term), management can be conservative because prompting a delivery may put your premature infant at more risk in the outside world than inside of your uterus. This is only considered, however, if there are no signs of infection. Any infection should prompt a plan of delivery no matter how early. As seems obvious, hospitalization, bed rest, and antibiotics are a given in these situations.

Premature, Thirty-Two to Thirty-Six Weeks
The time between thirty-two weeks and thirty-six weeks is the zone where risks equilibrate with benefits in weighing whether to deliver or to stand. The closer you are to thirty-six to thirty-seven weeks, the less concern there is of prematurity complications. Back the other way, the closer to thirty-two weeks you are, the scarier the situation, and your doctor may go to some extremes in trying to actively prevent labor. Once again, all of these scenarios involve

the use of antibiotics to prevent infection while a little more time is bought. If delivery can be prevented for a day or two, there may be time for steroids to work to help mature your baby's lungs. This protocol is recommended only before thirty-four weeks, and is contraindicated when infection is present.

Blood Pressure Problems: Chronic Hypertension and Pregnancy-Induced Hypertension

Pregnancy-induced hypertension and chronic hypertension during pregnancy are really very different conditions.

Pregnancy Complicated by Chronic Hypertension

There are three distinct types of high blood pressure that can complicate pregnancy. One type, not pregnancy related, is called chronic hypertension, and it has minimal impact on a pregnancy if well controlled.

Chronic hypertension is long-standing elevated blood pressure, usually greater than 140/90. High blood pressure is famous for banging up blood vessels and the organs supplied by them, not unlike a pressure wash. The hypertensive patient, feeling fine for years, may ultimately see this damage as a stroke in the brain, a heart attack in the heart, or kidney damage. Strokes and heart attacks are serious enough, but damage to the kidneys could escalate the hypertension because the kidneys play an important role in managing normal blood pressure in healthy people.

Substances called angiotensins are part of a cascade of chemistry in the kidneys, and they are important in raising blood pressure, ordinarily to maintain normal levels in healthy conditions. So it is not surprising that one of the newer drug types to treat hypertension is a medicine that blocks the chemical reactions that the angiotensins take part in. They are called ACE inhibitors (angiotensin-1 converting enzyme inhibitors), and they include catopril and the brand name Vasotec (enalapril).

But these popular medications are suspected of causing deformities to babies, specifically if given in the later trimesters, so pregnant patients with high blood pressure are left with the older treatments. Fortunately, there are a lot of them, and they still all work pretty well.

Fast Forward

Three types of blood pressure problems can occur in pregnancy:

- Chronic hypertension
- Pregnancy-induced hypertension (preeclampsia, or toxemia)
- Combination of the two

For example, Lopressor (metoprolol) and labetalol act by blocking the nerves that constrict the muscles in arteries and strengthen the heart's contraction efforts, lowering the blood pressure. Aldomet (methyldopa) works in a similar way but is less selective in the particular nerve effects, meaning there may be more side effects.

Besides being dangerous for you, untreated hypertension can also affect your baby. The same damaging effects to your own blood vessels can also damage the blood supply involved with placental exchange of oxygen and nutrition. This can age the placenta prematurely, and the result in hypertensive pregnancies is intrauterine growth restriction (IUGR—small babies) and oligohydramnios (low amount of amniotic fluid). Ironically, hypertension in you could so block the normal nutritional exchange that your baby would have the opposite problem—hypotension (low blood pressure)—which could endanger the fetal kidneys, decreasing the amount of urine the unborn baby produces. Since the urine is the most significant portion of amniotic fluid, this explains oligohydramnios.

ACE inhibitors will exaggerate hypotensive phenomenon in your baby considerably, so it is recommended that ACE inhibitors be discontinued as soon as pregnancy is diagnosed. One relief to the newly pregnant patients who have been on ACE inhibitors is that the danger seems to be in the later part of pregnancy, so getting off of them in early pregnancy is probably all that need be done to relieve any worries.

A-FACTOR

If you've been treated with ACE inhibitors (like Vasotec) before you knew you were pregnant, don't panic. It only seems to be a danger in later trimesters. There's plenty of time to switch you to a safe antihypertensive, and there are several to choose from.

Except for the ACE inhibitors, you probably won't need to stop any of the other antihypertensive medicines you may be taking if your blood pressure is well controlled.

Pregnancy-Induced Hypertension—The Plot Thickens

A particular condition unique to pregnancy is pregnancy-induced hypertension, which is quite different from the chronic type discussed above. *Pregnancy-induced hypertension* is the new term for the old-termed preeclampsia and the older-termed toxemia of pregnancy. Although the exact cause of it is unknown, it seems to be an immunologic reaction to or rejection of the pregnancy, the baby and placenta being treated as foreign substances by the immune system. This is a much more serious condition than chronic hypertension because there is much more alteration in the maternal body than just high blood pressure. Your clotting ability may be altered, your vascular volume will be affected, and growth of your baby slowed due to deterioration of the placenta. There's a whole chemical shift of maladaptative reactions that can even lead to seizures and death if the problem is ignored. Chronic hypertension, on the other hand, even in pregnancy is a slow-growing problem that allows plenty of time for management that seldom interferes with bringing a pregnancy to term. Chronic hypertension is the tortoise; pregnancy-induced hypertension is the hare. In this race there are no real winners, but as an obstetrician, I'd much rather go with the tortoise.

In pregnancy there are actually three conditions that involve hypertension: chronic hypertension (the most manageable of the three), pregnancy-induced hypertension (much more troublesome), and chronic hypertension plus pregnancy-induced hypertension (the sum is greater than the mere addition of the parts).

Telling the Difference Between Chronic Hypertension and Pregnancy-Induced Hypertension

One of the basic challenges for an obstetrician is to tell the difference between chronic hypertension and pregnancy-induced hypertension when a patient presents with hypertension.

First of all, just what is a normal blood pressure? I've always told my patients that the best blood pressure is the lowest one you can have without passing out. In the nonpregnant state we doctors like to see the blood pressures be under 140/90. In pregnancy, blood pressures tend to be a little lower, anywhere from 90s/50s to 110s/70s.

A patient with chronic hypertension will generally begin her pregnancy already on an antihypertensive medication from another doctor (a sure tip-off). Unless there are major changes during the pregnancy (like piling on pregnancy-induced hypertension too), the blood pressure of a chronic hypertensive patient will usually behave itself, rising only slightly over the course of the pregnancy.

On the other hand, a patient who develops pregnancy-induced hypertension will begin her pregnancy with a normal blood pressure, but it will rise sometime in the third trimester in typical cases, earlier in severe cases. The actual criteria that need to be met before suspecting pregnancy-induced hypertension is a rise in the systolic number (the top number) of 30 and/or a rise of the diastolic number (the bottom number) of 15. For example, a blood pressure that usually runs about 100/60 and then presents as 140/84 would warrant suspicion.

These blood pressure changes are only part of a classical tetrad of signs that are associated with the older referenced term, preeclampsia. These four noteworthy signs and symptoms are:

A. High blood pressure, as defined by the criteria above
B. Edema, or swelling—more suggestive of pregnancy-induced hypertension if it is central of the face rather than peripheral of the ankles
C. Hyperproteinurea, or spilling protein in the urine
D. Hyperreflexia, or exaggerated deep tendon reflexes (the knee jerk, for instance)

One of the most sensitive tests for how severe pregnancy-induced hypertension is involves collecting a twenty-four-hour urine (from you) for protein. In pregnancy-induced hypertension the amount of protein spilled in the urine increases because of the changes in the kidneys that are a result of the disease. The amount of protein can be measured and certain thresholds used to determine severity of illness. Chronic hypertension doesn't usually involve spilling protein into the urine, and the twenty-four-hour urine can be used to separate the two types of hypertension.

There Is No Cure for Pregnancy-Induced Hypertension, but the Treatment Is Delivery

In the famous Lying-in Hospital in Chicago is a place on the wall where important discoverers' names are etched. There is still a blank spot waiting for the one who discovers the cause of preeclampsia (pregnancy-induced hypertension). It's a safe bet it probably won't be me, but it's also a safe bet it may never be one particular person. This is such a complex condition that the final answer to its cause will be a very thick book spanning disciplines as diverse as immunology, biochemistry, genetics, and embryology. It will be quite a masonry challenge to place the names of the thousands of researchers whose combined knowledge will come together to identify the cause. They better get an extra wall or two.

If pregnancy-induced hypertension is "pre" eclampsia, and you're thinking that if it's bad enough as a *pre-*, then you surely don't want *eclampsia*, whatever that is, you're very right. Before the modern protocols of prenatal care became established, women would often show up at the hospital either having a seizure or having had one. Eclampsia refers to the condition in pregnancy when there's been a seizure. Seizures occur because of brain swelling, so eclampsia can kill you or cause brain damage. When you hear about all of those women who died in childbirth back in the olden days, if it wasn't due to bleeding or infection, then eclampsia was the culprit. So if you're being followed for pregnancy-induced hypertension, understand that this is a high-risk situation that commands close attention—usually hospitalization. If so, the trick will be to get your baby to maturity before your doctor is forced to "unload" because of the pregnancy-induced hypertension.

Testing You and Evaluating the Health of Your Baby with Pregnancy-Induced Hypertension

Fetal health is assessed by nonstress testing, stress testing, ultrasound, or the combined Biophysical Profile.

Sphygmomania

The sphymomanometer, that cuff contraption used to take your blood pressure, will get a lot of miles of mercury on it if you're being followed for pregnancy-induced hypertension. Depending on the stability of the illness, as determined by serial blood pressures and twenty-four-hour urine tests, your visits and blood pressure readings will be repeated anywhere from weekly to daily.

The Twenty-Four-Hour Urine for Protein

This test, mentioned earlier, will become a weekly part of your life if your doctor suspects pregnancy-induced hypertension. It's not the most glamorous of tests since you have to keep the jug of collected urine in your refrigerator until it's time to bring it to the lab. Whatever you do, don't buy any lemonade during this time—it's fraught with regrettable confusion.

Deep Tendon Reflexes

The amount of hyperreflexia—just how jumpy the knee-jerk reflex is—is a rather subjective way to add to the alarm in severe pregnancy-induced hypertension. But it does count.

Edema

Swelling is probably the least reliable indicator because all pregnancies involve swelling to some extent. But when central swelling of the face shows up, there are usually enough of the other things happening to make this a corroborating finding.

Hospitalization

There is no better way to get a feeling for the continuity of this disease than by doing the tests every day in a hospital. The academic teaching that all pregnancy-induced hypertension patients be hospitalized has fallen to the prideful false god of managed care. This is probably OK since you and your baby can be watched closely as an outpatient. But when things start worsening, your doctor isn't overreacting if she wants to hospitalize you.

Management of Pregnancy-Induced Hypertension

If you were to have only mild pregnancy-induced hypertension, even though this is usually followed conservatively, there are those who will argue that there is no such thing as mild pregnancy-induced hypertension and advise delivery as soon as your baby is deemed lung-mature. Bed rest, a low-salt diet, and peace and quiet are the treatment for mild pregnancy-induced hypertension, and this regimen hasn't changed in more than a hundred years. Of course the close observation with frequent blood pressures and serial twenty-four-hour urine collections go with this conservative treatment. That's how your doctor will watch you. To watch your baby, she will do nonstress tests and biophysical profiles. As soon as your cervix is inducible near enough to term, induction for delivery is recommended because it's not going to get any better.

If you were to develop severe pregnancy-induced hypertension, delivery will be indicated regardless of the gestational age, possibly creating peril for your baby if it's too early. But your baby won't fare well if you don't, so when the incubator gets this sick, it's time to change incubators.

In cases that are of intermediate severity, the judgment of your obstetrician and how fast your situation is deteriorating will determine courses of action individualized for your unique situation.

Magnesium sulfate is a muscle relaxer that is used to compete with calcium, decreasing the risk of seizure. This is the same stuff mentioned earlier that's used to quiet preterm labor. The amount used is increased until the knee-jerk reflex is just about absent (but it's really adjusted based on blood levels). It is a safe medicine but needs careful monitoring—levels too high will cause respiratory depression.

Treatment with antihypertensives won't improve pregnancy-induced hypertension. Merely making the blood pressure go down won't stop the disease. The damage and danger will still rage in the background. In pregnancy-induced hypertension the high blood pressure is not the disease, but an effect of the disease. In chronic hypertension, for the most part, high blood pressure really is the disease.

The longer you're pregnant, the more severe your pregnancy-induced hypertension can become. This is not so much a matter of how long you've been pregnant, but how pregnant you are. What I'm getting at is that twins and triplets can cause pregnancy-induced hypertension sooner than usual, and the severity can increase faster than usual. These are already high-risk conditions for premature delivery, so adding the complication of pregnancy-induced hypertension makes a multiple gestation even more dangerous.

A Bad Disease Gets Worse—HELLP Syndrome

There are some particularly sinister forms of pregnancy-induced hypertension. Thrombocytopenia (low platelet count) can appear as a sole problem.

Since platelets are part of your blood-clotting system, hemorrhage and strokes can occur if your platelet count gets low enough. That won't happen with good prenatal care. HELLP syndrome (low platelets associated with liver disease) is an obstetrical emergency and requires prompt delivery. It can happen even with the most overcautious of prenatal care because it can develop very quickly. The *H* stands for hemolysis, which means destruction of blood cells; *EL* stands for elevated liver enzymes, which go up, indicating a liver (yours) going bad; *LP* stands for low platelets—the thrombocytopenia described above.

HELLP gets very dangerous very quickly, and it necessitates delivery no matter what. It's a true obstetrical emergency, and your doctor knows all about it.

Since your liver is involved, right upper abdominal pain should be reported immediately to your doctor. Also, swelling in your retinas may cause the famous spots in front of your eyes, called scotomata. All of these things should be addressed ASAP.

Pregnancy-Induced Hypertension—In Summary

Pregnancy-induced hypertension is most commonly a phenomenon of first pregnancies, older pregnancies (women aged thirty-five to forty-five), and conditions wherein a patient is "more" pregnant than normal—twins, triplets, etc. In a well-managed prenatal program, pregnancy-induced hypertension won't come as a surprise, and intervention doesn't usually involve anguished decisions of delivering your baby prematurely. Mild preeclampsia can be followed conservatively if it occurs near the end of your pregnancy because the cure is imminent. The cure is delivery.

Gestational Diabetes

Just as with hypertension in pregnancy, there are two types of diabetes that can be present in pregnancy: insulin-dependent diabetes mellitus (IDDM), a preexisting condition, and gestational diabetes, a complication of pregnancy. There is also a combination of the two in which IDDM is just harder to control because of a gestational diabetes overlay.

Gestational Diabetes Mellitus (GDM)

Pregnancy causes a phenomenon called insulin resistance, which for lack of a better explanation means that a pregnant woman makes extra insulin when regular amounts don't seem to do the job. This is thought to be due to the pregnancy's tendency to make sugar metabolism less sensitive to it, hence the name, insulin resistance. In pregnancy insulin doesn't react to receptors at the cellular level as well, meaning it takes more of it to do what insulin is supposed to do—bring sugar into the cells for energy. Being overweight makes this worse. In pregnancy, when the insulin made just can't succeed anymore, we call this GDM (gestational diabetes mellitus). Since the insulin isn't as powerful, a diet low in sugar and in carbohydrates will mean less sugar in the system; less sugar in the system means less left over from the faulty insulin chemistry. This is what is meant by diet-controlled gestational diabetes, and it actually works fairly well with this condition.

Because diet does work well, very few women need insulin injections with GDM. As many as one out of ten to twenty pregnancies will have GDM. It used to be a sneaky disease until we started screening all pregnancies with the O'Sullivan test (a one-hour blood glucose determination after a sugar drink). Out of those with an abnormal test, a full three-hour glucose tolerance test (a fasting, followed by three subsequent sugar measurements after a sugar drink) will then pick out the real GDM patients. GDM can have the same complication as regular diabetes—large babies—so it is important to manage it aggressively.

And then there are the real diabetics.

Diabetes Mellitus

This isn't making insulin that is lackluster, but actually not making enough insulin at all. When there isn't enough insulin to bring sugar from your bloodstream (your bloodstream is what you eat) into your tissue, it builds up in your blood, gunking up the works. This leads to damage of the blood supply to your organs, resulting in kidney damage, eye damage, etc.

Women who are diabetic when they conceive are at twice the risk for abnormal fetuses, even when their blood sugars are well controlled. (But even with this doubled risk, the chances of having a baby with congenital abnormalities are only four or five out of a hundred.) But diabetic women who have blood sugars that aren't well controlled have a staggering increase in their risk—by about ten times what their normal risk would be for a well-controlled diabetic state. So the real deal breaker here is good control before conception.

Luckily, there's a test that can tell how well the diabetes has been controlled. It is called an HbA1c (Hemoglobin A1c) and measures how much sugar is stuck to a certain hemoglobin molecule in your blood cells. The beauty of this relationship between hemoglobin and glucose is that it's a firm interaction, meaning that it reflects how well the diabetes has been in control for a long time, usually months.

So a normal HbA1c in the first trimester will be a very reassuring test for a pregnant diabetic patient. And the risk of congenital abnormalities and miscarriage is directly related to how abnormally high the HbA1c is. This makes it, besides the serum-glucose measurement, the most important prenatal (and preconception!) test in a diabetic pregnancy.

But even with good control before conception and during the first trimester, the two natural enemies, pregnancy and diabetes, begin to fight it out. The very thing that can cause that normal variation known as gestational diabetes can make insulin-dependent diabetes harder to manage too, by driving up the insulin needs. Pregnancy with diabetes is usually a continuing medical challenge always at red alert.

Large babies make for more difficult vaginal deliveries. Besides the risk of cephalopelvic dysproportion (baby's too big to fit out), and shoulder dystocia (head delivers but shoulders get stuck), there is also increased risk of placental abruption (premature separation). Since the C-section rate is higher in diabetic patients for all of the above reasons, it's important to know that cesarean delivery is not the perfect answer to a pregnant diabetic's problems. Diabetic women don't heal well after surgery and their chances of infection are much greater.

In spite of all of these concerns, a woman whose sugars are well controlled can stack the deck in her favor, especially if she is evaluated preconception. But diabetes is definitely a problem in pregnancy that requires diligence on the part of the obstetrician and strict compliance on the part of the patient.

Complications Due to Advanced Maternal Age

Advanced maternal age is defined as any expectant mother who will be thirty-five by the time she delivers. This term is a throwback to the times when women married in their teens and began giving birth at a much younger age. In modern times, with women playing important roles in the marketplace alongside men and putting off their families for business or personal reasons, the magic number thirty-five still stands as a turning point in prenatal surveillance, because this age marks entry into a particular high-risk group with risk factors related to age. In my practice I never use terms like advanced age. In fact I can't think of a single euphemism that will keep me from getting the stink eye, so I do a lot of stuttering and slurring of a phrase or two, and the general idea is struck that extra testing is recommended "at this point in your childbearing career."

Down's Syndrome

At age thirty-three the chance of having a child with Down's syndrome is 1 in 625. Two years later at age thirty-five, the risk is doubled and it accelerates thereafter. This is why thirty-five seems to stick in the throat at this point in your childbearing career, and why your obstetrician is urged to pay special attention for abnormal pregnancies of a chromosomal cause, including aggressive screening via ultrasound and possibly amniocentesis or chorionic villous sampling. It's important, though, to factor in whether you would do anything with the information. Women who would never consider an abortion, no matter what, might not want to subject a probably normal baby to the very small risks associated with the invasive procedures. Even at age forty, the risk of Down's syndrome is 1 in 109.

It makes sense that chromosomal problems go up with advancing maternal age because the egg you conceive with is as old as you are. You were born with all of the eggs you will ovulate with for the rest of your postpubescent, premenopausal life. So if you're thirty, and your mom was thirty when she conceived you, then you're the product of an egg that developed sixty years ago! Isn't that depressing?

Or maybe not. Maybe you think you're lookin' pretty good for sixty. But the point is that the older you are, the older your eggs and their chromosomes are, and this is the reason for age-related risk.

The sperm, on the other hand, are young whippersnappers, so they don't play a role in the risk of Down's syndrome as related to paternal age. The father's age, however, will influence the chances of other genetic (autosomal dominant) diseases, like Marfan's syndrome, Huntington's chorea, von Willebrand Disease, and possibly schizophrenia.

Twins at This Point in Your Childbearing Career

Identical twins (monozygotic, or twinning from a single fertilized egg) happen spontaneously in 1 out of 250 pregnancies. This is unaffected by age, race, or any other factors. Fraternal twins (dizygotic, or twins from fertilization of two eggs), however, is a different story.

In dizygotic twins, not only maternal age but also the number of previous pregnancies ("parity"), increases the chances of having this type of twin pregnancy. Twins are three times as likely in women over thirty-five with at least four other children than in women under twenty who are pregnant for the first time. Taking parity alone, the chance of twins doubles from the first pregnancy to the fourth pregnancy. Racially, African-American women have a 1 out of 79 chance of twins; Caucasian women 1 out of 100; Asian women more rarely—1 in 155 pregnancies.

When women first get off of the birth control pill, their pituitary glands crank back up with higher amounts of stimulation than usual, so the chance of twins is greater with conception the first month off of the pill.

The ultrasound age is beginning to reveal a surprise. Now that ultrasonography is being done routinely at earlier gestational periods, it is becoming obvious that the occurrence of twins may be higher than what has been traditionally observed. The phenomenon of the absorbed twin has been observed more frequently than once thought. Occasionally, one of the twins doesn't make it, dies silently, then gets absorbed. This may present as bleeding in the first trimester, labeled as a threatened miscarriage. Fetal death even near the end of the first trimester may be hidden, showing no evidence at the time of the delivery of the single baby at term.

Other Risks

There is an increased tendency to pregnancy-induced hypertension with later pregnancies. Also, gestational diabetes, placental abruption, and even some disastrous events like stroke are more of a risk with advanced maternal age. But as there has been an increased number of pregnancies over age thirty-five, so too there has been a respect for increased vigilance. Today obstetricians aren't particularly fearful of women pregnant in their later thirties—they have their special set of risk factors just like teenagers who are pregnant have risks unique to them.

Genetic Testing: Invasive Prenatal Diagnosis

Besides Down's syndrome, other genetic problems can be diagnosed prenatally with sampling via chorionic villous sampling (CVS) or amniocentesis. CVS, usually done around ten weeks gestation, involves getting a very tiny biopsy of nonfetal (placental) pregnancy tissue by a needle through the cervix. Amniocentesis, typically done at fifteen weeks, is drawing out fluid for study from the amniotic sac, through your abdomen, guided by ultrasound. The advantage of CVS is that it can be done a full month earlier than amniocentesis, providing answers sooner.

Theoretically there are genetic problems of anatomy or metabolism that might make prenatal treatment possible if diagnosed by amniocentesis, but for the most part, amniocentesis is offered routinely to women thirty-five and older to diagnose those age-related genetic problems for which abortion is the only remedy. A pro-life stance means that a patient may base her decision on whether or not to have CVS or an amniocentesis on philosophical grounds.

The chances of miscarrying are very low with amniocentesis, but such a risk is often greater than the risk of carrying a genetically affected baby, depending on your age. People who aren't opposed to abortion (pro-choice) say that although this may be true, still the reality of a genetic problem is such a devastation as to be unacceptable.

Interestingly, even pro-life couples sometimes accept an amniocentesis purely for reassurance or alternately to know early on of any problems so they can prepare for their child and the problems that will come. I can't argue with this. I think that knowing about a serious problem makes available the time needed to deal with it. In this way, invasive testing need not be just a search and destroy mission, but a bonding to those children who will need the extra help and lengthier time for parents to appreciate a special circumstance. Is this important enough to risk the small chance of hurting a child? There is no solid answer to this because such a decision comes from the heart.

Medically Recommended Procedures Versus Medically Necessary Procedures

There is a big difference between a medically necessary procedure and a medically recommended procedure. Medical science has advanced to the point where a bad conception result can be eliminated, but that is the medical and technological reality. The philosophical reality is a personal position on the part of the prospective parents and should be taken into account as well. The recommendation by your doctor is a medical recommendation, and negligent malpractice could be alleged were she not to let you know amniocentesis is available and medically recommended. Whether pro-choice or pro-life, your doctor is obligated to inform you of your choices as part of routine and proper prenatal care. But if there are philosophical positions you can't deviate from, it becomes your call—medically, ethically, legally, and intellectually.

Rh-Negative Blood, Rh Sensitization— Sesame Street Hematology

We encourage our children to avoid strangers. Yet just as your baby is a foreign body to your immune system, so too you are a stranger to her. Sometimes you're seen—immunologically—as a bad stranger as dangerous as the sleazeball pulling over at the curb to offer her candy. Since reproduction isn't magic, but a complex system of rules and consequences, sometimes you can't have everything. The host versus graft reaction between mother and child comes close to blowing the whole thing.

Thankfully, good fences make good neighbors. The system by which your blood and your baby's blood remain separate and the membranes that segregate your pregnancy from the rest of your body act to maintain peaceful coexistence until delivery. But there are some holes in the system.

Antibodies you make can be small enough to slip through the exchange network to your child. Antigens, however, are usually attached to bigger structures, like red blood cells, and are too bulky to go from your baby to you. Your baby's red blood cells, usually different from the type you have—thanks to that big foreign body, your husband—don't get to you, and neither do the antigens they house. So you don't in turn generate antibodies, which is good because they are small enough to get back to your baby.

Why blood group incompatibilities have never been taught on Sesame Street is a mystery to me because it's all ABCs. There are the main blood types, A, B, AB, and O. A is only A, which means it can't mix with B, AB (it'll fight the B-part of AB), or O (which sees both A and B as foreign). The same goes for B. AB can only mix with AB (AB will strike discord with A, for instance, by showing up with a hostile B-part). And lonely O can only receive another O, seeing A, B, or AB as foreign (although A, B, and AB can accept O). This is why they're called A, B, or AB, because they have the A, B, or AB antigen that will generate an antiforeigner response, and no one does well with a war going on inside of them.

There's also the CDE system. The D, in particular, is a concern because of its frequency and possible severity of consequence. True, ABO incompatibilities between you and your baby are frequent, too, but the response is usually mild, which keeps the UV light industry in business. When you see blue lights going in the nursery, this is called phototherapy, which will break down the bilirubin that's released in the blood war going on in your baby.

D incompatibility, however, can be very serious. This antibody is called the Rhesus D antibody because of the initial research done with Rhesus monkeys. The C, c, E, and e are also in the Rhesus antibody group, but these are usually less severe. It's the D that's the problem.

If your baby ends up being Rh-negative like you, then there's no problem. If you're Rh-positive (D-positive), there's no problem. But if you're D-negative (Rhesus negative, or Rh-negative), that's fine until your blood first encounters blood that is D-positive (Rh-positive), usually when your and your baby's blood finally mix a bit with the sloppy blood-hitting-the-fan phenomenon known as placental separation. Then all hell breaks loose in your bloodstream. Fetal blood cells blunder into your system, evoking a lot of indignation that results in the production of your antibodies to fight them. They lose, but this is of no consequence because your baby's out of the blood incompatibility picture, instead getting into the relatives' pictures at the nursery window. Your antibodies remain—so many antibodies and so little to do—until your next pregnancy.

Your antibodies, able to pass through to your next baby, do just that. As stated above, the ABO incompatibility is mild, but if you're Rh-negative and your baby is Rh-positive, you'll be sending your anti-Rh army into battle, and the battlefield is in your baby. His red blood cells, which house the Rh-antigen, will be attacked and over time your baby will become anemic. This isn't good in a baby who's trying to grow and mature. The increased destruction of fetal blood cells stimulates an overproduction to make up for the deficit, which causes swelling in the fetal liver and spleen. This problem, called *erythroblastosis fetalis*, can worsen, and when fluid collects in the fetal spaces (abdomen, chest, etc.) it's called *hydrops fetalis*. Since such anemia and repercussions to the anemia can cause serious injury or fetal death, it's treated aggressively via a blood transfusion (guided by ultrasound) to your baby. A fetal transfusion involves inserting red blood cells through a needle into your baby's abdomen, where they are absorbed into his system.

Another victory of modern obstetrics: today erythroblastosis fetalis is rare because we give an injection called RhoGam to Rh-negative mothers of Rh-positive babies. RhoGam is also an anti–Rh-positive antibody. When you get it, your body is fooled into thinking there's already been an adequate response and makes no antibodies on its own. The antibodies of RhoGam don't attack subsequent babies because they're much bulkier molecules and don't pass through the placenta to the baby. It's a preemptive strike that has reduced the risk of erythroblastosis fetalis to a negligible frequency.

In cases such as miscarriage, where the amount of mixing of blood is theoretical, there's a test called the Kleinhauer-Betke test (a blood test done on you) that can quantitate the amount of blood mixing that could have occurred. This is also useful with occasions of bleeding during a pregnancy as in mild, stable placental abruption.

There are other blood antigens you may have. Usually named after their discoverer, these are rarer, and only a few put your baby at risk. (The only DiLeo antigen is to Brussels sprouts.)

Once again, prenatal care rules.

Right Upper Quadrant Pain

If you were to put a cross on your abdomen, a vertical and a horizontal divider intersecting at your navel, it would designate the four quadrants doctors often refer to in locating symptoms. These are the left and right upper quadrants above your navel (*your* left and right—not as seen by your doctor), and the left and right lower quadrants below it. It's true that anyone can have right upper quadrant pain, but in obstetrics the right upper quadrant (RUQ) has particular significance, which is why I include it. You won't find RUQ pain in the other books on pregnancy that share the rack with mine because most of them aren't written by doctors. But if you're really an inquiring mind, the RUQ is a terrible area to waste.

The right upper quadrant is where your liver lives and your gallbladder does what it does (concentrates bile). Also, especially in late pregnancy, the appendix hides there from its usual right lower quadrant location. So it's easily seen that when a pregnant patient complains of right upper quadrant pain, an obstetrician addresses that complaint most seriously. Pregnancy-induced hypertension often shows up as liver involvement. No one yet knows the exact reason a woman sometimes rejects a pregnancy with pregnancy-induced hypertension, but it's obvious that there's trouble in paradise because the cure is delivery. Even without the high blood pressure usually seen in pregnancy-induced hypertension, the liver can be the organ tipping off your doctor that something is amiss. In the severe variation of pregnancy-induced hypertension called HELLP syndrome, your liver enzymes can go sky high, and you will complain of right upper quadrant pain usually as a result of swelling in your liver against the sensitive liver capsule (you know that pain in your side when you run a long time?). With this type of presentation, it's usually necessary to effect delivery immediately because it may be life-threatening, and it's not going to improve until your baby is out.

Pregnancy (birth control pills, too) can affect the emptying of your gallbladder. Gallbladder symptoms—even stones—can present as right upper quadrant pain, but blood work for enzymes can usually exclude the HELLP syndrome described above. Gallbladder pain often radiates to the right shoulder blade and punishes the wrong diet, these symptoms varying from the more serious liver disease of pregnancy. Ultrasound, famous for showing you your baby, can also show you your gallstones if you have them. All the ultrasonographer need do is swing the ultrasound transducer north. Management of gallbladder disease is usually conservative and delayed until after the pregnancy. Kiss the Popeye's Famous Fried Chicken goodbye until then.

Plain ol' colic can hit your right upper quadrant too because a portion of your large intestines takes a turn at your liver, and small bowel is just about everywhere, this quadrant included. A kidney infection, usually more symptomatic in the midback to one side, can produce back pain to your right side; it might be very difficult for you to discriminate between where the right side of your back ends and your right upper abdominal quadrant begins. Therefore, ruling out a kidney infection is necessary with this complaint.

And then there's the sneaky appendix. Late in pregnancy your enlarged uterus pushes everything else upward. The appendix goes along as well. Unfortunately, this weird location can delay the diagnosis, which means that there are a lot more cases of ruptured appendix in pregnancy than in nonpregnant patients.

Did I mention labor? I was so busy describing the weird things that I didn't mention that irregular contractions can occur in any part of the uterus, the upper right as well. Premature separation of a portion of the placenta (abruption) can present in any particular spot as pain, but this is usually exquisitely sensitive in the uterus itself. This means that your obstetrician must run through the checklist to tell the difference between false labor and the complications discussed above. Luckily, that's what he does for a living and what he can do best.

I'm reminded of a Gary Larson cartoon in which three cavemen stare in wonder at a woolly mammoth lying dead on the ground, felled by only one tiny arrow in it's skin. "We should write that spot down," one says to the other. Doctors in training learned early which spot to write down. The right upper quadrant holds a special place for the obstetrician.

Babies Too Small and Babies Too Big

The beauty of prenatal care is if progress of your pregnancy goes awry, it can get picked up. One important serial determination is your baby's growth. Babies smaller than they should be are referred to as growth restricted (intrauterine growth restriction—IUGR); when larger than normal, they're called macrosomic (large for gestational age—LGA).

IUGR–Intrauterine Growth Restriction (SGA–Small for Gestational Age)

There are many possible reasons why your baby might not be on track in growth. When your obstetrician suspects IUGR, all of the causes must be ruled out. They include the following:

- **Infection:** usually an infection that you have or had, viral or bacterial—rubella, cytomegalovirus, hepatitis A and B, influenza, chicken pox, tuberculosis, and syphilis. In these cases of IUGR, the cause may not be self-evident because your own sickness may not be noticeable without prenatal care.
- **Hypertension:** either chronic hypertension or pregnancy-induced hypertension.
- **Genetic:** chromosomal abnormalities present a host of growth abnormalities.
- **Uteroplacental insufficiency:** decreased passing of oxygen and nutrition to your baby. Growth will be affected first, then fetal distress may develop. Delivery may be indicated, even with the risks inherent in prematurity.
- **Lupus coagulant and anticardiolipin antibodies:** the same antibodies that can result in recurrent miscarriage can affect your baby if you get past the first trimester. When you bump into other pregnant patients who have been placed on a baby aspirin a day, it's usually because of this.
- **Cord problems:** a mechanical partial blockage in the cord also affects what your baby gets.
- **Discordancy:** this phenomenon is with twins, in which one baby gets more than his share of the goodies, leaving what's left for his sibling. Strangely enough, the overload in the greedy twin is just as dangerous as the slim-pickings malnutrition in the other.
- **Familial:** growth parameters, like leg and arm measurements, may fall off the general population scale if one or both parents are shorter than average.

Symmetrical Versus Asymmetrical IUGR

In symmetrical IUGR all parts of the baby are symmetrically smaller. In asymmetrical IUGR the body is smaller than the head. This is sometimes referred to as head-sparing IUGR, meaning that most of the nutrition and oxygen are diverted to the brain so as to spare brain damage, with expectations of a catch-up of body growth after delivery. Once thought to be more protective than symmetrical IUGR, we now know that the symmetrically growth restricted babies do better.

Macrosomia (LGA—Large for Gestational Age)

If your baby is larger than what's expected, your doctor, besides wanting to rule out conditions that might prove dangerous, will also worry about what your baby's size will do to your chances of a vaginal delivery. Possible causes of LGA include the following:

- **Error in determining the estimated due date:** if you're really due sooner than the date determined, your baby is always going to be off the scale. This really isn't LGA.
- **Postdates:** if you go past your due date, your baby will grow at least one-half to one pound a week and keep growing until the aging placenta can no longer keep up with the demand. Then you have a different problem—fetal distress.
- **Diabetes:** either gestational or the real thing. That high maternal sugar gets into your baby's bloodstream easily, and he wants to use everything to just keep growing.
- **Congenital malformations:** problems in development of one part of the baby will cause distention or enlargement of that part or others due to the disruption of the balance.
- **Familial:** if your husband is the six-foot six-inch Dennis Rodman (not that you would want that), then you're liable to have a large baby. Ultrasound graphs are based on the normal population, and people as big as Dennis Rodman aren't normal.
- **Infection:** actually, referring to the whole pregnancy. For instance, in syphilis the placenta can be an exaggerated size. I once delivered a baby whose placenta weighed more than he did!

Infections Impacting Pregnancy

Sexually Transmitted Diseases (STDs)

We used to call them venereal diseases, the origin of this word coming from the goddess of love, Venus. (Interestingly, so does the word venerate.) Today, they're called sexually transmitted diseases, or STDs. The standard part of your initial pregnancy workup involves a screen for STDs, and this subject was covered earlier. Just because you're pregnant is no special protection from STDs. In fact, in pregnancy diagnosis is even more crucial because infections can affect your baby.

Herpes

This infection can be transmitted to your baby via direct contact with your vagina during vaginal delivery, so it is a common reason for C-section. The conventional advice is that if there's a recent lesion (within two weeks of delivery), C-section is indicated. If it's been more than two weeks, a vaginal delivery is acceptable (see "Controversies in Obstetrics" in Chapter 22). It used to be that half of all babies delivered vaginally over herpes lesions contracted the disease, and of those, half died! But with C-section availability and Zovirax (and medicines like it), newborn death is now very uncommon.

Hepatitis

It's easy to diagnose via blood work, but difficult to treat, and it can be passed on to your baby.

AIDS

It's also easy to diagnose via blood work. It's still fatal, but there have been great strides in preventing transmission to babies by the use of prenatal antiretroviral drugs like zitovudine and by C-section delivery to prevent direct inoculation (what is called vertical transmission).

Gonorrhea

Congenital gonorrhea can cause eye damage to your newborn. Most states have laws mandating antibiotic eye drops because the diagnosis can be missed. (Cultures aren't foolproof, symptoms aren't necessary, and a medical-sexual history is often unreliable. Of course, we're talking about all of those other people.) Easy to treat.

Chlamydia

This one has been implicated in preterm labor. Even sneakier than gonorrhea, chlamydia often has no symptoms. Easy to treat.

Human Papilloma Virus or HPV

This is a sexually acquired virus that's detected on Pap smear and confirmed with colposcopy. It can lead to genital warts and/or cancer of the cervix, especially in smokers. It can pass to the newborn through contact with your birth canal, but this is extremely rare so it isn't a strong indication for C-section.

Trichomoniasis

This infection is caused by little microscopic gyrating organisms. If you were to look at a vaginal smear under a microscope (the way to diagnose it), it would look like there's a party going on in there. The trichomonads would be cute if they weren't a venereal disease. It's harmless, although it's been suspected in preterm labor (unconfirmed) and causes burning, smelly vaginitis. It's easy to treat with pills, but your partner must be treated also.

Syphilis

This one is making a big comeback because everyone is so fixated on AIDS. It's easy to diagnose and easy to treat, but it can affect your baby by causing neurologic problems if untreated. It responds easily to antibiotics, but don't catch it on a deserted island where it'll go undiagnosed because its end stage in twenty years is ugly.

Molluscum Contagiosum

This one causes little painless bumps on the skin around your genital area. These can be popped off by a dermatologist, which is no big deal. No risk to your baby—just a pain in the neck.

Nonsexually Acquired Infections
Rubella, or German measles

This is a mild infection in you, but it can be devastating to your baby. It's easy to get, which means that you've probably had it and are immune; but it also means if you haven't, you are at a big risk in pregnancy. If so, you should get the vaccine when the baby's out.

There is an official congenital rubella syndrome, which includes deafness, heart defects, IUGR, eye abnormalities, and chromosomal abnormalities. The severity, however, is related to how soon you have the infection. At or before eleven weeks is worrisome; items in the syndrome after sixteen weeks are rare.

Toxoplasmosis

For all of you cat lovers out there (not that there's anything wrong with that), you can get this from eating infected raw meat. Even undercooked can pose a risk. You can also get this from cat litter when you don't wash your hands, making possible a fecal-oral route when you bite your fingernails, for instance. But for those with cats, the very thing that puts you at risk also protects you. I'm one who believes in the love-cats-once, love-cats-always theory that if you own a cat, you've probably had cats all of your life. All that exposure has probably exposed you to toxoplasmosis at some point, providing a nice immunity now. Nevertheless, anyone with cats should have antibody blood work thrown into the usual labs to check for immunity.

If you're not immune, do you have to have your husband take Whiskers "for a ride"? No. You should just be more sensitive to your hand-washing hygiene. And stay away from backyard parties where the host doesn't know how to barbeque.

Affected babies have low birth weight, eye inflammations, anemia, liver/spleen swelling, and/or jaundice. Severe neurological affects can be convulsions and mental retardation. The really weird thing about toxoplasmosis is that the earlier you get it, the less likely your baby will be affected (only 10 percent in the first trimester), but if so, the more severe the complications. The later in pregnancy you get it, the more likely your baby will be affected (60 percent in the third trimester), but if so, the less severe.

If you get toxoplasmosis, you probably won't even know you have it, so you should ask your doctor if you're at risk. The good news is that complications from toxoplasmosis happen in only one of thousands of pregnancies, so that would have to be one bad-ass cat. (Probably "Rotten Ralph"—a famous cat story you'll be reading to your child at some point.)

Listeria

A bacterial infection. Up to one in twenty adults have this bacterium in their feces, so the infection is a fecal-oral route, much like the feline-caused toxoplasmosis, and is probably everywhere. Foods contaminated with listeria, like soft cheeses and nonpasteurized products and cold cuts, can cause outbreaks, but in pregnancy it can have no symptoms at all or cause an illness that may be confused with a urinary tract infection or with just a flu that is managed with fluids and acetaminophen.

If contracted early, listeria can cause miscarriage. If the infection occurs later on, it can cause intrauterine growth restriction (IUGR). In the third trimester listeria can be a cause for premature labor, premature delivery, and ultimately can cause neonatal sepsis, meningitis, and death—it can be a baby-killer. The meningitis in the baby can even develop after the first few weeks of life. It is a fairly weak infectious bacterium, usually seeking out the immuno-compromised, like persons with AIDS or pregnancy. It is thought that exposure to it usually will not cause infection because it is so common a germ.

The true frequency of infection and infection affecting pregnancy is unknown for several reasons. Few obstetricians get routine cultures on miscarriages, assuming correctly that miscarriage is usually the result of genetic mishaps, especially in the absence of maternal symptoms. Because it is not checked for scrupulously and because it seems to be everywhere in contaminated products, the epidemiology statistics are still quite a mess. In the real world obstetricians don't obtain blood cultures and other tests for listeriosis on every woman with a low grade fever, headache, or muscle aches. They can't.

Listeria in pregnancy usually appears as flu-like, which can be scary when almost every pregnant woman gets flu-like symptoms at some point in her pregnancy. Low-grade fever, headache, and muscle pain are common, but there may be no symptoms at all. Less commonly there can be diarrhea and cramps. Delivery is indicated in the late third trimester so that treatment can be attempted on the newborn. In cases of severe prematurity, there is no best answer for a difficult question.

Accurate information on listeria can be obtained at the Centers for Disease Control website: http:/www.cdc.gov/ncidod/dbmd/diseaseinfo/listeriosis _g.htm

Group B β-Hemolytic Strep

Though it happens rarely, it can cause serious infection, as discussed previously, when associated with PROM or preterm labor.

Group A Strep

Very rare. This is the villain that causes toxic shock syndrome. Don't worry about this one, and don't make me eat my words.

Mumps

A common childhood disease involving the salivary glands and sometimes other structures, like the gonads, pancreas, etc. Treatment involves treating the symptoms only. It's rare in pregnancy because most people are immune by adulthood. Although there's no hard evidence that it causes miscarriage, the one case I had of it in pregnancy resulted in just that. It's not a reason to terminate a pregnancy because it doesn't seem to cause abnormalities in babies.

Influenza

There's no evidence that the A variety, our perennial plague, can hurt your baby. The risk is more from a high fever in early pregnancy than from actual infection to your baby.

Cytomegalovirus (CMV)

This is everywhere. Almost all humans end up getting it because there hasn't been a method thought up yet to keep you from getting it. By age three most children have gotten it and are only too happy to give it to you too, if you've escaped. You can even get it from the much maligned but seldom guilty toilet seat. In fact, if you're reading this, you've probably had it. If you haven't had it, you're probably getting it from this book if the last window shopper sneezed into it.

Because of its omnipresence, true cytomegalovirus syndrome is rare, and of those who are born with it, only one in ten have mental impairment. Other effects include hearing loss and anemia.

Chicken Pox and Shingles

These are actually the same thing. Both are caused by the varicella-zoster virus (VZV), a type of herpes virus. Chicken pox is the initial infection. After the skin heals from the pox marks, the virus retreats into the nerve roots of the spine and can migrate back out years later to form an irritating rash called shingles. The fact that the lesions are later distributed along parts of the body supplied by particular nerve routes (the nerves that harbor the virus) helps in the diagnosis. Both forms of VZV are contagious and if you're not immune, you'll more than likely get it (probably as chicken pox) if exposed within your household, so you should stay away from someone with chicken pox or shingles.

Chicken pox during pregnancy can cause congenital pox lesions or if contracted near delivery, it can affect your baby before you've had a chance to make any antibody to pass on to her. Such unprotected newborns can have life-threatening infection, so all newborns of mothers recently infected will get the VZIG antibody shot.

In pregnancy chicken pox is also extremely dangerous to you, both because it's dangerous in adults anyway and because pregnancy alters your immunological strength. You might develop varicella pneumonia which is a complication that can put you in critical condition.

I recently had a pregnant patient who was VZV nonimmune. I told her to stay away from Christmas shopping, crowds, theaters, etc., because in any crowd there's got to be some VZV floating around. If you know you've been exposed, you should report it immediately, and if you are less than twenty weeks pregnant, you can probably be given the VZIG shot. Certainly before or after a pregnancy VZIG should be given to immunize women of childbearing age.

In prenatal emergencies with VZV, the antiviral drug acyclovir, the same thing given for genital herpes, can be used in large doses. So far there is no evidence that acyclovir hurts the baby, and because it's been around for awhile, that's a meaningful safety record.

You need not stay away from people with shingles or chicken pox if you're immune. Your doctor can do a simple blood test to tell whether you're immune or not. If you are, you're OK. If not, ask your doctor about immunization after your pregnancy.

Fifth Disease

A common children's viral illness, this virus goes by the scientific name *parvovirus B19*. Typically infecting children aged five to fourteen, it causes the quaintly described "slapped cheek" rash, a redness similar to what a slap across the face might cause. It's called fifth disease because it was the fifth illness described in traditional medical texts of childhood diseases that cause a reddish skin rash, those being: (1) measles; (2) scarlet fever; (3) German measles, or rubella; (4) Duke's disease; (5) "fifth" disease, also called *erythema infectiosum*; (6) roseola. Spring is the most common time for outbreaks, most often blamed on breathing in infected droplets or by hand-to-mouth contamination.

Although there can be fever, headaches, sore throat, diarrhea, aches and pains, weakness, and the rash, some children have no symptoms at all. In adults the infection is milder than in children, a quarter of adults having no symptoms, but when there are symptoms, the aches, pains, and weakness reminiscent of a flu-like illness can be accompanied by paresthesia (tingling and numbness) in the fingers. Whether there are symptoms or not, there is an anemia that will probably go by unnoticed if the adult is healthy and the illness mild. Unfortunately, as mild an illness as it often is with children, it can cause concern for your baby if the virus were to cross the placenta.

> **✳A-FACTOR**
> "Fifth" disease infects women in only 1 in 400 pregnancies, then infects the baby in only 1 out of 3 such cases, and then might or might not affect the baby enough to cause problems. The arithmetic comes out to a 1 out of 1,200 chance of your baby getting hit, and then the effects are variable on top of that.

There is no risk if you've already had parvovirus infection before your pregnancy, and about 50 percent of all adults are immune. Even if you don't remember the infection you may be immune, having had an infection that wasn't recognized. Of those who are susceptible, about 50 percent get the infection after household exposure. Usually women at risk for exposure, like schoolteachers, have already had the infection and become immune.

Assuming you're in the half of adults who aren't immune, and assuming you're part of the half of those who would then get it, then there's less than a 10 percent chance of your baby being seriously affected. Doing the math, you're at a 2.5 percent risk (1 in 40). Adjusting for those who are pregnant, the risk goes to 1 in 400 pregnancies. Problems from the virus are less common in the latter half of pregnancy.

And that's if you're exposed. Keep in mind that if you're a schoolteacher or pediatric worker, this is an outbreak illness that you will know is coming because word of known outbreaks gets around.

Parvovirus infection occasionally reduces the production of red blood cells. In your baby this can cause severe anemia (low red-blood-cell count),

> **A-FACTOR**
> For most women, parvovirus fifth disease infection does not cause problems
> with their babies.

which may lead to a serious condition called fetal hydrops, similar to the hydrops fetalis seen in Rh-negative complications. Parvovirus infection does not seem to cause birth defects or other problems except for the hydrops.

Spontaneous miscarriage, fetal anemia, and swelling (*hydrops*) as well as fetal death have been reported. Recently, fetal transfusions correcting the fetal anemia have been shown to reverse the abnormalities with normal infants born near term. Ultrasound is used to see if there are signs of hydrops. The complications may occur weeks after maternal exposure, so an ultrasound every two weeks to look for signs of fetal anemia (hydrops) should be done for two months. If signs of hydrops are seen, fetal transfusion may save the baby's life. For most women, however, parvovirus infection does not cause problems with their babies.

There are two types of antibodies you will develop if you were to contract this illness after exposure. IgM antibodies develop first in about three weeks, lasting about four months, and then disappear. IgG antibodies develop in three to four weeks, but last for years. So the difference between the two antibodies can be helpful in determining whether a pregnancy has been recently exposed to the disease. Although those women in professions at risk can't go their whole terms getting IgM determinations every week, still those at-risk pregnant women should have this test thrown in with any other blood work that needs to be done. Might as well.

No vaccine is available for fifth disease.

Vaginitis

Usually yeast or bacterial vaginosis, both of which probably come from your rectum. Since your rectum is so close to your vagina, the greenhouse effect of underwear can cause colonization even under the most fastidious of hygiene, so don't get grossed out. The use of creams in the latter half of pregnancy is safe, and most doctors will even treat it in the first half too without a second thought. I think it's safe because I'm one of those doctors.

21

Pregnancy Complicated by Preexisting Conditions

Whether you're the Mercedes-Benz of incubators or just a Yugo is determined by what shape you're in to carry a pregnancy. But no matter what make, year, and model you are, your obstetrician is trained to work on them all. Backup is provided by the maternal-fetal medicine specialist (perinatologist), and your doctor will wisely consult one when serious maternal conditions warrant. Here we'll take a look under the hood at a variety of conditions a woman could have before conceiving that complicate her care when she becomes pregnant.

Chronic Hypertension

High blood pressure before pregnancy can sometimes worsen during pregnancy or mix badly with pregnancy-induced hypertension. This is fully discussed beginning on page 318 in Chapter 20.

Diabetes

Diet controlled diabetes can sometimes worsen into insulin-dependent diabetes (IDDM), and IDDM can sometimes worsen in pregnancy to increase a diabetic's insulin needs. This was also discussed at length in Chapter 20, beginning on page 325.

Abnormal Pap Smear

Just because you're pregnant doesn't mean you have special protection from abnormal Pap smears. This condition is typically thought of as a gynecological condition, but when it occurs in a pregnant woman, it's easy to modify the diagnosis and treatment somewhat so as not to compromise the well-being of your pregnancy.

Although it's true the dreaded abnormal Pap can run the gamut from mere harmless inflammation of your cervix (cervicitis) all the way to cancer, usually it's of the harmless variety. Pregnancy has certain affects on the pH of your vagina and the total vaginal environment that can cause inflammatory changes of the cervix that mimic disease.

The real test to judge the merits of a Pap smear result is an office procedure called colposcopy. A colposcope, although nothing more than a microscope on a stick, evaluates the entire Pap smear area stereoscopically, easily guiding your doctor to the areas that caused the abnormal Pap—areas that are biopsied with tiny clippings—perhaps with some mild cramping. These clippings, however, are not the scattered loose cells strewn over a slide as in a Pap. Instead they are actual chunks (microscopic, of course) of tissue the way it sits in your cervix. This yields a result of certainty that will be either no cause for concern or a need for treatment.

Most of the treatments involve simply eliminating the abnormal tissue. The slow development of abnormal tissue can safely see you through your pregnancy until it can be treated one to three months postpartum.

Colposcopy is safe in pregnancy even when there are biopsies, because those are done on the superficial cervix and don't involve the deeper layers responsible for holding a pregnancy in. Because of its safety, an obstetrician is obligated to use colposcopy to make the diagnosis during pregnancy the same as during nonpregnancy.

> **Fast Forward**
>
> A Pap smear is merely a screen. An abnormal Pap, like other screens, is in itself meaningless and merely identifies those who need a better evaluation. Colposcopy is a microscopic look that will give the answer.

> **A-FACTOR**
>
> Abnormal Paps may be due to simple yeast or other harmless infections, so don't panic. Even if colposcopy shows that there really is a problem, it can almost always wait to be addressed after your baby is born.

Rarely is there a condition that warrants immediate intervention. A GYN-oncologist (gynecological cancer specialist) can make recommendations that may include a cone biopsy to eliminate such a serious condition.

A cone biopsy involves cutting out a cone-shaped piece of the tip of your cervix so that the severity of the lesion can be identified better (diagnostic) and also to actually eliminate the lesion (therapeutic). It's not that dangerous actually, but you are involving deeper tissue in that structural part of your uterus that holds in your pregnancy. Premature delivery due to an incompetent cervix is a risk, but it's unusual, attesting to the safety of this procedure when done correctly and only when absolutely necessary.

The main cause of truly abnormal Pap smears is infection with the condyloma (genital wart) virus—the sexually acquired human papilloma virus (HPV). Also, as if you needed another reason to quit smoking in pregnancy, nicotine is concentrated thirty times more in the blood in the cervix than anywhere else in your body, making it a legitimate cocarcinogen for cancer of the cervix. You don't see much press on that, and I don't know why.

Specific strains of the condyloma virus cause both warts and cervical dysplasia (a truly precancerous lesion). Not all dysplasias become cervical cancers, but all cervical cancers most certainly begin as dysplasias. So if there are genital warts on either you or your husband, you must be examined for dysplasia with colposcopy, even if your Pap was normal.

As with all worries of pregnancy, prenatal care is the golden standard of a safe pregnancy. Anything else is out-of-sight/out-of-mind and could represent a time bomb the countdown for which is not heard.

Asthma

Asthma is an immunologic condition in which certain irritants or unknown causes result in increased secretions and bronchospasm that interfere with your air movement. In severe cases there is hypoxia (low oxygen) and hypercapnia (build up of carbon dioxide) in your body. Status asthmaticus, which is the most severe expression of asthma (unresolving asthma), can result in death.

In pregnancy half of asthma patients experience no change in the course of their disease. One fourth notice an improvement, but another fourth complain of worsening asthma. Most of the management of asthma during pregnancy shouldn't change because what worked to keep breathing smooth in the nonpregnant state works just as well in your pregnant state.

But because pregnancy itself is a challenge to your physiologic state, when things go bad (as in a bad asthmatic attack), things can go very bad. Therefore some obstetricians will be more aggressive with the use of antibiotics in pregnant asthma patients who present with an otherwise uncomplicated upper respiratory infection.

Treatment for asthma, besides eliminating the typical allergens of pets, cigarette smoke, household dust, and environmental allergens (pollen, etc.), is based on adrenaline-like substances that help dilate the bronchial tree. Terbutaline (see page 307 in Chapter 20), one particular agent, is also used to stop uterine contractions in preterm labor. Hydrocortisone and methylprednisolone, both steroids, can be used in severe cases. Aminophylline, the mainstay of chronic management, can be used safely under the direction of your obstetrician.

One of the biggest risks of asthma in pregnancy is when some other respiratory problem is thrown into the mix, like pneumonia. You can only add so many problems to someone's breathing before things can become very dangerous. Less oxygen for you means less oxygen for your baby. For this reason, your obstetrician would rather nip a new, developing problem in the bud than wait for it to become so unmanageable as to threaten both you and your unborn baby.

Women with asthma should be able to anticipate a full reproductive life. Your doctor is well equipped to handle even severe cases, but has other specialists available for their insight—pulmonologists, perinatologists, and internal medicine doctors. I'm not saying asthma is no big deal, but with few exceptions, asthmatic pregnancies can be managed without undue intervention.

Stomach Problems

Pyrosis is the medical term for heartburn, but no one, not even a doctor, says pyrosis. It's common in pregnancy, and the reasons are discussed on pages 46–48 in Chapter 3.

A sneaky problem with any complaint of stomach problems in pregnancy is that liver and gallbladder conditions could present (and be blown off) as simple heartburn. Liver disease as a result of pregnancy must be at least considered to make sure the symptoms aren't in the right upper quadrant of the abdomen. The same goes for the gallbladder. But if your discomfort is a burning sensation in the midabdomen right under the middle of your rib cage, is worse on an empty stomach and when lying down, then simple pyrosis (heartburn) is indeed the culprit, with remedies as described in Chapter 3. Keep in mind, though, that any heartburn not easily remedied could be an ulcer or other gastrointestinal problem worthy of further evaluation.

Treatments can also be found in the section "Drugs in Pregnancy and During Breast-Feeding" in Chapter 22.

Bowel Conditions

I'm not talking about constipation and common diarrhea here. Constipation is famous in pregnancy due to the decreased mobility of the bowels under the influence of progesterone. Common diarrhea is usually a brief self-resolving illness unrelated to pregnancy, although it can occur as a signal between latent phase of labor and active labor. (So can nausea.)

What I discuss here is maternal inflammatory bowel disease (IBD), of which there are several types, the most famous being Crohn's disease and ulcerative colitis. These are sometimes debilitating immunologic diseases that cause bowel damage that can cause pain and nutritional abnormalities and can even lead to surgery or death. Today, treatment (including steroids and the antibiotics sulfasalazine and metronidazole) have made such dire complications rare.

IBD is a chronic situation, so most pregnant women with IBD come to their obstetricians with a diagnosis way in advance. And thankfully, getting pregnant during times of quiet for these diseases usually means things will go smoothly for the pregnancy. But there can be flare-ups of both Crohn's disease and ulcerative colitis, most frequently in the first and third trimesters and then postpartum. So before attempting pregnancy, an IBD patient should consult with both her Ob-Gyn and her gastroenterologist.

Newly diagnosed IBD during a pregnancy is unlikely and therefore suspicious, so other causes need to be ruled out, like a weird presentation of appendicitis. And appendicitis often has a weird presentation during pregnancy because the location of the appendix is pushed up and away from the famous right lower quadrant of the abdomen. Also ovarian complications like benign cysts or torsion (twisting upon itself) can present with abdominal pain, nausea, and diarrhea, just like IBD. But it would be quite a coincidence to have a patient's very first episode of IBD occur during her pregnancy, so an obstetrician must always consider these other things when symptoms like this occur.

Statistics are not very helpful with IBD in pregnancy because one-third will get better, one-third will remain unchanged, and one-third will get worse. If you have IBD, you will find that no one can tell you what to expect because such balanced statistics provide no perspective at all on the likelihood of what you yourself might experience.

As bad a disease process as IBD can be, it shouldn't forbid pregnancy if you want children. Additionally, the treatments for IBD pose little risk to your baby, meaning that flare-ups can be treated. The sometimes heartbreaking aspects of IBD are because a person has IBD, not because they have it during pregnancy. But IBD as applied to your pregnancy brings up special considerations nevertheless. Nutritional needs are sometimes different for IBD patients, especially if you've had portions of your bowel removed previously. Also for this reason growth of your baby should be monitored closely with ultrasound, as dietary derangements can affect fetal growth.

Unless the disease has resulted in distortion of your anatomy—fistulas of the rectum or obliteration of your rectum surgically—a vaginal delivery can be anticipated. But if the anatomy there is abnormal with a chance of worsening by vaginal delivery, C-section is sometimes a better idea. Each case should be considered individually.

Some IBD patients also have depression, and most experts feel that the depression is not just because they're bummed out about having this disease, but that it is truly a related phenomenon—a co-disease state. Add in the psychodynamics of worry over a high-risk pregnancy and fluctuating hormones, plus the slightly hyperthyroid affects of hCG (the pregnancy hormone), and a woman's mental health must also be considered. If you have IBD, you have a lot on your plate.

Urinary Problems

Simply put, your pregnancy and your urinary tract will not get along. Besides the possible urinary retention of the first trimester and the postpartum period, there's the incontinence of the third trimester. This is all due to the distortion of your anatomy by cramming two people into the space of one.

Bladder Infection

As explained before, your body doesn't tolerate standing water. If you have urinary retention (urine left over in your bladder after emptying), this provides fertile ground for infection. Pregnancy makes you more prone to infection, and the typical symptoms aren't always there. Instead of burning with urination, you can experience pressure in your bladder, urgency to urinate, and even frequency of urination (which is a dirty trick since you're peeing your brains out anyway during pregnancy).

It's important to treat a bladder infection because it could possibly contribute to contractions that could be misdiagnosed as preterm labor.

Kidney Infection

Any bladder infection can literally rise up to become a kidney infection, but a kidney infection can happen all by itself. The bladder is just a muscular bag (with apologies to bladder physiologists), but the kidneys are complicated organs. An infection in one of them is a big deal and usually requires hospitalization to receive IV antibiotics. Your doctor may call in a urologist too.

Hydroureters

How can something that sounds so terrible be so normal? The weight of your uterus sits on the ureters (the tubes that carry urine from your kidneys down to your bladder). This results in a partial obstruction and distention in the ureters above the uterus-obstruction causing a sharp pressure pain in your side. Although normal, it can be extremely painful. Tubes meant to pass things through the system complain when distended—be it colic with gas in the intestines, the bile duct with a gallstone, or the ureter with obstruction (either within by a stone or without by pressure from a pregnancy sitting on it). If the obstruction is severe enough to interfere with the elimination of urine, a tube called a stent may have to be placed to keep the conduit open. This stent is a temporary treatment, usually removed if it causes pain itself or enhances your chances of infection.

Hydronephrosis
This is the same mechanism as hydroureters, but the "obstructed" liquid can back up into your kidneys. Use of stents provides the same relief.

Kidney Stones
Since kidney stones strike men more than women, it's not really a pregnancy thing per se. But it's not impossible. Usually made of calcium, they should be suspected if a kidney infection doesn't respond to adequate antibiotic therapy. A kidney stone acts as a foreign body, which makes infection hard to treat. The actual chances of a kidney stone in pregnancy are one in thousands.

Heart Conditions

Mitral Valve Prolapse
Mitral valve prolapse (MVP) is so common that many doctors are beginning to think of it as a normal variation. The reason it gets so much attention is because, as benign as it is, it still causes symptoms that are very disturbing.

The heart is an amazing organ, synchronizing the entrance and then ejection of your blood through two different chambered systems, depending on whether the blood is oxygen rich or oxygen depleted. It has four of these chambers, and the blood in each chamber is separated from the other chambers by a trapdoor effect of valves that slam shut then open repeatedly with each stroke of the heart. If there's damage to the valves, then blood can leak forward or be forced backwards.

The mitral valve sits between the left atrium and the left ventricle. Oxygenated blood from the lungs flows into the left atrium, then passes via the mitral valve gatekeeper to the left ventricle in preparation for the burst of propulsion to the aorta. In MVP the valve is weakened by causes unknown, and flaps backward into the left atrium during the ejection of blood from the left ventricle. Although MVP is associated with many serious heart defects, by itself it is usually a benign condition that merely provokes disturbingly weird symptoms.

Palpitations, then anxiety (either because of the palpitations or along with them), shortness of breath, unusual chest pains, and panic attacks are famously associated with MVP. It is difficult to separate the anxiety *with* as opposed to the anxiety *because of* the palpitations and chest pain, but the cluster is certainly a legitimately recognized symptom complex attributed to MVP. It's no fun to suffer from symptomatic MVP. In addition to the above discomforts, there are also the psychodynamics of being blown off as a hysteric. Anger, embarrassment, and the added expense of rotating doctors only make life worse.

It might be expected to be worse in pregnancy since the increase in blood and plasma and the changes in cardiac activity that are normal in pregnancy should challenge the valvular system more than usual. But actually MVP improves in pregnancy in most women because the physical changes in the heart tend to realign the mitral valve components into a more normal position. In other words, there's less prolapse of the mitral valve in mitral valve prolapse during pregnancy.

With most pregnant women who have MVP being symptom free, the biggest concern is whether to treat them with antibiotics at delivery as would be done with patients with other valve damage. Your dentist probably treats your MVP with antibiotics before dental procedures, so you may expect them at the time of delivery. But the current thinking is to forgo any antibiotics unless there are abnormalities of heart function along with your MVP or a complicated delivery is anticipated. Uncomplicated vaginal or cesarean deliveries don't necessarily need antibiotics for just MVP.

In summary, mitral valve prolapse for the most part poses no challenge in pregnancy, and its symptoms are even seen to improve. In fact, if you have troubling symptoms, your doctor may suspect another cardiac condition that may have not been challenged enough to be obvious before your pregnancy.

True valvular disease, usually as a consequence of childhood rheumatic fever, runs the spectrum from mildly symptomatic to life-threatening—after all, it is the heart. But you will know long before pregnancy if you suffer from heart disease for which pregnancy would be dangerous. Such patients have already had a lifetime of cardiologists and warnings.

Epilespy

Epilepsy itself is an enigma, with uncontrolled spasmodic muscle activity associated with an almost comalike amnesic episode called the postictal state. In fact, the postictal state is usually the determining diagnostic feature that sets epileptic seizure apart from merely "falling out," as in hypoglycemia, hyperventilation, or neurotic "spells." EEG test results demonstrating abnormal brain waves provide the ultimate evidence for a diagnosis of epilepsy.

The very severe uncontrolled jerking of the muscles in a seizure can cause a person to be in considerable danger of head injury, tongue injury, or even suffocation. Also, there is a seizure of the actual brain itself as well (of a neuron cell type), beginning from a point of injury of the brain, with a domino effect of stimulated brain cells, all of which fire off down the line to the muscles.

It is possible to have a sudden burst of brain-seizure activity without the convulsions of muscular stimulation if the nerve cells affected aren't ones that innervate nerves going to the muscles. Perhaps a seizure in the area of the brain responsible for mood could have a patient stare off blankly. Usually the convulsive seizures are termed "grand mal" (the big and bad) and the ones unaccompanied by convulsions are the "petit mal."

Epilepsy is serious business, and people still die from it—either from the seizure itself or because of having a seizure in the wrong place or at the wrong time.

Pregnancy is a very strange phenomenon in that it has its own disease processes that can mimic diseases seen in the nonpregnant state. But although both pregnancy and epilepsy can cause seizures, seizures in pregnancy are usually associated with pregnancy-induced hypertension (or preeclampsia).

Seizures due to pregnancy-induced hypertension can be easily distinguished from seizures of epilepsy, and the pregnancy-caused "eclamptic" seizures are more dangerous. But a patient with epilepsy is still considered high risk because epilepsy itself is high risk for the mother, who is the life support for the baby. In the United States there are two to three million epilepsy patients, so it is commonly seen in pregnancy. Morning sickness interfering with the ingestion of epilepsy pills can lead to a worsening of the epilepsy. But otherwise pregnancy seems to have little effect on epilepsy that is well controlled. It's only when the epilepsy is poorly controlled that the extra burden of pregnancy can make the seizures worse or more frequent.

When epilepsy is well controlled in pregnancy, the major concern is whether the medicines used to control the epilepsy are safe for the developing baby. The goal of therapy for epilepsy during pregnancy, like the goal of any therapy during pregnancy, is to use the least amount of medicine that will still control the seizures. In this respect evaluating the epilepsy medication is a risk versus benefit issue.

In my practice the most common drugs used are Depakote (Valproic acid), Dilantin (diphenylhydantoin), phenobarbital, and magnesium sulfate. Magnesium sulfate differs from the rest in that it's the only agent that is in the B category in the FDA classification of fetal risk, which means it poses no undue risk to the fetus. Magnesium sulfate is used in acute situations via IV to stop convulsions. Valproic acid is associated with brain and spinal problems in the offspring of epileptic patients, but even so the risk is less than 10 percent.

Phenobarbital is an old drug (since 1912) that used to be used fairly liberally in pregnancy to treat "mild" preeclampsia, if there is such a thing. Studies on abnormal development in babies exposed to phenobarbital have been inconclusive in that it isn't clear whether the increase in the minor defects (cleft lip, etc.) are a result of the phenobarbital or of the disease of epilepsy itself—or a combination of the two.

A definite problem with phenobarbital is that, being a barbiturate, it is addictive, and babies so exposed, once born and cut off from it, may have withdrawal. They may also experience bleeding problems because phenobarbital may interfere with the newborn's vitamin K, necessary for healthy clotting ability.

Dilantin, which is related to phenytoin—and phenytoin for that matter— is associated with a well-recognized fetal hydantoin syndrome (FHS), which includes abnormalities of the skull, face, and limbs.

I have to emphasize that as scary as all of this sounds, the risk of major problems is less than the disastrous outcome of epilepsy gone untreated. Risk to babies exposed to these necessary drugs is three to four times higher than the general population, but that may translate to anywhere from 2 percent to 30 percent, depending on the agent used. A maternal-fetal medicine consultation by a perinatologist can give the odds to a particular situation as well as provide a Level 3 ultrasound to look over the baby thoroughly for any telltale signs of abnormal development. These drugs may just have to be a necessary evil until newer drugs come along that can move the FDA-assigned risk up the alphabet into the A or B categories. Until that time, the nature of epilepsy is such that treatment with what we have is mandatory. Otherwise a baby has no chance at all if the epilepsy creates the worst scenarios for the expectant mother—complications from inadequate treatment.

Thyroid Conditions

Simply put, the thyroid gland is like a governor on a motor—it sets the speed of metabolism for your body. If it sets that metabolism too high, you can burn up your motor, in a manner of speaking. Weight loss, rapid heart rate, and a host of other unpleasant side effects can alter the way you feel with a higher than normal metabolism. In fact, if morning sickness of pregnancy increases in intensity into the uglier hyperemesis, an abnormality of the thyroid function should be suspected.

Euthyroid is a medical slang word meaning everything is just fine with this gland. Hyperthyroid means increased functioning into the abnormal range, as described above. Hypothyroid means decreased function, with resulting weight gain (you don't burn up the calories), lethargy and fatigue, and possibly goiter formation (enlargement of a lackluster thyroid that tries to overgrow to make up for the decreased function).

Hypothyroidism

Decreased functioning of the thyroid can be due to iodine deficiency (not enough iodine to make the hormones) or due to destruction of the thyroid gland (radiation or autoimmune disease). Being from the New Orleans area, I have iodine comin' out my ears, thanks to the seafood in my diet. But there are places where supplemental iodine needs to be considered. Autoimmune disease can produce an inflammation (thyroiditis) that can limit function. Partial removal of the thyroid, necessary to remove thyroid tumors, can remove enough functioning thyroid to cause hypothyroidism too.

In pregnancy there is increased excretion of iodine, plus the fetus sifts a lot of it out of the maternal circulation, so that if a woman has an iodine deficiency to begin with, there is an increased danger of hypothyroidism. Usually prenatal vitamins solve this dietary problem, though.

Symptoms of hypothyroidism are lethargy, cold intolerance, weight gain, and hair and skin changes. In its most severe form, called myxedema, there is excessive sedation, abnormally low sodium levels, respiratory distress, and possibly death. Myxedema is rare, usually seen in undiagnosed elderly patients, making pregnancy myxedema a nonissue.

Treatment of hypothyroidism is usually by way of supplementing a patient with T4 (e.g., Synthroid).

Out of control or undiagnosed hypothyroidism can complicate pregnancy by causing cretinism (growth and brain abnormalities) in the fetus if the maternal hypothyroidism is severe enough to be associated with iodine deficiency in the fetus too. But proper control of hypothyroidism should be plenty good enough to prevent these types of problems. Treatment is based on the cause, treated with either a prescription of levothyroxine (T4, as the drug Synthroid) or iodine supplementation, or both. Synthroid is in FDA Drug Class B, so it's considered safe, especially since not treating hypothyroidism carries the aforementioned risks.

Hyperthyroidism

Abnormally increased functioning of the thyroid is usually due to Graves' disease. In this autoimmune disorder, the thyroid is overstimulated, resulting in hyperthyroidism. Another cause can be an overfunctioning "hot spot"—called a toxic nodule (of thyroid tissue). And if you really want to get into some weird stuff, there can be thyroid tissue in a type of tumor of the ovary (dermoid cyst), which can be functional enough to cause hyperthyroidism (struma ovarii). I've even had a case of thyroid cancer arising from such ovarian tissue, but this is extremely rare.

Symptoms of hyperthyroidism include restlessness, fast pulse, intolerance to heat, and weight loss. The bulging eyes, called exopthalmos, are the most striking physical characteristic. How bad can it get? In a word, very. Thyroid storm is a name that's as bad as it sounds. It can result in fever, rapid pulse to the point of atrial fibrillation, shock, confusion, psychosis, seizures, coma, and death.

In pregnancy hyperthyroidism can aggravate morning sickness into the much more debilitating hyperemesis gravidarum, requiring hospitalization for rehydration. (In my practice anyone with morning sickness is evaluated for thyroid function again after the initial labs.) All this is just talking about the mother so far, but hyperthyroidism can impact the pregnancy too, with increased risk toward preterm labor, premature deliveries, low-birth-weight infants, and pregnancy-induced hypertension. The antibodies that make the mother's thyroid overreact can pass through the placenta to the baby, causing hyperthyroidism in the fetus too.

Because pregnancy tones down a woman's immune response to everything (so that she won't reject her baby), immune disease-caused hyperthyroidism might cool down after a temporary surge of activity at fifteen weeks, but there isn't agreement about the studies that have suggested this. But based on this, besides the postpartum time for a patient, her doctor will be wary of thyrotoxicosis in the early to midsecond trimester.

Treatment of hyperthyroidism in pregnancy is a little more challenging than treating hypothyroidism because medicines to tone down thyroid function are a bit more artificial. Since these are chemically constructed drugs, prescribing them may walk a patient down the FDA letters of risk.

PTU (propylthiouracil) is the time-honored therapy. This drug works by interfering with the thyroid gland's use of iodine to make thyroid hormones. Unfortunately, PTU crosses the placenta to the baby and can cause a mild hypothyroid condition—even goiters—in a minority of newborns. For this reason, its FDA risk category is D. The risk to the fetus is late in pregnancy because the fetal thyroid does not begin making thyroid hormones until the end of the first trimester. Still, it's considered the safest approach to hyperthyroidism. Not treating hyperthyroidism is even riskier. If steroids are used to help control thyroid storm, they have a significant safety margin in pregnancy.

In summary, autoimmune diseases can make the thyroid hyperfunction or hypofunction. Thyroid hormone supplementation treats "hypo," and "hyper" is treated with drugs like PTU that interfere with using iodine to make thyroid hormones. Both conditions are dangerous to mother, baby, and the pregnancy on the whole if untreated.

Depression

Depression is the most common psychiatric disorder, so it's a commonly encountered preexisting condition during pregnancy. Additionally, women have it twice as often as men, and among women there is an increased tendency toward it during the reproductive years. Where the menstrual cycle fits in as a contributing factor is unknown, as we've still only just scratched the surface of the whole PMS mystery. Certainly borderline depression can be affected by the hormonal impact of the menstrual cycle. And by pregnancy too.

Pregnancy is a particularly fertile field for depression to either start anew or worsen if already a problem. In fact, more women develop depression anew in the third trimester than develop it in the postpartum period. The extra physical, financial, marital, and sexual stresses come whether one is ready or not. On top of that, any new feelings of poor self-image can reinforce depression's already negative self-image problems.

Your obstetrician is qualified to handle mild depression, anxiety, the blues, and general moodiness. But severe depression is a very serious illness that requires the additional care of a psychiatrist because many people die from it! I'm talking about suicide (and possibly homicide), so all moodiness should be questioned.

Depression diagnosis can often be a confusing challenge. For instance, a common cause (co-illness?) of depression is thyroid disorder. Many women who have hypothyroidism will present first as a depressed patient, so thyroid function testing is a very good idea if you were to complain of depression. Also, depression can be overdiagnosed. For instance, if a woman's husband has just died in a car crash, her house has burned down, and she's been mugged and beaten up recently, depression is probably not an illness but a reasonable reaction to these things.

The point of this ridiculous example is that it's not inappropriate for you to be bummed out over really bad things in your life. Clinical depression, on the other hand, is when there is an inappropriate reaction to things, known or unknown.

Predisposing factors that make depression more likely are: childhood trauma, like death or illness of a parent or sibling; childhood sexual abuse, which will distort the well-being of a person on many levels; family history of depression; lower socioeconomic status (translated, poverty); stress; and substance abuse.

In any new depression during or after your pregnancy, it's important to understand the difference between merely feeling depressed and clinical depression.

Feeling Depressed

After delivery, feelings of depression can respond to an understanding ear and a reassurance that this is all too common. As a new mother (and father), what you will fail to anticipate is the selfish inner rebellion to the fact that you've been pushed to the #2 (or #3) position in your family and can't just do whatever you want anymore. For instance, let's take movies. As a couple you pretty much see all of the movies you really want to see—either at the theater or on cable or tape. Along comes baby.

Forget movies. No movies for about two years! And this is a colossal drag since life has been one big date up till now. Now, you can even forget seeing a movie at home uninterrupted by feedings or diapers or just checking on a suspiciously quiet baby. And if you go someplace, no more just hopping into the car and goin'. You've got to haul all of this crap along—bags of diapers, wipes, blankets, clicky toys, and the like. And as your baby gets older, add to this haul of paraphernalia collapsible rolling pods, strollers (two varieties—the deluxe and the umbrella), medicines, and snap containers of gruel.

It won't get any better until you realize and accept the new world order: you just have to put your life on hold for a couple of years.

On the surface, this is a bitter disappointment to your own inner child who wants to shuck 'n' jive and rock 'n' roll, but your thinking parental brain knows better—you are now a family and you're doing this for your children. Not that the li'l urchin will ever appreciate it! Fulfillment in life—trust me—is much better than just having a lifetime of fun.

During pregnancy, feeling depressed is usually a problem in which you experience nagging physical complaints caused by something you have no control over. As your abdomen expands in the mirror, this physical sign is symbolic of a shift from seeing yourself as a woman to seeing yourself as a mother—from seeing yourself as a sexual being to seeing yourself as a maternal one.

Unfortunately, "What have I gotten myself into?" isn't a question with a remedy, except for the cruel, "Deal with it." And because, I'm told, men are from Mars, they're often not the most sympathetic persons and often fail to come through. However, a couple who are pregnant for all of the right reasons or who have put themselves into the big picture of what pregnancy is all about will ultimately find a way to stay afloat on this endless sea of uncertainty. It's a sea-legs sort of thing and a matter of self-perspective. If the relationship between you and your husband is good, mild depression need only be a temporary reaction to a permanent change in your life.

Clinical Depression

Alterations in thinking, delusions, or hallucinations, however, push the diagnosis of depression, categorically, into a psychosis. After delivery, postpartum depression is a serious illness to be distinguished from the postpartum blues. Thought disorder can get fairly creepy in that a mother might start having threatening thoughts about her baby.

Clinically diagnosed depression is a psychiatric emergency because a woman is in a very difficult period of adjustment and less likely to climb out of her despair, hopelessness, and suffering. She poses a danger to herself and her new baby. And to her marriage.

Often a new father, dealing with issues of the new world order himself, won't understand why such a wonderful time is being ruined by such a bad mood, such an attitude, or such anger misdirected at the most likely victim in this drive-by shooting—him! Obstetricians, nurses, social workers, midwives, doulas—even lactation nurses can be a crucial help in recognizing depression and counseling a husband on the pathology involved and how this illness needs as much patience as convalescence from any physical illness.

During pregnancy clinical depression is a high-risk situation that tends to make patients prone to noncompliance with their prenatal care (keeping appointments, eating right, doing what's best for the baby). Substance abuse, either prompting the depression or because of it, doesn't mix well with a developing baby. The legitimate drugs for depression are also a concern, but they are weighed in a risk versus benefit decision. And in clinical depression, the benefit usually far outweighs any potential risks.

The woman who is doing fine on today's antidepressants but then gets pregnant will have worries over what a particular medicine might do to her baby. Luckily, there's been an explosion of effective, and for the most part safe, antidepressant drugs over the last fifteen years, and most of these patients will be on the newer, modern drugs. A seriously depressed patient may still begin prenatal care on the older stuff, and a switch to a safer medicine may present risks of worsening her condition.

Thanks to capitalism, the pharmaceutical investigations into neurotransmitters have brought about a revolution in new, safe, effective, and nonaddictive drugs. That's good news because pregnant people get sick too.

Complications Remembered

At any one time your doctor's patient load has 10 percent high-risk pregnancies, and this one tenth creates as much work as the other 90 percent combined. There are many obstetrical complications that are caught and handled well in a busy practice. It is a testimonial to your doctor that you continue on your way through pregnancy, reassured, your doctor secretly sniffing for the specter of complications that is always in the air nearby.

Every mature practice, unfortunately, has a handful of outcomes that, in spite of every watchful precaution, went very badly. There are things that no one can prevent. When one happens, a doctor will examine and reexamine every aspect of the case, trying to find out if there were any other subtle warnings or any telltale symptoms that might prevent a similar misfortune. You have no idea how much your doctor will care about a tragedy were it to happen to you, so I'll say it now: tragedies are shared with doctors.

Everyday, without exception, I think about the few very bad outcomes that have happened in my own practice. My patients who read this know who they are, but they realize that I will never forget each and every one of them. It goes beyond making a living, beyond reputation, and beyond fear of lawsuits. It has to do with why we do obstetrics and how every human being is important; how we know of the dreams that have been shattered; and how we feel the pain of that question, "if only . . . " God created a system that is miraculous but not magic. There are rules of biology, physics, and chemistry that come together, but have limitations. And we have to play by those rules.

Q & A–Pregnancy at Risk

Gas in Pregnancy

Question: What's the deal on gas in pregnancy? I'm halfway through my pregnancy and the gas has really increased.

Answer: There are many things that happen to increase gas during pregnancy. First, progesterone slows down your intestinal tract, which allows gas to build up. Second, the increasing size of your uterus crowds out the bowel, causing some extra kinking and trapping the gas in discrete pockets. Additionally, with the shortness of breath you can get as your uterus grows (decreasing the amount of movement that your diaphragm needs to do its job), you're likely to literally gulp more air than usual. Prenatal vitamins with iron add additional intestinal fartitude.

On top of all of this, normally gassy foods you might have been used to before pregnancy—and handled well—can have their effects exaggerated by the decreased bowel tone and sluggish gallbladder.

Now I'm not saying that people should run for their lives when you approach, but there are some things you can do. One is to quit smoking if you smoke (more gulping of air). Another is to avoid the famous gassy foods— fatty, greasy, and high carbohydrate foods. You can also take something like Phazyme or Mylicon (over the counter) which each have simethicone. Simethicone isn't absorbed, so it's safe in pregnancy; it works by breaking up the big bubbles into little bubbles (big bubbles are your problem).

Question: I'm seven weeks pregnant, and when I have gas, I have cramping. When I pass the gas, the cramping goes away. Is this uterine cramping or contractions? Is this normal?

Answer: It's hard to answer this with a straight face and a tight sphincter, but it actually is a really good question. The uterus and the entire bowel are covered with a lining called peritoneum. This lining is peculiar in its pain response: that is, you can burn it, you can cut it, you can do almost anything else and it won't hurt—unless you distend it. Gas building up will distend the bowel, and with it the peritoneum covering it. These are the same pain nerves you have in the lining covering your uterus, so it's easy for your brain, receiving pain nerve impulses from the same area, to misinterpret it as uterine cramping. Complicating matters is the fact that in the first trimester you are also experiencing growing pains, as the pregnancy starts to distend the uterus, and we already know what distension does to peritoneum.

So yes, it's normal. And I promise I won't tell anyone.

Excessive Vaginal Discharge

Question: I feel as if I've had an unbelievable amount of discharge over the last month. (I'm eight months pregnant today.) I've resorted to using panty liners but

I think their use has resulted in a yeast infection. My midwife has suggested stopping the use of the panty liners and just allowing it to flow and then air out, but I'm uncomfortable and am already changing my underwear numerous times per day! I know that the heat has aggravated the situation and when I'm home I try to go without anything; but being a busy working woman I don't have that option every day! Any suggestions?

Answer: Me? I'm hoping that all you have is a harmless discharge, but please excuse my using your question to emphasize that whenever a patient calls to complain about a discharge that is out of the ordinary—like your "unbelievable" discharge, I always want to evaluate that patient for premature rupture of the membranes (PROM). It's too important to blow off. And if all I find is bacterial vaginosis or yeast, then I'm obligated to treat it since some researchers suspect it to cause the very thing I would be evaluating you for—PROM.

Yes, yeast infections are common in pregnancy, but you shouldn't be changing undergarments several times a day. And if it is yeast, and PROM has been ruled out with a simple exam, then you should be screened for gestational diabetes, which can cause not only nagging, repetitive yeast infections, but also severe complications for the pregnancy.

In your situation and anyone like you: You need an evaluation to rule out PROM. A vaginal smear can do this as well as diagnose bacterial vaginosis, yeast, or other culprits that cause discharge. It may be that you have just a pregnancy-related hormonal discharge, but the microscope can make that call too. The fact that you've had the problem for a month probably speaks against PROM because it would've caused mayhem long before now. But stranger things have happened, so nothing should be taken for granted.

Changing Blood Type?

Question: I am forty-one and expecting my fifth child. Last September I had a miscarriage. My first son was born at twenty-six weeks, weighing one pound eleven ounces, but he is now a healthy twenty-one-year-old. But my concern is regarding my Rh-negative blood type. In my last two pregnancies (sixteen and fourteen years ago) my blood test results said I have Rh-negative blood and I received the antibody injections during pregnancy and after delivery. For this baby I'm going to a different doctor, which I am now feeling is a big mistake, because the blood test came back stating that I am O+ and that I am not an Rh-negative blood type.

1. *How can my blood type change?*
2. *What dangers are involved if I receive the RhoGam antibody shot while pregnant if I am not Rh-negative? I was already given an injection in my first trimester because of bleeding.*
3. *Is it possible for an Rh-negative blood type to switch by itself to Rh-positive?*

Answer: Rh, another marker for types of blood, can be either Rh-negative or Rh-positive. If a patient with Rh-negative blood were to receive blood from an Rh-positive donor, she would make antibodies to the Rh-positive blood given to her. The same thing happens if she has a baby, who, through inheritance from the father, would have Rh-positive blood like the father. At the time of delivery when the placenta separates, there is some mixing of maternal and fetal blood. Some blood does get into the maternal bloodstream, and this is just like receiving a blood transfusion from an Rh-positive donor. The mother would then make antibodies to this Rh-positive blood. But since she is Rh-negative, it's no big deal, because these antibodies will only attack Rh-positive blood, of which the mother has none. Until the next pregnancy.

If the next baby she's carrying is once again Rh-positive, then her old anti–Rh-positive antibodies, small enough to pass from her circulation through the filtering of the placenta into the baby's bloodstream, will attack the baby's red blood cells. Up to 15 percent of women have Rh-negative blood, but now we can give Rh immune-globulin (RhoGam), big bulky anti–Rh-positive antibodies that fool the body into thinking the defense has already been launched. Therefore, no antibodies are made by the mother. And since these are bulky molecules, they won't pass on to the fetus. These "blocking" antibodies therefore protect the fetus, and because they're too big themselves to get to the baby, getting a RhoGam shot when you're Rh-positive merely means you got a shot for nothing. But there's no harm done.

No, it isn't possible to change blood types. But Rh-positive women are identified by their Rh-positive red blood cells. There is a very weak variant called the Du variant. It is actually an Rh-positive antigen, which would make a woman Rh-positive, but since it is very weakly expressed in tests, it's possible to be mistakenly read as Rh-negative. Today, any Rh-negative woman should be tested further for the Du variant. If it's positive, then the blood type is corrected to Rh-positive, and no Rh immune-globulin need be given. If this is the case for you, then you received these shots for nothing with your previous pregnancies. Fear not, getting Rh immune-globulin when you're Rh-positive does no harm, except to your pocketbook. But before you go clobbering anyone on the head, do know that this is a recent test. So it may be that your new doctor has it right and that your previous doctors didn't have the technology back then to check for the Du variant.

Although you didn't ask, I'll also tell you that if you were truly Rh-negative, you would need the Rh immune-globulin even after a miscarriage since there can be mixing of maternal and fetal blood there too. We also give this shot to Rh-negative mothers who have undiagnosed bleeding during their pregnancy, such as car accidents and version (converting a breech to a headfirst baby).

Look for other current questions and updates regarding at-risk pregnancies at BabyZone.com, by going to babyzone.com/features/expertsqa.

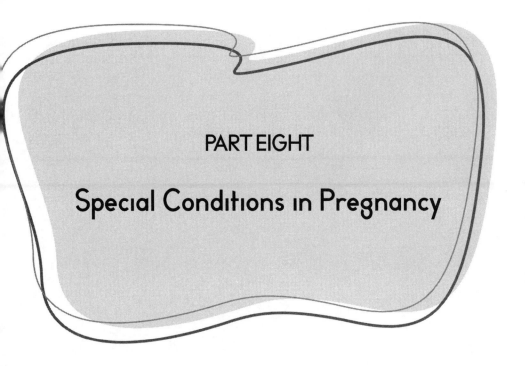

PART EIGHT

Special Conditions in Pregnancy

22

When Life Becomes Complicated

Your doctor has to be ready for any surprises that may come up in your pregnancy, but you also depend on her to offer choices and explanations on aspects of your pregnancy that are, thanks to prenatal care, well anticipated. Here I explore special aspects of pregnancy, each of which will seem exotic (unless they happen to you).

> **Fast Forward**
>
> Twins are a special gift, but involve possible risks:
> - Preterm labor and prematurity
> - Placenta previa and abruption
> - Fast-track onset of pregnancy-related conditions, like pregnancy-induced hypertension

Multiple Gestation—the Romance of Twins

There is a certain romance to twins. Generally what is envisioned is the double stroller being pushed down the street, garnering all of the attention; the identical outfits accentuating their likeness; and admiration from all for surviving such a grueling schedule. There's a certain glory to twins too. And all of this is fair because twins are special. They are a double blessing. Take the most important gift you can receive, double it, and you have twins.

But twins mean a high-risk pregnancy, and your obstetrician must watch this pregnancy very carefully because a twin gestation makes premature delivery much more likely. If a woman carrying a single baby were to wonder how much more pregnant she can get at, say, eight months, imagine what it feels like when hitting that point at six months with twins. If it seems like there's no more room in a single pregnancy, then twins get just plain ridiculous. Your body will think so too and tends to want to deliver what it thinks is just a single big mature baby prematurely—weeks or even months before your twins are really ready. Vigilance for premature labor can involve medicines for premature labor, hospitalization, and weeks of bed rest, and still result in a premature delivery.

Another concern is whether one twin will get more than its share of oxygen and nutrition at the expense of the other. Called discordancy, one twin will grow too big and the other not enough. Ironically, this puts both in grave danger, as the overload on the big one can be just as perilous as the deprivation to the other. Many, many ultrasounds are needed in twin gestations to make sure they're both growing at roughly the same rate.

A-FACTOR
Modern prenatal care has an incredibly successful record of getting healthy babies out of twin gestations.

If twins are identical, there's a chance that they might share the same sac, instead of having a dividing membrane between them. This makes cord entanglement a real possibility, putting them both in mortal danger. Once again, ultrasound comes to the rescue to show the membrane that would put that worry to rest.

All of the complications of a single pregnancy can have earlier onset in twins since there's an obvious increase in the give-and-take in the mother-baby physiologic relationship. Pregnancy-induced hypertension is more likely to occur (and earlier) in a twin pregnancy. Placental accidents are more likely too. Placenta previa is more likely because there's more placenta there but less space for it to occupy. Placental abruption, a premature tearing away of the placenta, is also more likely than in single pregnancies. This event could result in significant blood loss and danger of transfusion for you and mortal risk for your babies.

Delivery poses concerns as well. The jumbling together of two babies makes for frequent abnormal positioning of one or both twins. Breech babies are frequent as are impossible-to-deliver presentations like shoulder- or transverse-presentations. This higher incidence of malpresentation makes C-section the safest way to deliver.

And now the good news: modern obstetrical care and careful surveillance of two babies usually yields a good result. Even though it is definitely a high-risk situation, we have tools at our disposal that allow us to watch closely and to intervene—another dramatic argument for good prenatal care. The special gift of twins occurs in slightly more than one in a hundred pregnancies, but this number is increasing as more fertility drugs and fertility procedures are used in more aggressive attempts at pregnancy.

Let the romance continue; we're ready.

Drugs in Pregnancy and During Breast-Feeding

It's hard to hurt your baby, even on purpose. Most over-the-counter preparations aren't considered a major fetal threat, unless taken excessively or against precautions as printed on the label. Prescription drugs are the responsibility of your doctor, and if anyone's sensitive to safety in this regard, it's your obstetrician.

The biggest problem involves illnesses whose treatments pose some risk, but will have greater risk if untreated. Epilepsy is such an illness. Sometimes there isn't a perfect answer, and your doctor will weigh benefits versus risks.

Smoking

First, there's the risk to you, too. I just love that line, "Well, we all have to die somehow." True, but it's *how* you go. It's a bad death, and your whole family has to stop their lives to revolve themselves around your last six months of suffocation, chest tubes, and those other lovely parting gifts from the tobacco companies.

Then, of course, there's your baby. Are you crazy? The ill effects of smoking on your baby are too numerous to discuss, but include increased incidence of asthma, leukemia, sudden infant death syndrome (SIDS), and decreased intellectual potential. Even one of those should be enough, but the list keeps growing as cigarettes are put in the crosshairs of studies all of the time.

The Baby-Sitter Test

Here's a good test to see if you should smoke or engage in any other unwise consumption during your pregnancy: The baby-sitter test—would you hire a baby-sitter who you knew would make your infant smoke while you were gone? Well now you're the baby-sitter. Meet at least your own baby-sitter criteria. Would you hire a baby-sitter who you knew slapped your baby in the head while you were gone? You do this every time you take a drag.

The baby-sitter test is a chilling enough way to inspire you to stop—now—immediately.

C-Section Hysterectomy

Besides heavy cancer surgery, a cesarean hysterectomy is one of the biggest operations an OB-GYN surgeon can perform. A hysterectomy is performed after delivering your baby by C-section. The reason it's one of our biggest operations is because the organ being removed is just so very big. Your uterus, normally no bigger than a pear, is at delivery as big as your baby. And it is well supplied with blood vessels that would strike fear into even a cardiovascular surgeon. There's just a lot more clamping, cutting, and tying than with a regular hysterectomy.

Fast Forward

If you desire permanent sterilization and you had indications for a hysterectomy before the current pregnancy, then the advantageous combining of delivery with a hysterectomy will make a second hospitalization unnecessary. A cesarean hysterectomy will be the two-birds-with-one-stone solution: one hospitalization, one anesthetic, one price (albeit more than what a straightforward C-section might cost)—all are considerations that make sense.

There's two to three times more blood loss than usual, so there's more chance of transfusion and other complications. But a well-trained OB-GYN surgeon will usually have a very low complication rate when a patient is selected carefully for this operation.

And there are times when a cesarean hysterectomy is a good idea. Indications for hysterectomy can include precancerous conditions of the cervix (dysplasia), prepregnancy heavy periods interfering with work or lifestyle, prepregnancy relaxation of the uterus to a point wherein pain begins to cause severe limitations on sex, recreation, or just being vertical.

Strangely enough, recuperation from a cesarean hysterectomy can be easier than from a C-section because there's less remaining tissue to be a source of inflammatory pain. Also there are no afterbirth pains because there's no uterus to contract after delivery.

Of course, there are cases of uncontrolled bleeding with both vaginal and cesarean delivery that could result in an emergency cesarean hysterectomy, but patient selection under controlled circumstances can make this elective operation prudent when there's a hysterectomy in your future anyway.

Having Special Children

When you undertake pregnancy, you roll a pair of dice loaded your way, so it's an excellent gamble. Occasionally, however, things don't go the way you fantasized when you first encountered your pregnancy philosophically. Perhaps it happens as a big, rude surprise at delivery or as news from the nursery; maybe you knew about it since the second trimester and have been preparing for it. Regardless, nothing puts you firmly on the track of what's important in this world like having a special child.

There are many versions of the special child. Abnormalities can present physically, mentally, emotionally, and any which way, including unique combinations. And no one, including you, expects any of them. But the reality is that it happens. Should it happen to your child, you will go through stages, much like those of learning of a mortal disease.

> **Disbelief:** It'll all be a dream until you finally decide to wake up. Although you'll see yourself contrasted sharply with the rest of the "normal child" world, it'll be as a casual observer in an out-of-body family trance. But upon awakening, there's the anger.

Fast Forward

If you were to have a special child, you would go through the same four phases usually seen in the diagnosis of a fatal disease.

Anger: It's not fair. You're not bad people. You did everything right. You'll think, "Look at that woman, she's not even buckling her child! Look at that man, spanking that perfect little girl just for cutting up and acting like a two-year-old! And here I am, the best parent a child could have! I would never spank my child, never abort any babies, never let him play with sticks. Thanks, God, for nothing!"

Bargaining: Then you move on to hoping things will change: "Actually, God, I won't do this or won't do that. Let me close my eyes and when I open them I'll see my child as he might have been, and then I'll sing your praises. Please God."

Acceptance: Finally you accept and even appreciate your new gift: "This seventy or eighty years is nothing. I plan to spend the rest of eternity with my whole child. This is just a boo-boo. And life isn't just getting the most toys. The one who gets the most toys, wins nothing! This is what it's all about, making sure my child gets the most she can out of life. And suddenly, I'm not all that upset about a rude cashier or a broken shoelace."

Fast Forward

As we get older and get more of real life under our belts, we don't have to seek the meaning of life because it seeks us. It does this in many ways, and if you were to have a special child, this is your way.

True, you may not be able to take the kids rock climbing if one of your children has cerebral palsy. And your child won't be able to play competitive baseball if he can't see, or appreciate the fun of a rock concert if she can't hear. All of these things and many others are true.

But there are joys over the little victories that parents of "normal" children will never have—those little accomplishments that are otherwise unnoticed in other children but are the major hurdles in a special child. And, your child will never rob a bank, end up on drugs, hurt anyone on the way to the top, or abuse anyone with mean-spiritedness. I know parents of a lot of "normal" children who suffer over what their children have done—they were the ones who felt sorry for parents of handicapped children when their children were little. Even if your child doesn't have all of the choices he should have, he also doesn't have all of the bad choices. There are worse things children can do than be handicapped. And even the rawest of deals can become insignificant when overshadowed by a parent's love.

There is beauty in all children, even the ones who get all of the stares. And many of those stares make mental pictures that may touch the starers later—in the shower, while falling asleep, while daydreaming at church. Some will experience an epiphany, beholding the beauty in the parenting of a child who needs more than other children. And appreciating that beauty could touch a distant heart. And you'd never even know about it.

In the end, the beauty you've created in this world is giving your child the most wonderful life she could have—all with your help and love. The other parents will never experience the thrills of seeing the simplest goals attained, goals taken for granted in normal children. There is a fulfillment in life to having and raising children, and the fulfillment is all the greater when children need more.

Having Another Baby After Having a Special Child

There are two misconceptions in deciding whether to have another baby if the last one is handicapped. The first is that in some strange way you will feel the need to replace the good outcome that didn't happen. You can't replace it. Your child is the way he is, not another child that could have been. True, pulling off normal pregnancy outcome will go a long way toward making you feel better about life, but your handicapped child remains as he is.

The other misconception is the dangerous thinking that concludes that you shouldn't even try to have another child—look what happened last time. What's fair to all of your to-be-conceived children is that you don't decide on pregnancy because of what could happen, but because you want a child. That should be the deciding factor. If a geneticist tells you your genes are such that disasters will befall you every, single time, that's another story. But for the most part, delivery of a special child is an isolated event.

> ***A-FACTOR**
> It's possible to get more out of life by raising a special child. I know—been there, doing that.

Pregnancy After You've Been the Victim of Sexual Abuse

All of life is perceived in the brain. Just because a pain is "all in your head" doesn't make the pain any less real. All of our sensations are chemicals and electricity, firing off patterns of nerve combinations, each one perceived by all of the other nerve combinations that are responsible for self-awareness. This means that painful memories are sometimes not just remembered, but relived. This is what happens in post-traumatic stress syndrome. And this is the syndrome that children have who have been sexually molested.

We are complex creatures who have taken mating to a higher level because of our souls. Our souls mature enough to know right from wrong when we progress from self-awareness to being aware of our place. The sexual being within us needs a certain amount of maturation, just as our souls do, in appreciating the affection and dedication that sex is all about. The healthiest introduction to sexual intimacy can only happen after puberty when our bodies are ready, our minds are ready, and our souls are ready.

When you turn that sexual light on too early, the brain will get rewired.

You can kill a child with sexual molestation just as easily as sticking a knife into her heart. What's left, often, is another person who lumbers her way through this cruel world with all of the wrong worries. "Am I safe?" "Are all men evil?" "Don't all men beat their wives and molest their children?" The way to kill the child within a child is to kill her trust. Humor will go, fun can't be evoked, and love becomes a misdirected appreciation for what pleases someone enough so that he won't be abusive. And then, later, her children are at risk, thereby setting up a pyramid of potential abuse through generations.

Pregnancy when you've had a history of child sexual abuse is a particularly strange affair. The healthy expression of love, sexual intimacy resulting in making a baby together, gets distorted with corrupted sexual imagery. Any of the physical trials of pregnancy and the events of labor and delivery can trigger flashbacks—the actual reliving—of abusive episodes in your past. The flashbacks can be just as real as what happened, so a husband must be especially supportive when there's been a history of abuse. Your doctor should also know about your troubled past too because the fixations on your past that escape your control can contribute to pregnancy complications, including preterm labor, hyperemesis, and depression.

Your husband has a chance to fine-tune your sexual being a bit here. How he supports you in shaky times can make the love you share overcome anything, even your past. He can't undo what's been done, but he can help.

Controversies in Obstetrics

Obstetrics is an ever-changing specialty. There are no less than twenty obstetrics and gynecology journals that are constantly reporting improvements or new information in the field. What may be the best way to handle a problem today may be malpractice in five years. I present here a list of some of the hot topics that obstetricians argue over among themselves:

VBAC–Vaginal Birth After Cesarean

With the push toward lowering the C-section rate, primarily a financial imperative dictated by insurance companies, VBAC was embraced by managed care, natural childbirth enthusiasts who had "suffered" their previous delivery via C-section, and even obstetricians. It was deemed much safer than it ultimately proved to be, and although it is a legitimate way to deliver, it does have its risks—notably rupture of the previous C-section scar on the lower uterine segment. Most obstetricians I know feel the complication rate has been underreported; in fact, under certain conditions, the risk of uterine rupture can be as high as fifteen times the normal.

Herpes–When Is an Obstetrician Not a Gynecologist?

The current method of determining the need for C-section to prevent your newborn from serious complications of herpes infection is whether you've had a lesion within the last two weeks. Yet, in gynecology the official word on herpes is that there can be silent shedding, even without a lesion. This contradiction within the same specialty remains unreconciled.

PROM–Premature Rupture of Membranes

It used to be that if your membranes ruptured, even remote from term, you required delivery. Now with the later generation antibiotics and the mind-set of trying to get a twenty-four-hour window of potency from steroids to mature your baby's lungs, conservative treatment is considered. The only thing controversial about today's protocols is that they will most definitely change every year or so into the foreseeable future. PROM remote from term is a lousy dilemma, always, and every protocol will always have its trade-offs.

Home Delivery—Beauty and the Beast

In this life, do you really have to do everything yourself? I trust farmers to grow my food, Detroit to build my car, and Donna Karan to dress my wife. Let your doctor and a hospital do what they specifically are equipped to do. I think it's about time I go out on a limb here. In my private practice I've seen many welcome changes, and I've also seen many fashionable ideas about childbirth, many of which are lovely and befitting to this special event. Unfortunately, there's one that keeps resurfacing that remains dangerous. Home delivery still remains one of a baby's biggest threats. It poses significant risk to you as well.

This is because obstetrics is a specialty in which a prospective mother can be normal one moment and bleeding to death the next. An unborn baby can be normal one moment and suffering devastating fetal distress the next. Even in the most modern private practices and best-equipped hospitals there are still isolated disastrous outcomes that no one could have averted. But there are also many, many more miracle stories that just wouldn't have been so if a patient hadn't had a whole hospital wrapped around her. Hemorrhage, as in placental abruption, remains a major life-threatening complication in pregnancy. Unfortunately, it is usually sudden. Emergency cesarean section is lifesaving for the baby, and sometimes for the mother as well when emergency release blood can keep a mother from undergoing cardiovascular collapse and shock. Anesthesia is there to make the whole thing painless as well as manage the tricky fluid balances during the melodrama. In a bedroom in her neighborhood, a mother wouldn't stand much of a chance. Seeking the beauty of home delivery possibly means accepting the ugliness of death.

I cannot overemphasize the importance of cesarean delivery as a lifesaving measure. Maligning C-sections as overutilized, insurance companies and consumer groups have been successful in reducing the number of preventable C-sections. But this in no way takes away its importance in getting a baby out in the most expeditious way when disaster suddenly strikes. Sudden obstetrical hemorrhage, prolapsed umbilical cord, and seizures are all emergencies in which the distance between hospital and home is a dead baby.

Often a baby is born vaginally, every phase of labor and delivery having been completely normal. Yet within a moment the baby may not be breathing. A hospital has resuscitative equipment on hand, but your home does not. The riskiest time in a newborn's life is the first twenty-four hours, and except when your baby's with you, a hospital has a nurse watching the entire time. Any abnormalities can be immediately assessed and pediatricians notified.

Some people still choose home deliveries and their reasons are varied. Many see a certain beauty in the hearth. Some say birth is a natural event—I say that myself—and that the chances are slim that any regrettable mishap would occur. Others fear and distrust motives of doctors and hospitals. Still others do it to avoid the big hospital bills. As far as the beauty of the home for important events, save that beauty for important events like your baby's following birthdays, not *the* birthday. There's nothing beautiful about bringing your child to therapy every day. Stack the deck in favor of your taking part in the birthdays to come. As far as complications being rare, so are car wrecks; but I surely want my seat belt and air bag, thank you. The fear and distrust of doctors and hospitals is ridiculous. I never get tired of saying that I love what I do and I have nothing to gain in compromising a patient's well-being by unwarranted manipulation. As far as saving money by delivering at home, this is by far the saddest reason. Handicapped babies are expensive. Certainly a baby is more important than a car, so why don't we build our own cars at home? Is it because it can be done better elsewhere?

I wrote this book to allay anxiety, so I don't disparage home delivery as an antithesis to that goal. I merely tell the truth: your best anxiety prevention is having a whole hospital wrapped around you. So there.

HUAM—Home Monitoring for Preterm Labor

It's easy, has no risk, but is very expensive. An operation like this costs a lot to run. Add on a profit and your insurance company, the insensitive hustler that it is, will scream bloody murder when your expenses outpace your cumulative premium tally. How bad will they scream? Bad enough to help fund studies that prove the outcome in the general population isn't improved with HUAM. Which is true when you take the general population as a whole. But you are an individual, not a homogenized average. It's an interesting battle that's been going on between the insurance companies and the HUAM services. Your baby's the one caught in the middle.

The Business of Medicine—Modern Warm and Fuzzy Deliveries

Before the 1980s everyone made good money delivering good medical care. The ones who best benefited from the excesses of the '80s, however, were the insurance companies. They successfully whittled down the profits of both doctors and hospitals while simultaneously withholding full services. With this formula, no one made a lot of money. Except the insurance companies.

Because the insurance companies are exempt from antitrust regulations, they have pretty much run amok. They write their own policies, they handle any disputes against them, and they make the final dispositions on any disagreements between you and them. Guess who wins. Dealing with them is like dealing with The Terminator (my second Arnold reference): you can't reason with them, you can't beg for mercy. In fact, the only difference between insurance companies and kidnappers is that sometimes you can make a deal with a kidnapper. When you disagree with your insurance company's disposition on your case, you can appeal, but they manage the appeals too. And you lose again. Unless *60 Minutes* bursts through their doors or your Daddy's a judge, you fall victim to the American insurance way: *What's ours is ours, what's yours is ours.*

So you turn to your state's insurance commissioner. If you live in Louisiana, like I do, two previous ones went to prison. I wonder what coziness develops between insurance commissioners and insurance companies. Actually, no, I don't wonder—I *know* what coziness exists.

Was there anything good to come out of this at all? Actually, yes. With profits down, hospitals had to do something that up until then was considered unethical—advertise. They had to market themselves with whatever edge they could boast about. Unless you're an insurance company where you can rewrite anything short of the laws of physics any way you want, the rest of capitalism, including hospitals and doctors, have to compete. This always benefits the consumer, the only victim being the integrity of medicine.

Except at Circuit City, women run the show. If a woman has a good delivery experience at a hospital, this is the place where Grandma goes when she breaks her hip; the place little Jimmy goes when he breaks his arm; the place Dad goes if his gallbladder acts up. Every hospital knows this, so any hospital that gives up women's services will soon die. Hospitals with women's services will do almost anything to keep them.

And so the marketing to women was on, by way of sprucing up women's services. What came out of all this is the LDRP room for obstetrical patients.

And hospital administrators said, "Let there be carpeting, paintings, lounge chairs, Jacuzzis, curtains, thematic wallpaper, and that miraculous transforming labor bed that metamorphoses into the delivery bed." And it came to be.

And it really was good. And insurance companies, too mired in bean counting, don't even know what they accomplished for the human beans they count.

Your doctor stopped being a doctor sometime in the 1990s. The correct designation is now *provider*. The doctor-patient relationship has changed into the provider-patient relationship. This new partnership conspires to get the best medicine out of the stingiest of wicked stepmothers, so fear not, your relationship with your doctor is still a righteous bond. But it is fragile because someone somewhere in the managed care industry will degrade it further if they can figure out a way to make more profit.

At some point, therefore, managed care will become your doctor, using your doctor you think you have as a mere provider. In their defense, they'll vehemently deny this, stating that they are not dictating how your doctor should practice medicine. No, this is true. But they will also stand behind their right to say what portions of your doctor's advice they will pay for. I submit that this is the same thing.

Maternal Choice C-Section

Fact: In the private practice climate of good nutrition, adequate prenatal care, controlled circumstances, and advanced antibiotics, the risks associated with C-section (blood loss, infection, etc.) beyond that of vaginal delivery have narrowed considerably.

Fact: There is considerable evidence that vaginal delivery, especially with the last-minute judgment calls of the need for forceps delivery, has greater risk of vaginal prolapse, urinary and fecal incontinence, and uterine prolapse requiring surgery in the future; the risk for surgery to correct these time bomb complications needs to be added to the risks involved with vaginal delivery.

Nearly fact: When you add the risks of vaginal delivery with the risks of subsequent surgery in later years and the miseries of vaginal prolapse discomforts, the adjusted risk equals the risk of elective C-section. That's what the initial studies indicate. "Fact status" is probably forthcoming, though.

Fact: It has been ordained by law that you have choice over your reproductive health, but no one has applied this right to how you have your baby. In other words, why isn't there choice on whether you can choose between a vaginal delivery or a C-section? The insurance companies, quite in character, are hiding under a rock on this one. When this question comes to a head, they will no doubt spend millions of dollars in funding studies in an attempt to disprove the vaginal delivery-urinary incontinence relationship. Always interested in your health, right?

For those who think maternal choice cesarean delivery is unnatural and antiwoman, it's a private matter that is really only your own business. And every argument that can be used for choice at the beginning of pregnancy should be applicable at the end of your pregnancy. Unnatural? So are vitamins and antibiotics. Accept it; we all live past the age of thirty nowadays because of the unnatural advances we utilize. Unnecessary surgery? Then we would have to condemn plastic surgery. More expensive? I don't think so. The insurance companies, in their unbridled greed, are now reimbursing about the same amounts for vaginal delivery as they do for C-section. This was done to place a burden on your doctor to avoid C-section if at all possible. It is the insurance companies' latest attempt to introduce a conflict of interest into how your doctor practices so as to save them money while they are immune to legal responsibility.

Lawyers Versus Doctors

And speaking of legal responsibility, I would now like to debunk some myths. When a doctor makes decisions that are motivated by trying to avoid a lawsuit, this is called defensive medicine. This term is derogatory, but the practice isn't really a bad thing. Let's think about this.

If your doctor were to make a decision such that it would reduce the chances of a bad outcome upon which you might base a decision to sue, then he's making a decision to get the best outcome. How bad can that really be?

Isn't this really in everyone's best interests? (Except for the insurance company that bears the cost of extra testing ordered for this safety net.)

And that's if it were that cut and dried. It's not. It's not about avoiding getting in trouble. Your doctor wants a good outcome because that's what doctoring is all about. That's what ethics are all about. And integrity. And reputation. And looking at oneself in the mirror. There may be a little lawyer-phobic seasoning in the recipe of every decision, but the meal must be a success for all of the other reasons. If you were to compare doctors' paranoia with the perceived lawyers' stalking, you would find that the doctors overshadow the lawyers, which only benefits the patient.

Another myth: If a doctor makes a misjudgment, it's malpractice. Not true. If there is a reasonable set of circumstances that make such a misjudgment understandable, then your doctor is acting on what he has at the time. Through the cruel retrospectoscope, many people assume that if there's a problem outcome, it just *has* to be someone's fault. That's for the courts to decide, but most smart lawyers know that a case based on a doctor's judgment won't win.

Another myth: doctors hate lawyers and lawyers hate doctors. True, no doctor likes being sued, but most cases without merit never get very far. And lawyers don't want to throw good money after bad with frivolous suits—unless they're stupid lawyers, of course.

Post-Tubal Syndrome—Maybe It Does, Maybe It Doesn't, Exist

This theoretical syndrome is the deterioration of normal menstrual cycling after a tubal ligation. If your tubes were to be tied, burned, or cut—no matter how meticulously the technique—some of the auxiliary blood flow to your ovaries is affected. This allegedly interferes with the rheostat-like balance of hormones, which results in long, heavy, or irregular periods. It's an easy assumption to make because many women suffering from this troublesome bleeding began their symptoms soon after their tubal ligations. Critics who deny the post-tubal syndrome exists will say such a woman was regular before her tubal because she was taking birth control pills that manipulated her artificially into tidy monthly cycles; after the tubal, when the birth control pills were discontinued (no longer needed for contraception), her real cycling reared its ugly head.

There are just as many doctors who believe in the post-tubal syndrome as don't. I'm one of the ones who do, but I can't back that up scientifically because in every study on it, the findings are always equivocal.

Circumcision–Usually a Personal Preference

If you have a girl, skip this section. But if your new baby is a boy, you will be offered a procedure called circumcision. It is a word that is really self-explanatory: *cision*, meaning incision or cut, and *circum*, meaning around. The top of the foreskin, that part that slides over the top of the penis, or glans, is removed surgically, effectively exposing the area previously covered. In the newborn, it is usually done by the obstetrician or the pediatrician in a quick, simple manner.

Fast Forward

Circumcision is a cosmetic procedure only. If it's a toss-up for you, make your decision by what most of the boys have in the way of penises in your town. Ask your friends about their sons' penises. It's the only time you'll ever be able to do this and not get arrested.

One of the benefits of circumcision is the ease of hygiene. Smegma, the thick secretion that is seen to accumulate under the foreskin, is considered undesirable. Skin covering an area wherein urine can be trapped can be a theoretical concern for urinary tract infections and other inflammatory conditions. Also, phimosis, a condition in which the foreskin is stuck tightly around the penis once it's been forced down around it, can cause very painful episodes in a young boy's life. So circumcision, a practice as old as antiquity itself, is touted as the solution to uncleanliness and pain, all of which may be hogwash.

What is worth noting is that most parents make a decision for or against circumcision for religious or cosmetic reasons. This is reason enough because all of the above cautions are either easily avoided or extremely unlikely. The parents wonder whether most of the boys in the school gym shower will be just like their son—or more importantly, what can be done to make their son just like most of the other boys around. They don't want their son to be different—especially "there," in that part of the anatomy that has more than anatomical importance when someone falls for the myths of masculinity along with the realities.

It is strange that I can talk about circumcision as if it were just another usual expectation of medical care. Actually, it's really unusual, most of the world choosing not to circumcise their young sons. Except for North America and Israel, the practice may be looked at as deforming. In fact, many here feel the same. They say that because it really is only a cosmetic procedure, it shouldn't be forced upon infants. They say it is a breach, an uninvited altering of your son's privacy. They feel that it may forever diminish full sexual sensitivity. Additionally, they speak of the pain, even in an infant, which must go somewhere—even if it's not remembered.

On the other hand, proponents for circumcision argue that it just isn't that important, that no one who's had it regrets or remembers it. One thing is true—that it's easier done earlier than later, as demonstrated by the baby who sleeps untroubled in his mother's arms a moment after. Like most philosophical exercises, there can be no morally absolute, or obviously logical answer. It is a personal decision, and it is one of the first decisions you will make in raising your son.

Final Thoughts

What sets us apart from the animals on the Ark is that we do more than just mate. We fall in love, commit to each other, plan to grow old together—plan to "grow" together. We make the sum greater than the addition of the parts. Sex without love is mating with just the genital organs, a kind of cooperative masturbation between two people. Sex with love and living intimacy is mating with the soul.

When God created man, He made him in the likeness of God; He made them male and female. When they were created, He blessed them and named them Man.

So begins the fifth chapter of Genesis. If you look at this carefully there seems at first to be an error in grammatical agreement. God blessed *them*? And named *them* man? Them? How many people are we talking about?

Two, of course.

We take for granted that there could be such a difference between the genders in the same exact species. But because men and women are the same species, we fit together so nicely. While some have written bestsellers that claim men are from this planet and women are from that planet, we often forget that both belong to the same planet and the same species and the same ark. And they belong together, united—and not just physically and mechanically—if you know what I mean. The whole idea of sexual attraction and love goes so far beyond merely fitting tab A into slot B. This should be intuitively obvious. The ones who don't see beyond that are doomed to having nothing more than empty relationships in the shells they occupy.

The longing for reunion pervades our sexual beings on all levels, humans' more than other animals as we long to mate with our souls, not just our genitals. This is why we have an institution of fidelity called marriage. If God is Love, then love joins us together into that composite entity that is in His image.

We don't just seek to mate, we seek our soul mates.

Whether you're Jewish, Christian, anything else—even an atheist—it is naturally clear that in monogamy sex is special and represents more than just a physical union. When two people are so joined, they each feel they are part of the other's body—not unlike the composite creature ("them") that was named Adam.

And in monogamy this relationship can grow stronger over time. A couple fine-tune their affections. More than good sex being healthy sex, good sex is also a healthy union if it solemnizes the monogamy.

And out of this springs the family, the highest expression of loving and commitment. Just ask Noah.

Conclusion

I have the best job in the world. I not only get to see a new life beginning, I also get to see something much more: out of the cocoon of pregnancy exudes a beautiful butterfly—the birth of the family, which is what it's all about. What women do is special enough to warrant the most severe and swift punishment for physical abuse to them. What women are to accept this gift testifies to their unique place in their human condition and demands our attention, respect, and devotion. If life is a gift, women are the givers of the gift.

Christ said, "Greater love hath no man than this that a man lay down his life for his friends." It can be said that when you have babies, you and your husband give up your way of life forever, so that you can dedicate yourselves to making the world a better place because of what you're giving back with childbirth and how you raise them. I don't think it's hubris to add that there is no lover greater than a woman giving life for the benefit of everyone everywhere.

Index